Rasputin's Killer
and His
Romanov
Princess

RASPUTIN'S KILLER
AND HIS
ROMANOV
PRINCESS

PRINCE FELIX YOUSSOUPOV AND
THE TSAR'S NIECE IRINA

CORYNE HALL

AMBERLEY

To the memory of my parents Peggy and Ernie Bawcombe, who never lived to see my books and who are always in my thoughts.

First published 2023

Amberley Publishing
The Hill, Stroud
Gloucestershire, GL5 4EP

www.amberley-books.com

British Library Cataloguing in Publication Data.
A catalogue record for this book is available from the British Library.

ISBN 978 1 3981 1120 2 (hardback)
ISBN 978 1 3981 1121 9 (ebook)

1 2 3 4 5 6 7 8 9 10

Typeset in 9.5pt on 11.5pt Sabon.
Typesetting by SJmagic DESIGN SERVICES, India.
Printed in the UK.

Contents

Family Trees

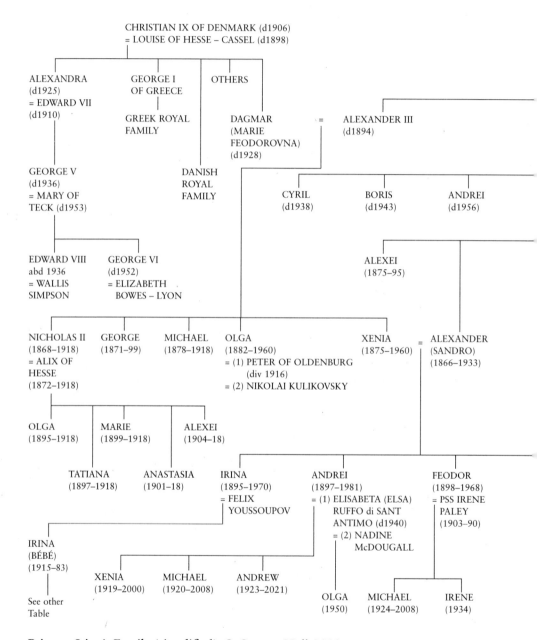

CHRISTIAN IX OF DENMARK (d1906)
= LOUISE OF HESSE – CASSEL (d1898)

ALEXANDRA
(d1925)
= EDWARD VII
(d1910)

GEORGE I
OF GREECE

GREEK ROYAL
FAMILY

OTHERS

DAGMAR
(MARIE
FEODOROVNA)
(d1928)

= ALEXANDER III
(d1894)

GEORGE V
(d1936)
= MARY OF
TECK (d1953)

DANISH
ROYAL
FAMILY

CYRIL
(d1938)

BORIS
(d1943)

ANDREI
(d1956)

EDWARD VIII
abd 1936
= WALLIS
SIMPSON

GEORGE VI
(d1952)
= ELIZABETH
BOWES – LYON

ALEXEI
(1875–95)

NICHOLAS II
(1868–1918)
= ALIX OF
HESSE
(1872–1918)

GEORGE
(1871–99)

MICHAEL
(1878–1918)

OLGA
(1882–1960)
= (1) PETER OF OLDENBURG
(div 1916)
= (2) NIKOLAI KULIKOVSKY

XENIA
(1875–1960)

=

ALEXANDER
(SANDRO)
(1866–1933)

OLGA
(1895–1918)

MARIE
(1899–1918)

ALEXEI
(1904–18)

TATIANA
(1897–1918)

ANASTASIA
(1901–18)

IRINA
(1895–1970)
= FELIX
YOUSSOUPOV

ANDREI
(1897–1981)
= (1) ELISABETA (ELSA)
RUFFO di SANT
ANTIMO (d1940)
= (2) NADINE
McDOUGALL

FEODOR
(1898–1968)
= PSS IRENE
PALEY
(1903–90)

IRINA
(BÉBÉ)
(1915–83)

See other
Table

XENIA
(1919–2000)

MICHAEL
(1920–2008)

ANDREW
(1923–2021)

OLGA
(1950)

MICHAEL
(1924–2008)

IRENE
(1934)

Princess Irina's Family (simplified). © Coryne Hall 2022

6

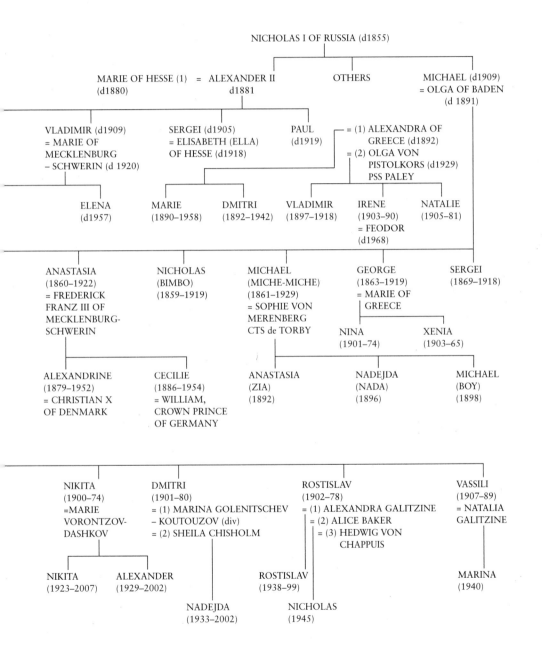

NICHOLAS I OF RUSSIA (d1855)

MARIE OF HESSE (1) = ALEXANDER II
(d1880)   d1881

OTHERS

MICHAEL (d1909)
= OLGA OF BADEN
(d 1891)

VLADIMIR (d1909)
= MARIE OF
MECKLENBURG
– SCHWERIN (d 1920)

SERGEI (d1905)
= ELISABETH (ELLA)
OF HESSE (d1918)

PAUL
(d1919)

= (1) ALEXANDRA OF
      GREECE (d1892)
= (2) OLGA VON
      PISTOLKORS (d1929)
      PSS PALEY

ELENA
(d1957)

MARIE
(1890–1958)

DMITRI
(1892–1942)

VLADIMIR
(1897–1918)

IRENE
(1903–90)
= FEODOR
(d1968)

NATALIE
(1905–81)

ANASTASIA
(1860–1922)
= FREDERICK
FRANZ III OF
MECKLENBURG-
SCHWERIN

NICHOLAS
(BIMBO)
(1859–1919)

MICHAEL
(MICHE-MICHE)
(1861–1929)
= SOPHIE VON
MERENBERG
CTS de TORBY

GEORGE
(1863–1919)
= MARIE OF
GREECE

SERGEI
(1869–1918)

NINA
(1901–74)

XENIA
(1903–65)

ALEXANDRINE
(1879–1952)
= CHRISTIAN X
OF DENMARK

CECILIE
(1886–1954)
= WILLIAM,
CROWN PRINCE
OF GERMANY

ANASTASIA
(ZIA)
(1892)

NADEJDA
(NADA)
(1896)

MICHAEL
(BOY)
(1898)

NIKITA
(1900–74)
=MARIE
VORONTZOV-
DASHKOV

DMITRI
(1901–80)
= (1) MARINA GOLENITSCHEV
– KOUTOUZOV (div)
= (2) SHEILA CHISHOLM

ROSTISLAV
(1902–78)
= (1) ALEXANDRA GALITZINE
= (2) ALICE BAKER
= (3) HEDWIG VON
      CHAPPUIS

VASSILI
(1907–89)
= NATALIA
GALITZINE

NIKITA
(1923–2007)

ALEXANDER
(1929–2002)

ROSTISLAV
(1938–99)

MARINA
(1940)

NADEJDA
(1933–2002)

NICHOLAS
(1945)

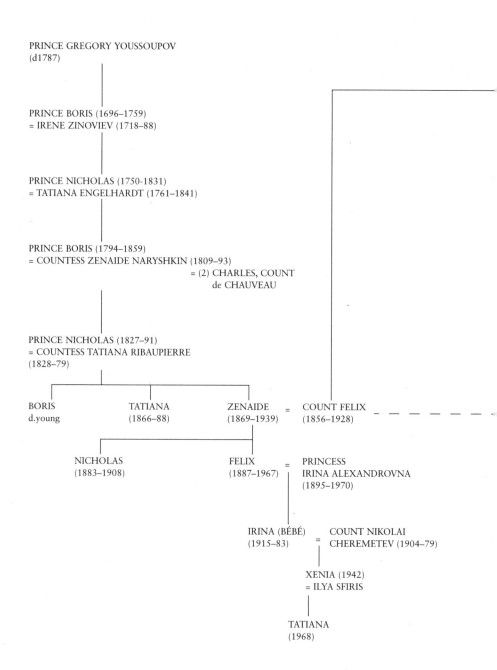

PRINCE GREGORY YOUSSOUPOV
(d1787)

PRINCE BORIS (1696–1759)
= IRENE ZINOVIEV (1718–88)

PRINCE NICHOLAS (1750-1831)
= TATIANA ENGELHARDT (1761–1841)

PRINCE BORIS (1794–1859)
= COUNTESS ZENAIDE NARYSHKIN (1809–93)
= (2) CHARLES, COUNT de CHAUVEAU

PRINCE NICHOLAS (1827–91)
= COUNTESS TATIANA RIBAUPIERRE (1828–79)

BORIS
d.young

TATIANA
(1866–88)

ZENAIDE
(1869–1939)
= COUNT FELIX
(1856–1928)

NICHOLAS
(1883–1908)

FELIX
(1887–1967)
= PRINCESS IRINA ALEXANDROVNA
(1895–1970)

IRINA (BÉBÉ)
(1915–83)
= COUNT NIKOLAI CHEREMETEV (1904–79)

XENIA (1942)
= ILYA SFIRIS

TATIANA
(1968)

The Youssoupov Family (simplified). © Coryne Hall 2022

Family Trees

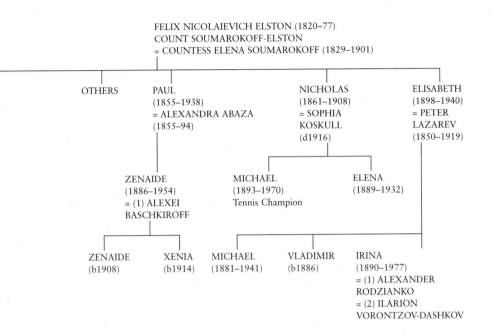

FELIX NICOLAIEVICH ELSTON (1820–77)
COUNT SOUMAROKOFF-ELSTON
= COUNTESS ELENA SOUMAROKOFF (1829–1901)

OTHERS

PAUL
(1855–1938)
= ALEXANDRA ABAZA
(1855–94)

NICHOLAS
(1861–1908)
= SOPHIA
KOSKULL
(d1916)

ELISABETH
(1898–1940)
= PETER
LAZAREV
(1850–1919)

ZENAIDE
(1886–1954)
= (1) ALEXEI
BASCHKIROFF

MICHAEL
(1893–1970)
Tennis Champion

ELENA
(1889–1932)

ZENAIDE
(b1908)

XENIA
(b1914)

MICHAEL
(1881–1941)

VLADIMIR
(b1886)

IRINA
(1890–1977)
= (1) ALEXANDER
RODZIANKO
= (2) ILARIÒN
VORONTZOV-DASHKOV

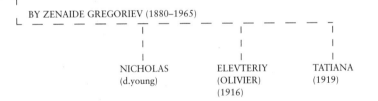

BY ZENAIDE GREGORIEV (1880–1965)

NICHOLAS
(d.young)

ELEVTERIY
(OLIVIER)
(1916)

TATIANA
(1919)

A Note on Names, Dates and Currency

Russians used the Julian Calendar until 1 February 1918. This was twelve days behind the west in the nineteenth century and thirteen days behind in the twentieth century. Dates have been used according to the Julian Calendar [OS] until February 1918, after which the Gregorian Calendar [NS] is used, although occasionally both sets of dates have been inserted for clarity. Where appropriate dates have been marked OS or NS.

The titles emperor, empress, tsar and tsarina are all correct and are used interchangeably. The eldest son of the tsar was the tsarevich, other sons were grand dukes. Daughters were grand duchesses.

From 1886 the title of grand duke/duchess was limited by Alexander III to the sovereign's children and grandchildren in the *male line only*; great-grandchildren of the sovereign were prince or princess. Although Irina's mother was a grand duchess, Irina was a princess as she was the great-granddaughter of Tsar Nicholas I *through the male line*. Her brothers were princes, not grand dukes.

Russians have three names – their Christian name, their patronymic (their father's name) and their surname. The sons of Alexander III had the patronymic Alexandrovich; the daughters were Xenia and Olga Alexandrovna. Nicholas II's daughters were Nicolaievna, so Olga was Olga Nicolaievna. Since the revolution, members of the Romanov family use the spelling Romanoff and this has been reflected in the text. There are several ways of spelling Youssoupov. The one used is simply my own preference.

In 1897 Russia left the gold standard. From then until 1917 the exchange rate remained stable at 10 roubles to £1. After the revolution inflation took hold and between 1917 and 1919 the rate was roughly 15 roubles to £1.

One thousand French francs in 1930 was worth roughly the same in pounds sterling in today's terms. In the next ten years it fluctuated between £760 and just over £1,000.

Other currency conversions are merely intended as a rough guide to show what the amounts mentioned are worth today.

List of Illustrations

Acknowledgements

Writing a book during a global pandemic, with archives, libraries and museums closed for much of the time, has been a challenge. The pandemic also closed off travel, barring several areas of research which I would have liked to investigate. Luckily, many of the Youssoupovs' letters are now available in Russian books or other sources, although I was not permitted to quote from the 14 November 2016 Paris auction catalogue.

I would therefore like to thank everyone listed below who, often working from home or under difficult conditions, took the time and trouble to reply to my requests for help or information.

Firstly, I owe a huge debt of gratitude to Geoff Teeter who generously copied and sent to me over a hundred pages of unpublished letters and documents he purchased at auction. These throw a new light on the Youssoupovs' life after the revolution and have enhanced my work considerably, as well as throwing up several surprises.

Oxford University played a part in Felix's early life. My thanks to Dr Robin Darwall-Smith FSA FRHistS, Archivist at University College and Jesus College Oxford, for providing so much information about Felix's time there and making us so welcome. Warmest thanks also to Dr Michael Nicholson, Emeritus Fellow of University College Oxford, who shared valuable insights and took us to see Felix's room at the college, a quite unexpected treat. Thanks also to the Master and Fellows of University College Oxford for permission to quote from Eric Hamilton's diary; and to Mrs Cordelia Uys who kindly gave permission to quote from the memoirs of her grandfather Sebastian Earl and provided other useful documents.

As always, Ian Shapiro has proved a stalwart friend and supporter, sending documents and introducing me to useful contacts. Huge thanks also to George Hawkins for help with GARF and for generously translating Irina's letters.

The plan for a book was given extra impetus by a friend's chance meeting with a relative of Felix's friend Oswald Rayner in a bookshop. My grateful thanks therefore go to the Malvern Bookshop, Valerie Cherrington, Dr David Lockwood (Oswald Rayner's great-nephew by marriage), Jeremy Frankel (Oswald's nephew) and Dmitri Kennaway (Jeremy's stepbrother). Special thanks to Paula Wrightson at Preston Manor, Brighton, whose sheer enthusiasm for the Oswald Rayner connection was infectious and who took us into her office, the room Rayner stayed in at Preston Manor. My thanks to the trustees of the Royal Pavilion & Museums Trust, Brighton for permission to quote letters in the Preston Manor Archives. Andrew Cook kindly gave his thoughts on the Sidney Reilly connection and generously made available to me his interviews with relatives of Oswald Rayner and John Scale.

Martin Elifolk at Åbo Akademi University Library, Finland provided some fascinating unpublished documents, and Tatyana Bukharina was an enormous help regarding the Crimea. Dr William Lee, the expert on Grand Duke Dmitri Pavlovich, provided valuable insights and translations. Valentina Nabok, Curator of Collections and Expositions of the Yusupov Palace, St Petersburg patiently answered my questions and Mme Xenia Sfiris, Felix and Irina's granddaughter, kindly permitted me to use the interview she gave in 2009 for the Nordisk Film television documentary *The Royal Jewels*. I thank Douglas Smith for the 1916 letter from Oswald Rayner to Felix and his researcher Tatyana Safronova who found it on an old, forgotten computer. Grateful thanks to Karen Roth-Nicholls, who has helped me for more than twenty years, for translating the German text and checking my Danish. Alex Kotchoubey and Eric Smiley put me on the trail of Count Foulques de Balliardei de Lareinty Tholozan. Timothy Xu at the Oxfordshire History Centre provided valuable information and documents, while Sarah Patton at the Hoover Institution Library & Archives, Stanford University provided help with Sir Paul Dukes's diary.

Some of the people who have helped are sadly no longer around – Prince Michael Feodorovich Romanoff, Prince Alexander Nikitich Romanoff, Prince Nicholas Romanovich Romanoff, Prince Andrew Andreievich Romanoff, Prince David Chavchavadze, Princess Margarita of Baden and Jacques Ferrand all provided valuable information on Grand Duchess Xenia's family many years ago, which I have made use of here.

I am extremely grateful to the following people for providing research material, photographs, help with translations and general support. I could not have written it without you. Mark Andersen; Arturo Beéche and the Eurohistory photo archive; Edgar Clin; Julie Crocker at the Royal Archives, Windsor; Diana de Courcy-Ireland; Det Kongelige Bibliotek, Copenhagen; Dominique Devaux, Conservateur en chef, Archives de la collectivité de Corse; Katya Galitzine; Paul Gilbert; Stewart Gillies at the British Library; Griffith Henninger; Susan Hutson, Secretary & Journal Editor of the Huddersfield & District Family History Society; Marlene Eilers Koenig; Galina Korneva; Elizaveta Krasnykh; Peter Kurth; Andrew Lownie; Dr Rainer Maass at the Hessisches Landesarchiv, Hessisches Staatsarchiv, Darmstadt; Giles Milton; Nicholas B. A. Nicholson; Stephen Noble at the British Red Cross archives; Huw Owen-Jones of Bibelots London Ltd; Professor Knud J. V. Jespersen; Peter Rogers at Burnby Hall Gardens and Museum, Yorkshire; Nadine Rouayroux, the Archives of Bayonne; Sarah at eliotsofporteliot.com; Maryl Strehmel; the State Archives of the Russian Federation (GARF); Ulla Tillander-Godenhielm; Jane Tippet; Blandine Turbellier, the Secrétariat des Membres, the Travellers' Club, Paris; Anna von Lowzow of Nordisk Film, Denmark; Katrina Warne (whose loan of a book for a couple of weeks just before the pandemic turned into more than a year); Marion Wynn; Charlotte Zeepvat; and a special thank

Acknowledgements

you to Barbara, John Rob and Tom at the Petersfield Bookshop for finding me so many brilliant Russian books.

My thanks also to everyone at Amberley, especially Connor Stait and my editors Alex Bennett and Shaun Barrington for having faith in the project and for all their hard work in seeing the book through to completion.

Last but certainly not least, extra special thanks go to my long-suffering husband Colin. He read and commented on countless drafts, dealt with the currency conversions, helped with the editing and was a fantastic support during an extremely difficult time. I owe him more than anyone could ever imagine.

Every effort has been made to trace all copyright holders. We will be happy to correct any errors and make suitable acknowledgement in a future edition.

Introduction

On 27 February 1934 the cream of London society flocked to the Royal Courts of Justice in London's Strand for the most celebrated libel case in British legal history. Society ladies, journalists and members of the public vied for space and by the time the session commenced at half-past ten Court No. 7 was crowded to capacity.

The atmosphere was hushed as a thirty-eight-year-old Russian princess walked majestically to the witness box to defend her reputation. Still showing traces of her stunning beauty, she was dressed in black with a spotted veil shielding her eyes. Her jewellery consisted of a single string of pearls, pearl earrings and many rings. Looking dignified and regal, she answered questions posed by her barrister about Nicholas II, the last tsar of Russia.

'In real life he had a niece?'

'Yes.'

'Who was that?'

'I was the niece,' replied the princess.

'Was there any other niece?'

'No,' was the emphatic answer.[1]

Sitting in court waiting to give evidence was the princess's husband. In 1914 eyebrows were raised when Princess Irina Alexandrovna married Prince Felix Youssoupov, one of Russia's wealthiest men. A flamboyant character who wore eye make-up long before the days of glam rock, Felix was believed to be homosexual, yet they stayed together for over fifty years.

As the princess gave evidence the court was transported back to the events of December 1916, when Felix Youssoupov was involved in one of the century's most famous crimes: the murder of Gregory Rasputin, the so-called 'Mad Monk' and perceived evil genius of the Russian court.

The following year revolution swept the country and like many other Russians, Irina and Felix lost nearly everything. Of the fifty-three Romanovs living in Russia in 1917 seventeen were killed by the Bolsheviks. These included Nicholas II, Empress Alexandra Feodorovna and their children Olga, Tatiana, Marie, Anastasia and Alexei – the cousins Irina played with during her childhood.

Yet the Youssoupovs were lucky. In 1919 they were evacuated from Russia on a British warship sent by Irina's close relative King George V along with her grandmother the Dowager Empress Marie Feodorovna (a sister of Queen Alexandra), her mother Grand Duchess Xenia Alexandrovna (the tsar's sister and a favourite cousin of King George) and other members of her family. With them went two Rembrandts and some of the most famous jewels in Europe. But this was only a fraction of their former wealth.

The tsar's niece and Russia's richest man went from a life of wealth and privilege to a life in exile in France, where most of their magnificent jewels were sold to make ends meet. How did they survive in the real world when the money began to run out? Why did they live their lives in the shadow of Rasputin? How did Rasputin save them? And how did Felix atone for Rasputin's murder?

The libel case made headlines around the world – but how had the tsar's only niece ended up defending her reputation in a British court of law?

ෲ ✳ ღ

The idea for this book has been in the background for many years. When I co-wrote the biography of Grand Duchess Xenia with John Van der Kiste I realised there were several books about Felix but Irina has largely been ignored. Accounts speak of her stunning beauty and her acute shyness, yet she was stronger than people suspected. Nevertheless, she flits in and out of books almost as a footnote, an unknown Romanov. Books and websites merely regurgitate the same few facts.

I wanted to put this situation right by concentrating on Irina but I soon discovered that without including the colourful character of Felix it would not work. I therefore decided to write a joint biography.

Most books have relied on Felix's own memoirs *Lost Splendour* and *En Exil* which, as in all memoirs, leave out much. The true facts are often very different, especially during the years of their exile.

As for Irina, her life began as a fairy tale and ended as a story of survival, faced with difficulties that someone of her birth and upbringing could never have envisaged. The first seeds were sown on that December night in 1916 when her husband killed Rasputin.

Although this is not an investigation into Rasputin's murder, it led to a fascinating trail of fresh information. Not everyone will agree with my conclusions but I hope this book will open some avenues for future research and throw a new light on Rasputin's killer and his Romanov princess.

1

The Tsar's Niece

'Her little girl is a real beauty.'
The Duchess of Coburg, 1899[1]

The tsar's estate of Peterhof bordered the Gulf of Finland. Peter the Great had built the Grand Palace, 'the Russian Versailles', with its water stairway leading to an ornamental lake and a long canal with fountains running down to the sea. In summer the park and fountains were illuminated by coloured lamps and the imperial ballet performed on a floating stage in the middle of the lake.

Among the villas in the private park was The Farm, where in 1895 Grand Duchess Xenia Alexandrovna awaited the birth of her first child. Peterhof held a special significance for the young grand duchess, having been the scene of her wedding the previous summer.

Xenia, the elder daughter of Tsar Alexander III and the Danish-born Empress Marie Feodorovna, had spent a happy childhood with her siblings Nicholas, George, Michael and Olga. In July 1894, aged nineteen, she married her father's handsome twenty-eight-year-old cousin Grand Duke Alexander Michaelovich (Sandro), one of six sons of Grand Duke Michael Nicolaievich, Governor of the Caucasus. It was a love match.

Their wedding was the family's last happy occasion, as Alexander III was suffering from nephritis. On 20 October 1894 he died, bringing Xenia's twenty-six-year-old brother to the throne as Nicholas II.

As 1895 dawned, Xenia was still trying to come to terms with her father's death – but by then she was pregnant.

C♈✶♌

By early July the birth was imminent and the Dowager Empress Marie Feodorovna arrived. Xenia was attended by midwife Evgenia Günst and gynaecologist Dr Dmitri Ott. She received a small dose of chloroform, 'causing her to laugh and say all sorts of funny things.'[2] As the baby's first cries were heard, Sandro followed the ancient Russian custom of lighting the candles he and Xenia held at their wedding.

Nicholas II issued a decree:

> On the 3rd day of the month of July H.I.H Grand Duke Alexander Michaelovich and H.I.H Grand Duchess Xenia Alexandrovna announce the birth of their daughter Irina.
>
> By authority of the Sovereign's Imperial Senate this new Princess is born of Imperial Blood and she shall have the Imperial title and all privileges alongside this shall be accorded.
>
> Signed by Order of His Imperial Majesty's Signature.
>
> Nikolai
Peterhof
3 July 1895[3]

As a granddaughter of Alexander III through the female line and in accordance with the succession rules of 1886, Irina was a princess, *not* a grand duchess.

Irina's first visitors were her uncle and aunt, Nicholas II and his bride Empress Alexandra Feodorovna, who described the baby as 'a tiny little thing with dark eyes and marked eye-brows'.[4] The tsar presented his niece with a travel set with her initial and the imperial crown. Irina's parents commissioned a triptych icon with the central panel depicting St Irene and the saints of her parents on each wing. '[T]he baby looks each day sweeter, as it has got a nice natural colour now,' the empress wrote.[5]

Custom demanded Irina's parents be absent from her christening, held at 3 p.m. on 12 July. Irina was driven to Peterhof palace church in a magnificently painted golden carriage drawn by six white horses, accompanied by Günst and the nurse. A guard of honour was formed by the *Guarde Equipage* (Marine Guard) and the tsar and the dowager empress were godparents. Irina screamed almost incessantly as she was completely immersed in the water three times, 'but old [Father] Yanishev held her exceedingly well'.[6]

Xenia and Sandro moved into the vast Winter Palace. A small bed and some baby clothes arrived from England and Xenia engaged an English nanny. Thirty-eight-year-old Elizabeth Jane Coster (Jane) had been under-nurse at the home of Lieutenant-General Sergei Plaoutine where her elder sister Frances was head nurse.[7]

In August Irina was left with the tsar and tsarina while Xenia visited her grandparents King Christian IX and Queen Louise of Denmark. She relayed news of her daughter to 'Aprak', her mother's lady-in-waiting Princess Obolensky. Irina 'now weighs 13 pounds and 36 zolotniks [5 ounces]. Both Nicky and Alexandra Feodorovna are absolutely thrilled and unwilling to give her back to us ... I miss her terribly (I'm talking about my own daughter, I'm sure you can't have realised it yet!) ... If the truth were known, I still can't believe I have a child! It all happened so quickly!'[8]

They returned to St Petersburg for the birth of the tsar and tsarina's baby, Grand Duchess Olga Nicolaievna, on 3 November. Soon the proud parents were comparing their offspring and Xenia was excited when Irina stood for a few seconds unaided. 'My grandchildren are sweet,' the dowager empress told her father, 'especially Xenia's little daughter, who is my favourite; she is terribly little, but so dear and clever.'[9] Maybe it was her daughter's attempts to say her own name that prompted Xenia to call her Baby Rina, but from her infancy, to most of the family, she was Titi.

In 1896 Sandro was dismissed from the navy after a disagreement. Sandro and Xenia spent more time together and soon she was pregnant again. 'I am so sorry we could not come to Denmark,' she told Queen Louise, 'and especially that you did not see my sweet baby, who is getting sweeter every day and is such a ... sharp little creature! She runs about all by herself now and chatters away!'[10] Irina quickly became acquainted with her cousin. 'Irina and Baby [Olga] drive together and are the best of friends – kissing each other and most amusing. Irina speaks much more already,' the empress wrote delightedly.[11]

On 12 January 1897 Xenia gave birth to Prince Andrei (Andrusha) at the Winter Palace. Later that year they moved into their St Petersburg home, Quai de la Moika 106, a huge palace with a large garden. Feodor (Odi) was born in December 1898.

Meanwhile, the empress gave birth to Tatiana in 1897, followed by Marie in 1899. Shortly afterwards the tsar's brother George died, leaving his other brother Michael (Misha) as heir. Nicholas's daughters could not succeed to the throne while male Romanovs were living. It was vital that the empress give birth to a boy.

❧ ✦ ☙

Nearly every year the descendants of Christian IX gathered for a reunion in Denmark. In 1899 four-year-old Irina was taken to Bernstorff Slot, where she met her cousins from England, Greece and Austria.

They spent the autumn at Ai-Todor (St Theodore), the Crimean estate Sandro inherited from his mother. The Crimea was the favourite holiday resort of the Romanovs and imperial estates were dotted along the coastline between Yalta and Sevastopol.

The scenery was spectacular. Prince Serge Obolensky described 'the blue waters of the Black Sea stretching away into the horizon. To the north, beyond the mountain slopes, were clean little villages of flat-roofed, white-plastered Tartar houses, each village with its mosque...'[12]

Xenia and Sandro settled into the Old House. As the family grew, new buildings were added. Ai-Todor 'became a flourishing country estate covered by gardens, vineyards, lawns and coves', stretching down to the sea.[13]

While staying there in 1900 Irina became very ill. 'Little Irina is really better now, thank God,' the tsar told his mother in October, 'the temperature is down but her condition was very grave before.'[14]

Then the tsar was stricken with typhoid and it was feared he might die. Nicholas recovered but his illness accentuated the uncertain future of the dynasty. Xenia had given birth to Nikita in January 1900, followed by Dmitri in August 1901 – but to everyone's disappointment, that June Alexandra had a fourth daughter, Anastasia.

Sandro had been reinstated in the navy, promoted to captain of the *Rostislav*. In 1902 he became Minister of Merchant Marine. When Xenia's sixth child was born in November 1902 he was christened Rostislav after his father's ship.

With all these children, Jane Coster, 'Nana', was indispensable. She was an unashamed Russophile who liked tea from a samovar but retained her liking for English soap and always travelled with a chest full of homeopathic medicines. Sometimes Nana staged tableaux for the children on an impromptu stage. On one occasion the curtains were drawn back to reveal them dressed as different flowers. Irina and her brothers had to sit motionless while the adults clapped.

෬ ✳ ෨

Early in 1904, angered by Russia's penetration of Korea and Manchuria, Japan launched a surprise attack on the Russian naval base at Port Arthur. Hostilities began immediately and proved disastrous for Russia, both on land and sea.

Irina, her mother and brothers spent the early summer with the dowager empress at Gatchina, 35 miles from the capital. With its towers, battlements, high walls, octagonal towers and secret passages it was an ideal place for children to explore.

They had picnics in the Finnish log cabin in the park, fed the deer, went fishing and romped in the woods. When his duties permitted, Sandro arrived in his new motor car (in those days a novelty) to take them on excursions. The family were keen photographers, snapping each other, the dog Bachka and the horse Flight.

In July they moved to Peterhof, where on 30 July Empress Alexandra gave birth to the longed-for heir, Tsarevich Alexei, the first heir born to a reigning monarch since the seventeenth century.

Alexei's lavish christening marked Irina's first appearance at an official ceremony. The tsarevich was carried on a pillow by Princess Galitzine, followed by a long procession of grand dukes and duchesses, ambassadors and dignitaries. Nine-year-old Irina and her cousins Olga and Tatiana wore short blue and silver satin court dresses with silver braids and buttons, silver shoes and blue velvet *kokoshnik* headdresses embroidered with pearls. An observer thought that 'the little girls were delightful'.[15]

Yet joy turned to despair days after his birth when Alexei was discovered to be suffering from haemophilia. Fearing for the future of the dynasty if the news became public, the dreadful secret was told to only a few trusted people.

෬ ✳ ෨

As the Russo-Japanese war continued, two of the villas at Ai-Todor were converted into convalescent hospitals. 'Today we went for a drive in a Tartar village and saw lots of children,' Irina told her aunt Olga. 'We went horse-riding ... Are you enjoying yourself in Gatchina? It is such a pity that you are not here.'[16]

They returned to Gatchina for Christmas but the atmosphere was gloomy. The disastrous war had fuelled the political instability of the country. On 9 January 1905 over 1,000 people were killed on Bloody Sunday, when troops fired on a peaceful demonstration headed to the Winter Palace to present a petition to the tsar, unaware he was not in the capital. In February Irina's great-uncle Grand Duke Sergei Alexandrovich was killed by a bomb as his carriage left the Moscow Kremlin. In May the Baltic Fleet was annihilated by the Japanese at Tsushima.

Irina's family found peace at Ai-Todor. As the only girl in a family of boys it was inevitable that she would become close to her cousins Olga, Tatiana, Marie and Anastasia. 'This morning we went for a walk and picked lilies-of-the-valley,' Irina wrote to Marie. 'We had a little ball with us and we played with it a bit. One time the ball rolled off into the grass and it was all we could do to find it ... Tell Anastasia I don't have time to write to her, because I have to prepare my lesson.'[17] And to Olga Nicolaievna: 'I really want to see you. I have just finished an art lesson. I have finished a black-ink drawing. Kiss Marie and Anastasia from us.'[18]

In the summer of 1905 as the war ended in Russia's defeat, the country erupted in strikes, riots and revolutionary activity. Nana was strict with the children and at the first sign of trouble threatened to 'get the Japs' onto them.

By the autumn a general strike brought the country to a standstill. A company of soldiers arrived as protection and the children were forbidden to go outside without armed guards. As the situation deteriorated, the guards were doubled and Sandro resigned as Minister of Merchant Marine.

The tsar was urged to give the country a constitution and a Duma. On 17 October Russia ceased to be an autocracy. There would be an elected parliament with two houses – the State Duma and the State Council, with Sergei Witte as chairman of the Council of Ministers. There would be freedom of conscience, speech, assembly and association.

Not until January 1906 could Irina's family return to the capital.

ɔ✶ɛ

When Irina was eight or nine Xenia appointed a governess, Maria Erchoff. For the older boys there was a physics master and a fencing master. The Swiss Monsieur Niquille taught French and Miss Coster remained as nurse to Dmitri and Rostislav.

In the summer of 1906 eight-year-old Feodor became seriously ill with scarlet fever. Sandro, who was commanding the *Almaz*, was immediately summoned home. Then Irina caught the illness. She and Feodor were quarantined, nursed devotedly by Jane Coster. Sandro then heard that his ship's crew had mutinied and intended to take him hostage on his return. The tsar ordered him to resign from the navy.

The doctors' insistence on a change of air provided the perfect excuse to go to Biarritz. With its superb weather and beaches, the Basque fishing village on the border between France and Spain had grown into a first-rate holiday resort for European royalty, including a sizeable Russian colony.

In September Xenia, Sandro, six children, three nurses, English and French teachers, Irina's governess, Xenia's lady-in-waiting, Sandro's *aide-de-camp*, five maids and four butlers settled into the Villa Espoir opposite the golf course. They intended to stay for three months but Christmas came and went with no sign of them returning home.

In March King Edward VII arrived. He entertained Xenia and Sandro at dinner and was indulgent with their children. At the Battle of the Flowers he sat in a tent while the children stood in front of him throwing blooms. 'His Majesty kept them supplied and also threw flowers himself,' a journalist reported.[19]

No sooner had the king departed than the dowager empress's train pulled into the Gare de Negresse. She took special delight in the company of Xenia's children. They went on excursions in Sandro's huge Delaunay-Belleville car and the children were spotted playing on the beach with their nurses.

They all left Biarritz on 25 April and were back at Gatchina in time for the birth of Xenia's last child, Vassili, on 24 June.

In August 1907 Irina's family annoyed the local Tartars by arriving at Ai-Todor by car for the first time. 'Everybody was much excited by that and very angry, because it frightened the horses,' wrote seventeen-year-old Grand Duchess Marie Pavlovna, who was staying nearby.[20]

Marie and her brother Grand Duke Dmitri were the children of Xenia's uncle Grand Duke Paul Alexandrovich and Princess Alexandra of Greece, who died in 1892 after Dmitri's birth. In 1902 Paul contracted a morganatic marriage with Mme Olga von Pistolkors, a divorcée by whom he already had a son. The tsar banished him from Russia and gave the guardianship of his children to Grand Duke Sergei Alexandrovich in Moscow. After Sergei's assassination in 1905 his widow Grand Duchess Elisabeth Feodorovna (Ella) remained their guardian.

Irina got to know Marie and Dmitri at Ai-Todor and the Kleinmichel Villa at Koreiz where they were staying. Sandro's brother Grand Duke George Michaelovich, his wife Marie (known as Grand Duchess George) and her brother Prince Christopher of Greece also joined them for picnics.

The tsar and his daughters often visited from neighbouring Livadia. In the summer of 1909 Tatiana was 'so happy we will be able to see Irina there'.[21] Olga told her tutor Petrov that 'it is a lot of fun for we three to be together'.[22]

Xenia's children loved the freedom of Ai-Todor, where they rode through the countryside on their ponies accompanied by Tartar grooms. Irina and her governess played tennis with Olga and Tatiana and on Alexei's name day they watched the Black Sea Fleet pass by in salute. When the girls were apart, they wrote. 'I hope I will see you soon,' Irina told Olga from Biarritz, 'but we have whooping cough at the moment. So strange that Nikita hasn't got it yet. Kissing you firmly. Lovingly yours, Irina.'[23] And she told Tatiana, 'We have wonderful weather and we are out in the fresh air all day, it is so nice.'[24]

They were among the few regularly invited for afternoon tea at the Alexander Palace. Greetings for holidays were always exchanged. 'I wish you a Happy Christmas and all the very best. What are you doing?' Irina wrote from St Petersburg. 'We go sliding down the (ice) mountain in our garden every day. Andrusha or Odi steer while I kneel behind. It is a lot of fun...'[25]

Olga and Tatiana tended to stick together, leaving Marie feeling left out. She turned to Irina for friendship, which made matters worse, as her sisters felt that she did not want to be with them. Irina was close to Tatiana, who as the girls grew older bore a striking resemblance to her cousin.

Herbert Galloway Stewart joined the household in 1908 to teach English. Mr Stewart was a keen photographer whose pictures provide an important record of the years before Irina's marriage.

ଓ ✴ ଓ

'Darling Tatiana!' Irina wrote to her cousin in February 1910. 'How are you? What are you doing? I haven't seen you for so long that I even forgot what you look like! ... We had fun in Livadia? Didn't we? ... Your cousin who has long loved you and has not seen you for a long time.'[26]

As Irina's family moved between St Petersburg, Biarritz, Ai-Todor and, occasionally, Denmark there was a complaint that became all too familiar. 'Why hasn't Irina written even once from Biarritz?' Olga Nicolaievna enquired plaintively in March 1910.[27] Tatiana, who was bored because she couldn't play with Irina, wrote several times and when Irina finally answered her 'dear Cousin Tanechka' it was only a short note: 'Thank you very much for your letters. How are you? Do you write down letters? [keep a list of them] ... I hug you and Olga firmly and remain your faithful cousin and ally.'[28] Not until 27 May did Olga receive a long letter.

Another undated note to Olga survives. 'Did you receive my letter? What are you doing? I have a runny nose of course and I am staying at home. Tomorrow, I hope they will let me out. When will we finally see each other?'[29]

Towards the end of June 1910 Irina was sent to Peterhof to stay with her aunt Olga Alexandrovna. 'Irina laughed from morning to evening,' Olga Alexandrovna told Tatiana. 'She would come to me when I was sitting in the bath – brushing my teeth – but of course we ended up laughing and all the water from my mouth – splashing around the room!' In the evenings they went to a concert, or explored Babignon Park. Aunt Olga was planning a dance on the eve of her name day. 'Irina will come, and is extremely happy!'[30]

Irina was going to Denmark on the *Polar Star* with her grandmother and her mother's young cousin Princess Margrethe of Denmark. Their destination was Hvidøre, an Italianate villa on the coast road north of Copenhagen which the dowager empress and her sister Queen Alexandra bought as a holiday home. Irina had first visited it with her family in 1908.

Space was limited, so Irina stayed on board the *Polar Star*. Olga Alexandrovna was worried. Irina 'seems to be very bored and the officers practically don't know her as she keeps to herself,' Olga lamented. It was a shame that neither she nor one of the young grand duchesses was on board. 'We would stir Irina up quickly! I am sorry for her because she could have a lot of fun ... It would have been better if they had sent her to me! I can vouch for it she would have had a good time.' Olga added that there would have been no embarrassment with Nikolai Kulikovsky (the ADC to her husband Prince Peter of Oldenburg who was thought to be Olga's lover) 'for she sees him a lot and seems fond of him'. Not until 5 October did Irina move to Hvidøre where guests included Queen Alexandra, her daughters Princess Victoria and Queen Maud of Norway, Maud's son Olav and Prince Christopher of Greece. Olga Alexandrovna continued: 'We would have gone horse-riding and gathered mushrooms in the woods etc. Of course, it would be much more fun than the life she is leading in Denmark, wouldn't it?'[31]

Irina seems to have upset Aunt Olga: 'Yes, Irina is such a pig, a rotter, mean and nasty that one should not speak with her let alone write to her! I haven't written to her for ages and I won't from now on, and hope that none of you will write to her either. I only hear about her from letters from officers...'[32] What Irina had done to merit this tirade remains a mystery. Perhaps the strains in her parents' marriage was a contributory factor to her change of behaviour.

In October Irina joined her parents in Paris. Whether she was sorry to leave Copenhagen was disputed by her relatives but she was undoubtedly sorry to leave her grandmother.

 CR ✶ ℛD

A replacement had to be found for Maria Erchoff, who was marrying Sandro's Marshal of the Court Vladimir Chatelain. On 9 December 1910 thirty-two-year-old Countess Ekaterina Kamarovskaia, who had been in charge of the Xenia Orphanage in Moscow, was summoned for an interview.

Two days later Ekaterina met Irina, a tall, very thin girl of fifteen. The countess noticed her 'beautiful eyes and the regular features of her face', but above all her acute embarrassment and shyness. She was persuaded to talk about a recent trip to Italy with her mother. 'She showed me many engravings and pictures ... She did not speak a smooth, coherent speech, [but] stammered, as if searching for words.'[33] Ekaterina was drawn to this shy child and agreed to take up the appointment at a salary of 216 roubles a month.

The countess took up her post on 13 January. She soon noticed that Irina's distinguishing trait was idleness and, although clever and talented, it was necessary to make her learn. She was conscious of her own superiority and the governess felt that nobody had ever told her the truth.

Lessons began at 8.30 a.m. Feodor Vinogradov taught Russian language, history and geography; Nikolai Youriev was in charge of mathematics. After lunch there was a free period to walk in the garden, go for a drive or, in winter, skate. The afternoon was mainly occupied with drawing, for which Irina, who had liked to paint since childhood, developed a talent. She had music lessons with her mother's former teacher and liked writing poetry. After dinner with her parents, she prepared for the next day's lessons before bedtime.

At first she was unruly, often jumping up and shouting, 'I am going to see papa or mama' before running away to their private rooms. Later, Ekaterina learned that Irina was sitting in her father's bathroom reading a forbidden English novel. Another time she rushed outside and stood silently staring at a tree for an hour. Finally, after the countess threatened to return to Moscow, Irina promised obedience.

In early summer the children stayed with their grandmother at Gatchina. They had lessons in the morning and after lunch with the dowager empress Irina walked or drove with her governess. Once, to Irina's embarrassment, they were challenged by a sentry in the park who refused to believe that the young girl was Princess Irina and tried to eject them. After this, Irina walked only with her grandmother. The Duchess of Coburg complained that the dowager empress 'never tries to amuse Irina – merely takes long walks with her round the lakes filled with ducks'.[34]

In July Irina's family went to London, where they visited Queen Alexandra and the dowager empress at Marlborough House. They then travelled to France and Italy. Olga Nicolaievna complained that Irina had not written to her once. 'I suppose she had a good time in England.'[35]

CR ✶ ℛD

In September 1911 the imperial yacht *Standart* berthed in Yalta harbour for the first time, bringing the imperial family to their new white palace at Livadia. Irina had tea on board the *Standart* at Sevastopol before going to Ai-Todor. The grand duchesses visited and they played *lapta* (a ball game) or *gorodky*, a form of skittles. Occasionally the tsar joined them for a game of tennis.

The princess was now developing a social conscience. On the steamer to Sevastopol she noticed an emaciated poor woman and wanted to help her. She and Countess Kamarovskaia gathered together all their needlework and held a bazaar. The 250 roubles raised were given to the woman. Irina was also asked to help on the empress's stall at a charity bazaar.

Irina had turned sixteen that July. At Ai-Todor she now had her own apartment with a room for her maid Lala. She also wore her hair up. Olga Alexandrovna was critical. 'I don't particularly like Titi's hairstyle,' she remarked, 'but I suppose it will be better later on when she gets used to doing it.'[36]

Olga Nicolaievna's sixteenth birthday was celebrated by a candlelit dinner at Livadia. The emperor led in Olga, followed by the rest of the imperial family, with Irina and the other young girls dressed in white.[37] The empress arrived later with Alexei. Dancing continued until the early hours of the following morning.

Dances were also held at the nearby estates of Harax and Djulber. 'Titi talked sweetly about the balls and how much fun she had,' Olga Alexandrovna wrote. Sandro teased Irina about Nikolai Rodionov, a dark-haired, good-looking twenty-five-year-old officer from the *Standart*, who was also a favourite of Tatiana. When Olga Alexandrovna asked about him Irina 'blushed and said, "foolishness, foolishness." What is it about him that you all like?' Olga Alexandrovna asked Tatiana. 'What do you all see in him? What kind of "come hither"???!!! ... Write to me whether Titi liked Rodionov.'[38]

A few days later a visibly upset Irina announced to her governess: 'Mr Fane, a friend of mama, has arrived!'[39]

Frederick Navarre Fane[40] was described by Kamarovskaia as of medium height, with a ruddy face and dark, rather cold eyes. He was a clever, educated man but it was no secret that he was Grand Duchess Xenia's lover. It was his first visit to Russia.

His family had connections with Biarritz, where he and his wife were regular fixtures at social events attended by Xenia and Sandro. Xenia gave him a photograph of her and Sandro inscribed on the back, 'For F.' In 1908, the grand duchess's diary recorded rumours that she and Sandro were divorcing and that it was 'to do with the flirtation with F.'[41]

Herbert Galloway Stewart photographed Xenia and Nikita with him at Le Tréport in 1910. Fane's face is partly obscured by a trilby hat, although his moustache can clearly be seen and he wears what were later called co-respondent shoes. In December 1910, when Xenia and Irina went to Naples, the newspapers reported that Monsieur Frederick Fane was part of their entourage at the Hotel Excelsior.[42] Irina disliked him.

At dinner that night Fane spoke in fluent French. He was staying in the now empty wing where the older boys once lived. From her apartment, Irina's governess could see Xenia, dressed in her negligée, going across to his rooms. The gossip had already started.

Sandro had been unfaithful to Xenia with a wealthy American lady whom Kamarovskaia identified as Mrs Warburton. Born Mary Brown Wanamaker in 1871, she was the daughter of department store owner John Wanamaker. Mary Warburton came to Europe every year.[43] Sandro disguised her identity in his letters and memoirs by calling her 'M. I.' – M for Mary and I for Ivan, the Russian equivalent of her father's name John.

Xenia reacted acutely to Sandro's betrayal, so he cunningly palmed her off with Fane. Sandro and Mary Warburton met discreetly but Xenia flaunted Fane, so Sandro refused to speak to him. Xenia's reckless behaviour put a strain on the household, especially Irina who was close to her father. While Fane and the grand duchess sat together looking at photograph albums, Irina and her governess did needlework.

On 14 November, the dowager empress's birthday, there was a second ball at Livadia. Xenia asked the tsar to invite Fane. Then Alexandra heard about it and rescinded the invitation. Xenia refused to go. She relented, but sat scowling angrily in the car with Irina.

Four days later, Xenia gave a party at Ai-Todor to which the tsar came with Olga, Tatiana and Grand Duke George Michaelovich. Xenia introduced Fane to Nicholas and his daughters and after dinner they danced to the accompaniment of a famous accordion player.

Soon afterwards they returned to St Petersburg, where Fane accompanied Irina and her mother to the Hermitage, before having tea with Olga Alexandrovna.

Then, to Irina's relief, the hated Fane went home.

ɔઓ ✱ ଚ

Xenia was careless about giving her daughter money. Instead of a fixed allowance, she suddenly gave Irina 200 roubles, or even more. Irina would then buy her favourite strawberry cake from Ivanov's and gobble it down quickly. Her governess put a stop to this, paying her an allowance of 25 roubles a month and asking for a full account of expenses, 'to accustom her to at least a small account and savings'.[44]

Countess Kamarovskaia received permission to take Irina for walks around St Petersburg to 'make small purchases, enjoy the marvelous view of the Neva embankment' and acquaint her with the history of Russia's capital. One day, Irina saw an old woman shopping with her granddaughter. The little girl had three roubles. '"You can't buy everything – there is not enough money," the grandmother insisted. "You have to give up the doll and buy a book for your brother." The girl's face fell.' Irina 'quickly took out 10 roubles in gold and just as quickly put it into the girl's hand' as she ran out of the shop. The little girl would never forget this act of kindness.[45]

Irina became very friendly with Sasha Leuchtenberg, the fun-loving daughter of Duke Nicholas (a great-grandson of Nicholas I). The girls rode, skated, tobogganed, visited picture galleries and went to the theatre. Irina was invited to their Christmas party and at a Russian evening ate pickled mushrooms, salted cucumbers and soaked apples. She played tennis and croquet with the Shouvalov girls and drove in a troika around

Orienenbaum on the Gulf of Finland with Maria (Merika) von Carlow and her sisters.

Seventeen-year-old Irina had blossomed into a real beauty and was attracting the attention of potential suitors. But by 1912 she had been seeing quite a lot of one of St Petersburg's most colourful and controversial characters – Prince Felix Youssoupov.

2

The Richest Man in Russia

'From now on, for betraying the faith of your ancestors, only one heir in the family will remain. If there are more children, they will die before they reach the age of 26.'

Curse said to have been laid on the Youssoupov family

Prince Felix Youssoupov was heir to the largest private fortune in Russia. The family's wealth before 1900 was estimated at over $500,000,000 in gold, over £10 billion today. They were rumoured to be even wealthier than the Romanovs.

It took two months to visit all of their estates, which numbered over forty, comprising some 250,000 acres. There were four palaces in St Petersburg, five houses in Moscow, three in the Crimea and eight apartment blocks, to name but a few. Some, like Spaskoie Selo near Moscow, had been abandoned or, like the house on the Bay of Balaclava in the Crimea, never lived in. One property had 160 miles of oil land beside the Caspian Sea on an estate the size of Belgium. There were five factories and the Dolzhansky anthracite mine in the Donbass, huge investments in railway construction and shares in the Russian Bank for Foreign Trade, the Belgorod–Sumy Railway, the Maltsov Commercial and Industrial Partnership, the South Russian Livestock Trading Society, and the British joint-stock company Elbrus.

Felix claimed the Youssoupovs traced their line back to a nephew of the Prophet Muhammad but according to Jacques Ferrand their history was embellished by Felix's grandfather, who hoped it would help his daughter Zenaide make a spectacular marriage.

In fact the story begins with one of Tamerlane's generals, Ediguey Manguite, who probably belonged to one of the branches descended from Genghis Khan towards the end of the fourteenth century. During the reign of Ivan the Terrible, Youssouf, the Khan of the Nogaïs, was a feudal Mourza, a Tartar prince rather than a reigning khan. The marriage of his beautiful daughter Soumbeca to the Khan of Kazan did nothing to change this. Two of Youssouf's sons served Ivan the Terrible, who granted them considerable lands.[1] Youssouf's great-grandson Abdoul Mirza converted to Orthodoxy and was created Prince Dmitri

Youssoupov by Tsar Feodor II. The Youssoupovs believed that the curse at the head of this chapter was laid on the family because of this change of faith.

Dmitri's son Prince Gregory supported Peter the Great when Tsarevich Alexei plotted against his father and was condemned to death in 1718. As Gregory signed his death warrant, Alexei is also said to have placed a curse on the Youssoupovs. Only one heir would survive in each generation and the name would disappear after seven generations. Felix's mother Princess Zenaide belonged to the fifth generation.[2]

Zenaide was one of three children born to Prince Nicholas Borisovich Youssoupov and Countess Tatiana de Ribeaupierre. She was a beautiful woman, whose talent for dancing and acting would, in any other walk of life, have led to a successful stage career. Her father dreamt of a royal marriage but on 4 April 1882 Zenaide married Count Felix Soumarokoff-Elston, a tall, good-looking lieutenant in the Chevalier Guards with little money. There is no truth in the story that his father, Felix Elston, was the illegitimate son of Countess Catherine Tiesenhausen and the future Frederick William IV of Prussia. Countess Tiesenhausen was Felix Elston's *foster* mother after the death of his own mother.[3]

Zenaide's brother Boris died young, and in the summer of 1888 her elder sister Tatiana also died. 'Princess Tatiana died at midnight without suffering, very quietly without regaining consciousness,' Count Felix telegraphed his father-in-law.[4] Some say it was typhoid, others maintain she drowned in the lake at Arkhangelskoe. Yet according to stories passed down by local residents, when the Bolsheviks broke open Tatiana's grave they also found the remains of a baby. It was assumed she died in childbirth, although there is a strong possibility of suicide. Tatiana's diaries for the last months of her life were destroyed but in surviving pages she recorded her love for a neighbour called Paul.[5]

With Tatiana's death Zenaide became sole heiress to her father's fortune. On 2 December 1891 Alexander III issued a special decree allowing Count Felix to be called Prince Youssoupov, Count Soumarokoff-Elston, in right of his wife. The title of Prince Youssoupov would be inherited by the eldest male heir after the death of the current title holder.

Of Zenaide's four sons, two died young, leaving only the eldest, Count Nicholas Soumarokoff-Elston, born on 16 February 1883, and the youngest, Count Felix, born at the Moika Palace on 11 March 1887. Remembering the curse, Zenaide continually feared for her children's lives.

ରେ ★ ଏ

Felix was a puny baby and Zenaide, who desperately wanted a girl, was disappointed with another son. Soon after his birth she left him in the care of his Soumarokoff-Elston grandmother while she took Nicholas to Bad Kissingen. Countess Elena was an eccentric, kindly old lady who became very fond of her grandsons, although later in life she became the victim of many of their pranks.

Much has been made of the fact that Felix wore dresses for the first few years of his life and the effect this may have had on him. This was the fashion of the times, as photographs of quite ordinary families show.

Felix and his brother were reared in an atmosphere of great luxury. They spent the winter in St Petersburg, late spring in Tsarskoe Selo, visited Krasnoe

Selo for the army manoeuvres and spent summer at Arkhangelskoe. In autumn they were at Rakitnoie for the shooting, then went to the Crimea at the end of October before returning to St Petersburg. All these journeys were accomplished in their luxurious private train with numerous staff.

Their main St Petersburg home was at Quai de la Moika 94, known as the Moika Palace, which was acquired by Zenaide's great-grandfather in 1830. He created an enfilade of state rooms with marquetry floors, ormolu-mounted mahogany doors and gilded stucco mouldings and cornices, where he displayed the family collections of ancient statues and French paintings. Zenaide's great-granddaughter recalled, 'The Youssoupovs were a family that travelled a lot, so by coming to France and England, they took all that was the most beautiful of these two countries…'[6]

On the ground floor was the Silver Pantry, a music room containing a collection of violins (including a Stradivarius) which nobody ever played, the Renaissance-style Henri II drawing room, the library with over 35,000 books and a billiard room. The exotic Moorish Room was an exact copy of a room in the Alhambra in Granada, with marble columns surrounding a central fountain, mosaics and couches upholstered in Persian fabrics. In later years young Felix would come to this room and, languishing on a couch wearing his mother's jewels, imagine himself an Oriental potentate surrounded by slaves.

A double staircase of white Carrera marble lit by French crystal chandeliers swept up to the first floor. The Gobelin Room contained French and Flemish tapestries and carpets which had belonged to Louis XIV. The classical enfilade included drawing rooms where crystal bowls containing uncut precious stones were dotted around as decoration. Later these were joined by Zenaide's collection of Fabergé snuff boxes.

Next to Princess Zenaide's bedroom was the small drawing room where she sometimes had intimate dinners with her sons. The furniture had belonged to Marie Antoinette and a rock crystal chandelier had graced the boudoir of Madame de Pompadour. Zenaide's Porcelain Boudoir boasted a chandelier in the form of a porcelain basket of flowers.

Priceless jewels were kept in long cabinets. Among them were the beautiful pearl La Pelegrina, Marie-Antoinette's diamond earrings, the 36-carat Moorish Sultan diamond, the Bengal Light ruby, and the Regent pearl from the French crown jewels.[7] It was said she had a dressing room just for her 3,000 pairs of shoes and boots.

On the left of the staircase was the ballroom, and in the east wing was the large banquet hall which occupied two stories. A further enfilade, with a picture gallery filled with priceless paintings and two huge halls of classical sculptures, led to a charming Louis XV-style theatre.

On the floor above were rooms for Felix and his brother and the private chapel.

The basement contained the wine cellar, storerooms full of *objets d'art* and china and plate for two thousand people.

All this splendour was run by 150 staff and overseen by the butler Gregory Boujinsky.

CR ✷ SO

In August 1893 six-year-old Felix was sent to the warmer weather of the Crimea accompanied by pets, tutors, the nanny Varvara Mikhailovna (Dydyusha), cooks and valets. 'We are bringing you an interesting surprise from Paris. Try to deserve it!' Zenaide told him. 'Are there many flowers in Koreiz?' she continued. 'Will there be many grapes? As the young master, you *must* know about these things!'[8]

As he grew older, Felix's playmates included his cousins Ekaterina and Zenaide Soumarokoff-Elston, and Michael, Vladimir and Irina Lazarev.

Felix disliked writing letters. In 1896 the elder Youssoupovs were hunting in the Ukraine. Felix, who hated killing, must have been horrified to read about his father's exploits. Then came a familiar refrain from his mother: 'I can't understand why you don't write … It is so boring without you, my dear…' Telegrams, Zenaide informed him strictly, 'are not enough'.[9]

Unlike Nicholas, who was preparing for the university entrance examination, Felix was lazy. At first he was educated at home. His tutors included Princess Zenaide's former governess Nadezhda Versilova (Ludusha) who married Felix's Swiss tutor Monsieur Pénard, and Nicholas Zhukovsky, but he wore them out in quick succession. Felix also had dancing lessons at the home of Alexander Taneyev, the Chief Steward of the Emperor's Chancellery, where he was partnered by the Taneyevs' daughter Anna, later Anna Vyrubova.

On 31 May 1900 Zenaide and Felix senior made a will. As their sons were aged seventeen and thirteen respectively, the curse was perhaps on their minds: 'In the event of a sudden interruption of our family … we bequeath that all of our movable and immovable property, comprising collections of fine art objects, rarities and jewellery, amassed by our ancestors and us … shall become the property of the state in order to preserve these collections within the Empire to satisfy the aesthetic and scientific needs of our Fatherland…'[10] Zenaide was taking no chances.

Upsetting his father, Felix failed the exams for military college. Instead, he entered the Gourevich Gymnasium, a private secondary school in St Petersburg where one of his fellow pupils was Gleb Deryuzhinsky, to whom he would later extend a helping hand.

Felix grew up unruly and undisciplined. He claimed to have his first sexual experience with an Argentinian man and his girlfriend whom he met in Contrexéville. During a tour of Italy with Professor Prakhoff he became bored, slipped off one night and ended up in a Naples brothel. To his amazement the door opened and the professor entered. After that they spent their days in museums and their evenings sampling the night life.

છ ✶ ૭

Every summer the family stayed at Arkhangelskoe, 12 miles west of Moscow, which would become Felix's favourite home. Bought by his great-great-grandfather Prince Nicholas, it became a paradise on earth, surviving occupation by Napoleon's troops and a catastrophic fire.

The ornate state rooms included a room for their collection of Tiepolo paintings, another for works by Hubert Robert and a sculpture gallery. The Gala dining room was decorated with Egyptian motifs on the walls and ceiling, with a musicians' gallery at one end. The library's many rare editions included a 1462 Bible. As a child Felix was afraid to go there because it contained a life-sized automaton of Jean-Jacques Rousseau dressed in seventeenth century clothes and worked by a spring. As Arkhangelskoe was designed to be a summer home, there was no heating.

Princess Zenaide and her husband lived in the left wing, with their sons' rooms on the floor above. Felix had an alarming habit of sleepwalking. One night he awoke to find himself on the balustrade surrounding the roof and was rescued by a servant.

Arkhangelskoe had 'a beauty all its own,' recalled Eric Hamilton who stayed there in 1910, 'the garden crammed with marble statues, some of which bear traces of mutilation by the French soldiery [*sic*] in 1812 when Napoleon burned Moscow. My room looks out on a most exquisite view.'[11] Near the Moscow River which fronted the estate were pavilions connected to large conservatories filled with palms, orange trees, orchids and hummingbirds. At one time there was a zoo, and porcelain and glass factories which made objects for the family's personal use. The porcelain factory perished in a fire in 1830 but the private theatre survived.

Zenaide took her guests for picnics in the woods followed by a line of servants carrying the food in silver dishes.

Francois Flameng's portrait of Princess Zenaide perfectly encapsulates the long, lazy days at Arkhangelskoe. She leans against a garden seat, parasol in one hand, dog at her feet, with her sons playing nearby and the terraces and south facade of the house in the background. It was a life of luxury and privilege.

CR ✶ ꝸ

Although he lived in splendour Felix was not the heir. That distinction belonged to Nicholas, with whom he had an ambivalent relationship.

Nicholas was tall and handsome, with black hair and brown eyes. After university he refused to follow the traditional path to the army or a position at court. The arts, music and literature were more to his taste. With no useful occupation, Nicholas became a dilettante. By the age of twenty-one he had a succession of mistresses.

At sixteen, Felix found his disreputable brother's lifestyle more to his taste and they became increasingly friendly. One night Nicholas and his mistress suggested visiting the gypsies but Felix was obliged to wear school uniform when he went out. To get round this they dressed him as a woman. For the next few years Felix said he led a double life – schoolboy by day, elegant woman by night, once dressing so convincingly that he attracted the wandering eye of King Edward VII at the Paris Opéra.

Felix liked to be surrounded by admirers. He recounted a story about a dinner at The Bear, a fashionable St Petersburg restaurant, which he and his cousin Vladimir Lazarev attended dressed as women. During the evening some officers invited them to dinner in a private room. To create a diversion Felix used his mother's long string of pearls as a lasso. It broke and the pearls scattered all over the floor. They scooped up most of the pearls before the head waiter presented their bill and they were forced to confess. The following morning the manager sent the missing pearls and the unpaid bill to the Moika Palace.

His memoirs have been accepted at face value but there is much that is invented and embroidered, in particular the story of how, dressed in a tunic-style dress of tulle and wearing Princess Zenaide's jewels, he obtained a two-week engagement as a cabaret singer at the Aquarium restaurant. All went well until the jewels were recognised by some of the princess's friends and a scandal ensued.

His Russian biographer Elizaveta Krasnykh checked contemporary newspaper reports, as well as the letters of Felix's close friends and his brother. She found no mention of this outrageous behaviour. There is also the question of when he did this. It would surely have to be before his voice broke. Also, how did he get his mother's priceless jewels out of the palace and through the streets to the restaurant without anyone noticing? Ms Krasnykh believes that Felix invented a lot, and in particular the cross-dressing. 'He may have done it once, but that's about all. It does not appear in contemporary letters etc.'[12]

At some point he also grew a moustache. His university friend Eric Hamilton mentions on 15 September [NS] 1910: 'Felix by the way, removed his little mustachios on this memorable day.'[13]

Felix's own writings show he was a rather banal character whom Nicholas completely outshone. Ms Krasnykh thinks that he used colourful incidents from his brother's life and passed them off as his own. After all, by the time his memoirs were published who would be able to correct him?

☙ ✶ ❧

In 1907 Felix was twenty. His father, a military man with no intellectual pursuits, was commanding the Chevalier Guards and the Youssoupovs lived in the regimental quarters, with a summer villa at the military camp at Krasnoe Selo. This did not suit Felix at all. He decided to go to an English university to read literature and philosophy, which would enable him to meet a larger cross-section of important people. Going to university was part of a gentleman's education, and as long as the young man was reasonably intelligent and could afford the living expenses, it was no problem. With the Youssoupovs' social connections, it would be possible to obtain introductions at the highest level.

In between lectures at the gymnasium, Felix began preparations to learn English. He begged his mother to ask friends if they knew an educated Englishman with whom he could go for walks or attend the theatre. He kept up his arguments throughout the autumn of 1907, planning to learn English during the winter. To Felix's joy his mother said nothing against his idea.

For the moment his life was spent travelling between Paris, Berlin and the Villa Tatiana in Crans-près-Céligny near Divonne in Switzerland, where he grew fond of the Pénard girls, daughters of his former tutor. He continued through Italy and by November was at the Hotel Vendome in Paris. His brother was at the Hotel Meurice and the Paris season was at its height.

They were due to return to Russia at the end of the month but Nicholas refused to go. 'I hope that you are living in peace and harmony and that all misunderstandings have been forgotten,' Zenaide wrote to Felix. She was conscious that her sons often had a fractious relationship and that they had only found common ground when they were young, delighting in being disdainful to visitors to the family estates. 'Agreement between you gives me great comfort,' she added. 'Think about this, both of you, and try not to upset things.'[14]

Nicholas had become infatuated with the courtesan Manon Loti and it was some time before he could be persuaded to leave. Felix, meanwhile, had a liaison with a young girl, visited an opium den in Montmartre and got high.

ભ ★ ୨୦

As heir to a large fortune, Nicholas was the object of constant attention by matchmaking mothers. But his meeting with Countess Marina Heyden was to have disastrous consequences and change his brother's life.

Marina was an occasional member of Nicholas's amateur theatrical group. She was 'much courted, extremely popular, and a great flirt'.[15] At supper after one of their performances in around March 1908 the beautiful Marina met Nicholas and Felix.

Nicholas at first appeared completely indifferent but she became infatuated with him. Felix stoked the fire, encouraging his brother and Marina to begin an affair, although she was shortly to marry Count Arvid Manteuffel, an officer in the Horse Guards. What started as a prank soon became deadly serious and Felix played a large part in the tragedy to come.

Marina said that on the eve of her wedding Felix tricked her into going with him to a restaurant to meet his brother. He asked her to write a note on the menu telling Nicholas they had arrived. 'Dear Count, I am waiting for you in room five. Marina,' she wrote hurriedly, giving the menu to Felix.[16] It was a grave mistake.

Nicholas was appalled when confronted by Marina. She was wearing a gaudy green cloak given to her by Felix, who claimed it was his mother's and that her own would be too easily recognised. Nicholas wanted to take her home to avoid a scandal but at that moment Felix returned with a crowd of actors. Nicholas and Marina were trapped. During the meal one of the actors, probably at Felix's instigation, implored Nicholas to save Marina from a man she did not love. Things then went badly wrong. Nicholas asked Marina to elope. At first she agreed but later Felix persuaded her that Nicholas was in love with someone else. Marina declared she wanted to go home and would marry Manteuffel as planned. Nicholas took her to an actor's apartment. It was almost six o'clock in the morning. Meanwhile Felix hurriedly went in search of Marina's mother, who took her errant daughter home.

Later that day Marina and Manteuffel were married and left for their honeymoon in Paris, where they spent most of the time apart. Alone in a foreign land, with a husband she did not love, Marina finally understood the horror of her position. Almost every day she entreated Nicholas to come to Paris.

Marina moved to the Hotel Meurice and when Nicholas arrived they resumed their affair. Their appearance together at the Opéra caused a scandal. Count Manteuffel demanded that Marina return home but she refused. Nicholas bought her a pearl engagement ring and told her that the green cloak she had worn at the restaurant had belonged to a fashionable prostitute.

Felix now arrived, later claiming he was sent to keep an eye on his brother. On discovering that Nicholas and Marina continued to meet he telegraphed his parents to come at once.

A furious Princess Zenaide informed Marina that divorce was out of the question, adding that she would soon be forgotten by the fickle Nicholas. Manteuffel's honour was tarnished, his family were incensed and he demanded that his wife leave Paris immediately.

After one last night together, Nicholas accompanied Marina to the Gare du Nord where her husband was waiting as she boarded the train to St Petersburg. Soon after her departure he challenged Nicholas to a duel but the seconds declared there were insufficient grounds.

Marina settled into her childhood home and waited. It was not long before the storm broke. Felix informed her that Manteuffel had found out about the prostitute's cloak. Marina begged him to prevent Nicholas's return to St Petersburg, knowing Manteuffel's regiment would demand a duel. She also asked him to destroy her letter. He did not do so. Only Marina's assurances to Manteuffel that the cloak belonged to Princess Zenaide calmed the situation.

Then a witness told Manteuffel that he had the menu with Marina's handwritten note, which Nicholas claimed he had never seen. Manteuffel's honour and that of his regiment were compromised. There was no way out.

On Saturday, 21 June, Princess Zenaide told Felix that she had been reassured by Nicholas that everything was settled and there would be no duel. Felix went to meet Nicholas but his brother never turned up. He returned to the Moika Palace and went to bed.

ᏯᏟ ✱ ᏕᎤ

In the early hours of the following morning Nicholas sat down at his desk and wrote a farewell letter to Marina on black-edged paper. Then he set out with his cousin Michael Lazarev to meet Manteuffel.

They met at dawn on 22 June/5 July on Krestovsky Island. Nicholas had chosen pistols. At thirty paces he fired into the air. Manteuffel aimed and missed. Commanded to move fifteen paces closer, they fired simultaneously. Standing sideways, Nicholas again shot into the air. Manteuffel fired towards Nicholas's raised arm and the bullet entered his side. The wound was fatal.

His body was brought back to the Moika Palace. For several days Zenaide refused to allow the coffin to be closed and the funeral was delayed. She never recovered from the death of her favourite son, her health completely collapsed and she was close to a nervous breakdown.

Felix senior, Marina's father and the tsar were aware that the duel was taking place. The tsar had consented on the assumption that neither party would be injured. Princess Zenaide was not informed.[17]

The funeral finally took place on 24 July at the little Church of the Archangel Michael at Arkhangelskoe. Nicholas was buried alongside Zenaide's sister Tatiana and one of Zenaide's baby sons.

Felix's feelings are difficult to determine. Yet it cannot have passed unnoticed by him that Nicholas's death (which he says incorrectly was a few days before his brother's twenty-sixth birthday) left him heir to a fabulous fortune. He found this intoxicating.

He had encouraged Marina and Nicholas to continue their ill-starred affair but the exact part he played and how much guilt he felt will probably never be known.

Princess Zenaide's close friend Grand Duchess Elisabeth Feodorovna (Ella) arrived at Arkhangelskoe to support the family and accompany them to their Crimean estate of Koreiz. Ella was an elder sister of Empress Alexandra Feodorovna, with whom Zenaide was not on particularly good terms. Widowed in 1905, Ella was in the process of divesting herself of her worldly goods and using the funds to build the Convent of Martha and Mary in Moscow, which opened in 1909 as something between a monastic order and a nursing institution.

Ella was joined by her ward Grand Duke Dmitri Pavlovich, who was nearly sixteen. Felix's parents had been frequent guests at Ilinskoie, the estate of Ella and her late husband near Arkhangelskoe, although Dmitri did not really know Felix. 'We don't see the Youssoupovs very often,' Dmitri wrote to his sister Marie. 'I saw them on the day of my arrival at Koreiz. Little Felix is living here, and is quite nice considering that we know each other only superficially. I want to get to know him better.'[18]

His wish was a prelude to murder.

ભ ✴ ৪০

By the end of 1908 Felix's plan to study in England was beginning to take shape. He returned to Moscow, where the English tutor Mr G. Stanning arrived.[19]

Felix now experienced a profound religious conversion. He went to see Grand Duchess Ella, who helped and encouraged him to work among the poor. Sometimes accompanied by Mr Stanning, Felix visited the slums to see the squalor and destitution in which the people lived. It opened his eyes to a world he had no idea existed. The nearest he had come to anything like that was when, as a joke, he and his brother posed as street beggars and suffered the indignity of rich people passing them by without a glance. He also visited the Moscow Hospital, where he envied the skilled doctors and nurses who were able to give proper help to the sick. Soon Felix spent all day there, returning home only for dinner in the evening.

Felix showed Mr Stanning the sights of Moscow but complained to Zenaide that the Englishman grumbled all the time. He was probably relieved when Stanning departed around 23 December.

A plan had formed in Felix's mind. He would turn the unused Youssoupov houses in Moscow and St Petersburg into hospitals, clinics and homes for the elderly, reserving a couple of rooms for his own use. These ideas were quickly scotched by Princess Zenaide.

Yet he had learned from Ella's example. It was something that would stand him in good stead in the years of exile.

ભ ✴ ৪০

To his consternation, Zenaide and Ella had decided that it was time Felix was married and, furthermore, they had put their heads together and chosen his bride. At this he rebelled. Faced with the conventional choice of a position at court or service in the army, neither of which appealed, he decided to travel. With his parents' permission, he embarked on a two-month journey to visit some of the Youssoupov estates.

Early in December he returned to Arkhangelskoe for the first time since his brother's funeral. Work had begun on a large mausoleum built with granite from Finland and costing 320,000 roubles. It was planned to move Nicholas's body there when the work was completed. In the meantime, a huge memorial angel marked the resting place of Nicholas and his aunt Princess Tatiana.

Leaving by car with his valet Ivan Nefedov, he then visited Ella in Moscow.

In the new year, the richest man in Russia would travel to England.

3

The Dreaming Spires
of Oxford

'It's like having a second life and I am sure it will give me strength and
moral clarity to face the future.'

Felix Youssoupov[1]

On 6 February 1909 Felix left for London, where he met Mr Stanning and
booked into the Carlton Hotel in the Haymarket. Although said to be 'a new
luxury establishment',[2] Felix found the rooms dark, cold and expensive.

Grand Duchess Ella had provided him with a letter of recommendation to
her elder sister Princess Victoria of Battenberg, who advised him to also see
her thirty-five-year-old cousin Princess Marie Louise of Schleswig-Holstein and
Arthur Winnington-Ingram, the Bishop of London.

With Mr Stanning and a new English friend, Mr Steel, Felix went to the Tate
Gallery, saw Shakespeare's *Henry IV* and visited Cambridge, Winchester and
Oxford, where Princess Victoria and the Bishop of London urged him to study.

Felix fell in love with Oxford. At University College he presented his letters
of introduction and was received by the Master, Reginald Macan, who showed
him around. A ground-floor room on the north-east corner of the front quad
caught his eye. When the master explained that the students congregated there
every evening, regardless of who was lodged there, Felix asked if he could be
the next occupant.

He returned home on 7 March, having caused pandemonium in the Carlton's
foyer by releasing all the rabbits and chickens he had bought. He was delighted
with the joke.

ଔ ✴ ଈ

In May Felix returned to Oxford to fill in in the official application form under
the name of Count Felix Soumarokoff-Elston. An affirmative answer was
received within a couple of days.

After spending the summer with his parents he returned in September for
the Michaelmas term. His 'splendid arrival' caused a stir. 'He burst on our

world like a man from outer space,' Reginald Merton remembered. 'He arrived in a bright-red open Delaunay-Belleville car (in those days only half a dozen undergraduates possessed cars). He was a magnificent looking person, very well groomed, extremely well dressed.'[3]

Felix completed the Admissions Register (written in Latin) in his own hand, stating that he 'willingly subscribed under the tutorship of Messrs Poynton and Farquharson and Dr Walker'. He gave his age as twenty-two.[4] Then, after a meeting with the master, he was lodged in VI, 1 (staircase 6, room 1). The charge was six guineas a term (£500 today), the most expensive in the college.[5]

From the front quadrangle, Felix's rooms were reached by a door on the far left by the staircase. The larger room, known as the Club, looked out over the street. An American from Oriel College remembered the 'chintz and deep wicker chairs and old engravings and silver boxes about on the tables, and innumerable photographs in silver frames'. The whole effect was of 'luxurious comfort'. Expense did not enter into it at all. 'He was not extravagant; it was only that he seemed not to be able to think in small quantities.'[6]

On the right was a large cupboard and a fireplace.[7] A small barred window overlooked the street and, after curfew, Felix often heard a knock from a locked-out student. He was always happy to run up to the roof and lower down some knotted sheets to save the stranded undergraduate. One night he caught a policeman and only the Bishop of London's intervention prevented him from being sent down. On the left was a door (now boarded up) to a long, narrow bedroom with just room for a bed and a few pieces of furniture. There was no heating, water froze in the washbasin in the morning and the carpet was so damp that it felt like walking through a marsh. Felix's scout Albert, who cleaned his room, called him Mr Elkins.

Felix suffered terribly and the coal bills were so excessive that the fire in the Club could scarcely have gone out. The college battels (accounts) show that this expenditure was only matched by Felix's kitchen bills. What he called the adequate breakfast and inadequate lunch were taken in his rooms; dinner was in hall.

To liven up the atmosphere he hired a piano. Soon the Club was filled with undergraduates drinking and talking until dawn. Sometimes he sang gypsy songs, accompanying himself on the guitar.

Felix had no trouble securing a college servant to collect messages (usually social invitations) from his pigeon-hole a few yards from his room. His tips were so lavish that 'the lure of working in his immediate vicinity threatened to paralyze the smooth running of the college'.[8]

Felix did not see why he had to be in by midnight, was reported if he was late and had to put on a 'ridiculous little gown' and wait on the dean, instead of sending his valet to summon him.[9] His Russian valet was not even allowed to sleep in college and was sent home.

CR ✶ ℘

The eight-week Michaelmas term officially began at the end of October. Felix did not take naturally to studying so finding a course presented difficulty. The college records show that he originally intended ('apparently uniquely') to read forestry *and* English and that this was later amended to just English.[10]

Lectures occupied most of the morning. After lunch he went rowing on six afternoons a week, which was soon discarded in favour of golf. After tea there were more lectures until dinner. Then, he told Zenaide, 'Everything that is musical in the college starts to play, and since all the windows are open, you get such a bacchanalia of sounds...'[11] Around ten or eleven o'clock all went quiet.

'There is no spoon-feeding, and everything has to be achieved by your own unaided efforts,' he told his mother. She was delighted. 'If you do learn to work independently then that will be the greatest benefit Oxford can bring,' she replied.[12] They exchanged 'pages of cablegrams' every day. 'She wants to know how I am today – not two days ago,' he explained.[13]

'Today is my second lecture on the same subject,' he reported on 29 September. 'Yesterday I already attended four lectures.' According to historian Evgeny Yudin, the Youssoupov archives contain numerous recordings of lectures in English made during Felix's first months at university[14] but, despite hiring a private tutor, Felix told the dean at the end of October that his English was not good enough for lectures on agriculture.

His English is best summed up by a telegram he sent to order a bull and three Jersey cows for Arkhangelskoe: 'Please send me one man cow and three Jersey women.'[15]

The dean suggested he switch to English, sixteenth- and seventeenth-century English literature, French literature and one lecture a week on philosophy.

The undated timetable Felix sent to Princess Zenaide shows that he read English literature with Mr Reginald Tiddy; French and English literature with Mrs Duff; sixteenth-century English literature with Mr Walter Raleigh; seventeenth-century literature with Professor Smith; eighteenth-century literature with the Reverend Alexander Carlyle; and French literature with Professor H. E. Berthon, whom Felix liked very much. There was also philosophy with Professor Edgar Carritt. Dr Michael Nicholson thinks that Felix was studying French 'on the side'.[16]

He founded the Oxford University Russian Club (now the Russian Society) and was president from 1909 until 1913. For the first time Felix found that he was genuinely liked, receiving regular requests for advice from students who were unhappy and struggling.

His mother worried about the company he was keeping. Felix 'lacked in a curious way the faculty of judging people's character' according to one friend. 'He likes everybody who is nice to him, and as everybody is always nice to him he takes the whole world into his good graces. And yet at the same time he is tremendously reserved. You never know exactly where you stand.'[17]

Felix made some lifelong friends. Through the Bishop of London he met Eric Hamilton, later Bishop of Salisbury and Dean of Windsor, who arrived at University College on the same day. Eric was three years younger than Felix. 'Your Bishop is a treasure,' Princess Zenaide wrote. 'How touching it is that he cares for you to such an extent and I am glad that you will have a real, good friend from the start...'[18]

In a meeting that proved pivotal in Felix's later life Hamilton introduced him to Oswald Rayner, who came from a very different background. A draper's son born in Smethwick, Staffordshire in 1888, Rayner won a scholarship to King Edward's School in Birmingham. He later taught English in Finland, part of the Russian empire, where he became friendly with Uno and Olga (Olly) Donner and stayed with Olly's mother Anna Sinebrychoff, a wealthy widow. In 1907 the Donners funded his education at Oriel College, Oxford where he read modern languages.[19] Rayner became fluent in Russian, Swedish, French and German and joined the Apollo University Freemasons' Lodge in 1908. He graduated with honours in 1910. Felix's other great friend was Austin Earl, whose father was the housemaster at Tonbridge School.

Felix often visited the Battenbergs, where he enjoyed discussing politics with Princess Victoria. The princess, a granddaughter of Queen Victoria, had married Prince Louis of Battenberg, an officer in the Royal Navy, in 1884. They had four children: Alice (Princess Andrew of Greece), Louise, George and Louis (Dickie, later Earl Mountbatten of Burma). Victoria's sisters Empress Alexandra and Ella had seen a chance to marry their niece Louise to the richest young man in Russia, a plan of which the Battenbergs approved.

Louise, born in 1889, was tall and slim with none of her sister Alice's classic beauty. Shy in public, in private she was vivacious and self-sacrificing. She had already turned down King Manoel of Portugal and in 1909 was reportedly secretly engaged to Prince Christopher of Greece but it came to nothing.

When Felix arrived in England, Princess Victoria began laying plans.

CR✶ℬ

During the first long summer vacation Felix invited Eric Hamilton on an all-expenses-paid trip to Russia. For Hamilton it was an unforgettable experience. He 'found the gaiety and charm of this handsome young Russian irresistible'.[20]

The prince showed him the Moika Palace ('about the size of Buckingham Palace') and the museums, galleries and sights of the capital, where Felix's name opened all doors. In Finland they visited the Imatra Falls and had tea with Anna Sinebrychoff, who they met several times in St Petersburg, probably through Rayner.

They visited Arkhangelskoe and went sightseeing in Moscow. One morning Felix's chauffeur stopped outside a jeweller's shop. The owner ran out and handed a small parcel to Hamilton, who instinctively passed it to Felix. He waved it away, 'saying in his best English "keep, keep,"' insisting it was a Russian custom. 'To my confusion and amazement, it contained a present of two large pearl studs.'[21]

Felix took him to the Crimea in the family's private train. Hamilton recalled 'all the Youssoupovs and 8 servants in their "wagon"'. From Bakhchisaray station, four cars conveyed them to Kokoz 20 miles away.

The hunting estate of Kokoz (Tartar for 'blue eye'), with its white walls, glazed green tiled roofs, Persian-style windows and marble courtyards, was straight out of the Arabian Nights. The blue-eye motif was everywhere. There were four fountains, including the Fountain of Tears, where the water trickled drop by drop from one small basin to another. It was an exact copy of the one in Bakhchisaray Palace immortalised in Pushkin's famous poem.[22] Hamilton described having lunch in the 'lovely white dining room'[23] where even the china was decorated with the blue-eye motif.

Princess Zenaide was delighted that her son had 'such a good and charming friend'[24] and gave him a beautiful icon.

From the Crimea they travelled 'north again ... to Kiev, Warsaw, Vienna, Munich and Paris'. Felix always booked a whole railway carriage to himself, 'because you don't know what dirty person might sit next to you'.[25]

In Paris Felix spent a day with Grand Duke Cyril Vladimirovich and his beautiful sister Grand Duchess Elena (Princess Nicholas of Greece) whom he had met at his brother's funeral. Elena was five years his senior and had the reputation of being rather wild.[26] Now Felix was falling under her spell.

'My grandfather was very fond of ... beautiful women,' recalled Xenia Sfiris, 'and he was very much in love with Princess Elena ... who ... I think was also in love with him, but it did not work.'[27] The reason it did not work was because lovely dark-haired Elena was already married and the mother of three daughters.

She was shortly leaving for Greece and Felix was sad that he would not see her for a long time. Princess Zenaide was worried. It was not Felix's closeness to the Vladimir family, whose opposition to Empress Alexandra was well known, that bothered her. It was Elena's reputation as a flirt.

ॐ ✱ ॐ

While in St Petersburg, Hamilton said that Felix went 'to meet a mysterious hypnotist whose powers F is trying to defeat in a very clever way of his own'.[28] The mysterious man was Rasputin.

Gregory Efimovich Rasputin was born in 1869 in Pokrovskoe, Western Siberia. As a young man he was a drunk and a lecher but he also acquired a reputation for second sight, with the gift of prophecy. He became a waggoner and after a journey to the monastery of Verkhoturye returned to his village, abandoned his wild ways and held forth on spiritual topics. After marrying a local girl, he claimed to have seen a holy vision and went on a pilgrimage to Mount Athos. Three years later he returned with an aura of saintliness which made people murmur that he was a Man of God.

Armed with a letter of introduction from the Bishop of Kazan, in 1903 Rasputin visited St Petersburg, where he impressed many influential churchmen and gained an entrée into the salons of the nobility. The unkempt Siberian peasant cut a strange figure in the elegant drawing rooms but men and women alike found it hard to resist the almost hypnotic influence of his eyes. Rasputin preached that to be purged of sin one had to have sinned. Bored society women soon discovered that by committing adultery with him and purifying themselves at the same time repulsion and disgust could be thrilling sensations.

In 1905 Grand Duchess Militza arranged for him to meet the tsar and tsarina. By 1907 Rasputin was a regular visitor to the Alexander Palace. Again and again, when Tsarevich Alexei suffered a haemorrhage, Rasputin stopped the flow of blood by praying at his bedside. The tsarina was convinced he had been sent by God to save her son. In her eyes, Rasputin could do no wrong and by 1910 his influence at the palace was becoming unassailable.

Felix said that he first met Rasputin in 1909 but a letter from his friend Munya Golovina dated 20 August 1910 mentioning 'your new friend' indicates a later date.[29] Maria (Munya) Golovina had been a fervent admirer of Rasputin for some time. Her extravagant descriptions aroused Felix's curiosity and he agreed to meet him at the Golovins' home.

Rasputin, wearing a peasant's caftan, baggy trousers and boots, attempted to kiss him in greeting. Felix found his self-assurance irritating but noticed his almost magnetic gaze. He left distinctly unimpressed. A few days later Munya said that Rasputin liked him and wanted to meet him again.

According to former Oxford students, Felix was already talking about getting rid of Rasputin. As Eric Hamilton recalled, 'even in the early Oxford years he [Felix] had spoken more than once of that sinister and evil power behind the Russian throne…'[30]

ଓ ✴ ଏ

In his second year the rules permitted Felix to live outside of college. In 1910 he shared lodgings in George Street with Austin Earl, two macaws and a French bulldog called Punch. Professor Carritt was invited to lunch and was surprised to find a bear cub there. 'You cannot imagine how pleased I am with my premises. It's so calm after college, and I can only see those of my friends whom I want,' Felix wrote home. For amusement he scattered coins, usually sovereigns, 'on to the street from an upstairs window because he enjoyed watching the ensuing scuffles'.[31]

Alongside his Russian chef Felix had a French chauffeur, his English valet Arthur Keeping and a housekeeper whose husband looked after the prince's hunter and two polo ponies. Felix had 'the most beautiful pair of pale brown riding boots that art could manufacture'. In 1908 his mother had told him that 'your killed Fox pleased Papa no end'. Now, at Oxford, Felix said he rode 'but I will not hunt'.[32]

At George Street only the best was good enough. Claiming that white bedlinen affected his mood, Felix insisted on it being dyed pale lavender. His mother complained that his taste in interior decoration was not sufficiently manly.

He also collected gramophone records and 'had every pink label His Master's Voice record delivered to him as soon as it was issued'.[33] He loved opera, especially Enrico Caruso.

Felix was more interested in his social life than in studying and he 'transferred from the degree-course to the Diploma in Political Economy'. There were other easy subjects but he would only be able to take a degree course, which would entail studying at Oxford for a fourth year.[34]

Although he claimed to be working hard he had a very full social life, both in Oxford and London. He smoked opium and had a series of affairs with both men and women (he was said to have liked 'rough trade')[35] but it seems to have been at Oxford that his interest in men became paramount. His memoirs, and those of his friends, only give us hints. According to his Russian biographer,

Felix 'became homosexual at Oxford, not before'.[36] It is likely that he came out of the closet at Oxford, although it must be remembered that it was illegal, punishable by a jail sentence.

Often on a Sunday Austin Earl's mother and brother Sebastian came to tea. Sebastian recalled that Felix's way of life, 'which mirrored his Russian background, was exceptional at Oxford'. The valet took the two macaws into the bathroom in time for Felix's morning bath, 'where they immediately started screeching so loudly as to be heard up and down George Street'. Felix also kept a tiny flat in Mayfair so that he could enjoy the delights of the London season. If he had to stay in London overnight, which was strictly against the rules, the valet still ran his morning bath in George Street and took the macaws into the bathroom, where their screeching 'provided the owner of the digs with sufficient evidence for him to mark the Count as having been present the previous night'.[37] According to an Oxford friend, Felix also 'had mysterious doings in Brighton at that time and kept a flat there'.[38] Others refer to a Brighton cottage.

Felix was a poor dancer, a bad tennis player and a reckless driver who was prosecuted and fined several times for being involved in accidents. Three late nights would mean expulsion but it did not take Felix long to notch up two. Returning from a dinner after curfew, he wrote one of his cars off when he crashed into some closed level crossing gates in the fog. 'Felix was knocked unconscious, while his friend ended up in Oxford hospital with several broken limbs.' This time his lateness was excused but the next time it took the intervention of the Bishop of London to save him from being sent down.[39]

ය ✶ ඊා

Felix often visited Grand Duke Michael Michaelovich of Russia. 'Miche-Miche' had been banished by his cousin Alexander III for contracting a morganatic marriage with Countess Sophie von Merenberg, despite her impressive list of royal relations. Sophie was given the title Countess Torby and they and their children Anastasia, Nadejda and Michael lived at Kenwood House, Hampstead. Nadejda (Nada) was nine years younger than Felix and Miche-Miche hoped that she and Felix would marry. Felix told his mother that the grand duke and his daughters were charming but Countess Torby was vulgar.

Grand Duchess Elena then told Felix that she had heard he and Nada were engaged but Miche-Miche was waiting until he graduated before making an announcement.

Felix's feelings for Elena were causing concern. Grand Duchess Ella suggested Felix spend the summer at Arkhangelskoe, instead of languishing at Tsarskoe Selo where Elena would be staying. 'I'm afraid of this meeting,' Ella told him, 'because playing with someone else's heart is very dangerous. You can't arrange her divorce and marry her – then why rush towards danger…?'[40]

ය ✶ ඊා

Felix knew all the leaders of London society. The Duchess of Rutland's daughter Lady Diana Manners fell in love with Felix, calling him 'breathtakingly' beautiful. Felix preferred her sister Marjorie and wanted to marry her. He sent Marjorie's photograph to Princess Zenaide, who was very angry, thinking her totally unsuitable. Diana recalled that Felix 'often wore, it seemed to me, cloth of gold, pearls and aigrettes', and sang Russian songs with his guitar.[41]

The Battenbergs were still throwing Felix together with Louise but they were so kind to him that it was becoming awkward. Before he returned home in 1911 they visited Oxford, went sightseeing and had lunch in his apartment. Eric Hamilton was there for moral support but Felix thought Louise looked bored. Princess Victoria's lady-in-waiting Nona Kerr said he should talk more to Louise but, as he told his mother, they did not seem to understand that he had no desire to marry her. Princess Zenaide called his position unenviable.

'We are not particularly wealthy and who can know whether she [Louise] will ever marry into a rich family or marry at all,' Victoria wrote to her sister-in-law.[42]

But she was hoping.

೮ ✴ ෨

In the summer of 1911 Anna Pavlova visited Oxford while she was on tour. Felix had seen her perform in St Petersburg and she had often been his guest for supper in the restaurants on the islands. Some of the undergraduates asked her to perform for them and, hearing that they were friends of Felix, Pavlova agreed.

On the day of the performance she arrived at his house with the entire *corps de ballet*. Felix took them sightseeing while Pavlova rested. When Felix returned, the family of a girl who many believed to be his fiancée were coming downstairs looking embarrassed. Expecting to find him home, they had opened the bedroom door and found Pavlova asleep on his bed. The identity of the supposed fiancée is unrecorded.

In 1912 Anna Pavlova bought Ivy House in Golders Green. It became her permanent home and Felix was a frequent visitor.

Another friend was the Marchioness of Ripon, who entertained at Coomb Court in Surrey. Queen Alexandra and other members of the royal family were often her guests, along with the dancers Nijinsky, Karsavina and Pavlova. At one of Lady Ripon's gatherings Felix was introduced to the now exiled King Manoel of Portugal, who lived at Richmond-on-Thames. They became firm friends.

In November 1911 Felix had lunch with Miche-Miche and his family. They invited him to join them in Cannes. At about the same time Princess Victoria invited him to stay with them on the English coast. Although flattered, Felix declined both invitations.

೮ ✴ ෨

For his final year at Oxford Felix rented 14 King Edward Street for himself and fellow undergraduates Jacques de Beistegui and Luigi Franchetti, the son of a famous Italian composer, who was at New College. Felix employed Russian cooks, an English butler and a French valet, Josef. The house was usually chaotic. Franchetti played the piano, while Felix's bulldog Punch and squawking parrot Florence caused mayhem. When Felix stayed away at night Josef took the prince's breakfast upstairs, ate it himself and brought the empty tray down so that the landlady thought Felix was in his room.

Felix's granddaughter recalled, 'My grandfather was a very friendly person because he had a very open mind ... He was ... kind to everyone and everyone liked him, because he had a crazy charm. And he knew all the great characters in the countries where they went.' In May 1912 he attended the Empire Fancy-Dress Ball at the Savoy Hotel, partnering Marjorie Manners in the gavotte. 'He went to the balls because it amused him. But he could not dance. He was dancing, but he was dancing very badly, but he knew it.'[43]

On 11 July Felix caused a stir at the Eglinton Ball at the Royal Albert Hall, arriving in an elaborate sixteenth-century Russian boyar's costume in gold braid embroidered with red flowers and edged with sable. It was studded with precious stones and had a hat to match. In his belt Felix thrust an elaborate dagger. The photograph is one of the most famous images of Felix.

At the ball he met Jack Seton-Gordon, another Oxford undergraduate. They rented two communicating flats at Curzon Street, Mayfair. The flat soon proved too small, so Felix rented a larger one at 15 Parkside, Knightsbridge overlooking Hyde Park. In a prescient move, he paid the rent for a decade in advance. He ordered 'new and unusual furniture' which gave an air of 'refined comfort'[44] and black carpets.

Jack Seton-Gordon had once shared a house with the president of the exclusive Bullingdon Club and around this time Felix also joined. 'I was chosen to be a member of yet another club at Oxford, but I'm completely dissatisfied with it, because for a whole year I have told everyone that I don't feel like joining this Company (cream of the Oxford aristocracy and rich students) but they obviously need money,' he told his mother.[45]

ଔ ✶ ଛ

It goes without saying that all this social life had not helped Felix's studies. In 1910 Eric Hamilton recorded that 'after dinner ... Felix composed a letter to the Dean of the University, with my help, re degrees and diplomas'.[46] By 1912 things were more serious and Felix was forced to abandon his frivolous lifestyle. He was still unable to write English without errors and his spelling in any language was bad.

While Austin Earl was awaiting the results of his civil service examinations, Felix asked him to stay on and coach him, as 'other interests had interfered with his reading'. A couple of weeks later, 'Austin asked him whether he should not start doing some reading. "I do not think so, my dear Austin," he replied. "I shall do what I did in St Petersburg. I shall ask the examiners to breakfast and I shall put an envelope with a cheque for £100 [nearly £8,000 today] on each one's plate."' Austin explained that, successful as this method might be in Russia, it would certainly not work at Oxford.[47]

Written examinations were at the end of June, with nine questions each on political economy, political science, public finance and political theories of the seventeenth and eighteenth centuries. Felix telegraphed home that he had withstood the tests well despite the tropical heat.

After an intense period of study he was so tired that he asked his college superiors if he could spend a week in Scotland. In Edinburgh he nervously awaited his results. 'I'm almost sure I passed the exam, but I am still afraid to announce it earlier than I know for certain. They were very, very difficult...' Felix failed the first examination and did not tell his mother the whole story. 'I look forward to your telegram about the final exam results,' she wrote. 'What confuses me is that you did not pass the first. How will they let you out?'[48] Finally, Felix said he had been told he passed and would know the result in early July.

Felix received a third-degree diploma (or certificate), the lowest award for those who had only passed, certifying that the proscribed course of lectures had been attended.

But that was not the whole truth. It is alleged by C. S. Lewis that Arthur Farquharson, a Fellow at University College, and the college chaplain Alexander Carlyle made a special certificate which they presented to Felix in a solemn ceremony. As Dr Nicholson said, he 'even contrived to finesse a pass, to his own professed surprise (though less, perhaps, to ours)'.[49]

Princess Zenaide was ecstatic. Felix was not academically minded and could not put his studies above social life but he was glad to obtain a diploma in political economy, even if it was third class.

∞ ✴ ∞

After leaving Oxford, Felix returned to London and threw himself into the social whirl. Two cousins, Maya Koutouzoff and Irina Rodzianko, came to stay, as did Prince Paul Karageorgevich, the later regent of Yugoslavia. King Manoel and Jack Seton-Gordon were frequent visitors.

Nearly every night there was a fancy-dress ball or party. At a charity performance at Earl's Court, Felix, dressed as a sixteenth-century Russian ambassador, greeted a fictional king played by Prince Christopher of Greece. Before another ball at the Albert Hall Felix gave his ostentatious Louis XVI costume to the Duke of Mecklenburg-Schwerin and came as a simple French sailor.

Felix and society leader Mrs Hwfa Williams organised a masked dinner and dance. As she recalled in her 1935 memoirs *It Was Such Fun*, they 'danced on till 3am when a crowd of us went off in Felix's car, with his old bulldog Punch sitting on the front seat'. At Covent Garden in the early morning they watched the fruit arrive for the market, 'discarding our masks on the way'.

Felix spent a few days in Jersey and visited Anna Pavlova, who had shipped her furniture over from Russia.

Before leaving England Felix gave a farewell fancy-dress dinner at the Berkeley Hotel, followed by a party at a friend's studio. The following day he returned home, taking with him 'a handsome, attractive chauffeur named Street' who had been employed by Austin Earl's father.[50]

It was usual for students' names to remain 'on the books' after they left Oxford and for them to pay a subscription. This enabled them to return for such things as voting in college elections. In January 1913 Felix replied to the college bursar from St Petersburg:

Dear Mr Poynton,

I only just got your letter as I have been away from Petersburg for a month.

It would be better to take off my name from the books, as I am very busy here and unfortunately want [*sic*] be able to come back to Oxford which I miss so much.

Sincerely yours, F. Elston.[51]

Felix's years at Oxford were probably the happiest time before his marriage.

His rooms at University College were later renamed the Youssoupov Rooms.

4

Irina and Felix

'I married my wife out of snobbery. My wife married me for money.'
Felix's wry sense of humour, recalled by a friend[1]

While visiting Grand Duke Michael Michaelovich in October 1910 Felix spotted the latest photograph of his fifteen-year-old niece Princess Irina. 'How beautiful she is,' he remarked to his mother. 'I trust my senses,' she replied. 'I know what I am saying when I praise her!'[2]

Encouraged by Zenaide, Felix began paying serious attention to Irina. The tsar's niece would be a good match but Zenaide warned him to be careful in front of Countess Torby.

Princess Zenaide may have considered Irina as a possible future bride for Nicholas, although Irina was not quite thirteen when he died. Now she spotted another opportunity to ally her family with the Romanovs. Felix's granddaughter recalled, 'At some point my grandfather's mother and "aunt" [Grand Duchess Ella] said that the time has come for my grandfather to get married and have a family. So ... they thought about my grandmother...'[3]

Then in 1911 a report appeared in the British press:

One of the provincial papers today gives credence to the rumour which has been circulating recently as to the impending betrothal of Prince Arthur of Connaught and Princess Irene [sic] of Russia. The journal predicts a formal announcement before the departure of the Duke and Duchess of Connaught for Canada next month. The Princess is closely related to the British Royal Family...[4]

No betrothal took place.

Zenaide passed on a rumour that Prince Christopher of Greece, twenty-three-year-old youngest son of King George I and Queen Olga, was courting Irina, a match hoped-for by the Russian-born queen. Christopher often stayed at Harax with his sister Grand Duchess George and had been at Hvidøre when Irina was there.

In November Princess Zenaide visited Ai-Todor. 'Irina was astonishingly beautiful,' she told Felix. 'In my opinion, she loses in society, and is much more beautiful in her home environment...'[5] Zenaide had been one of the passions of Sandro's youth and when Irina's parents enquired when Felix would graduate from Oxford, she realised she could probably influence him in Felix's favour.

Sandro had his eye on an even bigger catch – the Prince of Wales. History would have been very different if in 1936 Edward VIII had come to the throne with Irina as his wife.

CR ✱ ℰⴰ

To Felix's frustration, at the end of January 1912 British newspapers reported his imminent engagement to the empress's niece Princess Louise of Battenberg, 'the second daughter of Prince Louis of Battenberg, English Admiral and cousin of the Queen of Spain'.[6] *Le Figaro* followed suit.

It was an old trick. The Battenbergs probably banked on Felix not wanting to cause a scandal by denying it. Zenaide, afraid that all her plans would come to dust, told Felix angrily that it was for the Battenbergs to refute this, not him. 'How stupid and unpleasant all this is!'[7]

Louise was visiting her sister in Greece, so Felix had a very unpleasant talk with Nona Kerr who said that if he and Louise loved each other there was no reason why they should not marry. Felix replied that to love someone they had to know each other and he would not marry until he was ready. Princess Victoria tried to talk to Felix but he pretended he did not understand and changed the subject.

Although the Battenbergs failed, in 1916 the *Daily Mirror* reminded readers that 'Princess Louise of Battenberg ... some years ago was reported engaged to a great Russian nobleman'.[8]

To his mother's annoyance he was still friendly with Elena. In August 1912 Felix attended the centenary celebrations of the Battle of Borodino. Despite the empress's ban on grand duchesses attending, he persuaded Elena and her sister-in-law Grand Duchess Victoria (Ducky) to accompany him incognito.

Although they were constantly surrounded by people, the usually frank Felix was brief when he telegraphed his mother: 'Everything is safe, a lot of fun.'[9]

CR ✱ ℰⴰ

At the beginning of July [NS] Irina, her mother, governess, Mr Stewart, Miss Coster and the boys met up with Frederick Fane in Calais. Sandro had gone to Paris. Nikita irritably asked why Fane was there. The governess explained that Fane was his mother's gentleman-in-waiting. 'But I really don't like him,' Nikita protested.[10]

From Dover the royal train took them to London. Irina saw the sights and accompanied her mother to visit Queen Alexandra at Marlborough House. She and her brothers then went to the Holkham House Hotel in Bognor. Irina must have hated it, as she wrote 'a dismal letter' to Aunt Olga.[11]

Rumours pursued her. On 10 July the press reported again that Irina would marry Prince Arthur of Connaught. 'The report received from Paris today,' the

Western Daily Press said, 'is that the formal betrothal has not yet taken place, but is not likely to be long delayed. It is suggested that it will give King George grounds for visiting Russia before paying his ceremonial visits to France and Germany.' The Duke of Connaught lost no time in issuing a denial.

At the end of July Irina, her mother and governess travelled by special train with Queen Alexandra and her daughter Victoria (Toria) to Sandringham. Grand Duchess George, her daughters and Prince Christopher were also there.

They returned to Russia in August with Fane. Irina 'was very sorry to leave London where she had such a good time'.[12]

Irina's relationship with her parents was distant. Both were wrapped up in their own love affairs. The Duchess of Coburg said that Xenia's marriage had completely broken down. She 'is in love with an Englishman and longs to get away. Sandro is away with an American woman.'[13] The governess, with whom Irina had a closer relationship, felt there was no intimacy between Irina and her mother. She was closer to her father but Sandro never asked how his daughter was progressing.

Seventeen-year-old Irina was having her first forays into charity work. In December she organised a bazaar which raised 3,066 roubles for the Xenia Association for the Welfare of Children of Workers and Airmen. The following February she organised a musical evening, raising 1,626 roubles for the charity.[14] She also organised a bazaar to aid famine victims in Saratov district. One of the villages asked for her photograph. A large portrait was sent which, to Irina's delight, was hung in the village school.

❦✶❦

In the winter of 1912 Felix, under severe pressure to marry, singled out Irina. Neither of her parents objected, nor tried to stop their daughter from seeing him.

Quite when Irina and Felix met is unclear. Felix said that he spotted an unknown young girl while out riding in the Crimea and was struck by her loveliness as she walked by. Despite riding the same route for several days, he did not see her again. Then one afternoon Sandro and Xenia called on the Youssoupovs with their daughter and he had ample time to admire Irina's stunning beauty.

Countess Kamarovskaia believed that Irina was attracted to Felix because she could talk to him easily. The princess was still painfully shy, even among her own family. When she went with her cousins to Grand Duke Peter's estate for a tennis tournament Irina was too shy to go onto the court when it was her turn to play. Grand Duchess Militza gave her a consolation prize.

Irina confided her hopes and dreams to Countess Kamarovskaia. The governess was worried. Learning that Xenia and Sandro were going abroad, she asked to see the grand duke, thinking Sandro would discuss the matter more seriously. She felt that Irina 'was completely deprived of her mother's care'.[15]

After conveying her impression of Irina and Felix's relationship, she asked if Irina should be protected from Felix, if she should be with Irina when they met, or whether a courtship could proceed. Sandro seemed open to the idea of an eventual marriage but, in view of Irina's extreme youth, it would have to wait. He asked her to monitor the situation but not to push Felix away.

❦✶❦

Irina was frequently in the company of Grand Duchesses Olga and Tatiana. 'I hope that we will see her often,' Tatiana wrote to Xenia. 'She was terribly glad to see Aunt Olga…' Irina had been ill but Xenia's reply from Denmark was brief. After enthusing about Hvidøre and all the cousins, she added almost as an afterthought: 'I am glad that Irina is with you and finally got better.'[16]

During the early part of 1913, while her mother was again absent, Irina spent time with Olga, Tatiana and Aunt Olga to whom she remained close. 'I was terribly sorry to leave Irina!' Olga Alexandrovna wrote. 'She scolded me, clung onto my neck and didn't want to let me go, my poor Titi!'[17]

Although they saw their aunt in St Petersburg, Irina and her brothers were forbidden to visit her at Gatchina without telephoning first. Irina was dismayed but Xenia felt that her sister's unconventional lifestyle, living with her husband *and* Nikolai Kulikovsky, was unsuitable. Yet she was happy to parade Fane in front of her daughter. Besides, Irina had already met Kulikovsky. In August 1910 Olga Alexandrovna noted that Irina 'sees him a lot and seems fond of him'.[18]

Irina was invited to Aunt Olga's regular Sunday gatherings in St Petersburg. Felix was included, as were members of the Leuchtenberg family, Irina's friend Zoia de Stoeckl and various officers, including Nikolai Rodionov. Olga Nicolaievna disapproved of twenty-five-year-old Felix, who had no position at court and no army post. 'The last one to arrive was Felix, so awfully civilian that the Cossacks wanted to beat him up.'[19] In a society where nearly all the men wore uniform, Felix stuck out like a sore thumb.

Irina's friendship with the grand duchesses also held the risk that she might come into contact with Rasputin. Olga told Irina that 'Grisha [Rasputin] is the only man with whom Mama can forget that she is the empress. She can relax with him.'[20] Sandro instructed the governess not to let Irina meet him.

☙ ✶ ❧

In February 1913 the Romanov dynasty celebrated its tercentenary. After the thanksgiving service delegations from all over Russia came to the Winter Palace to greet the tsar and both empresses. An old, bearded farmer, overwhelmed by the splendour, approached the dowager empress who stood 'gleaming with diamonds like a costly icon'. Thinking he was in church, 'he crossed himself devoutly and sank to his knees'. Irina, standing just behind with her distant cousin Prince Roman Romanoff and his sister Nadejda, was unable to stifle a loud giggle. The Duchess of Coburg 'turned as quick as lightning, turned up her nose and threatened with her finger – not Irina – but Nadya [*sic*] who was completely innocent'.[21]

Around that time rumours circulated in the Crimea that Felix was in love with Zoia de Stoeckl, whose father was gentleman-in-waiting and later comptroller to Grand Duchess George. Zoia was two years older than Irina, with beautiful eyes and a lovely figure but terribly spoilt. Agnes de Stoeckl wanted her daughter to make a good marriage. After Agnes tried unsuccessfully to link her with ex-King Manoel of Portugal, Grand Duchess George suggested Felix.

The situation was further complicated because Grand Duke George was Sandro's brother; his wife, the former Princess Marie of Greece, was Xenia's cousin and her best friend since childhood. Their home Harax was close to

Ai-Todor and they saw a lot of each other. The Stoeckls shared their hopes for Zoia with Xenia and news of these conversations reached Princess Zenaide.

Agnes tried to throw her daughter and Felix together. He was forced to be nice to the Stoeckls without doing anything that could link him to Zoia, who was frequently present at gatherings attended by Irina and her cousins.

Irina's governess was so worried that she asked for a private meeting with Princess Zenaide. She described Irina's withdrawn 'broken character ... her inner alienation from her parents, especially her mother's complete indifference to her and my ardent desire to see her completely happy...' If the rumours about Felix and Zoia were true, she had a duty to protect Irina from unnecessary distressing experiences.

Zenaide listened carefully, then said: 'My son loves Irina. He really likes her alone. Zoia is out of the question.' Zenaide told the governess to let the couple get to know each other better.[22]

Xenia knew that Irina and Felix were seeing each other. 'They like each other, the stupid children! I even talked about it to Mama. She is not quite sure whether it would be a good thing!'[23]

'In Russia the family ... of the tsar and tsarina were not always happy with the way my grandfather lived,' Xenia Sfiris explained, 'because he went to the gypsies, he went to bed late and he was finally making too much noise around his name.'[24]

For Easter Felix sent Irina a small decorative egg on a chain to wear around her neck. She was longing to see him again but her brother Dmitri had measles and Irina feared she might catch the illness.

To take the heat off, Felix went to London and threw himself into the social scene. His letters describe parties with Lady Ripon and lunch with ex-King Manoel. The Stoeckls continued making trouble. He received a despairing letter from Grand Duchess George, who was sorry that she had interfered and was now in a difficult position with Agnes. Felix thought Stoeckl's behaviour disgusting.

Felix returned to Russia in April with Jack Seton-Gordon. News that Felix was not travelling alone upset Zenaide. It looked bad, especially when Agnes spoke out against Jack, whom she did not know, trying to start talk of a homosexual affair.

Felix was delighted that his mother had spoken to Irina's governess. Rumours about him and Irina were circulating in London and people had already asked whether they were engaged.

But Irina also had another suitor.

○✱ ○

Grand Duke Dmitri Pavlovich had transferred to the Imperial Horse Guards. As an *aide-de-camp* to the tsar he lived much of the time at the Alexander Palace, where the emperor and empress treated him as a second son. He was tall, elegant and extremely attractive.

Felix, although attracted to some women, quickly tired of the process of courting and found more loyalty in men. By now he knew Dmitri well. They went out in the Youssoupovs' motorboat in the Crimea, caroused in restaurants and nightclubs and visited the gypsies. Anna Pavlova was their frequent guest.

The tsar and tsarina disapproved of their friendship, so Dmitri moved to his own palace on the Nevsky Prospekt. Felix helped with the redecoration.

Dmitri was a robust heterosexual, although it is possible that he experimented with Felix. Elizaveta Krasnykh believes 'that there *may* have been a homosexual relationship with Felix at some time' but that most of the rumours about them appeared *after* the revolution. Certainly, there was no mention of it in the correspondence of the Russian courtesans among themselves. Hints of their relationship come when a cigarette case went missing. Felix told his mother that Dmitri again wanted to use his bathroom, they had a fight and the cigarette case must have fallen out there. For a long time afterwards Felix and Zenaide referred to Dmitri in their letters as 'cigarette case'.[25]

On 10 July 1912 [NS] *The Western Daily Press* stated that the tsar's eldest daughter would shortly be betrothed to him. But Dmitri had no intention of marrying Olga. In 1910 the Duchess of Coburg had reported that Dmitri 'finds evenings with the tsar's daughters at Tsarskoe Selo boring ... Dmitri wants to back out of an imperial marriage.'[26]

He now had his eye on Irina. 'There was also someone else who was interested in her,' recalled Irina's granddaughter. 'But she preferred my grandfather.'[27]

✩

Irina and Dmitri probably met in 1907 in the Crimea, when she was twelve and he fifteen. He appears to have been attracted to Irina, although there are only five references to her in his diaries. Most of the evidence comes from Felix's memoirs and Princess Zenaide's worried letters to her son. Family letters mention that Felix and Dmitri fought over Irina but there is no doubt that the enduring love of Dmitri's life was Crown Princess (later Queen) Marie of Romania, by whom he was seduced in his teens. His passion remained lifelong and she was the only woman he ever really loved.[28]

When Dmitri began visiting Irina's home Zenaide was afraid. Felix wrote to Irina fearing that she no longer liked him, that all his dreams were broken and happiness had eluded him.

Felix had been corresponding with Irina's parents. Irina would be eighteen on 3 July and when Xenia arrived he would probably be introduced to the dowager empress. Dmitri had told him that 'Maria Feodorovna wants Irina to marry him [Dmitri], but he thinks that if Irina doesn't love him, but loves me, he will not resist'.[29]

Felix believed that the dowager empress's plan was for Dmitri to eventually become tsar with Irina as his wife. The morganatic marriage of the tsar's brother Michael in 1912 barred him from the succession and the haemophiliac Tsarevich Alexei was not likely to reign long.

During tea with Irina's parents Felix explained the situation about Zoia and the rumours started by the Stoeckls, saying if they had anything against him seeing Irina perhaps he should end the relationship with her now. Xenia and Sandro seemed unconcerned. Sandro asked him not to rush as time would tell and, besides, they had to speak to the tsar and the dowager empress.

Xenia and Sandro then spoke to the emperor and empress, who in principle were not opposed, 'except that Alix says that he used to have a bad reputation,'

Xenia wrote in her diary. 'I know from people who know him well, that this is a lie. And even if there was something, then it's all past...'[30]

CR✶ℬ

Irina was enjoying herself at Aunt Olga's. 'Andrusha and Odi went there in Andrusha's little motor which he drives himself. He loves it terribly and drives us all the time,' she told her grandmother.[31]

Later that summer they went to Le Tréport. Irina begged Felix to join her, threatening otherwise to drown herself in the sea. She could not understand why he had to spend so much time supervising his estates. Without him she found life sad and empty. She was looking forward to joining her grandmother in England, where she would also see Felix.

He had been trying to forget Marjorie Manners but when he saw her again his opinion changed. Irina was 'a good, wonderful dream,' Marjorie 'a complete insincere comedy'.[32] He had irrevocably decided on Irina.

While Felix was enjoying Royal Ascot, Princess Zenaide and Irina's parents began long prenuptial marriage negotiations. The dowager empress still favoured Dmitri but Xenia 'would have nothing against [you] if Irina will hear of no-one else,' Zenaide told Felix. 'What I am afraid of is what will happen to your relationship with Dmitri, since I am certain of his duplicity. He is doing everything he can to arouse Irina's interest and is always by her side ... I am frightened of him and the fatal military tunic...'[33] Dmitri was in the regiment in which Manteuffel had served.

Dmitri told Felix that he had confided his feelings for Irina to the dowager empress. Zenaide called him two-faced and treacherous. He was constantly with Irina, meanwhile assuring Felix that nothing deep was starting between them. 'He tells you everything just as he sees it, only in the way he wants you to know about it,' Zenaide warned Felix. 'With you he seems genuine, but it is not certain what he thinks deep down. Even if this all turns out all right, I am afraid for the future. This must be borne in mind. I will not calm down as long as Dmitri isn't married.'[34]

CR✶ℬ

As Dmitri pursued Irina, Felix became indignant at his foul conduct. He found London unbearable without her and asked when she would arrive from Paris. 'Sometimes I want to see you so badly, talk with you, that I'm ready to take the train and to go there where you are.'[35]

The Stoeckls continued their games. They constantly telephoned Felix, who said he was busy. Zenaide was afraid that Felix was falling into a trap. She took her son to task: 'Concerning the Stoeckl family, I still regard them as dangerous "friends,"' she wrote, in a letter whose meaning is not entirely clear. 'Her letter is all lies – how can you not see this? How necessary it was to get out of this silly and nasty situation and come up on dry land. That's exactly what she did, thanks to their cleverness and your naiveté. Thank God that you never accepted this offer. It is better not to quarrel with them but to be cautious and not to trust them...'[36]

With Irina's arrival imminent Felix was afraid of complications from the Battenbergs and Miche-Miche, whose daughters were Irina's friends. Countess

Torby telephoned Felix every day and he did not want a repeat of the story with Zoia.

Irina had told Felix something bad about Zoia and this strained the friendship between her and Irina. Xenia told her daughter that it was mean to destroy a friendship. As the Stoeckls realised they had lost, rumours about Felix's sexual orientation began circulating. To Felix, this was no coincidence.

It was not rumours about homosexuality that worried him. He was afraid Irina's family would find out about his feelings for Grand Duchess Elena.[37]

QR ✶ ꝵꝍ

Irina and her parents arrived in mid-July [NS]. Her staggering beauty delighted London society.

While visiting a museum Irina told Felix she had irrevocably decided to marry him even if her grandmother was against it. She would insist on having her own way. Felix thought she must realise that her parents were leading separate lives. This became apparent when Felix lunched at the Ritz with Sandro, Xenia, Irina and Frederick Fane.

Felix had first seen Fane at the Café de Paris in October 1911, when Sandro with Mary Warburton and Xenia with Fane (whom Felix thought very handsome) were sitting near him. Felix found it incomprehensible that they paraded their lovers in public.

Now, in 1913, he thought that Fane was very likeable. He was very familiar with Xenia, reminding her about things she needed to buy for Irina. That evening they all went to the theatre, where Fane sat with them. Felix found it very odd that he travelled with Xenia as her gentleman-in-waiting. 'Wish I could keep him always!' Xenia told her sister.[38]

Princess Zenaide scolded her son for showing himself in public with Irina and her family *before* the dowager empress had consented to their marriage. 'If she doesn't meet you now, then this is a very bad sign!'[39] Significantly, the dowager empress stated that if their feelings were really serious, she would not object.

Princess Zenaide was also horrified to hear that Felix was going to a dinner dance where people were dancing the tango, which she thought disgusting. 'I am offended to think that Irina is also attracted there, and I find that it is time to sober up. Life is not given to turn it into some kind of bacchanal!'[40]

QR ✶ ꝵꝍ

Irina had given Felix her heart. He told her about his past life and she accepted it with understanding.[41] Yet it is doubtful if Irina, who led a sheltered life, had any real comprehension of what Felix was saying. She probably was unaware of the meaning of the words homosexual or bisexual. Years later she professed not to know the meaning of rape. Yet it suited both of them to marry. Irina would ally herself with the richest man in Russia, while Felix would link himself to the Romanovs. In 1913 Felix was 'spoilt, self-absorbed and neurotic'.[42] The principal female in his life remained his mother.

Felix wrote to Irina when he returned to Russia. Xenia had enquired how everything was going. 'I answered that for me, I had decided irrevocably and think that you also decided finally ... I'm so infinitely happy that my premonition about you came true and that you turned out to be exactly the person who I wanted you to be…' He signed it 'your devoted Felix'.[43]

He admired Irina's beauty, intelligence and sound judgement. Her shyness was in stark contrast to the free, easy and familiar English girls but whether he loved her is a moot point. Love came afterwards. In 1951 he wrote: 'Whatever I tell you, you know I love you the most in the world and that you are all my life.'[44]

⌒✶⌓

At the end of July [OS] Felix went with Ella to the Solovetsky Monastery in the north of Russia. He occupied a small dark cell, slept on a hard bed and ate the same food as the monks. Yet he enjoyed the experience, spending the day fishing while Ella spent hours at prayer.

He wrote to Irina, addressing her by her Christian name for the first time. 'How strange fate brings people together. Have I ever thought that there are such engrained views on life in your small inexperienced head and that you and I understand and feel this life in the same way … We both thought that nobody understood us and that only we felt like this…'[45]

Irina was back at Le Tréport. She played golf and 'since we are always out in the sun I am awfully tanned. I'm completely brown,' she told her grandmother. 'I am off to play a game of tennis with papa now.'[46]

They returned to Ai-Todor. On 26 September Empress Alexandra asked Xenia about Felix. 'She asks if we are sure of him – which, unfortunately, I cannot say.'[47] But Irina and Felix *had* decided. The parents agreed to make the official announcement when the dowager empress returned from Denmark.

Soon afterwards they all met the architect Nikolai Krasnov in the pine grove between Ai-Todor and the neighbouring estate of Djulber. Xenia and Sandro had chosen a place nearby for a small dwelling. Another site had been cleared so they could build a larger house in the future. Their home in St Petersburg would be a wing of the Youssoupovs' Moika Palace.

The following afternoon Irina and her family met the elder Youssoupovs at the old Morozov dacha next to Koreiz which they were giving Irina and Felix as a wedding present and which would be refurbished by Krasnov.

The private betrothal ceremony took place at Ai-Todor at five o'clock on 5 October. Irina and Felix were blessed by both sets of parents. Neither Olga nor Tatiana recorded their reaction to the engagement.

On 19 October, Irina and her parents drove with the Youssoupovs, Grand Duchess George and Krasnov towards Sedam Kaya, 'the Eagle's Flight', a rock with an observation platform above the woods built by Felix. After ninety minutes they arrived at the Eagle's Nest, a small tea-house on a cliff, and drove to a plateau with a view over Kokoz valley. What Xenia called 'this delightful place' and the Eagle's Nest was given to Irina by Felix.[48] Irina was so shy that Xenia had to persuade her to kiss Felix in thanks.

The engagement was an open secret. Felix was inundated with congratulations but Irina's parents still had doubts. The empress told Xenia that she would never let Felix marry one of her girls.

⌒✶⌓

In early November Xenia and Irina went to order the trousseau in Paris, where they were joined by Sandro's brother Grand Duke Nicholas Michaelovich and Fane. Alarming rumours were circulating about Felix's reputation. Sandro was worried.

When Felix arrived he was met by Sandro and Count Alexander Mordvinov, the ADC. Felix said that 'even if a quarter of what was being said about him was true, he would not consider he had the right to marry...'[49] Although Xenia and Sandro believed him, it was very unpleasant. Olga Alexandrovna's husband Prince Peter of Oldenburg was homosexual. Xenia did not want her sister's fate for Irina but, as Olga said enviously, her niece was terribly lucky in everything.

Felix saw this as another vile game of the Stoeckls. Sandro agreed. When Dmitri heard that people were trying to upset the wedding he spoke to Sandro for three hours, convincing him that the rumours about Felix were untrue. Zenaide believed Dmitri corroborated Felix's assurances as protection against homosexual allegations directed at *him*. She warned her son to be careful, as his last stay in Paris had made an unfavourable impression on Xenia. There was too much carousing and Xenia hoped he would not repeat this. Zenaide feared Fane might be influencing her. Dmitri saw it as the work of the Stoeckls. He told Felix that they should announce the engagement as soon as possible and shut them up.

On 6 November Irina chose an engagement present from her parents, a pink pearl suspended from a diamond chain. Sandro was still upset by the rumours, which were impossible to ignore. He was prepared to put Felix to the test to see if his behaviour proved satisfactory. If not, they could cancel the wedding.[50] In the meantime, he agreed that the couple could see each other and Irina gave Felix an emerald ring.

From the Crimea they went to Paris. 'I very much want to go to you and see you and because I love Denmark so much and haven't been there for so long,' Irina told her grandmother. 'I was such an incredible pig when I stayed with you at Hvidøre.' She was concerned that the dowager empress had not met her fiancé. 'It is such a pity you have never seen Felix. You most certainly need to meet him, he is awfully sweet. It is a lot of fun here. I have been to a small ball which Papa held and have been to the theatre once. I am very happy to be here now, but I was terribly sorry when we left Crimea. The weather was so wonderful there. From tomorrow I shall be doing wonderful gymnastics again. They say that within twenty lessons one becomes big and strong and maybe even has huge muscles so you certainly won't recognise me the next time you see me.'[51] Irina persuaded everyone to learn the tango but Felix disapproved, describing it as filth. Luckily, she understood.

Zenaide was concerned about the life her son was leading. She admonished him about a ball at the Paris Ritz and a list of guests associated with the Youssoupov name which disgusted her. Moreover, his letters were infrequent. 'I know that it is not all your fault that you are compelled to lead this sort of life which gives such a sad impression on people here [in Russia]! But although this state of affairs is not of your doing, thank God that you are getting used to it, but it is hell for Irina!' Zenaide had another concern. 'You do not tell me anything about Elena Vladimirovna... She is another worry to me as I know that she is in Paris and that it cannot be that you never saw her...'[52]

But Felix's relationship with Elena was a secret that he would not share with anybody.

ʘ⁎⦌

Irina's next stop was Copenhagen. Felix travelled separately, arriving on 6/19 December and booking into the Hotel Angleterre. It was the tsar's name day and Felix was invited to lunch at Amalienborg Palace. Princess Zenaide, an intimate friend of Marie Feodorovna, stressed that his first impression was very important.

After lunch the dowager empress took him into an adjoining room. Aware that Irina was her favourite granddaughter he used his considerable personal charm and the dowager empress promised to do all she could. Felix had won. 'Grandmother drank our health,' he wrote home proudly.[53]

'Irina is already engaged to the young Prince Youssoupoff [sic] and one says she is happy and delighted!' Olga Alexandrovna excitedly told her cousin.[54] Irina's betrothal caused considerable annoyance in some circles, as there had been talk of a Balkan prince.

On 22 December at four o'clock 'the betrothal was celebrated at the palace of Grand Duke Alexander Michaelovich ... of Princess Irina Alexandrovna and Count Felix Soumarokoff-Elston',[55] in the presence of the dowager empress, Grand Duke Cyril Vladimirovich, his wife Victoria, Grand Duchess Olga Alexandrovna and her husband Peter. Fifteen-year-old Feodor, who was particularly hostile to Felix, threatened not to attend. Xenia prayed for their happiness. 'I cannot believe that Irina is getting married,'[56] she wrote emotionally.

'My prayers and thoughts will be with you so, so much,' Alexandra told Xenia, 'it seems quite incredible your child is going to marry ... As we cannot be at your service of intercession I will send you Olga and Tatiana and shall place a candle for her at the Church of the Sign [Tsarskoe Selo]; I kiss you ever so tenderly & bless Irina (to whom we send a small bracelet she can also wear in her hair).'[57]

Nevertheless, Alexandra was upset because Felix had chosen Irina instead of her own niece Louise. 'Well, Irina's engagement to Felix Soumarokoff has at last been announced and one says they swim in happiness and she is beginning to wake up,' she wrote to her brother. 'God grant them happiness – they are so young and have little character I fear – she is lovely. I am sorry Xenia's only daughter making such a marriage – after all a false position (in England so easy) and he is a civilian.' She bemoaned Felix's lack of position and tact. 'Well I hope poor Xenia will have no bothers and that all will go well. Awful giving one's child away, not knowing what is in store for her – well here they have been ten months everywhere inseparable almost in Russia and abroad, so had time to know each other well – at least she remains in Russia and has everything one could only wish for...'[58]

Financially this was certainly true. In 1914 the Youssoupovs' income was 1.5 million gold roubles a year (equivalent to nearly £9 million today) with Felix's personal income estimated at 180,000 roubles (around £1 million today).

Irina spent her last unmarried Christmas Eve at the Anitchkov Palace with her family and on 29 December was present at Aunt Olga's Sunday gathering.

It was the end of an eventful year. Her wedding would be the major event of the 1914 season.

CR ✶ SO

Since 1902 Irina's parents had purchased two diamonds on her birthday and name day (5 May), with which jeweller David Hahn was assembling a diamond rivière necklace, adding two diamond solitaires every year.[59] Now Irina was showered with magnificent jewellery.

The tsar and tsarina gave her two rows of pearls and the tsar presented twenty-nine perfect diamonds. From the dowager empress came a diamond and pearl brooch; from Xenia and Sandro a sapphire and diamond necklace, Xenia's own emerald brooch with diamonds and rubies, three pearl sprays and a little diamond necklace. Xenia also gave a few loose emeralds for a diadem which Felix was having made for his bride. A note in Xenia's jewel book shows that she gave her daughter an ornate ruby and diamond corsage which had been given to her by Sandro on their wedding day.

The magazine *Stolitsa i usad'ba* published images of some of the presents displayed in the hall of Xenia and Sandro's palace. These included twelve items made for Irina by Chaumet using Youssoupov family jewels, among them the art deco Sunburst tiara. Other photographs show eleven pages of pearls, emeralds, rubies, sapphires and diamonds from the Youssoupov patrimony, including the pearl-and-diamond Lovers' Knot tiara.[60]

Felix gave his bride a Cartier tiara 'mounted with engraved rock crystal bars below a circular-cut diamond gallery' with a central diamond of 3.66 carats, and a bracelet with two large diamonds. 'The wedding was such a major event that the publicity photograph of the bride in her diamonds sold out' before Cartier's head office in Paris could acquire one.[61]

At Felix's request, the tsar granted him the privilege of using the imperial box at the theatre. For the man who had everything there was nothing more Nicholas could give.

It was traditional for people who had participated in the princess's upbringing to receive a present from the Office of the Minister of the Imperial Court. Awards were therefore given to Miss Coster and the nurse Marie Leviton.

The wedding would take place in the Chapel of St Alexander Nevsky at the dowager empress's Anitchkov Palace, so the invitations were sent out in her name. There was no ceremonial programme and no edicts for public prayer on Irina's behalf. It was a private event, not a state occasion.

Irina had one more duty to perform. As Felix was not of royal blood she was required to renounce her rights to the throne.

The night before the wedding Xenia recorded that her daughter did not sleep; she spent the night crying.

CR ✶ SO

On 9/22 February Irina lunched with her parents before dressing for her wedding. She was not obliged to wear a heavy court dress, mantle and imperial regalia. Instead, she chose a white satin gown with pearls on the bodice and long sleeves, with a long train embroidered with silver. She carried a small bouquet of lilacs and orchids. Her veil was held in place by Felix's gift of the Cartier tiara of rock crystal and diamonds. Felix says Irina wore Marie-Antoinette's veil but Grand Duchess Xenia's diary makes it clear that the wedding veil Irina wore was her own.[62]

Irina was blessed with an icon by her parents before leaving with her six-year-old brother Vassili in a golden coach drawn by four white horses and surrounded by a guard of honour.

As the procession passed through countless rooms to the chapel Irina was accompanied by the tsar and preceded by Vassili, who acted as icon boy. 'Whenever we came to a place where I didn't know the way to go, the Emperor would prod me with his knee in the right direction,' he recalled.[63] Irina's parents and her grandmother followed her to where the bridegroom was waiting to begin the service, which was held at around three o'clock that afternoon.

Felix wore the gold-embroidered black frock coat and white trousers of the nobility. His day started badly when the old lift up to the Anitchkov's chapel stopped halfway up. The tsar came to his rescue.

The bride's mother was almost overcome with emotion. 'They both looked so lovely, so young, happy and she – so lovely in the little diadem which he gave her … Nicky said he had never seen her so beautiful!'[64]

Among the guests were the British Ambassador Sir George Buchanan, his wife, daughter Meriel and the Danish Minister Harald Scavenius. Grand Duchess Ella was not present. She felt that a nun would be out of place among 'the glitter of jewels and decorations, of brilliant uniforms, and women's gaily coloured dresses'.[65]

In the small chapel, which the Danish Minister's wife thought not much larger than an ordinary sitting room, six groomsmen held golden crowns over the couple's heads. The nervous bride dropped her handkerchief and thirteen-year-old Anastasia darted forward to return it. Part of the ceremony involved the bridal couple walking on a carpet of pink silk. Traditionally, whoever put their foot on the carpet first would rule the household. Irina was determined to do this but she caught her foot in her train and Felix took advantage.

A champagne reception was held in the winter garden, where Princess Zenaide, in pale grey satin, a pale violet hat and 'a few beautiful diamonds', stood 'smiling faintly' as the long line of guests filed through. 'Her thoughts seemed very far away.'[66]

A wedding breakfast of *blinis* (Russian pancakes), consommé, roe cutlets and a baked apple desert was served on solid gold plates. Vassili went round drinking all the half empty glasses of champagne and had to be quickly removed.

As wedding favours male guests were given a pale blue satin bag embroidered with Felix and Irina's initials, which contained almonds; ladies were given a blue and white fan inscribed 'Anitchkov, 1914'.

Shortly after the wedding the tsar granted Felix the name and title of Prince Felix Youssoupov, Count Soumarokoff-Elston the younger. This permitted him to hold the title of Prince Youssoupov during the lifetime of his father.

The radiant newlyweds left for the Youssoupov Palace at six o'clock. They were greeted with the traditional bread and salt before going to Irina's childhood home, where her parents blessed them in the same manner and photographs were taken in the hall.

Both families accompanied them to the station. When Irina and Felix entered the railway carriage they found his bulldog Punch sitting among the profusion of flowers.

This should have been the beginning of a glittering new life for Irina, taking her place as the wife of one of Russia's wealthiest men. Rank, money and privilege all seemed to be hers.[67]

Fate, however, had other ideas.

5

Early Married Life

'They lived a very happy life together.'

Mme Xenia Sfiris

'Arrived safely,' Irina telegraphed to her grandmother from Paris. 'Wonderful weather. We remember the wedding at Anitchkov. How nice and cosy it was.'[1]

Irina soon found that Felix loved to buy clothes for her. She had fashionable waves put at the front of her hair and had her ears pierced. She enjoyed Paris and was sorry to leave, intimating to her mother that her marriage was ideal. Felix was equally happy. Despite the rumours, throughout their lives they shared a double bed.

They departed for Cairo and visited the Valley of the Kings. Irina was enchanted by the beauty of Egypt but the press followed their movements, giving them little peace. In Jaffa they had great difficulty in extracting themselves from the over-eager governor, whose attentions nearly made them miss their train. In Jerusalem so many dignitaries were assembled on the platform that Irina had to be persuaded to come and greet everyone. Along the road to the Orthodox Cathedral five thousand pilgrims, who had arrived for Holy Week, cheered the tsar's niece. The following day the Patriarch granted them a private audience. Conversation was difficult, even with an interpreter.

Problems with Irina's health had become apparent almost immediately. Four years earlier she suffered a bad fall and since then had been experiencing pain in her lower back. Further falls while riding had added to the problem. During Holy Week they attended services at the Basilica of the Holy Sepulchre but by Saturday Irina was unwell and spent several days in bed. This put a stop to many plans, although they held a reception for Russian pilgrims in the Mission gardens. At a service in the Orthodox cathedral so many pilgrims tried to enter to see them that there was a stampede. Irina and Felix barely escaped through a side door.

In Jerusalem a young Abyssinian man threw a petition into their carriage. He had fled his homeland after committing a crime and came to the Mission that evening to beg them to hire him. To Irina's displeasure Felix did so and Thespé became his devoted servant. He insisted on sleeping on the floor outside their door and constantly flushed the lavatory, which to him was a novelty.

From Alexandria they took a boat to Italy, collected their car and drove to Naples. There, probably more by accident than design, they met Grand Duke Dmitri.

In Rome their servants awaited them. They spent a week in Florence, from where Irina complained to her grandmother that Felix bought anything that pleased him. Moving on towards Milan, they took the train to Paris and collected Irina's reset jewels from Chaumet.

Irina had not kept in touch with her cousins. 'Where is Irina? Does she write a lot?' Tatiana asked her aunt Xenia. 'What is she up to?'[2]

☙ ✱ ❧

The season was in full swing when they arrived at Felix's Knightsbridge flat on 29 May/11 June. Irina's grandmother was at Marlborough House and the newlyweds were frequent guests for lunch. On Sunday Irina and Felix accompanied the dowager empress to the Russian Church. '[Irina] has completely grown up and looks charming,' she wrote in her diary.

One morning Irina and her grandmother went for a drive in Hyde Park, returning to Knightsbridge to find Felix still in his nightshirt. 'Did you see much of Irina and Felix?' Tatiana asked Xenia, unaware that her aunt was not in England. 'I heard from Aunt Olga that they are awfully lazy and they get up late, such pigs, it's awful. When are they returning to Russia and where will they go? Will they spend autumn in Crimea?'[3]

On 28 June Irina and Felix had lunch at Buckingham Palace with King George and Queen Mary, Queen Alexandra, Princess Victoria (Toria), the dowager empress, Queen Olga of Greece and Prince Aage of Denmark. Later that afternoon news arrived that the heir to the Austro-Hungarian throne, Archduke Franz Ferdinand, and his morganatic wife Sophie, the Duchess of Hohenberg, had been assassinated while on an official visit to the Bosnian capital, Sarajevo. Although everybody was shaken by this news, nobody thought it would disturb the peace of Europe.

Xenia and Sandro arrived but Xenia 'soon ran off to Paris after her flighty husband who wants to amuse himself there. Her daughter was also in London, very pretty indeed,' the Duchess of Coburg noted.[4]

'After tea' on 3 July, Empress Marie recorded in her diary, she and Queen Alexandra went to Knightsbridge 'to visit Irina in their sweet little apartment.' Felix's rather colourful memoirs place the visit in the early morning, when he and Irina were woken by a commotion. Downstairs, Thespé, under strict instructions not to let anyone in, tried to prevent the ladies from entering. Words had failed and the empress was threatening the unfortunate man with her umbrella.

☙ ✱ ❧

Irina and Felix went to Marlborough House on 11 July to say goodbye. From Paris they travelled to Bad-Kissengen, where Felix senior was taking the cure. The situation in Europe was growing more alarming every day. Austria was determined on revenge and by the last week in July it seemed war was imminent.

Shortly after the Youssoupovs' arrival Irina received a telegram from a relative advising them to leave Germany immediately to avoid being trapped. Troops were mobilizing in Russia and in Germany crowds began hurling insults at the Russians. Irina, Felix and his parents headed for Berlin.

It was too late. On 23 July [NS] Serbia was presented with a harsh ultimatum. Austria deemed the reply unsatisfactory and declared war on 28 July. Austrian troops bombarded Belgrade and Serbia appealed to Russia, traditional protector of the Slavs, for help. As the complicated network of European alliances came into play Austria, France and Germany mobilised and on 1 August [NS] Germany declared war on Russia.

At the Continental Hotel in Berlin chaos reigned. At eight o'clock in the morning of 3 August Felix and all his male companions were arrested. Felix senior telephoned the Russian embassy but was told everyone was too busy to help them.

In desperation, Irina telephoned her cousin Crown Princess Cecilie of Germany, whose response was not reassuring. The kaiser said they were now prisoners of war. Felix senior contacted the Spanish ambassador (who was looking after the interests of the Russians in Germany) and arranged for one of his secretaries to come over. Soon after his arrival the kaiser's adjutant appeared with a paper for them to sign.

The kaiser gave them a choice of three places of residence, guaranteeing that all consideration would be extended to them. They were to refrain from all political activity and remain in Germany 'for ever'. This was ridiculous. The adjutant agreed to have the text corrected to read 'for the duration of the war' and return at eleven o'clock the next morning.

The Spanish diplomat then accompanied Felix senior to see Sverbeev, the Russian ambassador. He had arranged a special train to evacuate the embassy staff and agreed that the Youssoupovs could leave with him. Sverbeev also said that the dowager empress and Grand Duchess Xenia had passed through Berlin earlier that day and had tried to contact them. However, with their train surrounded by a mob and the situation critical, they had been unable to wait.

The next morning Irina, Felix and his parents joined the convoy of embassy cars driving through a hostile crowd to the station. Their servants arrived only just in time, having lost all the luggage. A bag containing fifty thousand marks was mistakenly left in the hotel, 'but the family were so relieved to have escaped the German clutches that they willingly left that money as their ransom'.[5] Felix's English valet Arthur Keeping remained at the hotel to make it look as if they were still there. He was interned for the duration of the war.

To the Youssoupovs' relief, the train finally crossed into Denmark and they proceeded to Copenhagen.

CR ★ ÑD

On 4 August they booked into the Hotel Angleterre, where among Irina's first visitors were her mother and grandmother. They were both extremely agitated, having endured much indignity at the hands of the Germans in Berlin.

Germany had declared war on France and marched into Belgium; England entered the fray against Germany and would soon declare war on Austria. Denmark remained neutral but there were reports of insurrections in Finland.

Although Irina was in the early stages of pregnancy and feeling unwell, it was decided that they must return to Russia immediately.

On the evening of 5 August King Christian X, Queen Alexandrine and members of the Danish royal family assembled at Frihaven (Copenhagen's free port in the harbour) as Irina, Felix, his parents, the dowager empress and Xenia boarded the ferry for Malmö in Sweden. From there a train took them to Stockholm. Irina spent most of the train journey lying on a bed next to Princess Zenaide, who was also unwell.

In Stockholm they boarded a train going north towards the border with Finland. At 4.30 that afternoon they arrived at Kiruna and transferred to cars for the drive towards the Polar Circle. The weather turned stormy but they crossed safely into Finland.

At Torneo the old Finnish imperial train, unused for nearly eighteen years and rapidly refurbished, awaited them. While the family were having tea on board, a train arrived from Russia and, to their surprise, they spotted Princess Victoria of Battenberg and her daughter Louise (the one-time rumoured fiancée of Felix), who had been visiting their Russian relatives. They quickly exchanged news through the train window before Victoria and Louise hurried across the bridge into Sweden.

At two o'clock in the morning of 26 July/8 August they pulled away, finally arriving at Peterhof at noon the following day.

The Youssoupovs moved into The Farm. Olga Alexandrovna described Irina as 'terribly pretty and thin, talks a lot and is cheerful'.[6]

It had been a dramatic end to their honeymoon.

ℭℜ ✶ ℬⅅ

In Russia the war was greeted with jubilation. The tsar changed the capital's German name, St Petersburg, to the more Slavic-sounding Petrograd and appointed his imposing cousin Grand Duke Nicholas Nicolaievich (Nicholasha) commander-in-chief of the army. He also allowed his brother Michael, banished after his morganatic marriage to Natasha Wulfurt (given the name Brasova) in 1912, to return home.

Sandro was reunited with his family before leaving to be 'stationed in the headquarters of the fourth army'.[7] Felix was not called up. While he was studying at Oxford Princess Zenaide had campaigned through the Military Governor of Moscow to have him exempted from military service as the family's only surviving son. Felix senior deplored this inaction.

Felix began converting Youssoupov properties into hospitals. Seventy officers could be accommodated in the Moika Palace ballroom, while Felix's house on Liteinaia Prospekt became one of the best-equipped hospitals in Petrograd.[8]

At Peterhof Irina spent a great deal of time lying on a couch receiving visits from her relatives. Within a month she and Felix joined her grandmother, mother and brothers at Yelagin Palace, a summer residence on the island of the same name in Petrograd.

Felix was supervising the redecoration of their rooms in the Moika Palace with the architect Andrei Beloborodov. Sometimes Irina was present during the discussions but because of her shyness (sometimes interpreted by those who did not know her as coldness or even arrogance) she seldom uttered a word. Once, when Felix left the room, the architect and Irina sat in an embarrassed silence until he returned.

Their private entrance on the front facade was reached by white marble steps lined with statues, with the state rooms looking out over the Moika Canal. The interiors were a profusion of Louis XVI furniture, Aubusson carpets, *objets d'art* and rock crystal chandeliers. There was a ballroom which opened on to a winter garden, a large drawing room hung in ivory silk with French restoration furniture, and an amethyst dining room lined with cabinets of Arkhangelskoe porcelain. In the library, a bookshelf concealed a door leading to a strongroom.

Their private rooms overlooked the garden. Irina wanted a silver boudoir with a crystal bath and a fountain of tears like that at Bakhchisaray. The alcove's silver walls were painted with fantastic flowers, while bowls carved out of colourful stones from the Urals overflowed water from one bowl to another. A small hidden door opened into a narrow gallery carved into the thickness of the walls, leading to a low octagonal room with metal doors. When a secret button was pushed the door opened to reveal an Aladdin's Cave of jewellery, displayed in glass cases which were actually carefully concealed safes. Princess Zenaide loved to show off the family's gems. 'There was a room which was the vault where they put all their jewels ... I think that was during a party, that they opened this door so that any friends could see the jewels.'[9]

To the left of their entrance hall was Felix's *garçonnière*, a set of bachelor apartments. A small octagonal room 'about ten feet across and eight feet high' contained eight mirrored doors, four of which were false. 'One door led into a still smaller bathroom, beyond which was a no less diminutive bedroom...' Other doors led to 'Irina's apartments ... a hallway leading to the rest of the palace'[10] and stairs to the basement, with a door halfway down opening on to the side courtyard. Felix planned to turn the basement into a Renaissance drawing room.

It would become notorious for a completely different reason.

◌⃰◌

The war was brought home to Irina's family brutally when her second cousin, Prince Oleg Constantinovich, died from his wounds aged twenty-one.

The empress, Olga and Tatiana enrolled as nurses and Tatiana asked, 'What does Irina do?'[11] Sandro, anxious that Irina be seen to be doing something for the war effort, said that when the hospital was ready she should go there to take care of the wounded and cheer them up. 'Felix and Irina's infirmary will be ready in a few days,' Xenia reported from Yelagin. 'Poor thing, she can't go anywhere far by herself and just sits here, which makes her disheartened. He [Felix] works and she can't! It's a shame.'[12]

Irina never qualified as a nurse but when she was in Petrograd 'she always went to the [Liteinaia] hospital and, when there, wore a white uniform'. She was photographed in nurse's uniform with members of the Red Cross committee and Grand Duchess Marie Pavlovna in 1914/15. She was 'equally assiduous in attending the hospital and providing benefits for the suffering soldiers'.[13]

Irina wanted to visit the Youssoupov house in Moscow but Princess Zenaide advised her not to do anything without consulting the obstetrician. The pavement outside was uneven which might cause her to fall. Also, the house had no lift. By November Irina had measles and the family went into quarantine. On her recovery, she and Felix moved into the Moika Palace, occupying rooms once used by Felix and his brother.

Sandro held a shooting party at Ai-Todor in December, with Grand Duchess Xenia and Irina accompanying the guns.[14] They spent Christmas at the Moika Palace but Irina was unwell. She sent her grandmother a picture frame she had painted. 'How I wanted to give it to you in person, but I don't know when they will release me. I'm afraid it still won't be for a few more days. How tiresome to have to stay at home in the Holidays.'[15]

Olga and Tatiana often visited after work at the hospital. Once Olga came when Felix was at home. She was not impressed with his inactivity in wartime and wrote a scathing letter to her father describing him as a 'typical civilian' who 'dressed all in brown, walked about the room searching in some bookcases and magazines and virtually doing nothing: an utterly unpleasant impression he makes. A man idling in such times!'[16]

CR✱ℬ

On 8 March 1915 Irina gave birth to a daughter. She suffered terribly despite the assistance of Madame Günst, and bravely tried to lessen the anxiety of Xenia who had been worried about her daughter's poor health.

Soon Irina was feeling better. 'I am so glad Irina is going on well,' Alexandra wrote to Xenia, 'does she nurse the baby, or had she to give it quite over to the wet nurse?'[17]

The child was named after her mother. '[Irina] likes her name, & so wished the child to be called by it, funny little thing,' the empress commented. Tatiana thought differently. 'Strange to think that Irina had a daughter,' she wrote to the tsar, 'so tiresome that they named her Irina too – right?'[18]

At the christening in the Youssoupovs' private chapel on 28 March the tsar, wearing a 'drab wartime uniform', was godfather and the dowager empress was godmother. The empress stood nearby, with her daughters 'dressed very simply in white' behind her, giggling from time to time. Sandro's war duties prevented his attendance. The priest conducted the ceremony badly: the baby 'wailed plaintively', swallowed too much water and nearly drowned in the font. Afterwards, the Youssoupovs gave a 'magnificent tea with chocolate'.[19] Although the baby was christened Irina she was always called Bébé. By April Irina again had a fever. Later that month the empress thought she looked pretty but 'much too thin'.[20]

In mid-1915 the conscription exemption for only sons was rescinded. Felix decided to join the Corps des Pages, a military school for sons of the nobility, to undertake an officer's training course. He was thinking of joining the 3rd Baltic Squadron in Finland and planned to find Irina a house for the winter near the Finnish/Russian border so she would be close to her family.

In May Felix senior was appointed Special Plenipotentiary Military Governor of Moscow, where Princess Zenaide joined him.[21] This gave Irina the chance to visit the family's Moscow house.

The brightly painted house in the old Muscovite style had been built around 1551 as a hunting lodge for Ivan the Terrible and given to the Youssoupovs by Catherine the Great. The walls were 2 feet thick and there was a bricked-up underground passage several miles long with many exits, including one to the Kremlin. When the Youssoupovs opened it they found skeletons hanging on the walls inside.

The rooms were decorated in Oriental Tartar style with vaulted ceilings, medieval frescoes and magnificent porcelain stoves. 'Beautiful,' recalled Eric Hamilton, who visited in 1910, 'and the least English place I have seen since I arrived in Russia.'[22] The staircase was guarded by lions holding the family shield. Upstairs were rooms decorated with fantastic paintings of Chinese dragons, or colourful birds and foliage. Zenaide had added a new medieval-style wing of reception rooms and private apartments connected to the old house by a winter garden. None of the family were fond of the place, which they used only for parties and receptions.

From Moscow they went to Arkhangelskoe to see the progress of the mausoleum where it was intended that Nicholas Youssoupov would be buried.

Felix preferred Moscow to St Petersburg but he loved Arkhangelskoe above all else.

☙ ✴ ❧

The war was going badly for Russia. As the Russians retreated, many of the tsar's subjects came under enemy occupation and refugees fled before the German advance. In Moscow crowds gathered in Red Square shouting insults at the imperial family, demanding that the 'German' tsarina be sent to a convent and the tsar abdicate in favour of Nicholasha. Anger turned against all Germans and spy mania reached fever pitch. In the wake of the retreats the incompetent war minister Sukhomlinov was replaced by General Alexei Polivanov. Empress Alexandra now turned her attention to Nicholasha. She wrote letter after letter to the tsar, who was visiting the front, urging his dismissal. She hated Nicholasha because he was popular with the soldiers, his majestic stature overshadowed the tsar and, most of all, because of his opposition to Rasputin.

Rasputin's standing had been low when he returned to Petrograd in the autumn of 1914 making no secret of his anti-war sympathies. Then, early in January 1915, the empress's confidante Anna Vyrubova (Felix's old dancing partner Anna Taneyeva) was seriously injured in a train crash and seemed unlikely to live. Rasputin was summoned to the hospital and rallied her with a superhuman effort. As he predicted, Anna was disabled but survived. Later that year Tsarevich Alexei suffered a nosebleed on the imperial train while visiting the front. By the time they reached Tsarskoe Selo there was little hope. Again, Rasputin's appearance at the child's bedside stopped the bleeding. His position was once more assured.

In August 1915, urged on by his wife, the tsar took the fateful decision to become commander-in-chief of the Russian army. Princess Zenaide blamed Rasputin's influence and begged the dowager empress to speak to the tsar. It was to no avail.

The next day the tsar left for *stavka* (headquarters), now transferred to Mogilev, 500 miles from the capital. Behind him he left uneasiness. The empress, Zenaide told Felix, 'is simply triumphant!'[23]

The Duma was prorogued but no regency council was appointed. The vacuum was filled by the empress and Rasputin. From now on Alexandra's hectoring, almost hysterical letters to her husband were full of 'Our Friend's' ideas on everything from taxes to food supplies. As things went from bad to disastrous Alexandra nagged Nicholas incessantly to dismiss this or that minister who was opposed to Rasputin, the autocracy, or both. In just thirteen months, twelve ministers were replaced in what became known as ministerial leapfrog. The empress and Rasputin then turned their attention to the military situation. Alexandra faithfully transmitted his instructions but, when things failed to improve, the outcry against '*Niemka*' (the German woman) grew louder.

In early September Felix senior was removed from his post for his inept handling of the Moscow riots. The Youssoupovs blamed the German-dominated dark forces for his dismissal. There is only one way now,' Grand Duke Andrei Vladimirovich wrote in his diary, '... finish off Rasputin.'[24]

೧೩ ✴ ೮೨

Irina had been no stronger since Bébé's birth and by August was losing weight with alarming rapidity. When her cousin Olga called at Yelagin Palace she found Irina lying down with stomach ache. Irina was worried about Felix, although Polivanov had given a guarantee that he would not be sent to the front before December 1916 or even January 1917. To recover her strength Irina joined her parents-in-law at Koreiz where she spent two weeks in bed and lost more weight.

Koreiz was described by Eric Hamilton as 'one of the most beautiful houses I have ever visited ... with the mountains immediately behind and the deep blue sea below. In tropical surroundings it seemed to have been carved out of cool white rock...'[25]

It began as a small house built for Felix senior's mother, which was then placed inside a larger house designed by Krasnov. Wisteria and climbing roses covered the grey Crimean stone walls and, as it was built on a slope, the north side where the main entrance was situated was on two floors and the south side on three. The entrance steps, guarded by two stone lions, led into the hall where guests were received by a Tartar in gold-embroidered national costume. To the right along a corridor was a Moorish-style dining-room with a door leading to a balcony giving a magnificent view towards the Black Sea. Opposite the entrance door, a large arched window presented a wonderful view up to the mountain of Ai-Petri (St Peter).

Two flights of stairs led from the hall down to Felix's rooms. The furniture had been specially brought over from England. Princess Zenaide did not approve. 'Your furniture (armchairs, chairs and sofa) – the walnut items I don't like – has arrived. This old stuck-together rubbish will soon fall to bits. It wasn't worth bringing it,' she told him.[26]

The park overflowed with copies of antique statues and the terraces were filled with the scent of La France roses. Around the estate were some small villas for guests, a church and several vineyards. It was surrounded by high walls and the gates were closed to keep out the wild mountain dogs.

On the jetty was a statue of Minerva, while bronze statues on the shore recalled the legend of the beautiful Tartar girl captured for the Sultan of Turkey's harem who threw herself into the sea in despair. Felix senior once gave his wife the highest mountain in the Crimea, Ai-Petri, as a birthday present. She was given a certificate stating her ownership.[27]

Once recovered, Irina was joined by Andrei and Dmitri and visited by her eighteen-year-old cousin Prince Vladimir Paley, the son of Grand Duke Paul's second marriage. Vladimir was a talented poet and there are hints that he may have had feelings for Irina and dedicated poems to her.

By the autumn of 1915 Felix had decided that, come what may, he would spend the winter with Irina in the Crimea. Princess Zenaide was trying to obtain a deferment for him until February owing to illness, so that he would still be able to join the Corps des Pages, but if he was called up before then he would not be able to do so. She suggested that he ask Xenia to write to the war minister.

Irina spent her afternoons visiting the Youssoupov hospital on the estate. Zenaide Baschkiroff recalled 'continual parties for convalescent officers who were being restored to health'. On one of Irina's visits Lieutenant Colonel Vladimir Dogadin noticed that her heavy gold bracelet was severely bent and, as pure gold bends easily, he asked her to remove it so that he could correct it. The next time Irina visited, she took the bracelet off and asked him to straighten it, explaining that her brothers had damaged it again.[28]

The infirmary was costing 15,000 roubles a month (about £90,000 today) and Princess Zenaide was forced to make economies. A Renault Torpedo car, a Gaggenau truck and the family's motorboat were sold and they had to mortgage Rakitnoie to raise cash to keep all their properties functioning.[29]

Felix arrived and one evening they had a party at the Swallow's Nest, a three-roomed fairy castle of white walls and minarets perched on the edge of the cliff overlooking the sea.

Krasnov was building a Tartar-style country house on the land at Ai-Todor given to them by Irina's father. Sosnovaya Roshcha (Pine Grove), a little green-shuttered house, sat in the grove of pine trees near the cliff. Roses and wisteria covered the white-washed walls and the pergola surrounding the swimming pool. Reflecting Felix's preference, the interior was very English, although as it was built on a slope the layout lacked symmetry. Felix's ideas were both fantastic and original and Krasnov had difficulty curbing his more outlandish whims. One of the most original rooms, if it could be called a room, was less than 2 metres high, arranged as a sort of couch with a big window at the end, through which guests would be able to look into a large room full of exotic birds.

Zenaide was afraid that the couple would settle there and abandon Koreiz but Irina and Felix never had the opportunity to live there. It was the last house built for a member of the Romanov family in the Crimea.

They returned to Petrograd for Christmas. Felix's parents, Xenia, two of her sons and the dowager empress all came but Irina now seems to have had little contact with her cousins at the Alexander Palace. 'What is sweet little Irina like, and who does she resemble, the boys or Felix?' Tatiana enquired.[30]

It was their last Christmas at the Moika Palace.

ભ ✸ ৪০

After recovering from mumps, on 1 February 1916 Felix enrolled in the 4th Wartime Accelerated Course of the Corps des Pages wearing a specially tailored uniform. He moved to Grand Duchess Xenia's palace to be with Andrei and Feodor, who were also in the corps. Captain Nicholas Fogel, Sandro's ADC, was their tutor and later was assigned to Felix as his crammer. Every morning Felix was driven for training at the Vorontzov Palace further along the Moika, where he soon discovered that his studies were far from easy. There was little free time and he arranged frequent leaves of absence.

In March Irina and Felix returned to the Crimea with Andrei and Feodor. She was still unwell. 'We have wonderful weather here, but it is so tiresome that I still have to lie down so much,' Irina told her grandmother from Ai-Todor. 'They also give me arsenic injections ... Bébé is such a darling. I think she will start walking well soon. She always asks us to place her on the floor, and loves me very much, she doesn't let go of me. Odi is terribly happy to be here and he, Felix and Andrusha all but cry when they remember they are soon going back to the Corps de Pages.'[31]

Princess Zenaide wanted her daughter-in-law to rest. There was an unspoken, underlying element of unease. The elder Youssoupovs were anxious to have a male heir to prevent the name dying out. Irina's health was not strong and Bébé was the seventh generation since Prince Gregory's curse in 1718. Felix's Russian biographer says that in a bid to break that curse, Irina and Felix decided to limit their family to just one child.[32]

'Irina is always on the balcony, but goes riding in the morning,' Xenia told Olga Nicolaievna in May. 'She is feeling better. In a couple of days, they will probably go to Ufa province to [drink] *kumis*. So boring!'[33]

In June Felix accompanied Irina and Zenaide Baschkiroff to the estate of Filipov in Samarka, which belonged to relatives of Felix's grandmother Princess Zenaide Naryshkin. Bébé remained at Ai-Todor. 'Probably you are enjoying having your granddaughter to yourself?' Tatiana commented to Xenia.[34]

At the insistence of both sets of parents they stopped off in Moscow to see the obstetrician Redlikh and find out when Irina could have another child. Felix had omitted to tell them about the decision to limit their family.

Irina's health had deteriorated since Bébé's birth. She had kidney problems and a catarrhal condition of the renal pelvis. Redlikh advised them to wait until she was stronger and told her to remain outdoors to strengthen her health.

The abandoned estate of Filipov had a charming small wooden house with old furniture, no bath and few amenities. Irina drank *kumis*, a fermented mare's milk which produces valuable vitamins and antibodies, under the supervision of Dr Positov and went walking with Felix. The place was amazingly beautiful and she liked the isolated existence on the steppe, away from all social life. 'We go to bed early and get up early too,' she told her grandmother. 'In the morning, I drink *kumis* and we go for a walk, or lie in the sun when it is sunny. In the afternoon, we take some *kumis* with us and go for a drive somewhere in the woods and gather wild strawberries which I am not allowed to eat, which is very depressing. There are pretty much no roads here, and the ones that are here are so bad that you can't go on them, so we just go directly onto the steppe ... This *kumis* stuff is very tasty, but you get sick of it if you have it too much, so now I have four bottles a day, or I would like it less.'[35]

After Felix left for the camp at Krasnoe Selo, Irina stayed on with Zenaide Baschkiroff before returning to Moscow to see Redlkih again. He was satisfied with her condition but advised against having more children yet. This news reassured Princess Zenaide that another child could follow when Irina was stronger.

෬ ✶ ౭ට

Grand Duchess Xenia had always worried about her daughter's health but there were now worries about Bébé, who had been ill all summer with an intestinal infection. 'My poor baby was ill, but is now, thank God, recovering in Arkhangelskoe,' Irina wrote to her grandmother from Filipov. 'How awful it was to be so far away. I am always so worried when she is not with me. She will probably [not?] recognise me when I arrive. It will be such a pity.'[36]

Bébé's nurse was dismissed. 'Poor Nurse Shekina who has at last been sent away & an English one, "all teeth & glasses" (as you wrote), in her place!' Olga Alexandrovna wrote to Xenia. 'What did your granddaughter say to her?'[37] Princess Zenaide was also uneasy, especially as Irina and Felix had engaged a woman she called a cold English nanny.

Zillah Henton was born in Grantham, Lincolnshire in 1866 and had gone to Russia in 1906 to nurse 'children very close to the Russian throne'. Who they were and how she ended up working for Irina and Felix is unknown.[38] Princess Zenaide wanted to know why it had suddenly become fashionable in the Youssoupov family to hire foreigners to look after the children, especially when Miss Coster had seemingly done nothing for Irina's health.

During the summer of 1916 Bébé remained at Ai-Todor. After a while the grand duchess sent her to Koreiz. It was hot in the Crimea, so the Youssoupovs took their granddaughter to Arkhangelskoe where, unexpectedly, she fell ill and lost weight rapidly. They called in Dr Sergei Vozdvakhlanski, the head of Grand Duchess Elisabeth Feodorovna's orphanage in Moscow. Felix hurried to Arkhangelskoe, from where he telegraphed reassuringly to Irina.

He then told Grand Duchess Xenia and Princess Zenaide about his plan of going to Finland. Both thought that the climate in autumn would be no good at all for Irina.

On 12 August Alexandra told the tsar that Bébé 'is much worse again, lives here with the [Youssoupov] grandparents. Irina is at Krasnoe [Selo] with an "angina" – always ill, poor girl.'[39]

෬ ✶ ౭ට

During the summer of 1916 Felix may have learnt that he was not his father's only child. Whether this was Felix's first intimation that his father had another family is not yet established. Their existence remained a secret until 2007.

Felix senior had a mistress, Zenaide Gregoriev (Zina), who was also his goddaughter. She was born in 1880 in St Petersburg and he took an interest in her because she had the same Christian name as his wife. As she grew older they became close and he installed her as a companion to his mother until the latter's death in 1901. He and Zina remained in touch and, in around 1910, after Princess Zenaide suffered a near nervous breakdown following Prince Nicholas's death, Zina and Felix senior became lovers.

She bore him a son, who was baptised in Moscow while Felix senior was Special Plenipotentiary Military Governor. The baby, believed to have been born around 6 October 1914 and often referred to as Nicholas Elston, died.[40] In 1916 a second son, Elevteriy (later called Olivier), was born in Petrograd. By this point it appears that Zina Gregoriev was using the surname Svetilov (the name of Felix senior's secretary), the name by which she eventually left Russia.

With no end to the war in sight and the situation in Russia deteriorating, on 10 August 1916 Felix junior was instructed by his father that in the event of his death he should pay 500 roubles each month to Zina Gregoriev-Svetilov and to further place 2,000 roubles a year (taken from the income of his estate at Pokrovskoie in Kuban) to her son Elevteriy (Olivier) until he reached his majority. If Elevteriy died before then, the interest on the capital at the date of death should be paid to Zina. The capital would remain with Felix junior. A set of payment receipts from 1912 to 1914 has survived, 'established for the benefit of Zenaide Gregoriev-Svetilov on the farm and the benefits of the Bologoie estate'.[41]

Although his mother was aware of the affair and the children, all this may have come as a shock to the younger Felix.

ભ ✶ 80

In August Irina and Feodor collected Bébé from Arkhangelskoe and visited her grandmother at the Maryinsky Palace, Kiev. The dowager empress had given the tsar an ultimatum – 'either me or Rasputin.' When Nicholas refused to dismiss him she realised the situation was hopeless and joined her daughter Olga in Kiev, away from the pernicious atmosphere in the capital.[42]

On their return to Petrograd Irina and Felix had tea at Tsarskoe Selo. 'They were quite nice and natural,' Alexandra told Nicholas, 'she very brown and he looking very thin, short hair and as page [in the Corps des Pages] looks much better and holds himself properly.'[43]

By September Irina was at Koreiz with Zenaide Baschkiroff and her daughters seven-year-old Zenaide and baby Xenia, a month older than Bébé, who were staying in a villa on the estate. Bébé loved going to the beach and splashing in the sea with the two little girls.

Xenia hoped that Irina and Bébé would come to Ai-Todor but, as she told Tatiana in mid-September, 'now they have to go to Kislovodsk – and they will not get here for another month. Have you seen my little granddaughter?' she added.[44]

Before Irina left, she went riding with Tatiana. 'I did not see your granddaughter as she was asleep,' Tatiana replied to Xenia.[45]

Felix thought that the health-giving spa resort of Kislovodsk would benefit his wife and daughter, so he rented a secluded dacha called Calm from the Baranovskaya family.

Rosamond Dowse, a young English governess with the Miklashevsky family, recalled Felix's visit in September. Learning that Rosamond understood Russian, Felix ensured that 'only very general topics were discussed in her hearing. Later she came to the conclusion that the purpose of the prince's visit had been to find out whether Madame and her sisters would be willing to become involved in a plot to destroy Rasputin.'[46] On what evidence she based this far-fetched assumption is not stated.

Irina and Felix remained at Kislovodsk until 10 October, then left for Kiev.

ଔ✱ଛ

Felix was still trying to forge a life independent of his needy, controlling mother. 'Really,' he told her, 'I'm no longer a little baby who must be afraid that he might be punished. Don't forget that I'm almost thirty, that I'm married, and that we are entitled to our own private lives.'[47]

If he passed the examination for the Corps des Pages Accelerated Course he would graduate on 1 October. Newly commissioned officers applied to serve in one of the Imperial Guards regiments, so in August 1916 Felix applied to the Chevalier Guards, his father's regiment. His application was blackballed, with few of his so-called friends giving their support. Other prestigious regiments then made it known that Felix would not be welcome. Felix felt humiliated and betrayed, as many of these men had sought his help and support in the past. The blackballing was not only caused by disapproval of his 'sexual escapades and inclinations' but was a symptom of the openly expressed jealousy towards the Youssoupov family.[48]

Felix dropped out of the regular course work and discussed alternatives with the administrators. 'I am just back from the Corps,' he told Princess Zenaide. 'Matters there have been settled entirely to my satisfaction. I have been transferred to the infantry, and have been granted leave of absence from duty; and the final exams are to take place in February. Revisions are in full swing at present, so that I spend most of my free time at home cramming with Fogel.'

It appears that Felix 'subsequently received credit for much of his course work', because his final examinations were rescheduled for 17 December.[49]

This date would be significant for an entirely different reason.

6

Rasputin

'Ra Ra Rasputin, lover of the Russian Queen'

Boney M, 1978[1]

As early as 1912 Eric Hamilton recalled 'the atmosphere, sinister and mysterious, that seemed to overhang Russia in those days before the breaking of the storm ... And mixed with this strange melancholy were streaks of wild and wilful gaiety, gypsy songs, drinking and dancing, as if men were determined to forget something they knew in their bones was on the way...'[2]

By 1916 nothing had changed. The problem was Rasputin.

As the empress and Rasputin took over government affairs the people believed that dark forces were at work. They remembered the empress's German birth and believed she was spying for them, while Rasputin was said to be having regular discussions with German agents. Princess Zenaide, the dowager empress, Ella, Sandro, his brother Nicholas Michaelovich and Nicholasha called Alexandra and Rasputin the German Party.

Early in 1916 the senile Count Ivan Goremykin was replaced as chairman of the Council of Ministers by Boris Sturmer, an incompetent reactionary favoured by Rasputin. From now on the ministers reported directly to the empress and the cabinet ceased to function.

As scandalous stories about Rasputin's relationship with the empress circulated, it was not what Rasputin *did* that caused the problems, it was what people *believed* he had done. With Alexei's illness still a closely guarded secret, the Russian people had no idea why this debauched peasant was frequently at the palace. False stories that the empress and Rasputin were lovers damaged the prestige of the dynasty. The myth was more important than the man.

ଓ ★ ଯ

In the summer of 1916 Princess Zenaide went to Tsarskoe Selo to make one last attempt to persuade the empress to break off contact with Rasputin. Alexandra was irritated and asked her to leave.

Zenaide then complained to Felix about Rasputin and the crazy empress 'who has also driven her spouse mad. I'm literally suffocating from indignation and think that this [Rasputin's influence] cannot be tolerated any longer. I disdain everyone who tolerates this and remains silent!'[3]

Felix and Irina arrived in Kiev to celebrate the fiftieth anniversary of the dowager empress's conversion to orthodoxy on 12 October. The dowager was melancholy and in the same mood when they dined with her the following day. Her diary made no mention of whether they discussed Rasputin.

Irina returned to Koreiz but Princess Zenaide complained that she spent more time at Ai-Todor. In Simiez Irina also visited her uncle Grand Duke Paul, who had been allowed back to Russia with his morganatic wife Olga (created Princess Paley in 1915) and their children.

Meanwhile Princess Zenaide promised Khvostov, the Minister of the Interior, 'unlimited funds' to eliminate Rasputin. Khvostov said Zenaide acted as spokeswoman for the grand dukes and could see the harm Rasputin was doing to the dynasty.[4]

There had been attempts to get rid of Rasputin, either through investigations to discredit him or by assassination. All had failed. Although he had spoken about it in his Oxford days, Felix said in his memoirs that he first had the idea to do away with Rasputin in 1915, when he, Irina and Princess Zenaide discussed Rasputin's effect on Alexandra. Historian Douglas Smith thinks Felix decided to do it to please his mother.[5]

He now began making plans. The British Chaplain, the Revd Bousfield Lombard, said the prince visited him one afternoon 'full of plans for ridding the earth of this scourge Rasputin'. Lombard wrote in his diary: 'He suggested my trying to get into touch with the empress, on the score of certain knowledge of occult law which I happened to possess. I told him that to supplant "R" would be hopeless and also that probably the ambassador [Buchanan] would have a good deal to say if I attempted to interfere. He was very depressed and promised to come again and report progress.'[6]

The secret police, the Okhrana, were reading the imperial family's letters. Felix was worried that his correspondence would be intercepted, so on 3 November he told his mother to 'ask Irina to send a telegram whenever you receive a letter from me'.[7]

By the autumn the atmosphere was even more charged. 'I cannot imagine how all this will end,' Felix wrote to his mother. 'We live on a volcano; the same thoughts pass and repass in our minds.'[8]

Felix and Irina's new rooms at the Moika Palace would be ready by mid-December. 'Not all of them,' Felix explained to Zenaide, 'but enough to make life possible!'[9]

And enough to make a murder possible.

ଓ ✦ ଓ

The Duma sessions of early November could best be described as fiery. It is here that the accepted version of Rasputin's murder, which has been recounted so many times, begins.

On 1 November Paul Milyukov, leader of the Constitutional Democrats (Kadets), made a speech attacking the government. After each charge he paused dramatically, asking: 'What is this – stupidity or treason?'[10] The storm hanging over Russia was about to break.

Two days later Felix visited Ella in her Moscow convent, returning to Petrograd that night. The next day he was invited to Grand Duke Nicholas Michaelovich's palace. The Duma deputy Vladimir Purishkevich, leader of the right-wing faction, was also there and they discussed the disastrous influence of the empress and Rasputin.

Felix next visited the lawyer Vassili Maklakov, leader of the Progressive Bloc, who had made a speech in the Duma criticising the conduct of the war. According to Margarita Nelipa, Grand Duke Nicholas Michaelovich had told Maklakov why Felix needed to see him. Nelipa thinks the grand duke was masterminding the plan. His biographer Jamie Cockfield disagrees. Maklakov later said that Felix organised the murder.

Felix had no plan. He told Maklakov that killing Rasputin himself would amount to 'almost a revolution' because of his wife's close relationship to the tsar. Maklakov suggested using an assassin, although not a revolutionary, because Rasputin 'was doing more to discredit the regime' than any propaganda.[11]

Felix spoke to others, including his relative Michael Rodzianko. Something, or someone, changed Felix's mind and he decided to eliminate Rasputin himself. He began to assemble a group of conspirators, including a member of the imperial family.

Grand Duke Dmitri had long been hostile to Rasputin. In 1910 he complained to his sister Marie (then living in Sweden) that the empress was meeting Rasputin secretly in Anna Vyrubova's house. Felix and Dmitri had reconciled since they competed for Irina. In 1915 Dmitri was transferred to *stavka* as a liaison officer. He telegraphed Felix that he would return to Petrograd on 14 November. While waiting for Dmitri, Felix telephoned Sergei Sukhotin.

Lieutenant Sergei Michaelovich Sukhotin, an officer in the Life Guards Infantry, had been wounded and spent some time in the Youssoupov infirmary in Petrograd.[12] In 1915 Sergei and his then wife the pianist Irina Eneri (her stage name), who played regularly for Princess Zenaide, were invited to Koreiz and introduced to Felix. Later Sergei and his brother worked at the Youssoupov hospital on the estate.

By early 1916 Sukhotin, still unfit for front line service, was working at the Ministry of War. Zenaide often used the Sukhotin brothers to hand-deliver letters to her son to avoid the attentions of the Okhrana. Sergei Sukhotin had very friendly relations with the young Youssoupovs and readily agreed to take part in the plot.

When Dmitri arrived in Petrograd he invited Felix to his palace. He was close to his former guardian Grand Duchess Ella and knew her feelings about Rasputin. Disillusioned about events in Russia, Dmitri agreed to participate. This was vital. The involvement of a member of the imperial family would ensure immunity from prosecution for his co-conspirators.

On 15 November Felix, Dmitri and Sukhotin met at the Moika Palace. They decided to do the deed there, while Felix's parents and Irina were at Koreiz. As Irina was a member of the imperial family the palace could not be searched by the police. Firearms would be avoided, as there was a police station a short distance away along the other side of the canal.

It was now vital that Felix gain Rasputin's trust. They had not met since January 1915.

Felix claimed to have pains in his chest,[13] so Munya Golovina set up a meeting in her family's apartment on 17 November. Rasputin asked Felix to lie on the sofa and made 'mesmeric passes' over his chest, neck and head, all the time murmuring a prayer. Felix felt his 'tremendous hypnotic power' and, as he began to feel helpless, a struggle for control between Felix and Rasputin began.[14] All rather dramatic, but Felix was anxious to portray Rasputin as some kind of devil, although he was not an evil man. Rasputin had been learning hypnosis in 1912 and Felix was the only person on whom he allegedly used hypnotic powers.

CR ✴ ℰ○

The conspirators also decided to recruit a member of the Duma.

On 19 November Vladimir Purishkevich made a speech condemning 'the government, the tsarina and her advisor' Rasputin while hailing the Duma's patriotic commitment to the war. 'Go on your knees,' he begged the Duma members, 'and beg leave to open the eyes of the tsar to the terrible reality.'[15] Felix was sitting in the visitors' box wearing civilian clothes, breaking the rules of the Corps des Pages, for which he was scolded by his mother. Purishkevich's words made a deep impression and he arranged a meeting for 21 November.

Vladimir Mitrofanich Purishkevich was born in Bessarabia in 1870. His grandfather had worked his way up to the hereditary nobility and married a wealthy Polish aristocrat. Vladimir graduated from Novorossisk University, became chairman of the district *zemstvo* (elected local government council) and moved to St Petersburg. He worked at the Ministry of Interior and joined Russkoe Sobranie (The Russian Assembly), a monarchist organisation. By 1916 he was running a hospital train, spending a lot of time on the Romanian front.

Purishkevich suggested they also approach the Polish physician Dr Stanislav Sergeievich Lazovert, who had worked for two years as a senior Red Cross doctor on his train. Born in 1885 and educated in France, Lazovert is the least known of the conspirators.

Rasputin's murder was the first part of a plan. The second part was to persuade the tsar to banish the empress to a convent. Felix was convinced that once freed from the influence of Alexandra and Rasputin, Nicholas would become a good constitutional monarch. 'Now it is too late to mend matters without a scandal, whereas then everything could have been *saved* by the removal of the manager [Rasputin] for the duration of the war, and the complete non-interference of *Valide* [Alexandra] in affairs of state,' Zenaide wrote to Felix despairingly. 'I repeat *again* that unless these two questions are *settled*, nothing can be accomplished by peaceful means.'[16]

All the plotters saw Rasputin's murder as a patriotic act. Felix and Purishkevich were mainly driven by vainglory and the desire for a place in history. Elizabeth Naryshkin-Kurakin wrote about 'the passionate zeal' with which Ella urged Dmitri 'to commit the murder', a remark which seems quite out of character for the devout grand duchess. 'It was only after that, having convinced himself that there was little hope of a normal *dénouement*, that he decided to join with those few men who were ready to bring this *dénouement* about,' his sister wrote.[17]

Felix now spent a lot of time with Munya and Rasputin, often in Rasputin's apartment. Felix took him to visit the gypsies and eventually suggested he come to the Moika Palace to meet Irina. Her presence would allay any suspicions that Rasputin was going into a hostile environment. It seems that Rasputin's well-known powers of clairvoyance had weakened. Amazingly, he had no idea that a trap was being set.

ଔ ✱ ଛ

Irina remained in the Crimea. On 20 November Felix told her that he 'was awfully excited working over a plan about destroying R. This is now simply essential, since otherwise everything will be finished. For that I often see M. Gol [Munya] and him [Rasputin]. They've grown quite fond of me...' It was therefore vital, as Felix stressed, that she be in Petrograd. 'Dmitri Pavlovich knows all about it and is helping. All this will occur in the middle of December...' Felix desperately wanted to see her, but said there would be nowhere for her to stay until 15 December. '*Not a word to anyone* about what I've written to you,' he added. 'Tell my mother to read my letter.'[18]

Irina replied on 25 November:

> Thank you for your mad letter. I could not understand half of it but I can see that you are preparing for some wild action. Please, be careful, and don't mix yourself up in any bad business. My chief objection is that you have decided upon everything without consulting me. I don't see what use I can be now once everything has been fixed. That is disgusting of you. Who is this M. Gol? ... I have just understood what these words mean, and who the people are ... In a word, be careful! I can see by your letter that you are wildly enthusiastic, and ready to climb up walls.

She planned to be in Petrograd by 12 or 13 December. 'Don't you dare do anything without me,' she ended, 'or I shall not come at all!'[19]

Irina's participation was crucial. Rasputin had long wanted to meet her, although it was not intended that he would actually do so. They would give Rasputin poisoned cakes and wine and then dispose of his body from a bridge over the Malaya Nevka, a tributary of the river Neva. 'This is the only and most reliable way of saving the situation, which is practically hopeless,' Felix told her. 'Of course, not a word to anyone,' he stressed again. 'Malanya is also involved. You'll serve as the bait. Understand?'[20] Edvard Radzinsky identifies Malanya as Marianna Derfelden, daughter of Princess Olga Paley from her first marriage and therefore Dmitri's stepsister.

Nowhere does Irina agree, or intimate, that she would act as the bait.

ଔ ✱ ଛ

During the two weeks preceding the murder Felix, Dmitri and Purishkevich told more than a dozen people about their scheme. Rumours circulated about mysterious meetings in the National Club chaired by Purishkevich, attended by Felix, Dmitri and other young officers. One of those who had been warned of an approaching drama was the Honourable Albert (Bertie)

Stopford, a shadowy figure with high-powered connections. He and Felix had been friends since 1909. Stopford travelled regularly between London and the continent as the unofficial eyes and ears of the War Office. He is rumoured, although it has never been proved, to have worked for the Secret Intelligence Service (SIS).

The British ambassador Sir George Buchanan also heard something. 'I was told about a week ago by a friend who is in close touch with some of the younger grand dukes that a number of the young officers had sworn to kill him [Rasputin] before the end of this year,' he told the Foreign Office.[21] Did he know details of the plot, or had he picked up gossip?

With so many people in the know, it seems strange that the Okhrana were unaware of it – or were they?[22]

The conspirators' determination to act was strengthened by rumours that Russia would make a separate peace and that Rasputin had declared the war would end on 28 December. 'What is this sudden talk of peace?' Zenaide asked Felix on 3 December.[23]

On the same day Ella made one last effort to get the empress to see sense. Her sister refused to listen.

❀ ✦ ❀

Felix maintained that Irina was completely in agreement with his scheme. Yet she clearly did not like what was being planned. Suddenly she refused to come to Petrograd, seemingly in the grip of some kind of breakdown. 'You don't know how things are with me, I want to cry all the time,' she told Felix in early December. 'My mood is terrible ... But I can't go on anymore! I don't know myself. What is happening to me...' She begged him to come to the Crimea instead. 'Forgive me, my dear one ... Don't be angry with me, please don't be angry. I love you terribly. I can't live without you...'[24]

On 8 December Felix told Irina that he would leave Petrograd on 17 or 18 December. 'What happiness it will be to be together with you. You don't know how much I love you,' he said, adding that the rehearsals, as he called the plotters' meetings, had been going well. In a postscript he asked for a telegram to be sent on 16 December saying that Irina was ill and asking him to come to the Crimea. This would give him an excuse to leave Petrograd immediately after the murder.[25]

Irina had planned to accompany her mother to Kiev but she was confined to bed with a cold and the doctor forbade her to travel. Bébé was also unwell and staying with her Youssoupov grandparents at Koreiz. Felix was pleased that his mother had remained in the Crimea. Zenaide had obviously made more remarks about the health and treatment of Bébé, because Felix ended his letter, 'I was very much afraid that you might leave, and that Bébé would be moved to Ai-Todor ... I shall naturally keep to myself everything that you write about Bébé and Irina.'[26]

Apologising for pouring her heart out in her previous letter, Irina reported a strange occurrence with Bébé. 'A couple of nights ago she didn't sleep well and kept repeating, "War, nanny, war." The next day she was asked, "War or peace?" And Bébé answered, "War!" The next day I said, "Say peace." And she looked right at me and answered, "War!" It's very strange...'[27]

Princess Zenaide was worried about the company her daughter-in-law was keeping. Irina was frequently visited by a friend whose presence seemed to bother Zenaide. 'In my opinion she poses most impudently as a member of the family,' Zenaide told Felix on 11 December. 'She calls Irina by her Christian name, and even "Tata" [*sic*, she means Titi]. I strongly object to her behaviour. When I visit Irina I constantly find her there, lounging in a chair ... She sports a kind of operatic costume of a sister of mercy [nurse] and generally spoils the whole atmosphere by her presence. Irina seems to accept it all as inevitable...' Most books wrongly identify this 'sister' as Grand Duchess Ella, who at the time was away at a monastery. The young woman was Olga Vassiliev, a nurse at Grand Duchess Olga's hospital in Kiev, where she had been seeing rather too much of Sandro.[28] At the end of 1916 she was at Ai-Todor recovering from illness. Olga Vassiliev would cause Irina's family a lot of distress in the future, before redeeming herself many years later.

Ω ✸ ο

On 11 December Purishkevich approached Maklakov in the crowded lobby of the Duma, told him details of their plan and asked if Felix could see him again. Maklakov agreed, although he was unaware who else was involved in the plot. The lawyer's most important point was that Felix should 'mislead' questioners, so that the murderer's identity would remain a secret and the matter could not be brought to court.[29] He also suggested that during the evening of the murder they should telephone Rasputin's favourite restaurant and ask if he had arrived.

According to Felix, Maklakov gave him a rubber club in case it was needed to finish Rasputin off. However, Maklakov, writing in the émigré magazine *Sovremennye Zapiski* in 1928, said that Felix asked for a steel press which he saw on the desk. Maklakov later testified that Felix asked him to supply a club, which was made of 'tightly woven fabric'.[30] So who was telling the truth?

The rendezvous with Rasputin was set for the evening of 16 December, which Felix claimed was when he expected Irina to return to Petrograd.[31] It was also the first free evening in Dmitri's packed schedule and the day the Duma went into Christmas recess.

On 13 December Felix telephoned Purishkevich and said the code words 'Vanya has arrived.' Rasputin had accepted his invitation.

Ω ✸ ο

Underneath the Moika Palace were cellars. The architect Andrei Beloborodov was in charge of converting one of them, which had originally been part of the wine cellar, into a dining room. 'There were a lot of quirks in these ... "*garçonnière*" [bachelor apartments],' he recalled. 'There was a whole maze here of small rooms with a spiral staircase descending into the underground, which was supposed to serve as the dining-room.' On 13 December he recorded how Felix asked him to have everything ready by 'the day after tomorrow', as he would like to entertain some friends. Work continued throughout 14 December and only towards midnight on the 15th was Felix able to inspect the finished room.[32]

By 16 December all was ready.

℅ ✱ ℈

At 5.00 a.m. on 17 December Felix returned to Xenia's palace and was met by Feodor. 'Well?' Feodor enquired.[33]

The Revd B. S. Lombard heard of the murder soon afterwards. 'I was busy writing my home mail one morning when he [Felix] was announced. He flung himself down on the sofa and exclaimed: "Padre, we have done it." "Done what?" said I. Then Felix commenced to tell me the most gruesome tale I have ever heard.'[34]

In *Lost Splendour* Felix said that during the night of 16/17 December Irina suddenly awoke and saw the figure of Rasputin dressed in an embroidered silk blouse. The vision lasted only seconds and she went back to sleep. Irina was in the Crimea, so either she told him, or more likely he made it up for dramatic effect. Either way, that night Rasputin was murdered.

But what had happened?

℅ ✱ ℈

In fact, it is easier to say what did *not* happen.

The main versions of Rasputin's murder are in Felix's books *Rasputin* (1927) and *Lost Splendour* (1952), as well as Purishkevich's so-called diary published in Russia in 1918 and in Paris in 1923 after the author's death. This, as Maklakov explained later to the Paris publisher, was not an actual diary but a form of memoir. Much of it was second-hand, with dates and conversations mixed up.[35] It was probably written to shield Grand Duke Dmitri, who at that time was considered a serious candidate for a restored throne. Felix tailored his account to fit the broad outline of Purishkevich's version. Both played freely with the facts although they credit Purishkevich with firing the final shot.

The conspirators vowed never to speak about what happened that night. Dmitri never broke that promise. All that remains are a few allusions in his letters and diaries to the patriotic reasons for carrying out the deed. Lazovert told *The New York Times* that they shot Rasputin near Dmitri's palace as he was going to see the empress.[36] This was blatantly false. An account said to be by Lazovert published in *Source Records of the Great War* largely agrees with Felix and Purishkevich and attributes the final shot to Purishkevich but this account is a fake. Sukhotin left no memoirs or papers.

It is impossible to reconcile the accounts given by Felix and Purishkevich. Richard Cullen, a former Metropolitan Police Commander who conducted his own investigation, wrote that 'the differences are of too great a consequence to be accounted for as witness error'.[37] A later book by Margarita Nelipa builds on this but some of her conclusions disagree with Cullen.

According to Felix's account, he collected Rasputin from his apartment after midnight. Rasputin usually had two bodyguards and two covert agents monitoring him but 'the detectives responsible for surveillance were not on duty' that night. There have been rumours that these men were either agents from Scotland Yard or in the pay of the British. The chief of the guard that night should have been George Elvengren, a man who later turned up in connection with SIS agent Sidney Reilly, 'the Ace of Spies'. The Russian press 'asked whether the guards were withdrawn on British instructions'. The worried British Embassy telegraphed London to ask if a denial should be issued.[38] Alexander Spiridovich, head of the tsar's personal guard, said that the guards were removed at ten o'clock each evening so that the Minister of Interior, Alexander Protopopov, could visit Rasputin unobserved.

Felix and his 'chauffeur' (Lazovert) drove Rasputin back to the Moika Palace, the façade of which was separated from the Moika Canal by a narrow pavement. They drove into the courtyard at the left (eastern) end of the palace, which was separated from the street by a wooden grill fence with three entrances. Only the central gate was unlocked. This courtyard was normally associated with Moika 92, which also belonged to the Youssoupovs and contained offices and servants' quarters.[39] From the courtyard by Moika 92 a side door led into the palace, where a steep narrow spiral staircase went either up to the prince's study, or down to the basement. Each set of stairs comprised six steps.

The basement room to which Rasputin was taken was immediately below Felix's study. It was a low vaulted room with two small, high windows looking out onto the canal at ground level. A low arch divided the room into two but, once furnished, it looked small and cluttered.

As Felix and Rasputin entered the palace the prince's accomplices played 'Yankee Doodle Dandy' on the gramophone upstairs to simulate the party Irina was supposedly having.

Down in the basement Rasputin was offered poisoned cakes and wine and, when after two hours this failed to kill him, Felix went upstairs for a revolver and shot him while he was standing looking at a rock-crystal crucifix. The body was moved from the white bearskin rug and Lazovert pronounced Rasputin dead.

While Dmitri, Sukhotin and Lazovert went off on a failed mission to dispose of Rasputin's outer clothing, Felix shook the body violently to make sure he really was dead. To his horror Rasputin leapt to his feet with a wild roar and, as they struggled, tore the epaulette from Felix's shoulder and ran up the stairs. As Rasputin emerged into the snowy courtyard Purishkevich, hearing Felix's shouts, snatched up his pistol, ran outside and fired. Only at the fourth attempt did he succeed in hitting him in the back of the head.

Felix said he went outside to the snow mound which concealed Rasputin's body. A policeman, Stepan Vlasyuk, alerted by the shots, appeared. Felix told him that one of his guests had fired into the air to amuse himself. Vlasyuk left and the body was carried inside.

Later, Vlasyuk returned. The shots had been heard by Flor Yefimov at the police post across the canal. In Felix's study Purishkevich told him that Rasputin had been killed and asked him not to say anything.

Felix began pounding Rasputin's body (which was supposedly now on the narrow stair landing by the side entrance) with Maklakov's club until there was blood everywhere. He fainted. On regaining consciousness, he and his servant cleaned up the blood and tidied the basement. Having sworn the servants to secrecy, he decided to tell the police that one of his guests had shot a dog in the courtyard as he left. He ordered Ivan to shoot a dog and drag the body over Rasputin's trail of blood.

Purishkevich ordered the two soldiers guarding the palace entrance to wrap the body in cloth, bind it and put it in Dmitri's car. With Lazovert, Sukhotin and 'a soldier' in the car with the body, Dmitri drove through the empty streets to the Petrovsky Bridge, which led to Krestovsky Island where Nicholas Youssoupov had died in a duel.

There they tossed Rasputin's body over into a hole in the icy Malaya Nevka, forgetting one of his overshoes and the weights which should have ensured that it never surfaced.

ɔ✱ɔ

This is the accepted account – but it is problematic. The accounts left by Felix and Purishkevich disagree on everything from the car used to collect Rasputin to which of the cakes were poisoned and how many wine glasses were used. Nothing written by Felix or Purishkevich can be accepted as fact.

By the time Felix wrote his books he was desperate for money. Trading on his notoriety as the murderer of Rasputin was all he had to offer and he used it to the full. He needed a sensational story, so he invented the myth of the almost indestructible Rasputin.

It has now been established that Rasputin was not intoxicated when he died: there was no evidence of solids in his stomach, no water in his lungs (so he was dead before he hit the water) and no forensic evidence of poison.

Grand Duke Andrei Vladimirovich, who spoke to Dmitri by telephone on 18 December, recorded in his diary that Rasputin was interrogated about his relationship with the empress and Sturmer, who had been dismissed. 'After this, he was offered the choice of either taking poison or shooting himself. But he didn't take the poison, and took the revolver instead, and tried to shoot Dmitri with it. After this, they all fell on him and finished him off...' Dmitri denied participation but admitted that he had dined with Felix on 16 December.[40]

Rasputin's daughter Maria claimed she was told by Dmitri's stepbrother Alexander Pistolkors that Felix shot her father in the back and the others then finished him off.

Exactly who was in the Moika Palace that evening remains open to debate. There were rumours that Feodor and Nikita were there, as well as Felix's cousin Vladimir Lazarev. According to the *Stock Exchange Bulletin*, Princes Andrei and Feodor were present.[41] Grand Duke Nicholas Michaelovich told Buchanan that two sons of Grand Duke Alexander were *not* present, although Buchanan's original account to the Foreign Office has eleven men at supper, including two sons of Grand Duke Constantine, which is almost certainly untrue.[42]

Felix makes no mention in his books of ladies being there. However, he did mention it to the police and in the subsequent letter he wrote to the empress, where he referred to 'a supper party to which I invited my friends – several ladies'.[43] Perhaps he hoped to avoid awkward questions.

The ladies most frequently mentioned are Marianna Derfelden and the ballerina and movie actress Vera Karalli, with whom Dmitri had begun an affair earlier that year.[44] In the light of rumours about the relationship between Felix and Dmitri, did Felix fear that if it was discovered that these ladies, both of whom had been rumoured lovers of Dmitri, were present, tales of an erotic orgy in the palace would be spread?

Marianna was placed under house arrest and her apartment searched. It was thought that meetings planning the murder had taken place there but no proof was found. Correspondence was seized but she was soon released.

Vera Karalli's arrival in Petrograd was reported to the Department of Police[45] but no *primary* evidence has surfaced that either of these ladies was present that night.

The Danish Minister's wife Anna Sofie Scavenius heard that *four* women were there and claimed to have seen one of them a few days later at a party at the French Embassy. According to the ambassador Maurice Paleologue, 'there was no orgy at the Youssoupov palace ... no ladies were present at the gathering, whether Princess R–, or Madame D–, or Countess P, or the dancer Karalli'.[46]

A few days before the murder, Vera Karalli apparently noted that her evening with Dmitri was overshadowed by concern for the 'upcoming event'. He asked her to write a letter to Rasputin because they needed one 'in a woman's hand'. She wrote it wearing gloves and modifying her handwriting in order to confuse any future investigation. Was she writing a letter purporting to be from Irina? Karalli later wrote to her friend Galina Kradinova that Dmitri had told her to wait in his palace while he was at the Moika and that he kept phoning to say what was happening. But historian Oleg Shishkin says this letter was written when Karalli was trying to obtain Soviet citizenship at the Vienna Consulate and knew that her letters to Galina would be read by the security department.[47] She told police she had spent the evening in her hotel.

Even the timing of the shots is disputed. At around 2.30 a.m., four shots were heard at the police post across the canal from the Moika Palace, followed by a low scream. Others place the shots at around 4.00 a.m.

When Vlasyuk investigated he noticed no blood in the courtyard and no body lying in the yard. When he was summoned to Felix's study and told by Purishkevich that Rasputin was dead, he made no mention of blood on Felix or an epaulette missing from his jacket.

In a case with so many contradictory statements the one indisputable fact is that Rasputin was killed by three bullets.

In February 1917 Grand Duke Andrei Vladimirovich, who had attended the Military Juridical Academy, was told by Victor Sereda, the Investigator for Extraordinary Affairs, that the first shot was fired into Rasputin's left side below the heart, shattering the left lobe of the liver having passed through the stomach. The second was fired into his back (a jacketed bullet was taken from his spine). It entered the right side of the back and went through the kidney. The final shot, at point-blank range, was fired into his forehead. The first two shots were fired in fairly quick succession from about 20 cm (8 inches) away.[48] Any of these shots would eventually have been fatal but the final bullet *ensured* immediate death. In which case, why did Purishkevich say he shot Rasputin in the *back* of the head?

According to Richard Cullen this shot to the forehead has the hallmark of an assassin and all three shots could have been fired while Rasputin was seated.[49]

Grand Duke Nicholas Michaelovich said that Rasputin was shot while sitting down. His information must have come from Felix. According to his diary entry of 19 December, Felix 'sat right next to Rasputin and still talking to him fired a shot at point blank range. The bullet entered Rasputin's lung, passed through his liver, and he fell unconscious to the floor – to all intents and purposes a dead man.'[50]

Stopford mentions a shot 'fired point-blank at his forehead' in his account, which he says was 'recounted to me on June 6 1917 [NS] at Yalta by the perpetrator'.[51] If that is true, why did Felix change his story when he wrote his books? Was it to tie in with Purishkevich's published account? And why did Purishkevich lie?

Felix says he first sat down by Rasputin, then got up to admire the crucifix. Rasputin followed and he shot him while both were standing. The angle of the shots makes this impossible. They must have remained seated. Neither Felix nor Purishkevich mentioned the final shot to the forehead.

According to Cullen, Rasputin would have been incapable of escaping into the yard after either of the first two shots. Cullen further corroborates that there was no body lying in the yard, no blood on either Felix or Purishkevich and no missing epaulette on Felix's shoulder.[52]

Who fired the first two shots is unknown (probably Felix and Purishkevich) but for a long time suspicion regarding the final shot has centred on Oswald Rayner of the British Secret Intelligence Service, Felix's friend from Oxford.

ひ ✶ ஐ

In 1916 it was reported that the British government was worried about German influence on the imperial family and had asked the Danish royal family to intervene. It was proposed to send Prince Waldemar to Russia to see his sister the dowager empress. By this time, Marie Feodorovna had little political influence over her son and certainly none over her daughter-in-law. Whatever they hoped to achieve, the plan was abandoned because of Denmark's neutrality in the war.[53]

David Lloyd George, who became prime minister on 26 November/9 December and whom King George V disliked, was worried about pro-Germans in the Russian government. Warnings of 'impending disaster' also reached the king via his ambassador, who feared the tsar's rule was 'in jeopardy'.[54]

The British believed, rightly or wrongly, that Rasputin was involved in efforts to sign a separate peace between Russia and Germany, the consequences of which would be disastrous for Britain when considerably more German troops were released onto the Western Front. 'The British, likely including the king,' knew something urgently needed to be done to stop this happening. With many believing that the empress and Rasputin wanted a separate peace, they were 'a direct threat to the British Empire'.[55]

There is no evidence that Rasputin was involved in such a plan, unless of course it exists in intelligence files which are not released. According to Sir Basil Thomson, at the time Director of Intelligence at the Home Office, the assassins 'were convinced that Rasputin was engaged in a plot to persuade the tsar to make a separate peace with Germany, and just before Christmas [NS] Rasputin is said to have revealed the plan in a burst of confidence. The separate peace was to be proclaimed on January 1, 1917.' But, he added, 'how true this part of the story might be I was not in a position to judge'.[56] Princess Zenaide had reported this rumour to Felix on 3 December [OS].

Felix, who believed German agents were in Russia and rather fancifully claimed to have seen some in Rasputin's apartment, encouraged the British in their belief – and it is here that Rayner enters the frame.

After Oswald Rayner graduated in 1910 he worked for *The Times* in Paris as second assistant correspondent. By 1912 he was back in London as private secretary to the post-master general, Sir Herbert Samuel, where he got to know the then chancellor of the exchequer David Lloyd George. They remained 'in close contact' for the next ten years. All this time Rayner was reading for the Bar, to which he was called in 1914. He became a barrister at the Inner Temple in 1915. On the outbreak of war he joined the Inns of Court Officer Training Corps where it is believed his language skills were noticed. In October he was commissioned as a second lieutenant, interpreter and sent on special duties to the Intelligence Department of the War Office. He was recruited by the Secret Intelligence Service (SIS, later MI6) in January 1915. In November these duties took him to Russia at short notice as a temporary lieutenant in Military Intelligence.[57]

On 9 December 1915, Rayner wrote to his Finnish benefactor Anna Sinebrychoff from the Hotel de France in Petrograd. 'I don't know how long the work is likely to last, but it will be at least one month, and probably two, perhaps even longer.'[58]

He was sent there with Lieutenant Colonel Henry Vere Fane Benet (Croppy) as part of the Anglo-French Censorship Division, where co-ordinating censorship of telegrams and letters for intelligence purposes was among their duties. Hidden within the British Military Mission was a 'growing group' of personnel from MI6. Their reports reached the king, who was anxious about what they were saying.[59]

According to a family member, in London Rayner was briefed by the original 'C', Mansfield Cumming, chief of the SIS, who had known George V since they both attended the Royal Naval College at Greenwich. Even before the outbreak of war officials were spicing up the somewhat boring Foreign Office telegrams with secret service reports for the king's benefit.[60]

Croppy later said that they 'avoided all interference in purely Russian affairs', but it is also clear that the job gave them a pretty good insight into what was going on in Petrograd. Literally thousands of intercepted telegrams passed through their hands and some of the information was 'shared with their Russian counterparts without playing any active role in what ensued'. This was their definition of 'avoided all interference'.[61]

After completing his mission Rayner left Russia. Between 25 and 27 March he stayed at Preston Manor, Brighton, the home of Croppy's stepmother Mrs Ellen Thomas-Stanford. Croppy was the illegitimate son of Ellen's first husband Vere Fane Benet. In 1897 the widowed Ellen (heir to the Stanford estate in Brighton) married Charles Thomas. They moved into Preston Manor, taking the name Thomas-Stanford. Croppy kept in touch and introduced Ellen to Oswald Rayner. Charles Thomas-Stanford was the MP for Brighton and had important contacts. This may have been a factor in Rayner's friendly correspondence with Ellen during the war.

On 27 April [NS] a War Office minute confirmed that 'Lt. Col. Benet and Lieut. Rayner, the British delegates, are returning to Russia to assist censors in suppressing enemy communication and trade. Request inform Ambassador at Petrograd.' They took with them a diplomatic bag.[62]

Was Rayner sent back to Petrograd because he had known Felix at Oxford? It certainly looks like it when we see what happened next.

7

Cover-up

'The silent stone walls would always conceal the truth.'[1]

Felix Youssoupov

On 25 April [OS] 1916 Oswald Rayner sat in his room in the Hotel de France in Petrograd and wrote to Felix in English, addressing him as 'Dear Elston', the name the prince used at Oxford:

I can imagine you on receiving this letter turning at once to my signature, to find out who on earth can be the writer – so I have pinned my card to this sheet in order to help you in your search. Not that this will be of much assistance to you, however, for you have in all probability forgotten ever having met me. If that is so please take no further notice of this letter. I was at Oriel College Oxford from 1907–10 while you were at Univ [University College]; and together with one Cobb (of my college) used to meet you and [Eric] Hamilton from time to time – I used to try and play the piano. I arrived in Petrograd yesterday and shall probably remain here for some months as a member of an Anglo-French Military Mission. My work is at the General Staff [Building].

If you *do* remember me, I should so much like to see you again.

Yours sincerely,

O. T. Rayner[2]

Was Rayner instructed to write this letter to remind Felix of their former acquaintanceship? Was London anxious for him to cultivate his friendship with Felix, which had suddenly become of potential use to the government? Writing to his Finnish friends in May, Rayner said 'we have not yet settled down definitely to the work that brought us out here', but, he added, 'one part of my duties I have definitely begun and that is some consolation'. Was this duty the letter to Felix? He continued, 'I wish I could tell you some real news or tell you something about my work. You will know the reason why it is impossible for me to do this.'[3] By the end of May it was obvious that Rayner's stay would be longer than anticipated. 'I see no chance at present of being able to leave the city,' he told Anna Sinebryachoff.[4]

The semi-circular Russian General Staff Building overlooked Winter Palace Square and housed the British and French Intelligence Missions. Sir Samuel Hoare, a thirty-six-year-old former Conservative politician and Oxford graduate, was head of section of the British Intelligence Mission of the SIS in Petrograd. The liaison officer was his deputy Captain Stephen Alley, who shared a flat with Lieutenant Colonel Benet. Hoare had no expertise in intelligence. He arrived in Petrograd in the spring of 1916 'to forge links with Russian generals and monitor the fighting on the Eastern Front' but soon he was writing reports about the dark forces at work in Russia. He collected information about Rasputin and his camarilla, the 'hidden power behind the anti-war parties', and sent the reports to Mansfield Cumming in London.[5]

Hoare expected his men to play by the rules but not all of them agreed with 'his very British approach to espionage'. Nor did he realise that there was a far more nefarious side to the bureau's activities. Rayner and a few others had 'established a clandestine inner circle that members referred to as the "far-reaching system", the inner circle of the bureau'. They acted in 'absolute secrecy, spearheading underground missions that left no trace of their involvement'.[6] These professionals did not trust Hoare, whom they resented because he was responsible for the dismissal of his popular predecessor Major Thornhill.

The senior British agent was Captain John Scale, born in Wales in 1882 and educated at Repton and Sandhurst. A first-class Russian interpreter, he escorted the Russian delegation visiting England between April and June 1916. In August he was sent to Petrograd and billeted first at the Astoria, 'the "official" hotel, open only to diplomats, officers and officials'.[7] Shortly after his arrival the military control system was set up at Moika 19, officially called the office of the Bureau of Passport (Military) Control. Scale certainly believed that Rasputin was involved with the Germans and he was worried about his influence over Empress Alexandra. 'German intrigue was becoming more intense daily,' Scale wrote. 'Enemy agents were busy whispering of peace and hinting how to get it by creating disorder, rioting etc. Things looked very black ... The failure in communications, the shortness of foods, the sinister influence which seemed to be clogging the war machine, Rasputin the drunken debaucher influencing Russia's policy, what was to be the end of it all.'[8]

Scale's daughter Muriel was adamant that he was deliberately sent out of Russia before Rasputin's murder although 'he *was* involved in the planning of it; they were altogether, what they were going to do about it ... in fact he wasn't there when they actually killed him, he was somewhere else, so he didn't actually take part in that, but he was involved in all the planning and how they were going to get rid of him'.[9] Scale was in Romania destroying the oil wells before the Germans could get to them, although his *exact* location is unknown. Muriel confirmed that Scale knew Felix 'very well' and was 'often a guest at the Youssoupov Palace'.[10]

Scale met Felix through Captain Stephen Alley, whose father was a railway construction engineer and whose mother was born in Russia.

Stephen was born in 1876 in a house on one of the Youssoupovs' estates made available to senior railway construction workers. (It will be recalled that the Youssoupovs had huge investments in railway construction.) He was educated at Moscow's prestigious Fiedler school and King's College London, took a degree in engineering at Edinburgh University, worked at the family firm and then set up his own company. He also 'joined the Imperial Yeomanry, a reservist unit, and qualified as an interpreter in Russian, French and German'.[11]

In 1910 he returned to Russia. As a fluent Russian speaker who could pass for a native, on the outbreak of war he was sent to the Intelligence Mission in Petrograd and 'specifically tasked with investigating German agents and liaising with the Russian authorities'.[12]

Many people now believe that Rasputin's brutal death was arranged by British Secret Service agents, 'through the close personal relationship' between Felix and the men from the SIS.[13]

☙ ✷ ❧

Rayner's approach to Felix had borne fruit. By the time the prince returned from Kislovodsk in October, Rayner was integrated into his circle and knew several of his relatives. Robert Bruce Lockhart recalled that 'during the war years a junior lieutenant in the British Military Censor's Office probably went to more parties in high places than all of the members of the Embassy put together'.[14] He could well have been referring to Rayner.

On 9/22 November Rayner wrote to Felix from Moika 14, apartment 56, about a mile and three-quarters along the Moika Embankment from the Youssoupov Palace:

> Dear Elston,
> I have just received a letter from Countess Keller [probably Countess Kleinmichel's unmarried sister], who tells me that she met you at Kislovodsk, and that you expressed to her your intention of ringing me up as soon as you returned to Petrograd. I have left the Hotel and have moved into a flat at the above address – and it would afford me a very great pleasure if we could meet sometime before I return to England. I met a cousin of yours a few days ago, and it was from him I learned that this letter would reach you if I sent it to your Petrograd address.
> Yours sincerely, O. T. Rayner[15]

Yet this letter may have been a subterfuge.

Records show that in late October and during November Oswald Rayner and John Scale were driven to the Youssoupov Palace (Moika 94) several times by William Compton, a chauffeur from the Anglo-Russian hospital in Petrograd. Compton's account books give the dates [OS] as 13, 16, 21, 22, 27 October and 3, 9, 15, 19 and 25 November.[16]

Yet on 12 and 13 October Felix was in Kiev with the dowager empress; on 3 November he visited Grand Duchess Ella in Moscow, wrote to his mother and caught the night train back to Petrograd. His letter is postmarked 'Moscow

3/XI/16'. Did the meeting with Ella occur the previous day so that Felix could meet Rayner in Petrograd on 3 November?

It has not been possible to trace Compton's record to verify whether the entries say 'Youssoupov Palace', 'Moika Palace' or just 'Moika' – where after 9 November Rayner was living at Moika 14, where Felix was living in Grand Duchess Xenia's palace (Moika 106) and where the military control office was (Moika 19).

If Felix was present at all these meetings, by 9 November he and Rayner had already met several times. It also means Rayner and Scale had spoken to Felix about Rasputin *before* November, when Felix's plot is supposed to have taken off. Felix, Dmitri and Sukhotin met at the Youssoupov Palace on 15 November. It now appears that Rayner and Scale were also present.

The meetings were secret. 'But limelight is abhorrent, the work would suffer if it should obtrude,' Rayner told Ellen Thomas-Stanford. He complained to Anna Sinebrychoff about 'additional duties', adding that there were 'other difficulties too'.[17]

Felix and Rayner met again on 19 (with Scale) and 25 November. On 29 November Rayner told Ellen Thomas-Stanford that 'we struggle on with our war work which increases in volume week by week and threatens to overwhelm us. I have been sleeping badly of late but otherwise I am very fit.'[18]

After Scale left for Romania on 11/24 November, two more visits to the Youssoupov Palace occurred, 'the last of which was the night before the murder'.[19] The presence of Scale on the earlier visits, as well as their timing, points to something being planned, with the British agents probably acting as advisers.

Russian author Oleg Shishkin found an interesting letter in the Russian State Archive of Ancient Acts from Rayner to Sergei Sukhotin, dated 8 December 1916: 'Dear Sukhotin, I also have a big request for you. Can you come here tomorrow (Saturday) at ten o'clock in the morning? I would like to consult with you about Felix's affairs. It is impossible to get through – I tried for a long time. Your sincere friend Oswald Rayner.'[20]

On 14 December, Rayner told Ellen Thomas-Stanford that 'a general rearrangement of our respective departments has taken place, and we have greater hopes than ever before ... The political excitement in Petrograd has somewhat subsided,' he added. At the bottom is an interesting aside. 'You are the only friend I have who has access to the F.O. bag...'[21] Was this because her husband was the MP for Brighton? The Foreign Office diplomatic bag allowed official communications to go through border controls without being opened or detained.

☙ ✶ ❧

Felix confirmed that Rayner knew of the murder in advance. Margarita Nelipa believes Rayner was only sanctioned to confirm to Hoare that Rasputin was indeed dead. Author Joseph Fuhrmann suggests that they were discussing an idea that (if necessary) after Rasputin's murder, Felix would be able to seek asylum in Britain. This seems rather unlikely.

Rayner's cousin, who wrote his obituary, claimed Oswald said he was in the Moika Palace on the night of Rasputin's murder. This was also the view of

Gordon Rayner, as confirmed to me by Dr David Lockwood, Oswald's great-nephew by marriage: '[I] can confirm that there is, contrary to what some recent writers on the subject have said, very strong evidence indeed that he fired the fatal shot ... I had a long conversation with Gordon Rayner, Oswald's nephew, a couple of years before he (Gordon) died. Gordon was a man of the utmost probity, and revealed details that put the matter almost beyond doubt. Unfortunately, all the papers relating to the killing were destroyed by Oswald Rayner himself. Lloyd George ... had all mention of his presumed instructions to Rayner excised from official documents.'[22]

Andrew Cook, who investigated the Secret Service angle, believes that the operation was sanctioned either by Lloyd George (the secretary of state for war and later prime minister) 'or by senior officers of the [Secret] Service itself'.[23]

Further evidence comes from William Compton, who told his family that Rasputin's assassin was 'an Englishman'. He added that the man was a lawyer, who came from the same area of the country as himself. Birth records show that Compton and Rayner, who described himself as a barrister-at-law, were born just 10 miles apart.[24]

A different opinion about Rayner came from John Penycate: 'The former "C" of MI6, Sir John Scarlett ... assured me that he didn't [shoot Rasputin] – the official line now for a century, but probably true.' But as historian Vladimir Moss commented: 'Considering how Scarlett lied about the supposed weapons of mass destruction in Iraq in 2003, we are entitled to be sceptical of his testimony...'[25]

Rayner was not a professional assassin and nothing can be proved.

Two soldiers guarded the entrance to Felix's apartment that night and it has been suggested that they were Rayner and Alley. Cullen believes they were Felix's butler Gregory Boujinsky and his valet Ivan Nefedov, both of whom would have worn uniform. Felix said they had been told to wait in the servants' hall until summoned. The other staff were dismissed for the night. Boujinsky and Nefedov were sworn to secrecy by Felix. Boujinsky was never questioned and Nefedov's statement is, as Cullen states, 'a substantial lie'.[26]

Felix said that apart from the five known members of the conspiracy, 'those culpable of this disappearance [of Rasputin] had to remain ... unknown'. He would never say more. As Stephen Dorrill said, 'a particular hallmark of MI6 planning [was] plausible deniability'.[27]

ভ ✶ ৶

Rayner's colleague Croppy brought another element into the story. Croppy wrote to his stepmother Ellen on 14 February 1917 telling her how 'three men of royal blood, Boris, Dmitri and Youssoupof [*sic*]', with the help of 'two very smart ladies', lured Rasputin to a 'very smart supper party'. There they gave Rasputin a gun and told him to shoot himself. After a scuffle, Boris 'shot him as a dog, twice'. Rasputin's body was bundled into a car and 'they found he was not quite dead and that's when the second shooting took place' (the *coup de grace* into Rasputin's forehead).[28]

The only Boris with royal blood was Grand Duke Boris Vladimirovich, the brother of Felix's old flame Grand Duchess Elena, but there has never been any hint of his involvement. However, the letter continues: 'I do not care to *write* what I have heard (and believe to be true) was at the back of the affair but "it was the limit".' Was his reluctance to put the truth on paper because he had learned that Britain was involved in the murder?

There is further clue. 'The night of the murder I was discussing it with a highly placed individual who said, "Well, well, how slack these Russians are to be sure; it took an *Englishman* to do that for them" – because the history of the man, whose name is frequently mentioned, was at Oxford and a great tennis player, in fact about the best in the world until he hurt his arm.'[29]

Croppy seems to have put together a mish-mash of several people here. Felix Youssoupov had a cousin, Count Michael Soumarokoff-Elston, who *was* a tennis champion (he competed in the 1912 Olympics) and was forced to switch to left-handed play after surgery on his right arm. He was of course Russian, not English (some books confuse him with Felix, who was also Count Soumarokoff-Elston) but unlike Felix, he never went to Oxford. Rayner's family do have 'a strong tradition of tennis playing within the family generally' and a 1916 letter to Anna Sinebrychoff confirms that Rayner joined the tennis club in Petrograd's Tauride Gardens.[30] There is so far no evidence that he hurt his arm. 'When we meet I have much to tell you which it was quite impossible to write or hint at on paper,' Croppy told Ellen enigmatically.[31]

The mystery remains.

⊂੨ ✶ ੭⊃

There has been a lot of discussion about weapons, jacketed and unjacketed bullets and uniforms, which is beyond the scope of this book. It should be pointed out though that neither original pathologist Professor Dmitri Kosorotov in 1916, nor Professor Vladimir Zharov who examined the surviving post-mortem reports in 1993, could be certain about the make of gun that fired the shot into Rasputin's forehead.

The bullet extracted from the corpse was 'badly deformed'.[32] It is believed that the shots were fired by three different calibre revolvers – the first from Dmitri's Browning, the second from Purishkevich's Savage and the final shot from a .455 Webley, said to be 'Rayner's favourite weapon'.[33] Although a standard-issue weapon to British officers, Britain *did* sell the Webley to Russia. In the State Archive of the Russian Federation in Moscow Douglas Smith found a 1916 receipt for a Webley-Scott revolver issued to a Russian lieutenant colonel, proving that Russians also used this gun.[34]

Grand Duke Nicholas Michaelovich wrote: 'As for the true suspects, they haven't been found, and never will be. Why? Because the blow was delivered by very skilful Englishmen, who have disappeared. Meanwhile, public opinion continues to view Grand Duke Dmitri and Felix as the guilty ones, simultaneously [singling them out] as popular heroes who have liberated [Russia] from the yoke of Rasputin.'[35]

When news of the murder reached Tsarskoe Selo, Grand Duchess Olga immediately assumed that Dmitri had done it, perhaps because he was apparently an excellent shot. At the very least, he was guilty of conspiracy to murder.

Someone who knew Felix well said that for him it was probably a 'thrill killing'. In contrast, the sensitive Dmitri was so upset afterwards that General Laiming, his former tutor, sat up with him for hours.[36] Dmitri was certainly not an Anglophile politically. Later in life, the thought of accepting an honorary British Army commission horrified him as he knew that he would be marked out as having sold himself to the British. It is therefore doubtful that he would have sanctioned British involvement in an act he viewed as patriotic. Nor does it sound like a rogue operation, as the SIS were 'heavily involved'.[37]

Did Rayner step in when it became obvious that things were out of control? Were the SIS men supposed to be there only as observers? Was Dmitri's horror at betraying Russia by becoming involved with the British brought on by the knowledge that a British agent had fired the fatal shot and that Rasputin's death had brought the whole Russian house of cards tumbling down?

At the moment there are no answers.

൦൪ ✸ ଅ

Early on 17 December the policeman Stepan Vlasyuk reported the shots heard near the Moika Palace and Purishkevich's assertion that Rasputin was dead. They discovered he had not returned home from the Moika Palace the previous evening. Count Serge Zavadsky, Procurator of the Appellate Court, was ordered to investigate.

The news soon spread around the city.

On the morning of 17 December, Petrograd was 'roused by the news of [Rasputin's] assassination', wrote the British ambassador. The question of how much Sir George Buchanan *really* knew has dogged historians. He was a close friend of Grand Duke Nicholas Michaelovich, with whom he 'had frequently exchanged views on the internal situation' but there is no proof that he knew anything more than gossip that an attempt on Rasputin's life was being planned.[38]

Samuel Hoare, who in November had been told by Purishkevich that 'he and his friends determined to liquidate the affair of Rasputin', had not considered it 'a definitely thought-out plan'. He heard about the murder on the afternoon of 17/30 December during a meeting, where he was shown the headline on the *Bourse Gazette*, 'Death of Gregory Rasputin in Petrograd.'[39]

He told London that there was 'a crop of wild rumours about British participation' and he was contacted by Buchanan, who asked for his reaction. But, as Andrew Cook says, 'Hoare was not necessarily aware of what his own men were up to a good deal of the time.'[40]

On 18/31 December he sent an urgent telegram to 'C' confirming Rasputin's murder. This appears to be the answer to a query from 'C', so why had Cumming in London heard something before Hoare? Then on 2 January [NS] Hoare sent a further telegram asking if Cumming had any other information.[41]

Rumours of British involvement were picked up all over Europe. They were especially popular in Germany, where it was believed that Britain wanted Rasputin dead because he wanted a separate peace. Bulgarian reports had a

British agent travelling in the car to help dispose of Rasputin's body. But would an experienced agent really forget the weights and the overshoe?

Buchanan notified the Foreign Office about Rasputin's murder and Felix's involvement on 17/30 December, summarising what was known in a second communication. A few days later he reported a conversation with Grand Duke Nicholas Michaelovich, who had a 'gloomy view of the internal situation'.[42] Another telegram is summarised as 'Emperor's refusal to release Prince Youssoupov; former reactionary leader Purishkevich said to have planned murder'.[43] Duff Cooper recalled the 'thrilling telegrams' arriving at the Foreign Office, which 'read like pages from Italian renaissance history'.[44]

The two main Foreign Office files on Rasputin's death have never been released to the National Archives.[45] The only clue is an intriguing note from Stephen Alley to John Scale in Romania, dated 25 December 1916/7 January 1917. It reads in part:

> Although matters here have not proceeded entirely to plan, our objective has clearly been achieved. Reaction to the demise of 'Dark Forces' has been well received by all, although a few awkward questions have already been asked about wider involvement.
>
> Rayner is attending to loose ends and will no doubt brief you on your return.[46]

Alley's phrase 'not proceeded entirely to plan' bears a curious resemblance to a phrase in an intriguing letter to Felix from his cousin Count Michael Soumarokoff-Elston on 25 December (OS) which was published in a compilation of Felix and Irina's letters by Natalia A. Ganina in Moscow. Michael had been assigned to the Black Sea Fleet driving motor ambulances but was invalided out of the war and in December returned to Petrograd from Odessa. According to Natalia Ganina, the letter reads in part: 'Knowing a little of your plan of action, it seems to me that something did not succeed for you. Something happened that prevented you from exactly fulfilling your plan. What it was and how it happened – I, of course, don't know. You will tell me when I see you.'[47]

We don't know what the original plan was but Felix was recognised when he went to pick up Rasputin, the shots alerted the police, an overshoe and blood were found near the bridge and the body did not disappear out towards the Gulf of Finland as they had hoped.

Not everyone believed the British were involved. One member of the family said, 'If this was done by British agents, their agent was Felix.'[48] An intriguing idea.

In 2009 Felix's granddaughter Xenia Sfiris was asked about the murder. 'But the only thing I can say is that, a few years ago … there were Russian and English journalists and from other countries, who contacted me to tell me that apparently it was not my grandfather who killed Rasputin. And my reply was that, if I have no idea about who killed Rasputin, my grandfather had written that it was him and if he took on this murder, then he is even greater in my eyes. And I stop there, because I do not know.'[49]

The cover story suited everyone. The British needed to make it look as if Russians had carried out a patriotic deed; they could not be implicated in influencing Russian policy to keep Russia in the war by killing Rasputin.

Felix achieved notoriety as Rasputin's murderer. He would make full use of that in the years to come.

CR ✶ ℛ

At nine o'clock on 17 December, Procurator Zavadsky, Investigator for Extraordinary Affairs Victor Sereda and a police photographer went to Moika 92. No spent cartridges were found in the courtyard but blood was visible on the step at the basement entrance. The police were only allowed to take a blood sample from outside the palace, not inside where the blood came from.[50] Authorisation to search the palace was granted by the City Governor Alexander Balk. Felix only allowed the police to enter by his private entrance and to have a cursory glimpse inside the study. There was no forensic examination and no scene-of-crime photographs were taken.

At ten o'clock the Chief of Police of the Kazan District General George Grigoriev arrived at Grand Duchess Xenia's palace to question Felix, who was not obliged to offer any information. He denied that Rasputin had been in the Moika Palace but failed to give an explanation for the blood on the step. He told Grigoriev the story of the shooting of the dog and the superintendent left, apparently satisfied.

By now the empress knew that Rasputin had disappeared after a visit to the Youssoupov Palace to meet Irina. Alexandra was worried. She knew Irina was in the Crimea.

Rasputin's daughters asked Munya Golovina to phone Felix's home, unaware that he was staying at Xenia's palace. At midday Felix telephoned Munya and denied that Rasputin had been at his house.

With rumours of Rasputin's disappearance swirling around Petrograd, Felix rang to ask if the empress would receive him so that he could give his version of events. He was told to write a letter if he had anything to say.

Later that morning City Governor Balk summoned Felix, who said he had entertained friends at a small party the night before but denied Rasputin was present. This presented the police with a problem. The probable presence of members of the nobility meant that they could not even ask who had attended, only if Felix was willing to give his account of events. Felix again told the story of the dog and demanded that the order to search the palace be withdrawn, which it was that afternoon.

He then went to lunch with Dmitri, who was due to return to *stavka*. This was probably when Felix learnt that Rasputin's body had been successfully disposed of. Felix and Dmitri wrote to the empress denying that Rasputin had been in the Moika Palace. Almost the whole letter was a lie. Sukhotin and Purishkevich arrived and the conspirators agreed their story. Oleg Shishkin notes that during the interrogations the conspirators kept silent about Sukhotin and never mentioned his name.

During the afternoon Felix went to see Alexander Makarov, the Minister of Justice, to tell him the same story and get the case closed. 'Zavadsky and Sereda were instructed to stop the investigation'[51] and Makarov confirmed that Felix could leave for Koreiz that evening.

Felix called on Michael Rodzianko, the president of the Duma, whose wife was Princess Zenaide's cousin. He then visited Zavadsky for legal advice (Maklakov was in Moscow), as the police had interviewed his staff. Once Felix rescinded permission, no more questioning could take place and only three of the servants testified.

Minister of Interior Alexander Protopopov also began an investigation which he put in the hands of General Popov, an officer for special operations at the Ministry of Interior. That afternoon Rasputin's overshoe was found near the Petrovsky Bridge and blood was found on the bridge's railings.

Back at Xenia's palace Felix found Oswald Rayner, whom he said knew about the conspiracy and wanted to know what was happening.[52] Andrei, Feodor and Nikita were also there with Mr Stewart and the grand duchess's lady-in-waiting Sophie Evreinov. After dinner Felix and his brothers-in-law prepared to leave for the Crimea. Of those present, only Feodor and Rayner knew details of the plot.[53]

CR ✶ ঞ

When Felix, Andrei, Feodor and Nikita arrived at the Nikolaev station just after 8.30 p.m. accompanied by Oswald Rayner and Mr Stewart they were stopped by the police. Felix was informed that the empress had forbidden him to leave Petrograd and that he was to remain at Grand Duchess Xenia's palace until further notice. He was returned there under guard accompanied by Andrei, Feodor and Rayner. Nikita left for Ai-Todor with Mr Stewart.

Felix asked Feodor and Rayner to remain with him: 'Both of them worried and feared for my fate.'[54] He also asked Grand Duke Nicholas Michaelovich to come and see him. 'Felix was already in bed. I spent half an hour with him listening to his confidences,' the grand duke wrote in his diary. Felix reeled off the conspirators' agreed story and his visitor left looking unconvinced. 'I told him ... his fiction wouldn't stand up to any criticism, and that ... he was the murderer.'[55]

After the grand duke's departure Felix told Andrei, Feodor and Rayner that in the morning he was moving to Grand Duke Dmitri's palace while their fate was decided and explained what to say if they were questioned by the police. They all promised to stick to the agreed story.[56]

That evening Dmitri attended a performance at the Michael Theatre, where he received an ovation from the audience and was forced to leave early.

CR ✶ ঞ

On 18 December Irina received a telegram at Koreiz: 'I will leave tomorrow or the day after tomorrow. Feodor will stay, since Andrei has arrived. He will come with me. My delayed departure was disgraceful ... Kisses, Felix.'[57]

General Popov arrived to take Felix's statement. Later that morning, despite the empress's orders, Felix moved to Dmitri's huge neo-Baroque palace on the Nevsky Prospekt. The first-floor state rooms had been converted into the 200-bed Anglo-Russian Hospital. The private apartments were on the ground floor, with an entrance through a locked door near the foot of the grand staircase. Lady Sybil Grey (who helped set up and run the hospital) said that when it emerged that Felix had murdered Rasputin, 'there was an uproar of excitement and thankfulness, workers toasting him, nuns blessing him'.[58]

Purishkevich had immediately returned to the front on his hospital train. He sent a coded telegram to Maklakov in Moscow to say that Rasputin was dead.

Shortly after lunch Dmitri was informed that the empress had ordered him to be confined to his palace. He obeyed, although only the emperor could give such an order. He was not prevented from telegraphing members of the family to tell them what had happened. Most were convinced Alexandra had acted without the tsar's sanction. She called the Youssoupovs a 'wicked family' into which Irina had regrettably married.[59]

Only family members were allowed into Dmitri's apartments and many visited, including Grand Dukes Andrei and Cyril and Prince Gabriel Constantinovich, who said they would support Felix and Dmitri regardless. Dmitri told them he had left at 3.00 a.m. with the ladies and, as they left, he shot a watchdog that began attacking them. He escorted the ladies to Karavannaya Street and arrived home at 4.00 a.m. This was corroborated by Felix. Neither man named the others present apart from Purishkevich.[60]

Dmitri also rang Grand Duke Nicholas Michaelovich, who kept them informed about the search for Rasputin's body. According to Stopford, whose narrative is not always reliable, Felix telephoned Grand Duchess Vladimir and said there had been a misunderstanding. She later also spoke to Dmitri, who swore he knew nothing about it all.[61]

Two telegrams from Grand Duchess Ella, one to Dmitri and one to Princess Zenaide, were intercepted by the authorities and forwarded to Tsarskoe Selo. Ella had gone to the Deveyevo Monastery on 7 December and did not return until after Rasputin's death. Although she would normally have been 'appalled' by murder, she 'gave thanks' at the removal of 'such a malign influence'.[62] Her two supportive messages praising their patriotic action severely compromised Felix and Dmitri.

Late that evening the tsar returned from *stavka*.

Contrary to the expectations of most of the imperial family, the news of Rasputin's death did not cause a palace revolution, nor did the empress have a breakdown. The tsar seemed more distressed by the involvement of his family than by the murder itself.

Buchanan sent a telegram to the Foreign Office, which was circulated to the king and the war cabinet, explaining how he had emphatically denied British involvement although the tsar had no doubt about it:

At today's new year's reception the emperor spoke to me in his most gracious and friendly manner. As reports have been spread, evidently by German agents, that not only had English detectives been conducting an enquiry into Rasputin's murder, but that English officers had been actually associated with it, I told His Majesty that as I should be deeply grieved were either he or the empress to believe such an infamous story,

I wished to give him the most formal assurance that there was not a word of truth in it. The story had, I believe, arisen from the fact that a young English officer – Rayner, who was temporarily employed here, had been at Oxford with Prince Youssoupoff [*sic*] and had seen a great deal of him here. Rayner however positively assures me that the prince had never said one word to him about the plot, and I need hardly tell His Majesty that assassination was a crime held in abomination by British people. The emperor, who had evidently heard something about Rayner, said that he was very glad that I had told him and expressed warm thanks.[63]

Rayner had denied his involvement, allowing Buchanan a get-out clause of plausible deniability. According to an old adage, an ambassador has been defined as a man sent abroad to lie for his country.

೧✷ည

On 19 December Irina sent a telegram from Koreiz to Grand Duke Nicholas Michaelovich asking for news: 'We don't understand anything, we don't even know if the fact completed. Awfully worried. Telegraph further, tomorrow everyone leaving. Kisses, Irina.' Hours later a second telegram followed: 'Dmitri telegraphs that Felix leaves for Crimea the day after tomorrow. Is arrival still necessary? Kisses. Answer soon. Irina.' The following day her telegram begins, 'Answer quickly and don't get angry.'[64] The telegrams were intercepted by the authorities and preserved.

During the next few days Nicholas Michaelovich spent a great deal of time at Dmitri's palace, where he claimed to be directing Felix and Dmitri's every move, preventing them from doing anything rash. 'Your presence for us is a great comfort,' Felix telegraphed late on 19 December.[65]

Nicholas Michaelovich also telegraphed Felix's father at Koreiz: 'I consider your arrival here most desirable. I see Felix daily, he is calm, collected, makes an excellent impression upon me. Kind regards to the princess and to Irina. Come.'[66]

Felix senior made plans to leave, as the next telegram from the grand duke confirmed: 'I am glad of your arrival. I shall tell you what I possibly can en route.' Then he reported that Rasputin's body had been found that morning 'under the ice near the Petrovsky Bridge'.[67]

Nicholas Michaelovich rushed to Dmitri's palace with the news, writing in his diary that Irina and Princess Zenaide were delighted that Felix was the murderer.

Rasputin's body was frozen to the underside of the icy Malaya Nevka, his fur coat wrapped around him. Tied to his feet was a bag of blue material, the same as that found in Felix's apartment. The thin fabric had ripped and whatever was in it had disappeared. Felix was now directly associated with the crime. The body was taken away for an autopsy.[68]

That evening Dmitri was informed that by order of the tsar he was under arrest in his palace.

The following day, 20 December, members of the imperial family gathered at Dmitri's palace to talk about his arrest. The police had not believed anything

Felix said. Makarov, who a few days earlier had confirmed that Felix was free to go to Koreiz, was dismissed and replaced as Minister of Justice by Nicholas Dobrovolsky.

It had not yet been decided when Felix would be allowed to leave Petrograd, 'hence I consider your presence here desirable', Nicholas Michaelovich telegraphed to Felix's father. 'The princess and Irina can wait in the Crimea. I shall give you my opinion in writing.'[69]

As demonstrations in favour of Felix and Dmitri took place, Dmitri's sister Marie arrived from Pskov, where she had been nursing. She found Felix 'intoxicated by the importance of the part that he had played, and saw in it a great political future'.[70]

Both men were anxious about their fate. Dmitri was immune from prosecution as a member of the imperial family. Felix, married to a member of the imperial family, assumed he would be protected because of Dmitri's immunity. As Marie Pavlovna wrote: 'He believed in his lucky star and counted upon the protection of public opinion. Against that opinion, he held, the court would never proceed openly.'[71]

Dmitri's father Grand Duke Paul asked him to swear by his late mother's memory that he had not committed murder. Dmitri did so, although he never denied that he was at the Moika Palace that night.

 C3 ✱ 80

Sandro arrived from Kiev on 21 December. He went straight to Dmitri's palace for a family meeting to decide what to do if Dmitri was not released and the tsar pursued the matter.

Plainclothes police guarded the entrance to the Anglo-Russian Hospital, sent with Dmitri's permission by the prime minister Alexander Trepov, who was afraid that Protopopov might send agents to harm him. Soon afterwards a military guard also arrived. This was just as well. There was an attempt by Rasputin's followers to gain access to Dmitri's apartments through the hospital on the pretext of visiting the wounded. They were stopped by a sentry placed there by Lady Sybil.

On 22 December, as agreed, Sandro went to Tsarskoe Selo to persuade the tsar to close the case and be lenient with the 'misguided patriots'. He was concerned about 'the effect that this sensational news would have on the young tsarina and the responsibility of the imperial family for a murder committed in the presence and with the participation of two of its members'.[72] He could also see that in Alexandra's eyes Rasputin would now be a martyr and that any trial or court martial would reveal the depth of the imperial family's involvement in murder. The sympathies of the army and the public would be firmly on the side of Felix and Dmitri, leaving the tsar's isolation revealed. It would be impossible for them to receive a fair trial. Princess Zenaide later sent a message thanking Sandro 'for defending Felix and begging immunity for him'.[73]

At Tsarskoe Selo, Trepov and Makarov insisted 'that the case should be closed, whereas Protopopov ... insisted that the investigation should be continued'.[74] Sandro then telegraphed the dowager empress, saying he was hoping to bring Felix to Kiev where Irina and the elder Youssoupovs would join them. He asked her to telegraph the tsar and demand he close the investigation. This she did.

Nicholas's reply soon followed: 'Prosecution will be immediately stopped. Embrace you. Nicky.'[75]

The tsar signed a Manifesto of Clemency and on 23 December Dobrovolsky's investigation was terminated. The criminal investigation continued into January.

C꒤ ✶ ꒥

The tsar had promised to be moderate in his punishment. On 24 December Dmitri was informed he was to be banished to the Persian front. Felix was exiled to Rakitnoie, his estate in remote Kursk province. Both would leave that night.

Felix and Dmitri had one final conversation alone, which the grand duke recalled a year later in a diary entry written in Tehran:

> We discussed whether we should submit to the sovereign's orders, or remain in the capital and set off to the regimental barracks in order to launch a palace coup! Often thereafter – indeed, even now – I ask myself whether that wouldn't have been better? Presumably this revolution wouldn't have happened then! Who knows?
>
> But, of course, I couldn't bring myself to do it, because my participation in the assassination was only meant to give poor Nicky a last chance for a policy change, [and] allow him to stand openly against the friends of the deceased Rasputin – thus it's clear that I participated in that affair out of a desire to help the sovereign, out of devotion to him, and not for personal popularity...[76]

Rumours circulated that Dmitri had fired the fatal last shot and that this was being covered up in the hope that he could become the next emperor.

Felix was first to leave. Before departing, he gave Dmitri a wonder-working icon of the Holy Virgin, Mother of God.

Sandro drove Felix to the station. He was accompanied by Captain Zenchikoff, one of the instructors at the Corps des Pages, and Ignatiev, assistant director of the Okhrana. The train was due to leave at 12.30. Sandro was leaving Petrograd in the morning.

Dmitri's train left at 2 a.m. At Dmitri's request his father, whose health was not robust, remained at Tsarskoe Selo, upset that his son had been sent away in the middle of the night without being able to receive his blessing. Dmitri was accompanied by Laiming. Bertie Stopford reported that 'there was nothing to eat in the carriage, although he was assured there would be'.[77]

On 29 December sixteen members of the imperial family signed a petition asking Nicholas for leniency towards Dmitri. They requested that, because of his weak health, he be allowed to stay at his estates of Usovo or Ilyinskoe instead of the harsh climate of Persia.

The reply arrived two days later. 'No one has the right to kill. I know that many people are troubled by their own consciences, because Dmitri was not the only person involved in it. I am greatly surprised that you should have appealed to me. Nicholas.'[78]

Without realising it, the tsar had saved Dmitri's life.

CÆ✱ßO

Unaware of what had happened, Irina left Bébé at Ai-Todor with her nurse and set out for Petrograd accompanied by her parents-in-law. At least she and Felix would be together. The dowager empress was expecting Irina to stop in Kiev on her way, but by 23 December she had still not arrived.

Irina met her mother in Yekaterinoslav and they spent a few hours together. Xenia was on her way to the Crimea. Her reaction to Rasputin's death was: 'Thank God he's been killed.'[79]

Irina's train then became stuck in snow drifts and it was 7.30 p.m. on 24 December before she arrived in Kiev, where she learnt that Felix was being sent to Rakitnoie that night. 'Poor Irina only arrived Xmas eve after our church [service] – completely bewildered & whispered to me: "Just think how dreadful Christmas is for me!"' Grand Duchess Olga Alexandrovna told Xenia on 26 December. 'She assisted with all the "Christmas trees": one in each ward. This was awfully successful for my soldiers ... Irina is so sure of her spouse's *haut fait* [exploit] and only regrets not to have been there too. She is wonderful! Mama was furious when she heard that she was leaving again that evening & complained a lot – Titi only smiled complacently & muttered: "I must go."'[80]

Before leaving she had dinner with her grandmother at the Maryinsky Palace. The elder Youssoupovs remained on their train.

At 10 p.m. Irina left for Rakitnoie.

CÆ✱ßO

The normal ten-hour journey to Moscow took a day and a half. For Felix, the worst part was that he was forced to travel in a second-class carriage attached to a goods train without any food or attendants. Realising his correspondence would be read by the Okhrana, he had been unable to write more than a few words to Irina. To his delight, when he reached Kursk, 283 miles south of Moscow, she and his parents had already arrived.

Sandro arrived in Kursk at two o'clock in the morning, five minutes after Felix's train pulled in. He went straight to Irina's carriage where he found Felix and explained to them the basics of the situation. As he told Xenia, they sat talking until five o'clock in the morning and he said 'that under no circumstances should they undertake anything against the established regime, and that in general, they should keep calm, so that any counter-action from men such as Kuvaka [derogatory nickname of Voeikov, commandant of the Alexander Palace] and Protopopov would confirm the theory that I wrote about; and besides that it could reflect badly on the fate of Dmitri Pavlovich and Felix. They promised me that they would do everything I told them ... Irina is a fine person...' Another major blizzard prevented them from continuing to Rakitnoie, so they sat drinking tea and Sandro made them promise to take care of each other. He also 'got some promises out of Felix and I am sure he will keep them'. The elder Youssoupovs asked if Feodor could come to Rakitnoie for a few days. Sandro said he had no objection if Xenia agreed, but it would have to be for the duration of his regular leave.[81]

Sandro spent 26 December with Irina and Felix and at seven o'clock left for Kiev. Felix, his parents and Irina travelled to Rakitnoie.

From Ai-Todor, Nikita sent a postcard: 'Dear Felix, How sad that Christmas is cloudy, but how brave you are. I'm so glad you're with Titi now. Hurrah, Hurrah!! Rasputin was killed. But by whom?'[82]

Even today that is a very good question.

8

Rakitnoie and Revolution

'The revolution took place because I did not manage to kill Rasputin in time to stop it.'

Felix Youssoupov[1]

Rakitnoie was given to the Youssoupovs in 1729. The estate produced sugar beet, cereals and vegetable oils and boasted machine shops, woollen mills and factories. There was also a church, a hospital and even a zoo. Racehorses were bred at the stud farm and frequently won races in Moscow and St Petersburg. The U-shaped palace, built in 1840, was surrounded by a large garden and a magnificent park. The Youssoupovs usually stayed there for wolf and bear hunting, although Felix had long since given his hunting rifles away.

Isolated in the heart of Russia, its remoteness would provide no opportunity for Felix to make mischief. Captain Zenchikoff had been sent to monitor his movements and act as a guard. Protopopov had the estate under surveillance and Felix was watched by the Okhrana and the local police, who scrutinised his actions and correspondence.

Felix also organised his own guard. Ten Terek Cossacks were instructed not to let anyone come within several miles of his house. Perhaps he was afraid that Rasputin's followers would try to kill him, because along with letters congratulating him there was also hate mail and death threats. Irina was not excluded. Many correspondents felt that by not refuting the allegation that her name had been used as bait, she had betrayed her family.

Felix was forbidden to send letters or telegrams. Despite this, on 2 January he sent a letter to Grand Duchess Xenia at Ai-Todor, telling only Irina for fear of serious consequences.

Writing in the third person, Felix explained that he saw himself not as a murderer, but as a 'weapon of providence, which gave him [Felix] that inexplicable, superhuman strength and peace of mind, which enabled him to carry out his duty to his country and the tsar, by destroying that evil diabolic power'.[2] He added that they were content with their fate and living happily and peacefully. Irina supported her husband unconditionally, telling her mother that they had to accept the situation.

Bébé remained at Ai-Todor. 'My granddaughter lives with me – she is talking in such a lovely way,' Xenia told Tatiana.[3]

Felix had urged Sandro to encourage the dowager empress to speak to the tsar about the dire situation and Alexandra's influence. Sandro promised to do so, although he did not think it would work. He told them to burn all his letters in case of a sudden search for incriminating correspondence. He also advised Felix that it would be unwise to invite guests to Rakitnoie. It could lead to the family being transferred to some other place. Felix and his father ignored this advice. In the middle of January 'a group of sixty aristocrats, including two grand dukes, arrived for several days of hunting. Their visit was an obvious signal of support for Felix.'[4] He was also visited by one of his cousins, possibly Michael Soumarokoff-Elston, whom Felix sent on an errand to Purishkevich. We do not know what this task was.

Letters of support continued to arrive.

Several long letters in English signed 'W. W.' are from Oswald Rayner. W. W. was short for Wow Wow. How Rayner acquired this nickname is unknown but W. W. was used in correspondence by Felix and his Russian friends to disguise Rayner's identity. As previously stated, he used the name 'Billy' when writing to Anna Sinebrychoff, calling her 'dear Granny.'[5] His work for the SIS required this deception.

Rayner disingenuously said that the newspapers had reported a certain recent incident (although he knew full well why Felix had left Petrograd) and he realised that communicating with him might be difficult. He found it hard to believe that six years had passed since they were at Oxford and had enjoyed their time reminiscing. It all sounded very innocent.

At the end of January Rayner wrote again: 'I am about twice as busy on service as when you were here, and I'm extremely glad of it. However, my evenings are still free, after seven o'clock. I see a great deal of your various cousins, we very often talk of you … My love to Punch [Felix's dog] – I hope he has lost his grievance against me over his favourite chair … May everything that is good be with you and attend you, now and always. Yours ever and a day, W. W.'[6]

Felix also wanted news of Dmitri. Letters to Princess Zenaide from General Laiming's wife were not encouraging. Epidemics and diseases were rife in Persia and there were worries about Dmitri's health. On 18 January Dmitri sent Laiming back to Petrograd to oversee his personal affairs. Dmitri was now on his own.

By mid-January Felix had terrible toothache. With local help unavailable, the imperial dentist Sergei Kostritsky was summoned from Tsarskoe Selo. When Kostritsky asked him if he felt guilty about the murder Felix replied, 'Never. I killed a dog.'[7]

Irina profited from Kostritsky's return to send a letter to her mother. She missed her daughter and wanted to go to her family at Ai-Todor but had no idea whether this would be allowed.

In temperatures of -4C ('almost like summer') Irina and Felix went sledding in the dry sunny weather. Sometimes they walked round the estate or went for a sleigh ride through the crisp snowy countryside with Captain Zenchikoff. The captain wanted his wife to join him and demanded a separate room for her. He was informed there was no space at Rakitnoie. When it was too cold to go outside they played endless games of patience. The newspapers usually arrived after tea and, while Felix senior read some of the articles aloud, Irina played patience out of sheer boredom. During dinner they had the same tedious conversations as at lunch. Someone sent them a puzzle but they finished it in three days. The gramophone was more successful and Felix spent his time classifying the records sent from Petrograd. Irina was hoping her father and Andrusha would come. There was no way of knowing how long Felix's exile would last and he was now unable to take his examinations and graduate from the Corps des Pages. The elder Youssoupovs were in despair and could see no way out.

On 21 January Sandro reported the contents of a telegram received from his brother Nicholas Michaelovich, who had received a letter from Senator Stepanov, head of the First Department of the Ministry of Justice. Nicholas Michaelovich telegraphed to warn that someone else was now in charge of the case and that investigators would come to Rakitnoie soon. Sandro told Felix to remain calm and change nothing of his original testimony so that they could not catch him out. This interrogation was just the normal course of events.

By the end of January it had snowed heavily for three days and the post was unable to get through. It also prevented Sandro from arriving. Irina was anxious to speak to her grandmother, who was their last hope, but there had been no trains to Kiev for fifteen days. She was still hoping the case would be dropped.

Felix was anxiously awaiting the arrival of Stavrovsky, Forensic Investigator for Especially Important Cases, and the procurator. He had already received reports from Korneev, the general manager of the Youssoupov Palace, about the police searches.

On 31 January Irina thanked Nicholas Michaelovich (Uncle Bimbo) for his previous letter. 'We are very grateful to you for the letters of Stepanov that we return to you. They are very interesting. It is outrageous that the case has not yet been dismissed. We ... really want to see you. If there are interesting letters, send them to me. We frantically attack all kinds of news.'

And Felix added: 'Dear Uncle Bimbo, Thank you very much for your letters. I read them carefully, for the "Maestro" [Felix], you can be completely calm. He is on the right path and no one will move him from this path. About D [Dmitri] I also have news. He is well surrounded there and is now healthy. If you write to him, I ask you to convey that I feel good, constantly think about him and kiss him a lot, full of energy and hope. Irina and my parents often remember you and terribly regret that you cannot come here to hunt. We are all waiting for suitable weather...'[8]

Felix might not have been so calm had he known that the home of his secretary, Leonid Rambur, had been searched by order of the chief of the Counter-Intelligence Department of the Petrograd Military Headquarters. A letter dated 22 February 1917 confirmed that 'two photographs have been discovered of Gregory Rasputin's dead body, along with a key to deposit box No. 912 at the Azovsko-Donskoy Bank'.[9]

Rambur was released and no further action appears to have been taken.

Anna Rodzianko, wife of the Duma president, warned Felix to hide his journal so that it did not fall into the wrong hands if the Duma fell. The situation in Russia, she said, was critical.

ଔ✳ଓ

Investigator Stavrovsky and the procurator arrived during a terrible snowstorm. Felix refused to answer any questions which had been previously put to him in Petrograd, expressing surprise that they were interrogating now, when he was serving his punishment and after the case had been closed by order of the tsar. After several hours they concluded that the press had blown the matter up and that Felix was not implicated. The evidence was insufficient and no guilty parties had been found.

When the men returned home the next morning Felix gave one of them the reversible coat he had worn to Rasputin's apartment that fateful evening, a gesture which the prince thought 'exceedingly funny'.[10]

Towards the end of February Captain Zenchikoff officially informed Felix that the case would be closed. Rasputin's murderers were never put on trial.

03 ✳ 80

In mid-February Sandro arrived, having been delayed by the storm which Irina feared would prevent him coming at all.

Sandro found both of them well; Irina had put on some weight and they were 'buoyant, but militant'.[11] He told them he would take Felix to serve on his staff in Kiev, so that they could live there. Irina was delighted; she would be able to see her grandmother more often and hoped Felix would be promoted soon.

Felix told George Michaelovich that although Dmitri would not be questioned, Purishkevich *had* been interrogated. Felix had written to him the day before and Purishkevich's answer was published in the newspapers. Felix was now hoping that their luck would hold. He suggested that at the end of February, after the tsar returned to *stavka*, the dowager empress should go to Petrograd and, together with the generals, demand that the empress be sent to Livadia and that Protopopov, Ivan Shcheglovitov (former Minister of Justice) and Vyrubova be arrested. This, he said, 'was their only hope'.[12]

Felix realised that if change did not come from above, it would come from below.

There are hints that by late February he was planning to leave Rakitnoie for Kharkov to meet someone. It would prove difficult, as all his movements were watched. Who Felix was planning to meet and why remains mysterious.

03 ✳ 80

Irina wanted to go with her mother to Petrograd but Felix said it was too dangerous. He was right.

By February 1917 there were protests on the streets and serious unrest was in the air. The decisive day was 27 February, when demonstrations against the government and the war turned to revolution and the elite regiments of the Imperial Guard fraternised with the mob. As the situation spiralled out of control Michael Rodzianko assumed chairmanship of the temporary Executive Committee. In another wing of the Tauride Palace a Soviet of Soldiers' and Workers' Deputies was meeting. Rodzianko's power was waning rapidly.

The Duma and the Soviet reached a compromise and a provisional government was formed, with Prince Lvov as Prime Minister and Alexander Kerensky as

Minister of Justice. The tsar's ministers gave themselves up to the protection of the Duma.

At *stavka* the tsar finally agreed to make concessions and appoint an acceptable ministry – but it was too late. Prevented by revolutionaries from reaching the capital, isolated 100 miles south of Petrograd and unwilling to plunge his country into civil war, Nicholas took the course urged on him by the provisional government and the generals. On 2 March he abdicated in favour of Alexei with his brother Michael as regent. Later that evening Nicholas changed his mind and abdicated for himself *and* Alexei, leaving the throne to Michael.

The following day Michael, informed that the provisional government could not guarantee his safety, refused the crown unless it was offered to him by an elected Constituent Assembly.

Grand Duchess Xenia was already receiving telegrams from Irina at Rakitnoie and the dowager empress in Kiev, the latter 'asking what is going on and where is Nicky?'[13]

After a tearful meeting with Michael, Xenia telegraphed that the Romanov dynasty had fallen.

ᙓ ✱ ᙒ

On 7 March Alexander Kerensky informed Felix that he had been pardoned and they could return to Petrograd. Irina and Felix decided to go to the Moika Palace. Before they left, a service was held in Rakitnoie church, which was full of weeping peasants distraught at the fall of the monarchy.

They travelled via Kharkov, where at the station buffet they were almost suffocated by the crush of the enthusiastic crowd who wanted to see Felix. Then the train of the former commander-in-chief Nicholasha pulled in. Making their way through a cheering mob, they exchanged a few words before their own train departed.

The Youssoupovs reached Petrograd on 12 March and were met at the station by the family chauffeur wearing a red bow on his jacket, which he was promptly ordered to remove. Imperial portraits and emblems had been removed from buildings. It was now treason to buy, or even display, the former tsar's picture.

A constant stream of people visited Felix and Irina at the Moika Palace. Nicholas Michaelovich noted the couple's rapturous spirits. The suffragettes Emmeline Pankhurst and Jessie Kenney were given a guided tour, which included the famous basement dining room. Emmeline related Felix's story of the murder to the American journalist Rheta Childe Dorr, whose first-hand account was one of the earliest to be published.

In his memoirs Felix said Rodzianko offered him the throne, which he refused point blank. Rodzianko's memoirs make no mention of this.

Vladimir Samoilov from *Russkaya Volya* published an interview with Felix on 13 March. Asked who killed Rasputin and why he was killed, Felix refused to answer, maintaining it made no difference now. He said he had not been questioned about Rasputin in Petrograd but that a court investigator came to Rakitnoie. When asked his name, Felix said he could not remember. The reporter insisted that it was pointless not to give out that information but Felix maintained that there was now no reason to talk about it. 'Please note that I never belonged to any political party. I was educated in England and I liked the political system of that country.' He then professed allegiance to the provisional government.[14]

In a second interview in April, he said that during the past year Nicholas II had been 'unrecognisable', and that the influence of Alexandra was fatal because she 'believed in Gregory Rasputin's miracles and for him and his accomplices she sacrificed the nation's approval and national interests'.[15]

Felix gave yet another account to Charles de Chambrun, First Secretary at the French embassy, which did at least include the significant fact that he fired the first shot to Rasputin's left side but gives the impression that they were standing up. 'Chambrun and I feel this account must be accurate,' Louis de Robien reported. 'There are details in it which could not have been invented. Besides, the characteristics of each person are found here ... Prince Youssoupov, superstitious, nervous, a mystic event even at the moment when he kills his victim while contemplating a crucifix. And then the sadism which drives him to go back and gaze at the corpse...'[16]

On 18 March Felix visited Bertie Stopford, telling him that the tsar and his family should be sent away and 'kept under surveillance till the end of the war. Otherwise ... there would always be the fear of her corresponding with Germany,' Stopford noted. 'Felix is working with the army here to promote order and discipline,' he added.[17]

But remaining in Petrograd was unsafe.

ରେ ✸ ଜ

Succumbing to family pressure, Irina left for the Crimea where life was peaceful and the Tartar population remained loyal. She arrived at Koreiz to be reunited with her daughter and found that the servants had introduced an eight-hour day.

Bébé was currently living at Ai-Todor. She had been there with Zillah Henton when a crowd of revolutionaries came up the drive. Henty stood on the balcony with Bébé and Irina's younger brothers while the Swiss tutor Monsieur Niquille congratulated the crowd on the revolution, to loud applause. They then moved off singing revolutionary songs.

Princess Zenaide and Felix senior left Petrograd on a train crowded with noisy, unruly soldiers who had deserted from the front. Before leaving, they granted a temporary 'Power of Attorney for the Management of all Estates and Houses' to retired Lieutenant G. P. Orlik, a former employee. Korneev was required to keep a careful account of all expenses, as the family were responsible for maintaining their properties. Day-to-day issues would be dealt with by Gregory Boujinsky.[18]

Xenia left for Ai-Todor on 25 March, her forty-second birthday, with Andrei and Feodor. In the Crimea they joined her other sons, the dowager empress, Sandro, Grand Duchess Olga and her second husband Nikolai Kulikovsky who were all at Ai-Todor. The tension was palpable. 'Papa has changed very much in the last month, becoming irritable, terribly silent, and only rarely does he smile as before,' Feodor wrote to a friend. 'Mama is serene, but also somewhat dejected ... She eats in her room and stays there all night long.'[19]

Nearby at Djulber were Grand Duke Peter, his wife Militza and their children Marina, Roman and Nadejda, while at Tchair were Nicholasha, his wife Anastasia (Stana) and the children of her first marriage.

Felix went to Moscow to visit Grand Duchess Ella, who listened closely to his account of Rasputin's death and told him he could not have taken any other course.

Easter eve was celebrated in Petrograd at the Youssoupov hospital on Liteinaia Prospekt with Oswald Rayner among the congregation. Afterwards he had supper with Felix, telling Anna Sinebrychoff that he could 'well imagine what a festival Easter must be in Russia under ordinary conditions of life!'[20]

Before leaving Petrograd Felix gave an interview to *Novoye Vremya*, saying that he was pleased that the imperial ministers ('criminals') who had been arrested by the provisional government were imprisoned in the SS Peter & Paul Fortress. 'All these people ... deserve the most severe punishment. They sold Russia.'[21]

He also wrote to Dmitri, who was still in Persia and not in the best of health. Dmitri replied to his 'dearest friend' from Kazvin:

Yes! It has happened [the revolution]. The development of events, the possibility of which you and I had visualised, has come to pass. The final catastrophe has been brought about by the wilful and short-sighted obstinacy of a woman. It has, naturally, swept away Tsarskoe and all of us at one stroke, for now the very name of Romanov is a synonym for every kind of filth and indecency... Ah, how desperately I long at times to have a talk with you! How intensely I long to share my thoughts and opinions with you! We have lived through so much together; it is not often that people meet under such strange conditions. You used to understand me so well; you knew how to support me in moments of trial. For God's sake write to me. What is happening? How are things?

He asked Felix to make tentative inquiries about the advisability of his returning to Russia, thinking it impossible to return without categorical instructions, although he had no idea from whom these would come. He was eventually informed that no decision had been made. 'So I must again restrain my urgent desire to see you and to speak to you,' he told Felix, adding, 'I wish to assure you of my sincerest affection.'[22]

Felix advised him *not* to return.

All court properties, including the palaces and private estates, had been transferred to the state and all the members of the imperial family ceased to receive their income from the appanages (land purchased by Catherine the Great to provide their incomes). This did not affect Irina, who had received a payment of £100,000 at birth (around 14 million pounds today), but Sandro had to dismiss Monsieur Niquille and Mr Stewart because he could no longer afford to pay them.

The palace administrator at Kokoz was in despair over what to do with the estate and wondered if he should sell it. But it was too late. Soon revolutionary sailors arrived and looted the property. Then the villagers moved in, bringing their chickens and cattle, the telephone lines were cut and the administrator was turned out.

Felix decided to see what was happening to the Youssoupov properties in Petrograd. Feodor insisted on accompanying him.

CR ✹ ℬ

The revolution had reached the Crimea, where the Bolsheviks were divided into two groups – the hard-line Yalta Soviet and the more passive and far more powerful Sevastopol Revolutionary Regional Committee. They both claimed jurisdiction over the Romanovs.

On 26 April there were early-morning house searches by rough soviet sailors at Ai-Todor, Djulber and Tchair, which left all the occupants shaken. Letters were gathered up, along with anything else with writing on it, and taken away in the hope of finding compromising documents.

The next evening Irina joined her aunt Olga and Andrei for dinner with the dowager empress, where she heard about the rough treatment experienced by her grandmother. The empress was unwell, depressed and unsettled by the whole episode. Sandro decided to protest to the provisional government.

On 5 May Felix and Feodor returned from Petrograd bringing letters for the dowager empress, some easily transportable jewellery, as well as two Rembrandts cut from their frames in the Moika Palace, *The Man in the Large Hat* and *The Woman with the Fan*. Felix hung them on the walls at Koreiz, concealed behind some paintings done by his cousin Elena Soumarokoff.

Later that month Irina and Felix visited Irina's step-great-aunt Princess Catherine Yourievsky (the youngest daughter of Tsar Alexander II and his morganatic wife Princess Catherine Dolgoruky) and her husband Prince Serge Obolensky at the Mordvinov Palace near Yalta. Bertie Stopford was also present. Felix had already managed to secure some of the family's assets but 'could only save possessions that could be easily transported without attracting unwanted attention'. Perhaps he was hoping Stopford could help.[23]

As they sat in the garden Felix told him the story of Rasputin's murder. Stopford later said that he suspected 'that there had been some relationship between Felix and Rasputin'. This was also the opinion of Noel Coward. 'The only thing I query,' he wrote in 1967, 'is that Youssoupov lured Rasputin to his house to meet his wife Irina, who was in the Crimea. Rasputin would have known this perfectly well. The truth, I think, is that Rasputin had a tiny little lech on Youssoupov himself.' The French embassy staff thought that Felix, 'strange and vicious man that he is, must have profited by these meetings [with Rasputin] to get himself treated a little lower down'.[24] But this supposes Rasputin was that way inclined and there is no evidence that his leanings were anything but heterosexual.

For Irina, dinner with her grandmother became a regular occurrence, sometimes with her brothers and sometimes alone. She had reclaimed Bébé and on 27 May took her to Ai-Todor for breakfast, where the little girl took delight in sitting on Olga Alexandrovna's lap. The young Youssoupovs had decided that Irina should try and see Kerensky and ask him to intervene to ensure better treatment for her grandmother. They would leave for Petrograd immediately.

CR ✹ ℬ

On 28 May Irina and Felix left for the north. Sandro, who was concerned for the family's safety, gave Felix a letter for Kerensky to see if he could gain concessions from a personal interview.

After a stop in Moscow, by mid-June Irina and Felix were at the Moika Palace. Rheta Childe Dorr interviewed Felix at around this time and called him 'something of a popular hero'. She described him as 'barely thirty years old but looks much younger ... tall and slender and almost too handsome. With his fine features, dark melancholy eyes and ivory skin he might even be called effeminate in appearance...'[25] They had lunch with Nicholas Michaelovich, who seemed very agitated about the situation and visited them nearly every day.

Tours of the notorious basement were now a regular feature of Felix's life. The Revd B. S. Lombard went with him to see the room. 'I cannot describe the horror of the atmosphere,' he wrote. 'It felt filthy and unclean. The only other place where I have experienced the same feeling was in the museum at Scotland Yard. I gained his consent to cleanse that room ceremonially which I did very thoroughly with both Holy Water and incense, after which it felt quite different.'[26]

The Youssoupovs continued to host small parties where they welcomed everyone, including people who needed shelter from the Okhrana. Sometimes Felix hired gypsy singers to provide entertainment. Lady Muriel Paget described a party where Irina, 'in red against green – lovely', drew 'extraordinary creatures from her imagination, and a magnificent woman pianist played. Later, at midnight, we all went down to the cellar dining-room and listened to the gypsies' while guests sat on cushions on the floor.[27]

Irina's twenty-second birthday on 3 July was celebrated by another dinner with Grand Duchess Marie Pavlovna and her half-brother Prince Vladimir Paley among the guests. Later the guitarist Sasha Makarov played and other friends joined them, including Bertie Stopford.

In between parties, Felix was busy hiding the family's valuables. Around 1,182 paintings were removed from their frames, rolled and stored above false ceilings or in specially concealed locations, as well as '100 packages of silver, 184 musical instruments, antique sculptures, snuffboxes, coins, weapons, jewels and tapestries'.[28] Heavy iron doors concealed storage rooms whose shelves and cupboards were stacked with gold and silver plate, porcelain and china. A column in the ballroom contained valuable violins, including two by Stradivarius. The family's personal archive was hidden in a secret room behind bookcases in the library. In all, some forty-seven thousand different items were hidden.

The provisional government was becoming increasingly insecure and Irina still had not seen Kerensky. Between 3 and 7 July the Bolshevik party very nearly pulled off a successful coup and shortly afterwards their strongholds were stormed. As their leader Vladimir Lenin fled over the border into Finland, Prince Lvov resigned and on 8 July Alexander Kerensky became Prime Minister and Minister of War in a new provisional government.

Every day (and often at night) there was shooting in the streets, frequently near the Winter Palace where the whole government – the Duma, the soviets, the workers and soldiers – were installed. One morning while Irina and Felix were walking nearby, a battalion of infantry riflemen was disarmed in Palace Square and access to the Winter Palace was completely closed.

Then they heard that Bébé was very ill. Irina told her grandmother that they had been previously unaware of this, otherwise they would have returned. 'My poor granddaughter … has some kind of stomach infection and is weak,' Xenia wrote cautiously to Tatiana on 6 July. 'Her obnoxious parents are still in P [Petrograd] and I do not know when they will return. They've only been 8 times at L [Livadia?].' Obnoxious is a strange way for Xenia to describe her daughter and son-in-law but the tsar and his family were under arrest at Tsarskoe Selo and Xenia was aware their letters were being read. It was also a reference to the murder of Rasputin, which had upset the young grand duchesses considerably. Several times Tatiana and Olga enquired after Bébé's health, with no mention of Irina at all, although they had once been close.[29]

Irina and Felix were visited by Vladimir Paley and had lunch with Vladimir's father Grand Duke Paul. Vladimir had written some pieces for his sisters Irene and Natalie to act. Irina was very fond of them.

Nicholas Michaelovich paid long visits and thundered his outrage at the house search of Ai-Todor. Irina also visited her great-aunt Queen Olga of Greece, who was living at the beautiful palace of Pavlovsk outside Petrograd.

She was still determined to see Kerensky, who since the failed Bolshevik coup had been living in some style in the Winter Palace with guards and a red flag flying when he was in residence, but he had disappeared. Irina and Felix waited for two hours at the palace but he did not arrive.

Finally, Irina's persistence paid off and Kerensky received her in Alexander II's study. Looking rather embarrassed, he invited her to sit down. Irina immediately sat in the tsar's armchair, leaving the visitor's chair to Kerensky. She described the search at Ai-Todor and the rough treatment of her grandmother. Kerensky protested this was not his responsibility but, as she continued speaking, he promised to look into the matter. Irina promptly rose, gathered her imperial dignity and left the room. It would be many years before another Romanov set foot inside the Winter Palace.

'I think it was brave of her,' Stopford wrote to a friend, 'there is so little of her! But she told me that, once in the room, she was no longer frightened, and although at first Kerensky declared he could do nothing, he ended by acceding to all she asked. She is a plucky little thing and clever. Kerensky did not kiss her hand nor open the door for her, because she got to it before he did. He did not keep her waiting. The result of all this will be – at least we hope so – that the Empress Marie will come to Finland and eventually get to Denmark.' While Stopford was lunching at the Moika Palace a telegram arrived saying that Irina's grandmother 'was no longer under arrest' but was 'not allowed to leave the house'. Felix had been taking considerable risks by going to Petrograd so often and Stopford advised them to leave as soon as possible.[30]

They left for Moscow on 1 August. From Arkhangelskoe Felix took away some toys and a folding stool for his daughter. Then they returned to the Crimea.

Irina never visited Petrograd or Moscow again.

ᲗᲒ ✳ ᲒᲗ

On 7 August Irina arrived at Ai-Todor very agitated. The shocking news she brought from Petrograd nearly gave her grandmother a heart attack. On 31 July the tsar and his family had been moved to Tobolsk in Siberia, even though they were all under the impression that they would be sent to Livadia.

A permanent guard had been established at Ai-Todor since the beginning of June. There were now restrictions, including a list of people who were allowed entry. These included Irina and Felix, her brothers' tutors, the doctor and various tradesmen.

There were renewed tensions in the house. Irina's friend Olga Vassiliev had moved into Ai-Todor. She and Sandro had become close in Kiev. The dowager empress recorded in her diary: 'The three eldest [grandsons] dined with me, told me how they had been scolded by Sandro because they are so unfriendly towards O. K. [Olga Konstantinovna Vassiliev] They cannot stand the fact that she had put herself between their father and them. I well understand that this annoys them, but all the same there is no need for them to be so unfriendly towards her, especially as they originally liked her.'[31]

On 12 August Irina's thirty-five-year-old aunt Olga gave birth to a son, whom she called Tihon. The dowager empress called this 'the only good news'.[32]

Then another blow fell. On 29 August they were placed under house arrest, cut off from the outside world. Nobody was permitted to enter or leave Ai-Todor. Irina, married to a 'commoner', was not considered a Romanov by the guards and was allowed to go free. She was now isolated from her parents, brothers and grandmother, who was ill. Only the doctors were allowed inside.

Her aunt Olga and Nikolai Kulikovsky, also considered 'commoners', went to live in the flat over Sandro's wine cellar, taking with them the jewels belonging to the dowager empress and Xenia. Olga hid them in cocoa tins and at the first sign of trouble concealed them in a hole in the bottom of a rock down by the sea.

On 3 September Kerensky declared Russia a republic.

Contrary to the impression normally given, letters and diaries show that the family were occasionally able to meet. On 8 September Irina and Felix were permitted to visit the dowager empress, who was gravely ill with influenza and bronchitis, and on two occasions when Irina was ill her mother was allowed to go to Koreiz.

On 17 September Commissar Vershinin arrived at Ai-Todor, sent by Kerensky.

Perhaps unwisely, Felix returned to Petrograd in early October. He delivered another letter to Sir George Buchanan for the dowager empress and took her favourite portrait of Alexander III from the Anitchkov Palace, but it was impossible to obtain the box containing her important jewellery as it had been sent to Moscow.

Felix and Gregory Boujinsky then travelled to Moscow, taking with them some of the family diamonds. These and many of Princess Zenaide's other jewels were hidden in seven leather trunks behind a false wall under the staircase of the Moscow house.

Before leaving, Felix visited Grand Duchess Ella. He found her very alarmed about the tsar, tsarina and their family. After joining her for a short prayer, he left for Petrograd. They were never to meet again.

But things were about to become a lot more serious.

9

Last Days in Paradise

'I am not sure that it was not Youssoupov ... who without himself
realising it, struck the first blow.'
Oswald Rayner to Ellen Thomas-Stanford
about the revolution[1]

On 25 October 1917 the Bolsheviks seized power. Stealthily, and with few
casualties, Lenin became master of Petrograd.

Felix took refuge at the Moika Palace where Oswald Rayner had moved into
the bachelor apartment. 'I am very comfortable in my new quarters,' Rayner
told Anna Sinebrychoff.[2] Felix was glad of his company.

Anarchy reigned in the capital and there were rumours that the provisional
government had been arrested. Soon banks were nationalised, private bank
accounts frozen and army ranks abolished, along with private ownership of
land and the rights of inheritance. The only titles were 'citizen' and 'comrade'.
In the Red Terror that followed, a man's class would seal his fate more than his
political sympathies. Vladimir Paley, other friends and even strangers arrived at
the Moika Palace, some hoping for shelter thinking it would be safer there. The
foreign ambassadors wanted to depart but were unable to obtain permission
from the Bolsheviks. The Winter Palace had suffered great devastation but the
other palaces were intact.

A detachment of soldiers came to occupy the Moika Palace. Felix impressed
upon them that the building was more suited to a museum than a barracks.
Although they left, he had the feeling they would return.

The Youssoupovs' financial situation was serious. At the beginning of the
war Princess Zenaide had heeded the tsar's request to repatriate all funds held
abroad, so 95 per cent of their wealth was now in Russia. All their funds had
been seized and Felix was busy trying to conceal more of the family's valuables.
He hoped to send some of the things out of Russia. Works of art were put into
crates ready for transportation but there was shooting in the streets and they
never knew what might happen next. Part of the Moika Palace would be placed
under the protection of neutral Sweden. If the embassy moved, the consul would
take care of things.[3]

One morning he stumbled over some soldiers sleeping, fully armed, on one of the marble floors. A German officer informed him that they had been ordered to guard the house.

Felix decided to leave everything in the Moika Palace, either safely in crates or hidden, and also to give the Moscow house over to the protection of Sweden.

Irina was afraid for his safety, reminding him that passenger trains would be cancelled after 10 November. She had no idea how he would return. 'Rumours are reaching us that in Petrograd the devil knows what is happening and I'm terribly worried about you!' Felix was now urgently trying to arrange his departure. 'If you can't leave, I'll try to come somehow,' Irina told him. 'Understood?'[4]

Felix thought that the guards inside the house signified that the Bolsheviks considered him a sympathiser. He decided to leave at once for the Crimea.

An officer commanding the district, whom Felix knew, arrived with a stranger in civilian clothes who gave him some false identity papers and said he should accompany them to Kiev. Felix later discovered that they were Freemasons, acting on instructions from their order. It is worth recalling that Oswald Rayner had been a Freemason since 1908.

As Felix got into their car he noticed a large red cross painted on the front of the Moika Palace. At the station he was ushered into a private compartment of a packed train. The door was then locked.

When they reached Kiev all the hotels were full and, disinclined to stay with the officer, Felix was glad when Princess Gagarine offered him a room. The next day he braved shooting in the streets to go to the post office to telegraph his family. A few days later, he noticed in a newspaper that the police were looking for a well-known criminal and that his identity papers were made out in this man's name. He contacted the officer, who gave him a new set of papers.

Felix realised that he must return to Petrograd to pick up the valuables he had left behind on his hurried departure. The officer did not seem keen on this but promised to pick him up in a couple of days.

He managed to contact Irina. 'Felix communicated to her that he had to escape from Kiev – for what reason she does not know,' the dowager empress recorded. 'Later he sent a telegraph that he was going off again to Petersburg [*sic*]...'[5]

In Petrograd, Felix saw a newspaper report that he was under arrest in the SS Peter & Paul Fortress. He had supposedly corresponded with the Cossack Ataman Alexei Kaledin, who had assumed power in the Don region after the October revolution and was 'preparing troops to march on Petrograd and overthrow the Bolsheviks'. This report reached Grand Duke Dmitri in Teheran, who remarked that Felix 'is too sly and slippery to allow himself to be caught so easily'.[6]

Dmitri was right. It was Vladimir Purishkevich who was arrested. He had gone underground after being released from prison and was corresponding with Kaledin.[7] These erroneous reports were followed by a rumour that Felix had been killed. This news reached Tobolsk but was soon contradicted. 'Someone told us that Felix was killed in Kiev, and the next day they told us that it was not him but someone else,' Tatiana wrote to Xenia.[8]

When Felix reached the Moika Palace he found the household in tears because they thought he was in the fortress. He found the reaction of friends touching. 'W. W. [Rayner] and the embassy are thrilled,' he told Irina. Apart from trusted friends, he followed advice to see nobody and did not answer the telephone. 'I saw Sergei Sukhotin and asked everyone to say that Tipty [Felix] is in Kiev.' He intended to hide Andrusha's paintings in the Moika Palace.[9]

Felix's schoolfriend the painter and sculptor Gleb Deryuzhinsky had spent time with him at the Moika. Felix now persuaded Gleb to return with him to Koreiz, promising him lucrative orders for work. He planned to leave on 9 November and asked Irina to remind the chauffeur not to tell anyone at Bakhchisaray station that he was meeting Prince Youssoupov.

Felix left the Moika Palace in the care of Rayner and three attachés from the Swedish Legation. 'My Oxford Friend left three weeks ago for the Crimea, where he will re-join his family and probably remain with them for many months to come,' Rayner wrote. 'In fact I doubt whether I shall see him again before my return to England.'[10]

By 13 November Felix had still not arrived at Koreiz, although he was expected the previous evening. Irina was concerned. Writing from the Moika Palace, Rayner told Uno and Olly Donner that 'we have had no news of him' and 'his people were getting anxious for his safety'.[11]

☙ ✶ ❧

At last Felix reached Bakhchisaray station and was met by a huge chauffeur-driven Delaunay-Belleville complete with the family coat of arms, pennant and crown. The restrictions had been lifted from Ai-Todor and he arrived in time to celebrate the dowager empress's birthday on 14 November. The mood was spoilt by his account of the dire situation in Petrograd and Moscow.

Soon afterwards, the Romanovs were again placed under house arrest at Ai-Todor. Only Dr Malama and Irina were allowed inside.

Commissar Vershinin was afraid to make any decisions without reference to the Sevastopol Soviet. Towards the end of November he was replaced by Commissar Philip Zadorozhny, a former member of the Black Sea Fleet who had served at Sandro's aviation school in 1916.

Sailors from the Yalta Soviet then arrived at Koreiz, confiscated the car and put everyone under arrest, including Gleb Deryuzhinsky who had set up a workshop. They were saved by Zadorozhny, who appeared with his detachment, freed everyone and ordered that they should not be disturbed.

On the final day of 1917 Irina and Felix had a visit from Grand Duchess Xenia. 'The Bolsheviks are coming this way,' the grand duchess recorded.[12]

Olga Alexandrovna had been promised Bébé's spare pram but amid all the anxiety the Youssoupovs had forgotten it and she was ashamed to remind them.[13]

☙ ✶ ❧

In February 1918 the Bolsheviks changed the Russian calendar to bring it in line with the rest of Europe. 1 February now became 14 February, although many Russians continued to use the Old Style dating, or both dates.

That month the Crimean Tartar National Party attempted to take power from the Yalta and Sevastopol Soviets. They were repulsed by the Black Sea Fleet who then mutinied, set up their own Sailors' Soviet and turned on their superiors. The so-called Naval Cavalry roamed the countryside looting and murdering.

Brandishing flags with slogans like 'death to the bourgeois', they were heavily armed and rode stolen horses, putting terror even into the hearts of the Soviets.

Bands of sailors broke into houses, looting, murdering, raping women and torturing men to discover where their valuables were hidden. They then roamed the countryside, festooned with stolen pearls and diamonds on their necks, wrists and fingers. When the Youssoupovs went to bed at night, they never knew whether they would be alive the next morning.

Miss Henton recounted how she heard shooting as she sat in the palace grounds. Three of the outside staff were shot in cold blood. One man tried to escape by crawling under the floor of the granary but they killed him. She 'spoke of all-night vigils, sitting beside little Irina's cot, a packed suitcase at her feet'. One night Felix 'tapped her on the shoulder and picked up Irina while she grabbed the suitcase; the pair had walked what felt like miles to a waiting car, then driven to safety'.[14]

One day a band of sailors arrived to arrest Felix senior. Zenaide recorded how Irina came running in, imploring her father-in-law to go to bed. Meanwhile, Felix invited their leader into the dining-room and told him his father was sick so they could not see him. He asked to see their warrant, which of course they did not have, so he told them to go and fetch one. Two of them left. After several hours they had not returned, so the others gave up and departed.

Another time Irina returned to find a band of sailors in the kitchen taking refreshments, while Felix was in his room with two more, both wearing blood-stained uniforms. One wore a diamond bracelet, the other a brooch. As Felix sent for some wine, one of them asked if he was the man who murdered Rasputin. They drank his health and settled down to a pleasant chat, which finished with Felix playing his guitar and singing. As bottle after bottle was emptied the men joined in the choruses, which became ever more rousing. Finally they rode off saying that the Youssoupovs had nothing to fear from them.

ೞ ✱ ೞ

On 3 March 1918 Russia signed a separate peace with Germany at Brest-Litovsk. The terms were harsh and a quarter of Russia's territory, including the Crimea, now came under German rule. A local government was formed in Simferopol but, in reality, power was in the hands of the local soviets. This brought more danger for the Romanovs and their relatives.

Zadorozhny decided to take action to protect them. On 10 March the occupants of Ai-Todor were moved. Their destination was Djulber, the nearby home of Grand Duke Peter Nicolaievich, Grand Duchess Militza and their younger children Marina and Roman. With its white towers and Moorish-style minarets it resembled something from the Arabian Nights but it had the advantage of high, stout walls making it easier to defend. Once again Irina and her aunt Olga were allowed to go free. Before her parents left, Irina was permitted to take Bébé to see them.

Conditions inside Djulber were cramped. As well as the contingent from Ai-Todor, Peter's brother Nicholasha and his wife Stana (Militza's sister) were among the forty-five people confined there. 'I can imagine how hard it was to leave Ai-Todor,' Olga Nicolaievna wrote to Xenia sympathetically from Tobolsk. 'And you can't even see T. O and I. [Tihon, Olga and Irina]. So disgusting, but nothing can be done about it.'[15]

Determined to stay in touch, Irina smuggled letters into Djulber with Bébé, who toddled in and out with them hidden inside her coat by the resourceful Miss Henton.

Koreiz was one of the neighbouring estates, so Irina and Felix began walking their dogs beside Djulber's walls. As the princess called to the dogs, one of her brothers would pop up on top of the wall. This trick was soon discovered and walks in Djulber's park were forbidden. Irina received a letter from her mother saying that they were prisoners in a fortress under siege. They could only go out as far as the front of the house, where they spent their time sitting with the children, not even allowed to walk in the garden. Food was eaten from a common dish and they were all suffering from boredom. Xenia begged Irina to send Bébé again as soon as possible. Luckily, Irina and Felix were permitted a two-hour visit on the grand duchess's birthday.

The only cheerful news was the birth of a daughter (yet another Irina) to Grand Duke Peter's daughter Nadejda and her husband Prince Nikolai Orlov, who were living at Stana's nearby estate of Tchair.

As the Germans began to march towards the Crimea, word reached Djulber that the Yalta Soviet planned to execute the Romanovs before the Germans arrived. While out walking, Felix met Zadorozhny and asked him for news. Seeing the commissar's embarrassment he invited him to Koreiz. Zadorozhny came secretly, climbing in over a ground-floor balcony. In a conversation lasting several hours it became obvious that he was anxious to preserve the lives of Djulber's residents but he feared the Yalta Soviet would attempt to seize them by force.

A few days later Zadorozhny said he had received reliable information that men from Yalta were coming the next day to take the prisoners away and shoot them. He decided to be away, knowing his men would not admit anyone during his absence. To Irina's relief, he had also handed out arms to the Romanov men in case of need.

As he predicted, the men from Yalta arrived the next day and were turned away. Meanwhile, Zadorozhny went to Sevastopol to fetch reinforcements. It could only be a matter of time before the Yalta men returned.

Irina and Felix spent that night on the roof at Koreiz anxiously watching the road to see who would arrive first – the execution squad from Yalta, or the reinforcements from Sevastopol. At dawn, as the Sevastopol contingent drove past, they went to bed relieved. Later they heard that the Yalta men had crashed on a bend in the road during the night.

The next morning Irina awoke to news that an advance party of German soldiers, sent personally by the kaiser, had arrived in the Crimea. The Romanovs still regarded them as enemies and refused to receive the German officer who had saved them from the firing squad. Tartars now took up guard duty at Djulber, as Empress Marie refused to have Germans.

That afternoon Irina arrived at Djulber with Felix, Olga Alexandrovna and Stana's children Sergei of Leuchtenberg and Elena, and the latter's husband Stefan Tyszkewicz. Militza's cook went shopping and that night they all had a magnificent dinner. Shortly afterwards, the dowager empress commissioned a plaster bust of Zadorozhny from Gleb Deryuzhinsky.[16]

CR ✶ ဆာ

After Easter Xenia and Sandro left for Ai-Todor and Empress Marie moved to Harax, the nearby English-style home of Sandro's brother Grand Duke George Michaelovich. Olga and her family lived in one of the smaller houses on the Harax estate.

During the next few weeks Irina visited her parents and grandmother regularly, as they settled down to a more normal existence of tennis parties, fishing and gardening.

Felix and Irina were joined at Koreiz by Gleb's wife the poet and socialite Pallada Bognanova-Belskaya and Felix's cousins Michael and Elena Soumarokoff-Elston. Felix supported Gleb and Pallada financially and moved them into Sosnovaya Roscha, which was now almost finished. He was attracted by Pallada's artistic nature and visited her almost every day. The artist and stage designer Sergei Sudekin and his wife Vera Schilling also arrived. Sudekin intended to paint the inside of Sosnovaya Roscha but the plan was never realised.

Irina and Felix attended gatherings at the Sudekins' home, were constant visitors to the concerts, performances and exhibitions held around Yalta, and visited Roman and Marina at Djulber. 'Sometimes Felix brought his guitar and sang Russian songs and romances with an English accent,' Roman recalled.[17] They had picnics at Sosnovaya Roshcha. Although everyone brought their own food because of the shortages, wine was plentiful as all the Crimean estates had their own vineyards.

Irina, Felix and some of the younger people published a weekly newspaper *The Merry Arnolf*, which was edited by Olga Vassiliev. Irina copied out poems and also wrote some.

Contributors met every Sunday evening at Koreiz where the articles, which ranged from accounts of imaginary foreign journeys to adventure stories, were read aloud. The older generation were uneasy, knowing that in these uncertain times even the most innocent-sounding pastimes could prove dangerous.

Their joy was only disturbed by rumours from the north, where Moscow and Petrograd were under the reign of the Cheka and there were wholesale massacres of the aristocracy.

It may have been around this time that Felix, realising how dangerous the situation was becoming, made an attempt to retrieve the jewels hidden in the Moscow house. He turned to Robert Bruce Lockhart, who had been appointed British agent in Moscow in January. Lockhart asked Galina von Meck, who 'knew the house to be a labyrinth of passages', to go and see if she could help recover the hidden treasure. Although she thought it unlikely that a 'mere superficial examination' would yield results, she agreed. 'The house was empty at the time,' she recalled. 'I told the caretaker that I had come from the government offices to see if the building was worth taking over. He showed me round and I noticed that, in one of the passages, the wall seemed to have been replastered and repainted fairly recently. Shortly after, the building was taken over by a government office and, as far as I was concerned, that was the end of the affair...'[18]

The Bolsheviks had also turned their attention to the Romanovs.

First came news that Irina's uncle Grand Duke Michael Alexandrovich had disappeared from Perm, where he and his secretary Johnson had been living in internal exile in comparative freedom since March. Shortly before dusk on

12 June they were taken away by a group of men. Nothing had been heard from them since. Another of Irina's uncles, Grand Duke Sergei Michaelovich, was imprisoned at Alapayevsk in the Urals along with Grand Duchess Ella, Prince Vladimir Paley and Princes Constantine, Igor and Ivan Constantinovich, who were Irina's distant cousins. There were rumours that they had all vanished, believed killed. Grand Duke Paul Alexandrovich was in a Petrograd prison with Grand Duke Dmitri Constantinovich and Grand Dukes Nicholas and George Michaelovich. But the most disturbing rumours concerned the tsar's family.

Nicholas, Alexandra and Marie had been moved from Tobolsk to the Ipatiev House in Ekaterinburg in April; the other children joined them when Alexei had recovered from his latest haemophiliac crisis.

In July they disappeared. The Bolsheviks announced that Nicholas had been shot and the empress and her children had been sent 'to a safe place'. When the White Army arrived, the Ipatiev House was empty. There was only the sinister ground-floor room, with blood on the floor and bullet holes in the walls. Nobody knew whether they were alive or dead. For Irina, news that her childhood playmates may have been killed was traumatic.

ᏬᎡ ✴ ᏅᎥ

On 10 November a rumour reached Koreiz that the kaiser had abdicated and Germany's collapse was imminent. The armistice was signed on 11 November and defeated Germany now had to evacuate the Crimea.

In the middle of all this there was a family wedding. On 25 November Irina's brother Andrei married Elisabeta Ruffo di Sant' Antimo (Elsa), a young widow with two children, Alexander (Sandrick) and Elizabeth (Betty) Friderici. The wedding was hastily arranged because Elsa was around five months pregnant with Andrei's child.[19]

The Russian officers who had made their way to the peninsula to protect the imperial family rushed to join General Denikin's White Volunteer Army. Felix, Andrei, Feodor, Nikita and Michael Soumarokoff-Elston decided to do the same. Denikin replied that because of their connection with the imperial family they were not welcome.

Gleb Deryuzhinsky wrote anxiously to Felix from Yalta because the dowager empress had indicated that she wanted to have his bust of Zadorozhny. 'My request is, perhaps, if it would be possible for you to ask Her Majesty for permission to bring her the bust...' He wanted to go abroad and offered to take a letter to Queen Alexandra.[20] As the Bolsheviks closed in, Gleb, whose marriage had broken down, left for the Caucasus.

It was feared that as the Germans left, the Bolsheviks would arrive in the Crimea before the Allies. Dramatic pleas arrived from relatives in England, Denmark and Romania begging the dowager empress and Xenia to leave while there was still time.

On 24 December, to Irina's dismay, Sandro announced that he was leaving on a British cruiser to see the heads of the Allied governments in Paris and impress upon them the seriousness of the situation. He left on 26 December for Taranto in Italy on board HMS *Forsythe*. Andrei and Elsa went with him. Irina received a letter when the ship reached Constantinople. 'Incredible that yesterday I was at Ai-Todor in prison and today I am free,' Sandro wrote.[21] It was impossible to describe his feelings but, at the same time, he was worried about Irina. He intended to go via Rome to Paris and then London.

Grand Duchess Olga (who was again pregnant) also departed. On 1/14 January 1919 Olga, Nikolai Kulikovsky and their small son Tihon left for the Caucasus, where the Red Army had been pushed back.

'The newspapers write about the imminent liberation of Petrograd by the Estonian and Finnish troops. God grant!' Princess Zenaide wrote in her diary on 17 January.[22] That same day Sandro telegraphed from Taranto, stressing that they *must* all leave Russia.

ʘ✳⠊

Early in February a British cruiser arrived in Yalta. Miss Henton set off to the dock and returned with bread, coffee, jam, matches and postcards, in raptures at her reception. The crew wanted to see Felix but he refused to go.

Irina received another letter from her father reporting the progress of his discussions with the Allies. He heard rumours that Felix had been assassinated and begged her to leave for France because the Bolsheviks were not far away. He added that he now had no more hope that the tsar and his family were alive.

Then news arrived that Irina's great-uncle Paul Alexandrovich, her uncles Nicholas and George Michaelovich, as well as Dmitri Constantinovich, had been shot by a Bolshevik firing squad in the SS Peter & Paul Fortress at the end of January. Prince Gabriel Constantinovich, who had been imprisoned with them for a while, had been released and reached Finland with his wife Antonia. There was no news of the tsar, nor of his brother Michael, who had completely disappeared.

Among all this bad news Irina and Felix had a muted celebration of their wedding anniversary at Harax. The dowager empress noticed that Felix was wearing a skull cap to hide his hair loss.

Irina became an aunt on 23 March, when Elsa gave birth to Princess Xenia Andreievna in Paris. The good news reached the Crimea by telegraph from a member of Sandro's staff.

ʘ✳⠊

By mid-March the French had pulled out of Odessa after their sailors mutinied, the Bolsheviks were closing in and only the poorly trained volunteers of the White Army stood between the imperial family and disaster.

The family were at Harax celebrating Xenia's birthday on 25 March/7 April when Captain Charles Johnson of the battleship HMS *Marlborough* arrived. He stressed the seriousness of the situation and produced orders to evacuate the dowager empress and her family that very evening. They must be ready to go within hours.

Marie Feodorovna at first refused to leave. She finally consented on condition that the British evacuate everyone else who wanted to go. This gave Captain Johnson quite a headache, as HMS *Marlborough* had to be hastily rearranged to accommodate many more people than originally planned. Meanwhile, the dowager empress asked Felix to take a letter to Djulber, asking Grand Dukes Nicholas and Peter to leave with her.

As preparations commenced on board, Irina and her relatives hastily packed their most precious items. Irina grabbed the travel set given by the tsar when she was born. Felix took the two Rembrandts, as much jewellery as he could and many family letters. Princess Zenaide concealed several items of jewellery in her luggage, while Felix senior took with him 7,000 roubles.

Travelling with them would be the invaluable Miss Henton and her maid, Irina's maids Lala and Leviton, Felix's servant Thespé and two other menservants named Harpin and Pierreoff.[23] Irina's young brothers brought small bags of earth from Ai-Todor and Vassili took his canary.

It was a bittersweet moment. All knew that they were leaving their homeland for the foreseeable future. Nobody could be sure of their final destination and there were many decisions to make before the family gathered at Koreiz cove for embarkation.

Before leaving Russia, Felix senior took steps to secure the future of Zina Gregoriev, who was installed in the nearby village of Alupka with their son. On 7 April he wrote a letter on Koreiz-headed notepaper leaving his property of Kermentchik in the Crimean Tauride province to his illegitimate son, to whom he now gave the surname of Elston: 'The income of the estate until his adulthood will be given to his mother.'[24] Felix senior had been unable to arrange for the evacuation of Zina, who was pregnant again. Her daughter Tatiana was born at Alupka on 7 July 1919.

As the Youssoupovs made their way down to the cove they took a last look at the back of Koreiz, towering over them out of the cliff. 'God, how hard it was to leave Koreiz,' Felix senior wrote in his diary.[25] He looked even more imposing than usual in his Cossack uniform, while the normally flamboyant Felix junior was conventionally dressed in a lightweight coat and plain trilby hat. Irina wore a belted coat, cloche hat and a single string of pearls.

Those making their way to the ship included the intimidating Grand Duke Nicholas and his milder-looking brother Peter, with their wives and Peter's children. They arrived early and bagged all the best cabins on the *Marlborough*.

Lieutenant-Commander Pridham welcomed them on board. Conditions were extremely cramped. While Irina's younger brothers were allotted hammocks in the schoolroom, Bébé and the four other children under six were each given a mattress.

As the ship sailed for Yalta that evening the Youssoupovs stood on deck watching Koreiz disappear from view. Their last sight was the statue of Minerva on the jetty and the Tartar landscape all around.

ᖇ✭ᖃ

On 8 April they awoke in Yalta, where more refugees and luggage were embarked. As the ship's guns covered the port, the evacuation continued for another three days. When the rumour spread that the dowager empress was leaving, panic set in as people abandoned all their possessions and hurried to the waterfront in a desperate attempt to board the Allied ships. Irina, who to Pridham had seemed 'much too frail to have such a healthy child',[26] now spoke to her grandmother about the desperate plight of these refugees, who if left behind would be shown no mercy by the Bolsheviks. The result was a further nightmare for Pridham, as the empress insisted that the *Marlborough* must not leave until the last Allied ship had sailed from Yalta.

Extra bedding now had to be fetched from the imperial estates. By the time the evacuation was complete, there were nineteen members of the imperial family, with their maids, menservants, governesses and officials of their households, in addition to 1,170 evacuees and crew, 200 tons of luggage, and jewels and other treasure with an estimated worth of £20 million.

When it became obvious that the ship would be in Yalta for some while, Felix and two companions asked permission to go ashore and spend some hours in the port. Stories that Felix wanted to see Oswald Rayner, who was on the quayside to say goodbye, are untrue. Rayner was at the British Military Mission in Vladivostok.[27]

As an endless succession of stranded people begged to be taken away, a group of officers from the White Army approached Felix. They wanted Nicholasha to accompany them to Novorossisk 'on a ship with a Russian flag' and take command. Felix, who was a little afraid of Nicholasha, gave the message to his mother to pass on. The grand duke dismissed the proposal as unrealistic.[28]

As other British ships arrived, Irina stood by the railings with Feodor, Nikita and Roman. Beside them was Thespé, holding Bébé. To Pridham, Irina had appeared 'shy and retiring at first, but it was only necessary to take a little notice of her pretty small daughter to break through her reserve and discover that she also was very charming and spoke fluent English'.[29] Felix, he said, spoke English well.

Roman recalled Felix standing beside him at the ship's railings and holding up a long tube, saying, 'You'll never guess what this is.' Inside were the two Rembrandts he had cut from their frames at the Moika Palace.[30]

⋆

The morning of 11 April 1919 dawned cold and dull as at 8.30 a.m. HMS *Marlborough* set sail towards Constantinople. Irina and Felix were up early to witness the raising of the flags and the playing of both national anthems.

As the ship slipped quietly, almost imperceptibly, into the open sea nearly all the imperial family were on deck. Irina stood with Roman and her brothers by the gunwale on the ship's starboard. They could just see Livadia and the park stretching down to the sea. Some contemporaries recalled the dowager empress hiding behind binoculars, which she asked Irina to hold up for her.

Grand Duchess Xenia took a last look at the coastline through the captain's binoculars. 'What are those little black things left along the shore?' she enquired. 'Madame,' he replied, 'that is your silver.' The servants had been so afraid that they would be left behind that they had not loaded the fifty-four chests. Although Xenia said it did not matter, in the years to come all of her family would regret that loss.[31]

They sailed along the Crimean coast past the familiar landmarks – Livadia, Kishkine, Djulber – Irina had known since childhood. Her last sight was the Ai-Todor lighthouse, a final glimpse of home as they sailed into exile.

Yet few of them believed that they would remain in exile for ever. Felix summed up the family's feelings in 1952. 'Who could have dreamed that thirty-three years later it would still be impossible to foresee the end?'[32]

1. Irina's birthplace, The Farm in the Alexandria Park at Peterhof. (Photo: Katrina Warne)

2. A family group in 1895. Front: Irina's grandmother the Dowager Empress Marie Feodorovna holding Grand Duchess Olga Nicolaievna; Irina's aunts Grand Duchess Olga Alexandrovna & Empress Alexandra Feodorovna. Back: Grand Duchess Xenia holding Princess Irina; Irina's uncle Tsar Nicholas II. (*Det kongelige bibliotek*, Dept. of Maps, Prints & Photographs, Copenhagen)

Left 3. Irina (right) and Andrei riding in the Crimean Mountains, 1898. (Private collection)

Below: 4. Irina with some of her British and Danish relatives at Bernstorff Slot, Denmark, 1899. Back: Princes Waldemar, Carl & Christian (later Christian X) of Denmark; King George I of Greece; Prince Hans of Glücksburg; Tsar Nicholas II. Middle: Princess Victoria (Toria) of Wales; Princess (later Queen) Alexandrine of Denmark holding her son Frederik; King Christian IX of Denmark; Alexandra, the Princess of Wales (later Queen Alexandra); the Dowager Empress Marie Feodorovna; Princess Marie of Denmark; Empress Alexandra Feodorovna. Front: Princes Axel & Viggo of Denmark; Prince Andrei and Princess Irina of Russia; Princess Margrethe of Denmark; Grand Duchesses Olga & Tatiana of Russia; Princes Erik & Aage of Denmark. (Private collection)

5. Irina, her brothers and the tsar's daughters, 1906. Back: Princes Nikita, Dmitri & Rostislav Alexandrovich, Grand Duchess Olga Nicolaievna, Princess Irina Alexandrovna, Princes Andrei and Feodor Alexandrovich. Front: Grand Duchesses Tatiana, Anastasia & Marie Nicolaievna. (Eurohistory photo archive)

6. Irina with Andrei, Feodor, Nikita & Dmitri, early 1900s. In the custom of the time the younger boys are wearing dresses. (Private collection)

7. Irina (centre) with her cousins Grand Duchesses Tatiana and Olga, Peterhof 1909. The girls were close during their childhood. (Beinecke Rare Book & Manuscript Library, Yale University)

8. The family of Grand Duke Alexander & Grand Duchess Xenia, 1912. Left to right: Rostislav; Grand Duke Alexander; Grand Duchess Xenia with Vassili; Irina with Nikita in front; Feodor, Dmitri & Andrei. The tensions in the marriage were already becoming apparent. (Private collection)

Above left: 9. Nikolai Rodionov on the *Standart*, 1912. Irina blushed when teased about him. (The Beinecke Rare Book and Manuscript Library, Yale University)

Above right: 10. Felix in the 1890s. He was not yet heir to his mother's vast fortune. (Private collection)

11. The massive Youssoupov Palace at 94, Quai de la Moika, described by one visitor as 'about the size of Buckingham Palace.' (Eurohistory photo archive)

12. Arkhangelskoe near Moscow, Felix's favourite home. The family were rumoured to be wealthier than the tsar. (Photo: Katrina Warne)

13. The Youssoupovs at Arkhangelskoe in the early 1900s. They led a life of luxury and privilege. From left: Felix, Nicholas, Felix senior and Zenaide. (Private collection)

14. The ornate large salon in the Youssoupovs' Moscow house, once the hunting lodge of Ivan the Terrible. Pictured on the left is Tsar Peter I, on the right Tsar Peter the Great. (Photo: Katrina Warne)

Above left: 15. Felix during his early years at Oxford. The handwritten dedication reads: 'Remember me kindly. F. Soumarokoff-Elston, 1909.' His moustache is just visible. (Courtesy of Mrs Cordelia Uys)

Above right: 16. The beguiling Grand Duchess Elena Vladimirovna, wife of Prince Nicholas of Greece. Princess Zenaide was worried about Felix's obvious feelings for her. (Mark Andersen)

Above: 17. The wedding of Irina's cousin Countess Nada de Torby, 1916. Left to right: The bridegroom Prince George of Battenberg; his sister Princess Louise of Battenberg (one-time rumoured fiancée of Felix); Countess Nadejda (Nada) de Torby; her sister Countess Anastasia (Zia) de Torby; Princesses Xenia and Nina, daughters of Grand Duke and Duchess George of Russia. The parents of both Louise and Nada hoped their daughters would marry Felix. (Eurohistory photo archive)

Right: 18. The elegant Grand Duke Dmitri Pavlovich. He and Felix fought over Irina but what was his true relationship with Felix? (Private collection)

19. The wedding of Prince Felix Youssoupov and Princess Irina Alexandrovna, 9/22 February 1914. It promised great wealth and privilege but fate had other ideas. (Courtesy of Likki Rossi, St Petersburg)

Left and above: 20a & 20b Irina's wedding presents on display in 1914. After the revolution Felix hid many of the jewels but the hiding places were discovered by the Bolsheviks in the 1920s. (*Stolitsa i usad'ba*, No. 5, 1914)

21. Irina (seated left) and Felix during their honeymoon journey, 1914. (Geoff Teeter collection)

Above left: 22. Irina with her daughter, also called Irina but known as Bébé, after her christening in 1915. Although the baptism took place at the church in the Youssoupovs' palace, the picture may have been taken at Xenia and Sandro's palace further along the Moika. (Eurohistory photo archive)

Above right: 23. Gregory Efimovich Rasputin, the supposed evil genius of the Russian empire. Felix was determined to end the influence of Rasputin and Empress Alexandra. (Eurohistory photo archive)

Left: 24. The modern waxworks of Felix and Rasputin with poisoned cakes and wine in the basement dining-room of the Youssoupov Palace. Is this what really happened? (Photo: Diana de Courcy-Ireland)

Below: 25. Oswald Rayner in uniform. Did he fire the final shot that killed Rasputin? (Courtesy of the Oxfordshire History Centre. Image ref. P23/1/P/1)

Right: 26. Koreiz, the Youssoupov estate in the Crimea where Irina and Felix spent the tumultuous months after the Bolshevik revolution. (Photo: Coryne Hall)

Below right: 27. A meeting of the *Merry Arnolf* newspaper, Koreiz 1918. Felix (second left) and Irina (third left) with other contributors. (Private collection)

Below: 28. Felix, Irina and her family in exile in Biarritz, 1919. Left to right: Felix, Nikita, Andrei, Grand Duchess Xenia, Grand Duke Alexander, Irina, Feodor, Elsa holding her baby Princess Xenia. Felix and Irina's own daughter was living with the elder Youssoupovs in Rome. (Paul Gilbert collection)

Above left: 29. Bébé in the 1920s, probably at Frogmore Cottage. Her character was very similar to that of her father, making the task of her governess difficult. (Courtesy of Bibelots London Ltd)

Above right: 30. Irina in 1925, taken by Krog in Denmark. Although Irina loved cats, Felix preferred dogs. (Private collection)

Above left: 31. Irina modelling a gown from their couture house Irfé, late 1920s. She had the ideal figure for the androgenous fashions of the time. (Private collection)

Above right: 32. A fashion magazine advertisement from February 1927. The Irfé design is on the right. (Private collection)

Right: 33. Bébé, Irina and Grand Duchess Xenia around the 1930s. (Geoff Teeter collection)

Below: 34. A press photo of Irina and Felix taken after the successful court case against Metro-Goldwyn-Mayer, 1934. (Geoff Teeter collection)

35. *Parfums* Irfé. An advertisement for the London showroom which opened in 1935. (Geoff Teeter collection)

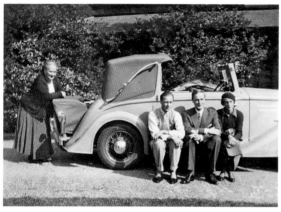

36. Rostislav with Felix and Irina, date and place unknown. (Bibelots London Ltd)

37. Irina, Feodor, Andrei & Rostislav relaxing in deck chairs at Frogmore. The lady behind is probably Andrei's wife Elsa with their sons Michael and Andrew. (Geoff Teeter collection)

38. Irina, Felix and Bébé, 1930s approx. Felix was close to his daughter but Irina's relationship with her in childhood was more distant. (Bibelots of London Ltd)

Above left: 41. Felix Youssoupov in old age. For many years he had tried to hide his hair loss. (Eurohistory photo archive)

Left: 42. Irina and Felix. Against all the odds, their marriage survived for over fifty years. (Ian Shapiro collection)

Below: 43. Felix and Irina's grave at St Geneviève-des-Bois. Also buried there are Princess Zenaide Youssoupov & Countess Irina (Bébé) and Count Nikolai Cheremetev. (Photo: Coryne Hall)

10

A Nomadic Existence

'I hope the time will not be long before I can return to my house
Felix Youssoupov to Mrs Ethel

As HMS *Marlborough* sailed through the Black Sea the weather turne
and foggy, matching the despondent mood on board. Once the Crimea
had faded away many passengers disappeared below. Nothing could d
the fact that they were now stateless. Irina and Felix were given a certifi
Captain Johnson attesting that they 'had left Russia in HMS *Marlborou*
the 11th April 1919'.[2]

On the first evening the younger members sat on cases and trunks
hold listening to Felix singing gypsy songs to the accompaniment of his g
To their surprise they were joined by the dowager empress who signalle
to continue.

The Russians were permanently hungry after the hardships of the revolu
so Irina and Felix spent most of each day waiting for the next meal. As sup
dwindled, the captain worried that food meant to last for several weeks w
disappear within days. Irina played endless games of patience but Bébé wa
high spirits, running around on deck.

On the grey, overcast morning of 12 April they dropped anchor at Prink
the largest of the Prince's Islands in the Sea of Marmara. Clocks and watc
now had to be advanced by thirty minutes. There was still no indication
where the *Marlborough*'s passengers would be disembarked. After load
provisions they sailed on to Halki, the second largest of the islands. The n
day was Palm Sunday and the ship's chaplain conducted a service on deck.

The older people were melancholy but the younger ones were becomi
restless, so some British officers organised an expedition to Halki island. Irin
Felix, Nikita, Dmitri, Rostislav, Roman, Marina and Nadejda were among tho
who had a picnic in a small cove and explored the surroundings. The weathe
was hot and some of the men went swimming.

There was also an opportunity to see the bustling city of Constantinople
which they mostly remembered for the heat and flies. One of the highlights wa
Hagia Sophia, where they were all required to don special slippers over their

shoes before going inside. Irina lost one of hers 'and completed the tour hopping through the building on one leg'.[3]

The crew did their best to amuse the children. A rug was placed on part of the deck, where Bébé happily played with Princess Nadejda's one-year-old daughter Irina Orlov and four-year-old Olga Dolgoruky. The better weather lifted everyone's spirits. The only sour note came when one of Irina's brothers released Vassili's canary through a window.

The following day Grand Dukes Nicholas and Peter with their families left for Genoa on HMS *Lord Nelson*.

The *Marlborough* left Halki on Good Friday. Their destination was Malta, which had been a British colony since 1814. Easter was celebrated with a midnight service in the captain's cabin. At breakfast time hard-boiled painted eggs were given to the children, a gesture which Irina and the other mothers appreciated. For the adults there were hard-boiled eggs with the Cyrillic mark XB (Christ is Risen) and their own initials in Cyrillic characters painted on the shells.

Shortly before 5 p.m. on 20 April HMS *Marlborough* anchored in Valletta harbour. After dinner 'Felix sang most beautifully to his guitar while the rest of us played patience and listened'.[4]

During the voyage Felix also spoke several times about the killing of Rasputin, a custom he would continue in the years to come.

☙ ✲ ❧

They disembarked the following morning to the strains of the Russian national anthem and were welcomed by Lord Methuen, the island's governor. The empress, Xenia and her sons were driven to San Antonio Palace, the governor's lovely seventeenth-century summer residence at Attard. Irina, Felix, Bébé, the elder Youssoupovs and the Soumarokovs left for the aptly named Imperial Hotel in Sliema, a town on the promontory to the north. With them went Zillah Henton and her maid, Irina's maids and the three manservants. They were to be guests of the British government.[5]

Princess Zenaide was annoyed at the amount of luggage the Romanovs had put on board the *Marlborough*. 'If I had known that they had so many trunks, I wouldn't have left so many of our own possessions behind for the Bolsheviks,' she wrote grumpily.[6]

The Imperial Hotel looked out onto the seafront but the Youssoupovs were given rooms on the other side with balconies overlooking the terraced gardens. With the certainty that their lives were no longer threatened, a feeling of security returned.

Irina and Felix were enchanted by the picturesque Maltese streets, where a goat wandered along supplying the local people with milk. Sofka Dolgoruky recalled 'watching the women come running out of the houses with jugs as the goat-herd's bell resounded. Then the pause as jugs were filled ... and coins passed from hand to hand, before the flock was driven on with incomprehensible cries.'[7]

That evening the hotel's manager 'screened off part of the dining-room so as not to embarrass the poor refugees, only to find his indigent guests coming down in full albeit old-fashioned evening dress and glittering with jewels'.[8]

39. The funeral of Grand Duke Alexander Michaelovich in Roquebrune, 1933. Left to right: Prince Dmitri, Felix, Prince Andrei (slightly behind), Grand Duchess Xenia, Christian X of Denmark, Irina, an unidentified woman, & possibly Karabassov, Sandro's major-domo. (Geoff Teeter collection)

40. Rue Pierre-Guérin, Felix and Irina's final home in Paris. The portrait is of Felix's brother Nicholas. (Geoff Teeter collection)

The following day Irina's brothers took the train to Sliema. Free from the threat of Bolshevik execution squads, the boys were in high spirits. One evening Felix and Feodor slipped into town and did a tour of Valletta's nightclubs with some English and American sailors. With so many offers to buy them a beer they had to return home quickly before they became too drunk.

There was a lunch party for twenty-two people at San Antonio on 27 April. The young equerry Robert Ingham, who had been left in charge by Lord Methuen, described Irina as 'a lovely girl ... dressed in soft black silk'. She was sitting on Ingham's right, with the empress on his left. Etiquette required Irina to open the conversation and Ingham regretted that she rarely did so, 'for as everybody knows one does not open any topic with royalty, so when Her Majesty was not speaking I found it a little trying'. Felix, sitting two places away, was wearing a velvet skull cap. Ingham was told 'that the prince had received head wounds at the time of the killing of Rasputin'.[9] This was untrue. Felix's hair loss was nothing to do with Rasputin's murder.

As their eight-day stay neared its end, Irina and Felix had to think about the future. Their chief concern was Bébé. The dowager empress was going to England with Xenia, Dmitri, Rostislav and Vassili but Felix could not be certain what sort of a welcome, if any, he would receive there. He still had the London flat on which he had paid the rent for ten years in advance, which enabled him to claim legal-alien resident status. Although they were not barred, King George, who had refused asylum to the tsar and the grand dukes, was anxious not to receive and possibly finance more dispossessed Russian relatives. There were even problems about how many of their entourage would be allowed into Britain.[10]

Irina desperately wanted to see her father in Paris, so it was decided that they would go to Italy, then Paris and then to London where Felix hoped to see Grand Duke Dmitri Pavlovich. Feodor and Nikita would travel with them. Felix senior, Zenaide and the Soumarokovs were going to Italy, taking Bébé with them.

On 29 April Irina took Bébé to San Antonio to say goodbye to her mother and grandmother. The empress told Miss Henton sadly that she had no idea when she would next see her granddaughter.

That afternoon Felix and Irina were on the quayside as the empress, Xenia, her three youngest sons and attendants boarded HMS *Lord Nelson* for the journey to England.

The following day Irina, Felix, Feodor and Nikita left Malta to go into an uncertain future.

CR ✳ ৪০

They arrived in Syracuse on Sicily's south-east coast on 1 May to find communist demonstrations in the streets, a general strike and red flags everywhere. Amid cries of '*Evviva* Lenin! *Evviva* Trotsky!', which reminded them rather too much of the Russian revolution, there a wait of several uncomfortable hours for a train to take them northwards. From Punta del Faro they could take the ferry across the Strait of Messina and continue to Rome.

Money now became an unexpected concern. The Youssoupovs had never carried cash unless it was for charitable purposes or to give to the poor.

Anything they purchased was placed on account and delivered to their palace. In 1914 they had 3.2 million roubles in Russian stocks and bonds (nearly £19 million today). 'With such resources, the extravagances of ... Felix and the family's annual deficit of expenditure over income could be survived,' wrote Dominic Lieven. By 1915 their securities holdings were 5.1 million roubles (about £30 million today).[11] Until 1914 there had also been investments in Europe, South America and the United States but all this money had been repatriated to Russia at the tsar's request and was now lost. All they had was the Villa Tatiana on Lac Leman, which they had been unable to sell during the war.

Now they had to become accustomed to a new way of living. They had no foreign currency but Felix had the jewels of Irina and Princess Zenaide. As their granddaughter explained: 'They took with them the black pearl Azra, and the black pearl necklace of Catherine the Great. And apart from that of course all the other jewels they had, La Pelegrina ... their silver and diamonds etc which were quite known worldwide. In addition, there were also the earrings of Marie Antoinette, that it appears had a sensational beauty.' These earrings, traditionally said to have belonged to the queen, had a dramatic history all their own. According to Youssoupov family tradition, 'when Marie Antoinette and Louis XVI left to escape [from Paris in 1791], she sewed in her hems everywhere in the blouse the earrings and the other jewels ... Unfortunately, they caught them in Varennes, and they were guillotined.'[12] The earrings were later bought by Princess Tatiana Youssoupov, Felix's great-great-grandmother.

Felix pawned Irina's diamond collar so they could continue their journey to Paris, meeting up briefly with Prince Roman in Genoa on the way.

ল ✸ ৪০

The Youssoupovs' arrival in France was delayed by customs officials who were under the impression that Irina's maid was a spy. Passport controls had also been reintroduced and all foreigners over the age of fifteen had to provide an identity card. Irina and Felix only had the certificate signed by Captain Johnson.

When they finally reached Paris, Sandro accompanied them to the Hotel Vendome. Andrei, Elsa and their baby Princess Xenia had 'a comfortable flat' in the city.[13]

Sandro had tried to plead Russia's cause at the Versailles Peace Conference but the politicians would not listen. Then, to his dismay, he was refused a visa for England. Neither King George nor Arthur Balfour, the Foreign Secretary, wanted the Russian grand dukes in Britain where their presence would be blamed on the king's influence.

That night they all dined at the Ritz. Paris had changed since the Youssoupovs' last visit just before the war. Everything closed at 11 p.m. but they had suffered too much for gaiety and declined all invitations.

The bond between Irina and her father remained close. There now began a struggle for influence over Irina between Sandro, who had left his family in danger in the Crimea, and Felix.

ল ✸ ৪০

While in Paris, they received some pleasant surprises. The jeweller Joseph Chaumet arrived with a bag of diamonds left over from a necklace he had altered for Irina. Felix's old Panhard car was discovered in good condition in a garage. He engaged a chauffeur so that they could take it to England. A Frenchman who had recently arrived from Petrograd said that the Moika Palace remained intact, and the valet Arthur Keeping brought the things they had left in Berlin in 1914. A more unpleasant shock was the bills which remained unpaid, some dating back to 1911.

Some of Irina's jewels were used as security. Her pendant earrings had secured a loan of 11,000 lire. Felix sent a letter to his mother asking her to let him know if she did not have the money to retrieve them.

There were problems about where they were going to live. Felix was puzzled by his parents' decision to settle in Italy and tried to persuade them to live in Finland, which was closer to Petrograd. Irina wanted to be close to her family, so many people advised them to settle in England. Felix knew of a charming place near the sea which would be ideal for Bébé and, of course, there was the London flat.

Felix travelled to London, where one of the first things he did was dine with Austin Earl. His flat had been sub-let and the housekeeper cried when she saw him. Felix could see no obstacle to them moving to England but a lot of work was needed to put the flat in order. Felix remained convinced that they would be able to return to Russia and he planned to go to Petrograd at the first opportunity to assess the situation. He stayed at the Ritz until the flat was vacated.

One evening in May, as Felix was playing his guitar and singing in his hotel room, there was a knock at the door. Expecting to find an irritated neighbour, he was surprised to see Grand Duke Dmitri, who had recognised his friend's voice through the wall. It was the first time they had met since December 1916.

Earlier that year Dmitri learnt the dreadful details of his father's execution by firing squad in the SS Peter & Paul Fortress and the death at Alapayevsk of his former guardian Grand Duchess Ella and his half-brother Vladimir Paley, who were thrown alive down a disused mineshaft by the Bolsheviks. Dmitri's sister Marie and her second husband Prince Sergei Putiatin were also in London, having escaped from Russia through Romania. Felix found them much changed, especially Dmitri, who had lost nearly everyone he loved. There was no money awaiting *him* when he arrived penniless in London. Felix felt unable to leave him and tried to help, as Dmitri recorded: 'Because all my own money is gone, and now I've already squandered 500 pounds of the 1,000 pounds of credit [around £29,000 today] that Marling arranged for me. I simply can't imagine what will happen [when it runs out] ... Then, Felix told me that he could obtain as much money as I need, because there are Russians who are offering it to him. He would then take money from them and transfer it to me. That seems like a more feasible and believable proposition to me. But all these matters are ... unpleasant.'[14]

Dmitri wanted Felix to live with him in the environs of London but Felix refused. He felt it his duty to support the Russian refugees. There was also Irina to consider. Her mother was staying at Buckingham Palace and Irina did not want to be far away. Felix still thought they should all move to London. He had a long frank conversation with Xenia and a rather cool meeting with

Grand Duchess George, now living permanently in London and still upset by the Stoeckl affair.

⊰✶⊱

Irina was with her father, Andrei and Elsa in Biarritz. The main hotels were closed and the place was nearly deserted. The season did not begin until June but by then they hoped to be back in Petrograd.

Sandro had turned towards faith and introspection, finding the Orthodox religion a great comfort. He also become interested in spiritualism and infected Irina with the craze. One evening they took out the Ouija board but Irina was scared stiff when a message appeared saying that Rasputin was there. All the family were worried about Sandro's new interest but Felix was particularly upset and annoyed. In his youth he had professed an interest in spiritualism but it stopped with his brother's death in 1908. He begged Irina to stop the sessions immediately.

She had begun to paint and draw again, had taken up golf and sometimes played bridge with her father in the evening. She was delighted with Biarritz and did not want to leave.

Irina also missed Bébé, who remained with the elder Youssoupovs in Rome while they awaited their expected return to Russia. Irina could not understand why they did not go to Finland. Nobody knew when the Crimea would be liberated and whether Koreiz had been completely destroyed. As Xenia Sfiris explained: 'After the revolution, all Russians believed that within six months they could go home and that's why they spent so much money. Because they thought we were going home... having what we had before. They did not expect at all that they would not see their homeland again.'[15]

There was another problem. Much as Irina liked her parents-in-law she could not live with them again for a long period and she wanted Bébé with her, even if Princess Zenaide considered it selfish.

⊰✶⊱

By 20 June Felix had moved into the Knightsbridge flat. 'What a relief to be back in England and to see all one's old friends, but how sad to miss so many,' he wrote to Austin Earl's mother. 'Austin and his wife came to lunch with me at my flat in London and it was quite like old times to be with your son again. Our poor country is passing through awful trials, but we hope soon, that the good will prevail over the evil, as from my point of view it is the struggle between those two forces, which brought Russia to the present state.'[16]

Felix and Dmitri continued to meet, usually for lunch at the Ritz. After one meeting Dmitri called on his aunt Grand Duchess George, 'so she could talk to me about what Felix had said to her when she saw him recently. She's terribly afraid that he'll drag me under his influence again, and that his nasty reputation will spread to me.'[17]

Grand Duchess George and Agnes de Stoeckl were causing more problems for Felix, spreading untrue stories about him in London. The king's sister Princess Victoria (Toria) was also involved. His reputation left nobody indifferent.

King Manoel of Portugal, the Duchess of Rutland, her married daughters Marjorie and Diana and Mrs Hwfa Williams were in London and Felix met up with Jack Seton-Gordon. Irina's brothers Dmitri and Rostislav visited every day. Felix said that Feodor should move to England and prepare as soon as possible to go to Oxford University.

Serge Obolensky and his wife Catherine were in town, and Dmitri frequently visited the flat. 'I didn't like Felix's apartment very much,' he wrote. 'True, it's very cozy, but two of the rooms are too much in the style of [Leon] Bakst...'[18]

On one occasion Dmitri stayed until 3 a.m. the next day. He and Felix obviously had much to discuss. 'And this time our conversation was very interesting and *sympathique*...' Dmitri recorded. 'He wanted to accompany me back to the Ritz on foot, and we parted friends, but on a different footing than before.'[19] When Marie and Sergei Putiatin moved into a house in Kensington, Dmitri went with them.

Felix plunged into work for the Red Cross while awaiting news about the military action on the south-west front of Russia and the expected taking of Petrograd. His time was divided between London, where Feodor had joined him, and Paris, where he attended a costume ball given in his honour by the famous courtesan Emilienne d'Alençon. Irina remained in Biarritz. He reassured his mother that staying in Paris and London without Irina was not improper.

☙ ✦ ❧

In summer Felix and Feodor left Paris by car. This may have been the vehicle purchased from Irina's aunt Grand Duchess Vladimir, who was trapped in the Caucasus. Using 'American, Swedish and French contacts as go-betweens', she wrote to Alexander Ouchakoff in Paris asking him to sell the car she had bought there in 1913. 'The assassin', as she called Felix, paid Ouchakoff nine thousand francs.[20]

Felix and Feodor were joining Irina for a reunion to celebrate Xenia and Sandro's silver wedding anniversary on 7 August [NS]. The grand duchess and her sons had left Buckingham Palace in June, moving first to the Savoy Hotel and then to Draycott Place, Chelsea. To Irina's probable relief Fane seems to have disappeared from the scene. 'Have you met F [Fane] and were you pleased, or not particularly?' Xenia's sister Olga wrote to her from Russia in May.[21]

Andrei and Elsa were in Biarritz with baby Princess Xenia but Irina's own child remained with the elder Youssoupovs, although Zenaide had sent a photo. Irina still found it difficult to live without her daughter, even though she knew that Bébé, who had been ill again, was in good hands. It was almost impossible to take her to Switzerland as it was difficult for Russians to obtain permission to go there. Miss Henton wanted to return to England and Felix thought it would be best to find a governess in Italy, even if she was Italian; Irina did not want an Englishwoman under any circumstances and they did not find Frenchwomen friendly.

While Felix returned to Paris Irina faced problems with her own family. The dowager empress had gone to live in Denmark. Grand Duchess Xenia had taken Nikita to London and in the autumn Dmitri would be sent to a crammer to prepare him for university, but Feodor refused to live with his mother. He disliked the fact that Prince Sergei Dolgoruky now accompanied her everywhere.

Sandro was gloomy and the relationship between parents and children was very tense. The situation broke Irina's heart. She wanted to go and see Bébé but didn't want to leave her father. Felix was afraid to leave Irina with Sandro for too long because of his influence on her. At the same time, she did not want to be far from her mother and brothers.

It was decided that Irina and Felix would live in London and Feodor would live with them. He was a great moral support to Felix and a good influence on his sister. If the elder Youssoupovs intended to stay in Italy for a long time then Irina wanted Bébé to come and live with her and Felix.

Irina had a strong sense of duty. She wanted to do something for Russia and asked Felix to find her some work. Helping her compatriots would be better than doing nothing. They could not be involved in anything political so he suggested she work for the Red Cross. Felix hoped that working with Lady Buchanan or Lady Egerton helping Russian refugees would give Irina some stability.

They needed money and Felix was making arrangements with his mother to pawn more jewels. He was intent on organising a Red Cross detachment to go to Russia and wanted to get to Petrograd and Moscow as soon as possible but the thought of returning via the Crimea was disagreeable.

ભ ✴ ક૭

To Russian exiles like the Youssoupovs, who had been used to travelling around Europe, it must at first have seemed as if they were on an extended holiday. At the end of 1919 their hopes of returning home were raised when General Denikin marched towards Moscow and General Yudenich advanced on Petrograd. Soon these hopes were crushed.

It was now beginning to dawn on them that they would not be returning to Russia any time soon. Many of the émigrés had lost their families and their livelihoods. Mentally and physically they all had to come to terms with a new life in exile.

Irina and Felix returned to Knightsbridge. King George, worried that Felix might influence his own sons, was probably not happy about him moving to London but as Felix had a flat there and Xenia was living in the capital, he could hardly ban her daughter's husband. Author Christopher Dobson says 'there is nothing about Felix's arrival in Britain' in the National Archives.[22]

Felix was soon in contact with Paul Ignatiev, president of the Russian Red Cross, who was anxious to provide work for the refugees. Felix set up a workshop in a beautiful old mansion in Belgrave Square, which also became a centre where refugees could go for help or advice. The energetic Countess Natalia von Carlow (widow of Duke George of Mecklenburg-Strelitz, a distant cousin of Irina) took charge. The place was consecrated on 24 October by the priest of the Russian embassy in the presence of Grand Duchess George and Grand Duchess Marie Pavlovna junior. Marie was envious: 'The cutting tables and sewing machines stood in a room decorated with gold mouldings, the windows of which looked out onto one of London's most aristocratic squares.' The refugees were paid for their work and Felix 'spent thousands of pounds' out of his own pocket. Her own efforts could not compete.[23]

As civil war raged between Trotsky's Red Army and General Wrangel's Volunteer White Army, Felix made all his Crimean villas 'available for charitable purposes to Baroness Wrangel'.[24] Feodor and Nikita packed up food and clothes to send to the White Army and many English friends offered assistance. Irina directed the ladies and attended fundraising charity bazaars.

As the available money quickly disappeared, Felix knew he had to do something, so he toured the industrial areas to raise funds. Friends organised charity events which brought in more donations. The most successful was a performance of Tolstoy's *The Live Corpse* at the St James's Theatre in London, with the Shakespearian actor Henry Ainley in the title role. Afterwards, Ainley made a speech urging the audience to help their recent Russian allies.

Among those who stayed with the Youssoupovs was Princess Sophie Volkonsky. She recalled Felix, whose 'witty butterfly hedonism' she enjoyed and who 'knows the secret of rendering his faults as attractive as his good qualities. If not more so…' His flat, she said, was always filled with 'extraordinary people'[25] who discussed art in Italian and sport in English.

The six-room apartment soon became so crowded that in 1920 Mr P. Zelenov, a rich Russian industrialist, helped Felix to buy a large house and garden in Chiswick to accommodate the refugees.

Irina and Felix lived a Bohemian lifestyle, with guitars, gypsy evenings and a parrot called Mary. Among those who slept on the couch at various times was Serge Obolensky, who was looking for a house for himself and Catherine. His chef Vassili arrived to cook for them. Felix, who was conscious of his increasing hair loss, hired a barber who gave him and Serge scalp massages. Serge claimed that Vassili could do it better but his treatment proved less than successful and he returned to the kitchen. 'He always makes me feel he is pounding a cutlet,' Felix complained.[26]

Obolensky described evenings which included 'Thespé, Felix, Irina and others including a bizarre array of gypsies', as well as Uncle Kotia, a plump gypsy guitarist who had accompanied many lively evenings in Russia. 'The Russian evenings began almost as in the old days,' he recalled.[27] Guests included the Prince of Wales and his mistress Freda Dudley Ward, his brother Prince Albert and his latest love Sheila Chisholm (estranged wife of Lord Loughborough), Irina's brother Prince Dmitri and Anna Pavlova.

Grand Duke Dmitri and his sister, who were considerably less well off, attended these parties. Marie criticised the Youssoupovs' lifestyle, keeping on 'innumerable and useless servants' while Irina seldom had a new dress and their car was old and dilapidated.[28] Marie and Felix soon began to fight over control of the White Russian émigré relief effort.

Felix met another old friend from Oxford, Duff Cooper, now married to Lady Diana Manners, who had been in love with Felix years ago. 'He seemed in no way altered by having murdered Rasputin – but rather sillier,' Cooper recorded in his diary. 'He says that Russia can only be saved by the Cross – Good can defeat Evil. Attributes all the trouble to Jews and Germans and believes the latter will restore the monarchy.' He described a dinner at Felix's flat with Mrs Hwfa Williams, Serge Obolensky and some refugees. 'The food was excellent and the wine though erratic in appearance, beginning with port and ending with champagne, was good in quality and sufficient in quantity. They sang Russian songs and drank Russian toasts and it was all rather charming … I left Diana to enjoy the music after dinner.'[29]

Felix still saw a lot of Dmitri Pavlovich. 'I dined at home,' Dmitri recorded. 'Felix and Irina ... were there, along with Feodor. We all drank quite a lot, as a result of which Feodor got plastered and took all his clothes off (with a little help from us), then sat there completely naked for almost the entire evening. What a mess!'[30]

Felix also caught up with other old friends. In 1919 Stephen Alley set up the Bolshevik Liquidation Club (Bolo for short), an unofficial lunch club for diplomats and intelligence officers. Members included George Hill, Sidney Reilly (an active member, whom Felix may have met in St Petersburg before the war), Paul Dukes and Sir Basil Thomson, head of Special Branch. The first Bolo lunch took place at the Café Royal, Regent Street in December 1919. According to someone who knew Felix later in Paris, he was regarded as an 'honorary member' of this club at which they drank a toast to the 'liquidation of the Bolos'. Alley's stepson later gave the impression that it was an excuse for them all to get together over a good lunch and copious amounts of alcohol and 'reminisce about the past and fantasise about the future'.[31]

At the end of 1919 Irina, Felix and Feodor left for Rome to celebrate the Russian Christmas and help Princess Zenaide set up a Red Cross centre. Hélène, Duchess of Aosta, invited them to lunch at Capodimonte near Naples and provided letters of introduction which opened many doors.

Irina remained in Rome, delighted to be reunited with Bébé, whom she had not seen since they left Malta. The elder Youssoupovs had moved into the Villa Kvitka, owned by Colonel Andrei Kvitka whose name was virtually a passport for Russians to gain entry to Italy.

Felix had been ill and was still unwell when he returned to London. Oswald Rayner was back in town and visited Felix every day.[32] By March, to Felix's delight, Rayner had moved in to keep him company.

Sandro was worried about a trip to America that Irina and Felix were planning and hoped Felix could take Feodor instead. Xenia was concerned that the couple spent so much time apart, leading a nomadic existence and separated from Bébé. Irina adored Felix but she accepted that he frequently needed to go away. She was astute enough to realise that she could do nothing about his need for men without breaking up their marriage. Felix, in his own way, needed Irina and was grateful for her understanding. In his letters he never failed to say how much he missed her.

ↀ ✸ ↂ

One evening during a party a bag of diamonds was stolen from Felix's study. He called the police. Sir Basil Thomson arrived and asked for a list of the guests but Felix did not know all their names. Those he did know were personal friends and he was unwilling to provide their details.

With the enquiry going nowhere, the newspapers seized on rumours that the stones were part of the Russian crown jewels, smuggled out of Russia by the Youssoupovs. *The Star* reported that they were worth £15,000 (nearly half a million pounds today). Scotland Yard immediately issued a statement that they were the 'absolute property' of Prince Felix and 'had nothing whatsoever to do with the late Tsar's jewels'.[33]

Felix took up the matter himself. By a process of elimination, he worked out that the thief was a man named Kolar. He took some of the man's letters to a clairvoyant, who verified that he was indeed the culprit. Felix returned home and invited Kolar to see him. Opening the study drawer, Felix looked him straight in the eye. Kolar fell on his knees, begging forgiveness. Felix pardoned him and promised not to tell anyone on condition that Kolar gave back all the stones or their monetary value and made a handsome donation to the Red Cross.

At these parties and other gatherings Felix had begun to speak about the assassination of Rasputin, seeming to glory in the publicity and the financial gain he could obtain for the refugees. Dmitri, hearing that Felix had broken his oath of silence, was angry, offended and 'could not forgive his chatter'.[34] He wrote to Felix giving his reasons for their changed relationship.

Felix was so outraged that he wrote to Marie Pavlovna saying that he was unable to answer and was sending Dmitri's letter back. It led to a series of very long letters and a bitter, acrimonious falling out between Felix and Dmitri.

On 26 February 1920 Felix wrote to Dmitri, saying he did not expect a reply. 'At one time you were my very best friend. I poured out my soul to you because I believed in your friendship. But what remains of that friendship now? We meet each other almost as enemies, and at the very moment when all those Russians who love their motherland and are devoted to her should be united by a single goal...' He knew that people were turning Dmitri against him but believed that the truth eventually would triumph. 'We've lived through too much together to stand so far apart from one another now. I know you so well that, in the present instance, I understand just what you might not know about yourself. You have unwittingly removed your mask in front of me, and I have seen what you hide behind it, the very thing that is best and most noble about you. Having come to know you, I love you all the more, and am all the more strongly devoted to you. Be assured that I don't need anything from you, and the only sentiment that guides me is one of deep devotion to you, and sad recognition of the fact that the person I so ardently loved and believed in has cast me aside. It's not easy in life to gain friends, and not everyone does. When you have them, you need to keep them.'[35]

Dmitri saw through him. In a long answer from Paris he denied that anyone was turning him against his former friend, indeed nobody ever spoke to him about Felix. He saw now that little was left of their friendship and that it was best to be honest. 'I parted from you as a friend on 24 December, 1916. We met again in May 1919, and only the memory of our friendship remained. Why? Because we are looking at that subject through such very different eyes, from such an absolutely different perspective, that in itself is enough to ruin any friendship...' Rasputin's murder, he continued, would always remain 'a dark stain on my conscience' which he never spoke about, believing that murder is murder 'no matter how hard you try to give it mystical significance! That notwithstanding, I am very well aware of the fact that it is exclusively thanks to my participation in that affair (and consequently thanks to you, who lured me into it) that I got out of Russia and didn't suffer the horrible fate of the poor sovereign or my father. But I know just as well that if it hadn't been for my presence among the conspirators of the December drama, you would probably have been hanged as a political criminal. Thus we are even!'

He and Felix looked upon the Rasputin affair from a completely different perspective, he added. He never mentioned it. 'You talk about it. You practically brag about the fact that you did it with your own hands!' He was annoyed that Felix intended to talk about the murder to collect money for the Red Cross. 'Have you really stooped so low that the only means you have of gaining the attention of the American public is to stand in front of them and say: "Look at me – I killed Rasputin!?"' Dmitri said he would give everything to 'erase the blot from his conscience', but Felix gloated, seeing it as a way to raise money. 'So, Felix, there you have the real reason for the change in our relationship. Believe me – that change is very unpleasant for me … I would love to be able to look upon you the way I did until 16 December. But alas! That's impossible…'[36]

Felix returned Dmitri's letter unopened. It was found tucked into the grand duke's diary.

Felix then heard from Marie, who also objected to him using his fame to collect money in America. Dmitri then wrote again from London, saying how surprised and upset he was that Felix had written to Marie, who knew nothing about their reasons for falling out.

It was a sad end to a friendship.

ॐ ✱ ॐ

While Irina spent Easter in Rome, Felix was at the Manoir de la Trinité in Jersey, a seventeenth-century house where he had gone for a few days' rest with Oswald Rayner. The *seigneur de la Trinité*, John Athelstan Riley, was a friend of Rayner's from Oxford. Felix told Irina that he and Serge Obolensky planned to rent a small house in one of the villages outside of London where they could keep pigs and cows. She and Catherine could feed the pigs and milk the cows while their husbands were working in London. Irina was unimpressed. She made it quite clear that if they were going to live in England she wanted to be just with him. When he was away, she preferred to be alone.

Princess Zenaide reproached Felix for going to Jersey without Irina, giving the world a bad impression. She insisted that he come to Rome immediately but after Rayner returned to London Felix moved to Guernsey, saying he hoped to be in Rome in two or three weeks.

The stress of living with her parents-in-law for the past three months was getting to Irina. Her hair was falling out quickly and she did not know what to do. She loved Rome and wanted to remain there, only visiting her parents-in-law from time to time. There was also the problem of having to ask them for money and she begged Felix to send her a few pounds. At least Feodor had arrived.

Felix returned to London to organise the Blue Ball in aid of the Red Cross, which was under the patronage of Queen Alexandra. Andrei Beloborodov, the young architect who had worked on the Moika Palace and was now staying at the London flat, was in charge of the décor.

In the middle of all this Felix had to have an operation for appendicitis. Then Irina received telegrams saying that the operation, originally planned to be in Paris, would take place in London. A room in the flat was converted into an operating theatre. For several days Felix was gravely ill and friends arrived with presents and flowers. Irina and Feodor hurried from Rome, arriving several days later.

There still remained the problem of the Blue Ball, which Felix was determined to attend. Six thousand invitations had been sent out and it was impossible to cancel. King George and Queen Mary, Queen Alexandra and King Manoel had all donated lottery prizes. Felix gave a solitaire diamond ring worth £2,000[37] (around £58,000 today) and Anna Pavlova agreed to perform.

Felix was transported to the Albert Hall in an ambulance, having told Irina and his nurse that the doctor had made this a condition of his attendance. Irina was incredulous and tried to telephone the doctor but luckily for Felix, who was telling a brazen lie, he was out. Irina, Feodor, Nikita and the nurse accompanied him, all wearing black masks. Many members of the royal family were present, Pavlova performed, the *corps de ballet* danced to the Blue Danube Waltz and Russian dances were performed by Vera Karalli and Lydia Kyasht. The ball raised a considerable sum of money for Russian refugees in Britain, as well as British nationals who had fled from posts in Russia.

☙ ✶ ❧

By August, Irina and Felix were at Divonne with Feodor and Nikita, accompanied by a nurse and their butler Andrew Bull, a part Russian, Danish and English man whom Felix had met at the London Red Cross centre. The doctor had ordered total rest and they hoped to spend time alone. Unfortunately, the enormous Hotel Chicago had replaced the smaller hotels, so they kept meeting people they knew, including Felix's former teachers Monsieur and Madame Pénard who lived in Geneva. They took the opportunity to visit Villa Tatiana which was currently leased to some Americans. It was a spacious, pleasant villa with a garden running down to the lake. They thought of living there once the lease had expired but were put off by the overwhelming view of Mount Blanc, which was framed in almost every window.

During their stay Irina almost persuaded her husband to liquidate the London flat and buy or lease a farm in France. Although Felix did not want to leave his refugee work, it was possible to rent a house very cheaply there but everything depended on the sale of the two Rembrandts.

Felix had tried to sell them in the new year of 1920 but his potential buyer had returned to America. During the autumn he was in contact with the art dealer George de Maziroff, a former captain of the Imperial Guards who, although under sentence of death by the Bolsheviks, dyed his hair, had his face altered, shaved off his moustache and lived in Russia for eighteen months before his disguise was penetrated. De Maziroff now acted as Felix's agent. They received an offer for the Rembrandts from Sir Joseph Duveen and another from Senator William Andrews Clark. But it was a saga that, despite hopes of a quick solution, was not going to end quickly.

☙ ✶ ❧

Irina's parents had not reconciled and were both having affairs. 'From the theatre I went to Xenia's for tea,' Grand Duke Dmitri recorded. 'Seryozha [Sergei] Dolgoruky was there. The two of them are currently the main focus of London gossip. No one is talking about anything but them. I mentioned that to Dehn in passing, and he said it was already old news, and Dolgoruky was constantly at Xenia's side in the Crimea. She is so sweet – I love her terribly, and if she has truly found support in Dolgoruky, then good for her, especially since Alexander Michaelovich does exactly what he pleases in Paris.'[38]

The émigrés had still not given up hope of returning to Russia but it would be impossible to return to the Crimea in the coming spring. By mid-September, Felix and Irina were thinking of moving to a farm near Cannes where they could live quietly with Bébé.

At the end of September, they took the train to Venice, before going to Florence and Rome. Irina wanted to take Bébé back to London. Felix was opposed, saying she needed a regular routine rather than their own nomadic existence. For the moment she remained with her grandparents, who spoilt her dreadfully, while Irina and Felix returned to Knightsbridge. It was an error Felix later regretted.

At the end of 1920 General Wrangel's forces in the Crimea were finally beaten by the Bolsheviks. This ended the civil war and was the end of the émigrés' hopes of an imminent return. It also removed the principal reason for Felix and Irina's refugee work in Belgrave Square.

Leaving the Rembrandts for safe keeping at the National Gallery in London, they moved permanently to Paris.

11

Bohemian Rhapsody

'Old Russia ceased to exist and will never be restored.'
Grand Duchess Marie Pavlovna[1]

Paris in 1921 was the centre of the Russian émigré movement. Many Russian aristocrats already had homes in Auteuil or Passy and they all spoke French, the language of the Russian court. The less privileged congregated around the Russian shops and cafes of Montparnasse.

Irina's family were scattered. Her father remained in France. Her mother lived in Chelsea with several of Irina's brothers. 'There does not appear to be any objection to their being allowed to accompany their mother as they do not possess grand ducal title or rank,' an official wrote when the grand duchess returned from Biarritz in 1919.[2] Nikita was studying at Cambridge, Andrei remained in France with Elsa and baby Xenia. Their son Prince Michael Andreievich was born in 1920.

Russian princes who once owned large estates now drove taxis, while former tsarist officers worked as waiters or chauffeurs. Lenin's hold on Russia seemed secure and removed all expectation of returning to their former lives. Felix refused to give up hope. Dining with Duff and Diana Cooper in July 1921 ('his pockets full of diamonds and pearls which he wants to sell,' Duff Cooper remembered), Felix said he was 'confident that he will be back in Russia under a tsar within a year'. Cooper added: 'He has great charm.'[3] Felix also wrote to Austin Earl's father, 'stating his absolute confidence that the old order would be restored in Russia and he would once again enter into his vast possessions'.[4]

Wherever Irina and Felix went their presence was accompanied by an extraordinary aura. Yet by the spring of 1921 their resources had been absorbed by refugee work and their finances were desperate. Felix never turned anyone away, sometimes leaving himself without money to buy essentials. In March the Russian industrialist Zelenov, who had helped to buy the Chiswick house, gave him £5,000 (about £145,000 today) for three months.

Felix decided to sell *The Man in the Large Hat* and *The Woman with the Fan*. He again approached George de Maziroff and offered 2 per cent commission. Irina warned Felix that de Maziroff had a reputation as a rogue, but Felix insisted he was doing everything he could. They had tried unsuccessfully to sell the Rembrandts to the Dutch but there had been a second offer from the British art dealer Joseph Duveen.

Felix was arranging for an extension of the lease on their flat and Irina needed money to pay the rent. It was a sign of the times that, once attended by hundreds of servants, Princess Irina asked her husband where she could find the iron to press her silk dressing gown.

୧ ✱ ୨

Felix had already raised money by pledging Irina's jewels; now he was forced to consider actually selling them. Unfortunately, the market was depressed by the sheer amount of seized Russian jewellery coming up for sale by the Bolsheviks. It was not going to be as easy as he thought.

He was also reluctant to sell the Rembrandts. Nevertheless, he had lunch with the American art dealer Joseph E. Widener and proposed lending the paintings to him in return for a loan of £100,000 (just under £3 million today). Widener replied that he would only buy them. He returned to America and negotiations proceeded via cables and letters, one of which asked Felix to keep the transaction secret.

Finally, an arrangement was concluded whereby Widener would pay £100,000 for the paintings but Felix had the right to buy them back for the same price, plus interest of 8 per cent, 'if on or before January 1, 1924 ... a restoration of the old regime in Russia made it possible for Youssoupov again "to keep and personally enjoy these wonderful works of art"'.[5] If they were not redeemed by that date the paintings would become the property of Widener.

After much to-ing and fro-ing, a contract was signed by Felix on 12 August and witnessed by Oswald Rayner, by that time a Treasury Solicitor of King's Bench Walk, Inner Temple. It was then sent to Widener. But in September Widener refused to see de Maziroff.

Confident that the deal would go through, although he did not yet have the money, Felix bought a small house at Boulogne-sur-Seine. Number 27 rue Gutenberg was the former stables and servants' quarters on the estate once owned by Felix's great-grandmother the Countess de Chauveau. It consisted of a main building and two pavilions, one giving onto the entry courtyard and the other onto the garden. It was close to the house that Irina's great-uncle Grand Duke Paul had occupied with his morganatic wife Olga. Felix planned to move there in September and began writing cheques to pay for alterations, settle debts and move their furniture from London. Then he received a letter from Widener's American lawyers.

Widener wanted him to sign a second contract promising that if he repurchased the two pictures *before* January 1924 he would not sell them again within ten years. Otherwise Widener would not pay the £100,000 and the deal would be off. Left with no choice, Felix signed the contract in the office of Widener's London agent, Arthur J. Sully, who said Felix was accompanied by several friends who tried to snatch the cheques before he had signed the agreement. Two cheques were then handed over, one for £45,000 and the other for £55,000.

Along with the contract Felix sent a letter explaining that the money for the paintings was to help the refugees. There was no reply.

෬ ✸ ෩

With work ongoing at the new house Felix and Bull left for the south of France where Felix booked into a clinic. In typical style he had a piano installed in his room and spent evenings with people singing gypsy songs to his accompaniment. The cellars were well stocked and there was no shortage of champagne to keep the party going. One evening he was surprised to see Vladimir Makaroff, a former Russian officer whom he had known in St Petersburg, who was working nearby as a cook.

In October Feodor arrived, followed by Irina. She was astonished to find that the place was a maternity clinic where many women gave birth secretly to their illegitimate children.

All through the summer Irina received regular letters from her father. His financial situation was worse and, despite all his efforts, he was unable to find any money. He asked Irina to help by sending back the money he lent her for the apartment, adding, 'I no longer remember if I told you that O.K. [Olga Konstantinovna Vassiliev] is in Menton, at the Villa Sabatini. Write her a few words, she will be very happy...' Olga was now the wife of Captain Nicholas Tchirikov, whom she had married in Malta in 1919.[6] Whether Irina wrote to her is unknown but Sandro made many visits to the Tchirikovs' home.

Then in December 1921 Felix heard that Sandro wanted a divorce in order to marry Mrs Addison, a British woman he had met in the spring of 1919 in Biarritz. Described as tall with auburn hair, she was around the same age as Irina and separated from her husband. Sandro pursued her back to Paris, the relationship developed and she demanded marriage. Sandro had even introduced her to Grand Duke Dmitri.

It was now imperative that Irina and her brothers explain to their mother that, if she agreed to the divorce it would destroy their father's reputation for good, but if she refused then perhaps there was a chance that Sandro could be extracted from the woman's clutches. Mrs Addison remains unidentified and the grand duchess did not agree to a divorce.

෬ ✸ ෩

When Felix and Irina arrived at rue Gutenberg they were forced to camp there for several days while work was completed.

The house's décor in tones of blue and green recalled the London flat on a grander scale. Their neighbour the designer Erté recalled 'silk lampshades, a large fireplace and murals on the walls'. Here the Youssoupovs lived with their chauffeur and servants, some 'huge violently-coloured parrots' given to them by King Manoel, Felix's dog and Irina's dog Mops, a present from Felix. One room was a Tartar tent, another lined with 'strange pictures of monsters', which Felix had drawn in the time after the murder of Rasputin when he felt 'invaded by evil-spirits'.[7]

The pavilions contained rooms for Russian refugees. On the ground floor of one Felix installed a small theatre, decorated with murals by his friend Alexander

Yakovlev. Vladimir Makaroff was engaged as a cook, probably because he was also a remarkable balalaika player with a deep bass voice.

Some of the actors, artists and writers who formed the strange selection of permanent guests were not to Irina's taste. Felix liked oddities. Among them was Hélène Trofimoff, a woman of uncertain age whom Felix used as an accompanist on the piano, and a Polish count who said he would sleep in a corner of the attic if Felix employed him as a gardener. Irina was furious; she had suffered enough with Bull and Hélène without this new clown. The house was not a circus, she said. It made no difference. Every morning 'the mad gardener raked the gravel, attired in the remnants of a dress-suit, greenish top hat and drooping tails, like a tired swallow'.[8] When Felix was absent Irina had to sort out their differences and settle their quarrels. If she showed any strain at all, it was by chain-smoking.

Another friend was the Polish aristocrat Alex-Ceslas Rzewuski, the former head of Grand Duchess Vladimir's hospital train. In exile he became a fashion illustrator, theatre designer and artist before taking Holy Orders as a Dominican monk in 1932. He remained a regular visitor to Felix and Irina throughout their lives.

Then there was the wealthy, eccentric Bertha Stern, Lady Michelham of Hellingly (sister of Boy Capel, one-time lover of Coco Chanel). Her fantasies included dressing up as the mythical Princess Lointaine, the unattainable love of medieval romances. She tried in vain to persuade Felix to obtain a divorce so that she could marry him. She introduced Felix to Jai Singh Prabhakar, the Maharaja of Alwar. Felix visited him at Claridge's, where the Maharaja dressed him in Indian costume, complete with priceless jewels, and invited him to India. Felix declined.

The Saturday evening parties at the theatre pavilion soon became legendary, with friends bringing other friends and everybody contributing food and drink. The dancing, guitar-playing and gypsy songs were a reaction to the terrible times they had all lived through in Russia. Felix's cousins Irina Vorontzov and her brothers Michael and Vladimir Lazarev were often among the guests, as were Feodor Chaliapin, Serge Lifar, Arthur Rubenstein, Elsa Maxwell and Feodor. Irina, 'eternally draped in tasselled slinky dresses', gazed enraptured as Felix sang and played his guitar. 'But, suddenly exasperated, she would shatter the spell with a dry remark in her husky, blurting Romanoff voice. Quite unruffled, Felix would smoothly bring in the next entertainer.'[9]

'I first met the Youssoupovs around 1921 at Ganna Walska's house in Paris,' recalled Erté in later years. 'What a handsome couple they were! The prince had been regarded as one of the best-looking men in Russia. Even in old age his finely structured face, though wrinkled, was still striking.'[10]

To raise money for émigré causes they formed a group of amateur actors who staged comedies and reviews under the stage management of the celebrated Russian actress Ekaterina Roschina Insarova, who had a drama studio and a Russian theatre in Paris. Grand Duchess Maria Pavlovna was among several friends recruited to take part. None of them had any acting experience, so some short humorous sketches were performed. The grand duchess recalled being asked to play 'a dizzy blonde in a sketch by Chekhov'. After several weeks of rehearsals the first performance took place amid 'feverish excitement'.[11]

Another feature was the Easter celebrations. On Easter Saturday they and their friends attended the 11 p.m. service at the Russian Church on rue Daru.

Many friends then stayed to enjoy the traditional supper afterwards. On Sunday, everyone was greeted with three kisses and the words '*Khristos Voskres!*' ('Christ is risen!'). Instead of Fabergé masterpieces there were painted eggs, the traditional Easter bread *kulich*, a rich creamy desert called *paskha* and gypsy songs.

 CR ✶ ഇ

All this time Felix was keeping an eye on events in Russia in the hope that the Bolsheviks would be overthrown and they could return home.

Early in 1921 he became involved with Vladimir Grigorievich Orlov, an associate of SIS agents Sidney Reilly and Paul Dukes in their anti-Bolshevik intelligence service. Orlov was a former Okhrana agent who later worked for Moisei Uritsky, head of the Petrograd Cheka, where he provided information on a number of people from the former tsarist government who were later arrested and executed. Orlov established an extensive intelligence network in Berlin and was receiving funds 'partly from Paris and Warsaw from the French and Polish General Staffs, partly from wealthy Russian émigrés in Paris'. The émigré who gave the largest amount of money was Felix.[12]

At the same time Orlov did not cease his connection with Soviet agents. He was a confidant of the surviving Romanovs and claimed that Felix was trying to bring about an economic crisis in Soviet Russia by running a secret organisation counterfeiting Soviet banknotes.[13]

True or not, by his association with Orlov, Felix was wading in very dangerous waters indeed.

CR ✶ ഇ

Felix had lost the taste for society and concentrated on assisting the refugees. Through his Oxford friend Walter Crighton he met the second Mrs William Kissam Vanderbilt. She gave three rooms in her house in rue Leroux so that they could open an employment office, supported by Crighton and Prince Victor Kotchoubey. In 1923 Felix helped Gleb Deryuzhinsky visit Italy in order to work. Dorothy Paget, a friend of Grand Duke Dmitri, donated money towards a retirement home for old people at St Genevieve-des-Bois. A church and cemetery were erected nearby. Then there was the School of Art, where the students were taught various trades which would enable them to earn a living. Felix and Irina also opened an *institute de beauté* where Russian ladies could learn massage and make-up and were taught to create beautiful things, ensuring they would have a livelihood.

Irina and Zenaide thought Felix was overdoing things. As Marie Pavlovna recalled, Felix 'preferred to work independently ... he would have nothing to do with committees, nor would he listen to advice. But though he always wanted to dominate, he was not an organiser; he worked at times with feverish energy, yet his efforts were mostly ineffective.'[14]

The Russian Emigration Office in Paris was headed by Vassili Maklakov, the lawyer to whom Felix had spoken before Rasputin's assassination. He had been appointed Russian ambassador to France by Kerensky but by the time he took up his post the Bolsheviks had taken power. Maklakov lived in the Russian embassy until France recognised the Soviet Union in 1924, undertaking the tasks normally done by consulates. He and Felix met in Paris in 1919 and no doubt kept in touch.

On 5 July 1922 the Nansen passport became the identity document for the stateless Russian refugees. It was recognised in thirty-eight countries and had to be renewed every year. Irina was still renewing hers in 1955.

ભ ★ ૭

On 19 February 1922 Nikita married Countess Marie Vorontozov-Dashkov, granddaughter of the former Minister of the Imperial Court. The wedding at the Russian Church was followed by a reception at Irina and Felix's home attended by Xenia and Sandro, who still had not resolved the question of their crumbling marriage.

Another problem was Bébé. Irina went to Rome, where she remained for Easter. Her seven-year-old daughter was disobedient and out of control. She spoke very good Italian but mocked Irina, who could not speak it at all.

The elder Youssoupovs were now living at via Boncompagni with Princess Maria Radziwill, whose ancestress Alexandra Engelhardt was the sister of Princess Zenaide's great-grandmother Princess Tatiana. Princess Radziwill, dubbed Aunt Bichette by Felix and Irina, treated her guests royally, despite the fact that she had lost most of her immense fortune in the revolution. Felix senior collected wine corks and Russian paper money for use when they returned to their estates. In contrast, Zenaide became 'increasingly depressed' as the years ticked by and their circumstances did not improve.[15]

Irina was more and more convinced that she should bring her daughter back to Paris but her parents-in-law now thought of Bébé as the daughter they never had and could not envisage life without her. Even though Zenaide had health problems, they refused to come and live in Paris. Irina remained in Rome for her daughter's birthday and returned home with the problem unresolved.

Back in Paris in October Irina was learning new skills: 'I am taking lessons in stenography with Irina B,' she told her mother. 'Three times a week we go to school. Apart from that we study to type on the typewriter.' She then gave an example of the shorthand they were taught – 'you must pay the taxes set' – with the appropriate transcription in French. 'Awful!' she wrote at the bottom of the page.[16]

Sandro had been sharing an apartment in Paris with his sister Anastasia, the Grand Duchess of Mecklenburg-Schwerin, but on 11 March she died in the south of France following a stroke. Sandro was sad without her and still determined to remarry. 'Papa had breakfast with us today,' Irina told her mother, 'also I was at his place a few times. He is in a good mood. He is ... nearly the same as he was before ... Staying in Thesin [?] in my view was good for him ... We would like to come to London at the end of next week or the beginning of the week after. Will you have space for two of us? ... I could not come earlier because I did not have a warm coat – we took it for alterations. Now I can!'[17]

A letter to her mother from 1 September may refer to Sandro's visit. 'It is a terrible pity that I cannot come to you. If only I could live with you everything would be much easier but it is impossible. I will try to come soon. How long do you think to stay in London? So would like to see you and live with you. I have to stop. He is going away. I thought after his visit I won't be in the house. It was so nice to have him here.'[18]

On 5 December Irina and her mother attended the Russian Red Cross sale at the imperial Russian embassy at Chesham House, London. Xenia, Irina and her sister-in-law Marie had also been invited to the Chesham House ball. This caused Irina some panic. She asked Felix to have the dress she wore in Rome dyed a different colour and sent to her.

She also went to Marlborough House for a lunch to celebrate the seventy-eighth birthday of her great-aunt Queen Alexandra. Thirty royals were present, including Irina's grandmother the dowager empress, King George and Queen Mary and their sons Edward, Prince of Wales and Albert (Bertie). The Empress Marie spoke proudly about her grandchildren, whom the king and queen had not seen for some time. King George flirted with Irina, coming over several times to speak to her. She told him she was learning stenography, which seemed to puzzle him. He also asked about Felix. Irina told him about his work for the refugees but she felt that the king did not really understand. Irina, it seems, did not have a very high opinion of King George, perhaps because he failed to save many of her relatives.

ରଃ ✷ ଅ

The year 1923 started badly as Felix tried to sort out their catastrophic financial affairs. He once more fell back on the Youssoupov jewels. Princess Zenaide was also short of money and had given Felix the necklace of thirty black pearls and Marie Antoinette's earrings to sell in Paris.

Felix senior had also tried to raise money, as Xenia Sfiris recalled: 'My great-grandfather took La Pelegrina … to Cartier and he showed it so that it could be estimated. Monsieur Cartier, when he saw this pearl, which he knew very well, said, "I have a thief in front of me," because he did not know my great-grandfather. And he called the police and [also] my grandfather [Felix]. Then the police arrived and my grandfather came to save his father.'[19]

Felix went to London, where Zelenov had promised to find him some money. There were also hopes of a serious buyer for the black pearls.

Irina definitely wanted to take eight-year-old Bébé back to Paris in the spring. Despite their wish not to have an English governess they had hired Alexandra Coombs, who was previously governess to Grand Duchess George's daughters Nina and Xenia. Miss Coombs insisted that she needed a second nanny but they could not decide whether to take Miss Bell, the nurse to Grand Duchess George's children whom Irina had known almost all her life, or leave forty-two-year-old Gwendoline Digby, a Norland nanny to whom Bébé was accustomed but Felix disliked.[20]

Felix remained in Paris, afraid that if he left the house all their things would be seized by the bailiffs. Feodor was due to go to Rome to accompany Irina back to Paris but Felix thought this an unnecessary expense. Irina insisted on bringing Miss Digby and Xenia felt sorry for Princess Zenaide, who would soon be separated from her granddaughter.

Meanwhile a rumour circulated that Lenin had died. It proved to be untrue.

ରଃ ✷ ଅ

Feodor had become part of Felix and Irina's lives. He lived with them in London and Boulogne and usually accompanied them to Rome. He was currently in Paris, where he saw a lot of his mother's cousin Princess Irene Paley. By April 1923 Feodor and Irene Paley were engaged.

Princess Irene Paley was the daughter of Grand Duke Paul Alexandrovich by his morganatic marriage. Sandro had befriended the family in Biarritz and was pleased with his son's choice. Feodor went to London to discuss his forthcoming wedding with his mother, taking an Easter egg as a gift from Irina. The couple wanted to live in one of the pavilions at rue Gutenberg.

They married on 31 May at the Russian Church in Paris in the presence of a large contingent of Romanov relatives. The bride entered the church on the arm of her half-brother Grand Duke Dmitri. Felix was noticeably absent.

Princess Paley now hoped that her other daughter Natalie would marry Feodor's brother Dmitri but the young woman was not interested in the Romanovs. In 1927, against her family's wishes, she married the couturier Lucien Lelong.

⚮ ✷ ⚭

By the autumn of 1923 time was running out on the agreement with Widener. Felix sought advice from his London lawyer Mr Barker, who said that the second contract could not be enforced and if Felix came forward with the money the paintings would have to be released. The only way they could raise money was to sell more jewels but the market was again saturated. Irina and Felix decided to try their luck in America.

Felix returned to Rome to collect Princess Zenaide's other jewels, which they also intended to sell there. The elder Youssoupovs were unhappy about this and upset that Irina and Felix were finally taking Bébé away.

Among the jewels Felix took were Marie Antoinette's earrings, which nobody would buy as they were believed to bring bad luck. Felix and Feodor had lunch at the Paris Ritz with two elderly women wearing outrageous make-up and covered with flashy jewellery, who wanted to buy the earrings and the black pearls. Felix took an instant dislike to them. To make matters worse King Manoel, seated at a nearby table, sent over a note asking Felix if he was not ashamed to be seen in such company. Felix pretended he had left the jewels at home and quickly departed with Feodor.

He was then approached by a representative of a Hollywood movie company who offered a considerable sum for Felix to play himself in a silent film about Rasputin. The man was surprised when the prince refused. The price was raised. It made no difference. The man called Felix an idiot.

Time was fast running out. If Felix did not raise the money to redeem the paintings by 1 January 1924, he would lose them forever.

In Paris he approached the Armenian oil tycoon Calouste S. Gulbenkian, one of the world's richest men and owner of the world's most valuable art collection. Gulbenkian was interested in the pictures, which he said were worth £100,000 *each*. Hearing this, Felix asked Widener to give them back. Widener 'wanted to know what revolution had taken place that would enable the prince to enjoy the pictures again'. Felix replied 'that it was none of his business'. Widener maintained that the contract had stipulated an 'economic revolution'. With Felix refusing to answer the question, he refused to return the Rembrandts.

Gulbenkian then agreed to lend Felix the money to redeem them, requiring only Felix's word that if he decided to sell the pictures he would offer them to him. Felix offered to pay $520,000 (about £6.5 million today) to redeem the paintings but Widener refused. Widener's lawyers claimed that Felix only wanted the paintings back so that he could re-pledge them. Felix said he would take him to court.[21] On 17 January 1924 the *Edinburgh Evening News* reported that Felix had served papers on Widener for the return of the paintings. The case would be heard in the U.S. Supreme Court the following year.

Irina and Felix returned to Boulogne with Bébé and Miss Coombs. The governess's task was not easy, as Bébé's character was unfortunately similar to that of her father in his youth.

Having retrieved their daughter, Irina and Felix now had to leave her. There was no question of taking Bébé to America.

CR ★ &O

On 17 November 1923 they sailed from Cherbourg to New York on the *Berengaria*. With them were jewels, gold snuffboxes and cigarette cases, diamond-framed miniatures and other valuable artefacts which they hoped to sell to wealthy American collectors. Although Felix and Irina travelled as Count and Countess Elston the newspapers reported their arrival on 23 November, adding that the couple were carrying jewels worth a million dollars and would be the guests of Mrs William K. Vanderbilt. On the passenger list Irina was described as 5 foot 4 inches, with brown hair and grey eyes. Felix was 5 feet 9 inches with brown hair and grey/green eyes.

A hoard of journalists boarded the *Berengaria* just before the liner docked at 8 a.m. and hassled the couple for stories about Rasputin's murder. The liner was also boarded by immigration officials who, to their horror, said that Felix would not be allowed into the country because an acknowledged assassin could not be granted a visa. Felix had to convince the authorities that he was not a professional assassin. No sooner was this difficulty sorted out than the jewellery was seized by customs officials, who suspected that the pieces were part of the Russian crown jewels. Irina and Felix protested vehemently but nothing they could do or say could convince them otherwise. Felix was given a receipt and the jewels were impounded. It was not a propitious beginning.

Newspaper reports of these incidents made the couple instant celebrities. Mrs Vanderbilt took them to a suite at the Plaza Annexe which was reserved for them. Felix's notoriety preceded him; the hotel manager said he would be guarded by police and that a special chef was in charge of preparing the couple's meals. Felix assured him these precautions were unnecessary. So many visitors and invitations arrived that Felix had to engage two secretaries.

At one sumptuous mansion they mounted a white marble staircase and were met at the top with great solemnity by the hostess, who had been cautioned not to mention Rasputin. Irina, who still suffered from shyness and hated this sort of thing, was quite ready to turn and leave. Then the hostess crossed into the salon and announced to her guests in a loud voice: 'the Prince and Princess Rasputin'. There was a stunned silence, then Irina had a fit of the giggles. The incident was reported in all the newspapers and made them more popular than film stars.

Irina was photographed by Edward Steichen for *Vogue* and painted by the White Russian émigré artist Elisabeth Shoumatoff. She described the princess as 'a classic beauty with strangely lifeless grey-green eyes'. Irina took the opportunity to show Elisabeth some of the 'Arnolfs', her small paintings 'of female heads with bloody tears and cut throats'. Felix, 'divinely handsome' despite his rouged cheeks, then brought out some of his own pictures. These 'were even more peculiar than his wife's – large charcoal drawings of horrible men with beards and hair sticking out of their nostrils'. Felix was, she said, 'still haunted by Rasputin', and wanted to give lectures about him in America.[22]

The Plaza Annexe soon proved too expensive so they moved into a minuscule apartment which was comfortable and, above all, cheap. Among their friends was the gypsy singer Vera Smirnova, who became fond of Irina and kept an eye on Felix while Irina spent a few days in the countryside. She came to see them at all hours, often still in her gypsy costume. With their money running out Vera helped by bringing back leftover food from the nightclub where she sang. On some days this was the only meal Irina and Felix had. Early one morning she arrived with a huge bouquet of flowers. When Irina protested, knowing that Vera had little money, the singer confessed that she had taken it from a vase in the hall of the Plaza Hotel.

On 27 December the newspapers reported that the Youssoupovs had recovered forty-two black pearls from the customs officials on payment of duty of $12,000 (around £145,500 today). The remainder of the jewels could be redeemed on payment of 80 per cent of their value, a sum beyond their means. Elsie de Wolfe, the fashionable interior decorator, offered them space in her gallery to sell the jewels and bibelots. Society flocked to view the precious objects and, above all, to see the famous Youssoupovs – but nobody bought anything.

They were still lionised by society, where they had to keep up appearances. This led to a bizarre situation. In the evenings they attended a function in a splendid dwelling, with Irina wearing Catherine the Great's black pearl necklace. Afterwards they returned to the cold apartment where she washed their underwear in the bath.

Irina's brother Dmitri arrived from Paris for a short holiday and moved in with them. He thought by now they must have sold the jewels and become millionaires, so was surprised to find them at such a low ebb. He found employment in the Foreign Exchange department of the National American Bank of Manhattan.

Finally Felix went to see Pierre Cartier, whom he knew he could trust. Pierre was anxious to acquire Russian jewels ahead of his competitors, so he was offered 'watches and snuffboxes, miniatures in diamond frames, and oriental daggers with handles enriched with precious stones'. Then there were the diamonds – the 41-carat Polar Star, the 35-carat blue Sultan of Morocco, Marie Antoinette's earrings, and Catherine the Great's light-rose Ram's Head diamond on a black pearl necklace. All were sold by Cartier during the 1920s.[23]

Cartier had made some of the Youssoupovs' finest jewels and Pierre had no hesitation in advancing Felix $75,000 (about £912,000 today) for the black pearls.[24] Felix handed over another necklace of thirty-one pearls as a guarantee.

Discreetly, Cartier put the word around his clients and waited for the right buyer to appear.[25]

Once more the Youssoupovs had money in their pockets and they began to enjoy themselves, with Gleb Deryuzhinsky and other friends from the Russian colony. At the Red Eagle restaurant there were three Caucasian dancers, one of whom, Taoukan Kerefoff, was a remarkable performer and would become a great friend.

Irina particularly appreciated the home of General Philipoff in the mountains about four hours from New York which gave the illusion of being back in Russia. During the day they went tobogganing. In the evening Russian specialities were served.

Typically, the Youssoupovs did not forget the Russian émigrés. The American branch of the Russian Red Cross was in difficulty, so Irina and Felix created a new international organisation, the Russian Relief Society of America and Europe, to help refugees earn a living. Irina made a personal appeal to America and another to Europe, asking for help to give the émigrés the possibility of re-joining society. When the day came that they could return home to Russia, she wrote, they would remember with love and gratitude those who had helped them during their ordeal.

Committees were formed and prominent people organised sales, balls and charity concerts. Irina and Felix were patrons of the Russian Ball at the Hotel Lorraine but their greatest triumph was the ball in aid of Caucasian émigrés, where Taoukan Kerefoff and dancers in national costume performed at the end of the evening. Taoukan spent freely to help them organise the event, also taking charge of the dances and becoming the star attraction.

Taoukan Kerefoff was a Tcherkess Muslim from the Caucasus who had fled to Constantinople following the defeat of his White Russian cavalry regiment in the Crimea. In the Turkish capital he earned his living as a dancer performing for the Sultan, gradually dancing his way to Paris and then New York. When the Youssoupovs left for Europe, Tao followed them.

After redeeming the so-called crown jewels from customs officials, Irina and Felix left New York on 7 May, having placed the money for the objects confided to Cartier in a real estate deal.

On 19 May, *The Times* reported that Prince and Princess Youssoupov had arrived on the Cunard liner *Aquitaine*. They had funds in the bank and were reunited with Bébé, now nine. She had inherited her father's enormous charm and soon discovered the power it gave her, which she knew how to use skilfully.

In their absence Feodor had become a father when Irene gave birth to Prince Michael Feodorovich but there were worries about Felix's father, whose health had deteriorated and who was now bedridden. Felix was shocked at his appearance, but reassured by the doctor and the care of Princess Zenaide and Aunt Bichette.

CR✴ഏ

On 21 January 1924 Lenin died. His body was embalmed in a mausoleum in Red Square and Petrograd was renamed Leningrad. He was succeeded by Joseph Stalin. On 28 October 1924 France recognised the Soviet Union and established diplomatic relations. The stateless Russians could have no relationship with the new Soviet officials. Vassili Maklakov and the Central Émigré Office in Paris continued to carry out the work of the former Russian consulates but the brief ray of hope that the old order might be restored was shattered.

Grand Duke Cyril had dismayed the émigrés by declaring himself 'Guardian of the Throne' in 1922 and, with the presumed deaths of Tsar Nicholas, Tsarevich Alexei and Grand Duke Michael, he proclaimed himself emperor in 1924. Cyril's declaration not only broke the unwritten rule that no member of the family would claim the throne in the dowager empress's lifetime, it also caused a rift in the Romanov family which has never healed. Neither Irina nor Felix supported him.

Meanwhile, a Russian-language paper of Soviet allegiance, published in New York, printed a story purporting to come from Moscow alleging that Felix was a crook who had defrauded at least two people during his stay in America.

Sometimes Felix was himself the victim of crooks. In order to establish a workroom in Boulogne he had paid 23,000 francs to Czech-born Jean Dojetchak to terminate the lease of a building which later proved to be non-existent. Felix complained to the police, who then began trying to trace Dojetchak. He had of course disappeared.[26]

By July Irina and Bébé were in Saint-Gervais, south-east France, where they spent three or four weeks. Felix was 50 miles away in Divonne with Tao and a group of friends.

Irina and Felix had been glad of their time alone in America, which reinforced their marriage and would enable them to cope with the difficulties life threw at them.

There would be many more of these in the years to come.

12

The House of Irfé & Other Ventures

'Prince Youssoupov ... brings to his clothes his refined taste and striking personality, which expresses itself exceptionally well in the choice of lines and range of colours.'

Vogue, Paris, 1926

In 1924 Irina and Felix set up a Paris fashion house called Irfé, after the first two letters of their Christian names. It is an idea they may have taken from their friend the Russian-born artist and designer Roman Tyrtov, who while working for Paul Poiret took the pseudonym Erté (R.T.).

Fashion took its lead from Coco Chanel. In 1921 she had an affair with Grand Duke Dmitri Pavlovich, who persuaded her to employ several Russian aristocrats.[1] Soon Russian designs were all the rage.

Paris had several Russian fashion houses, among them the Bery House of Fashion established by Irina's distant cousin Prince Gabriel Constantinovich and his wife Antonia (Nina), a former ballerina, who lived with the Youssoupovs, but the Russians were often resented by the French couturiers.

Irfé started life on the cramped ground floor of a building on rue Obligado rented from a Russian friend. Princess Zenaide was not too pleased, disliking the idea of trade in Felix's home. Irina explained that the shop was nearby, with an entrance directly from the street, but she feared clients would not want to travel so far from the centre of Paris.

Irina and Felix, like most people of their class and upbringing, had little idea of what to do with money apart from spend it. New to the world of business, they launched their first collection without any advertising. Luckily, in the winter of 1924 the large couture houses were holding a fashion show at the Ritz followed by a ball. It was an ideal opportunity for Irina and her aristocratic friends to model the dresses.

They arrived at the Ritz around midnight. Even at this late hour the seamstresses were working feverishly to finish the garments. Nevertheless, when Irina led the models out the clothes made an unforgettable impression on Parisian society and French journalists. 'Originality, refined taste, meticulous work and an artistic sense of colour immediately placed this modest atelier in the ranks of the big houses of fashion,' gushed one reporter.[2]

This early success was followed by fashion shows in the theatre pavilion at rue Gutenberg, where clients from Europe and America flocked to the home of the notorious Prince Youssoupov to hear his stories about Rasputin's death and see the tsar's niece model the gowns. In the early 1920s the *kokoshnik* headdress was especially popular and in Irfé's designs 'variations on motifs from the Russian headdress and the Russian boyar costume also appeared'.[3]

The Youssoupovs were not the only Russians setting up a couture house but they 'managed to achieve the impossible: to gain respect, authority and clientele in a country forever known as a trendsetter. The picky French praised the exquisite taste and new lines of models of the Irfé House. The press published laudatory articles about the new Yusupov [sic] collections, with the smallest details...'[4]

The enterprise was so successful that they moved to the first floor of a house at 19 rue Duphot near the other large fashion houses in the Madeleine quarter. This bolstered Irfé's reputation. Felix had the walls of the salon covered in grey velvet and the panelling painted light grey. The reception room had grey floral cretonne walls, yellow silk curtains and mahogany furniture. In Irina's office was an art deco knotted woollen rug by the French designer Edouard Benedictus and they brought in showcases filled with Russian bibelots. Irina left unusually shaped crystal bottles on the tables and shawls draped over the backs of chairs. The effect was as if the princess had invited clients into her sitting room, from which she had just stepped out for a minute. Nearly all the staff and workers were Russian.

Felix patronised the Stroganoff School of Applied Arts, 'a professional teaching institute set up with the assistance of Zemgor', an organisation registered in Paris to help Russian émigrés. The school 'prepared its students to work in emigrant art enterprises and for the Fashion House of Felix Yusupov [sic]. The students' best works were selected for sale in the prince's shop.'[5] Some of them were subsequently employed by Irfé and many others were saved from unemployment and poverty.

At various times Irfé's staff included Nikita and his wife Marie, and Michael and Nona Kalachnikoff. The models were Russian aristocrats, including Baroness Anastasia von Nolken whose father Felix had known in St Petersburg. The cutter was a Russian woman whose eccentric designs 'were beautiful but difficult to wear'.[6] By law a percentage of the workforce of every Russian business had to be French citizens, so the experienced French-born Mme Barton was employed as directress. She struggled to enforce discipline among the typically Russian disorder. Felix's butler Andrew Bull answered the telephone and made appointments very inefficiently, causing many misunderstandings.

Several hundred invitations were written for the opening of the new showroom. Gilded chairs were hired and flowers arranged. Everything was ready – but nobody came. Bull had forgotten to post the invitations.

The opening was rearranged but then Irina remembered that she needed someone to look after Bébé. They had no choice but to bring their nine-year-old daughter to the party. As society feasted on canapés and cocktails Bébé grew bored. Hiding under the table, she spotted a leg and sunk her teeth into the man's calf. It was her father's main financial backer, who was less than pleased when the culprit was discovered. The incident earned Bébé a beating from Felix.

The Irfé showroom was 'reminiscent of an Eastern palace: all the fitting rooms were lined in grey velvet, as if they were in Turkey'. The eccentric Felix, who wore 'pink rouge and green eye shadow', received clients dressed 'in a turban and Eastern robe, looking like a khan with his favourite bulldog'. He was apparently not averse 'to trying on one dress or another to show how it should be worn'.[7]

In contrast, the presence of the modest Irina, who did not like the models to curtsey to her, lent the whole enterprise some gravitas. She had the ideal figure for the rather androgynous fashions of the 1920s. Her photographs appeared in newspapers and magazines wearing elegant Irfé gowns and she soon became famous. Grand Duchess Olga Alexandrovna was astonished to learn that her niece did everything herself and did not even have a chambermaid.

To attract French society they employed the Chilean-born Marquis Jorge de Cuevas as an agent. Thanks to his efforts they soon had so much work that Felix rented the floor above for the workshops. Jorge's time with the Youssoupovs was short. In 1928 he married Rockefeller's granddaughter.

People of all nationalities came to the showroom, where tea was served from a samovar and the models discussed the clothes in many languages. One of their clients was the eccentric, enormously large and extremely rich Mrs Hannah Whobee, an Egyptian millionairess known as Bibi, who ordered a *kokoshnik* and fifteen dresses while holding a shot of vodka in her ringed and braceleted hand. She would become important in the Youssoupovs' lives.

The success of the Paris atelier led to the opening of a branch at Le Touquet managed by Nina, followed by one in London. On 25 November 1926 the *Hull Daily Mail* reported that Princess Youssoupov and her husband were opening a shop at 42 Berkeley Street. When Mrs Ronald Armstrong-Jones (mother of the future Lord Snowdon) wanted a maternity dress in 1927 she turned to Irfé for a 'white silk crêpe dress with a black art-deco print depicting wheat flowers'.[8]

A Berlin branch followed in 1927, in the former private residence of the Radziwill family on the Pariserplatz, run by Princess Pauline von Thurn und Taxis. Even Felix was astonished when one night the unpredictable Pauline took him to a transvestite club to look for models.

Irfé was designed to capture the American market. 'Rich American women, gluttons for titles and sensation, paid crazy sums for their designs – not so much because they were so good, as for the right to meet the man who had killed Rasputin'[9] and see elegant clothes worn by a genuine relative of the last tsar of Russia.

Irfé also sold coloured shawls and woven fabric belts made by the Russian artist Maria Vorobyova-Stebelskaya, known as Marevna. She had a small daughter and needed a steady income. '[At Irfé] Marika could be with me,' she recalled. 'We would live in a servant's rooms with an attic, and I could cook on an alcohol burner.' Irina offered 350 francs a month. 'Alas,' Marevna continued, 'this wasn't enough to live on and feed a child.'[10]

Irfé was also the first *Russian* couture house to introduce its own perfume. Felix had previously approached Molinard to create a fragrance. They asked Leon Bakst to paint the baccarat crystal bottle and proceeded to make the scent. Then Felix stopped the project.

The perfume was finally launched in 1926 in a rectangular bottle with a black glass cap. Irina and Felix both took part in the creative process, which produced a perfume with a sharp, spicy, Eastern quality. The advertising promised a perfume 'for each type of woman, Blonde, Brunette, Titian and Silver Grey'. Later Irfé also produced an exotic refreshing bath essence. The perfume formula was lost during the Second World War.

Irfé was also sold in Copenhagen. The dowager empress's lady-in-waiting was permitted to set up a small shop in the living room of a private house selling perfumes, cosmetics and soap sent directly from Paris by Irina and Felix.

Youssoupov-mania was so rife that the menu of a London restaurant included 'Fatted fowl *à la Youssoupov*'.[11]

◌❧ ✦ ☙

Irfé's success led to other business ventures. With Belgian-born Baron Edmond de Zuylen, Felix opened the porcelain shop Monolix. He also became involved in three restaurants. There was La Maisonette Russe du Mont-Thabor where Felix supervised the interior decoration and was involved in the management of the place, which was patronised by Chaliapin and other celebrities. Russian music, singers, Caucasian dancers and gypsy orchestras provided entertainment as the patrons sat down to traditional Russian cuisine. There was also the Venetian-style Le Lido, which was more a nightclub; and the peasant-style Mon Repos where Vladimir Makaroff was installed by Felix as director.

Felix was a regular at Le Boeuf sur le Toit, the cabaret bar frequented by his friend Jean Cocteau. There were other old friends to catch up with, like Princess Sophie Volkonsky, whose daughter Sofka Dolgoruky had played with Vassili on board HMS *Marlborough*. Sofka remembered the Youssoupovs as a 'glamourous' couple and she listened avidly while Felix 'gleefully' recounted his part in Rasputin's murder to 'an entranced American visitor'.[12]

In the 1920s Russian beauties with titles were popular in Paris. Irina was just one of the women who frequented charity balls in aid of Russian refugees.

◌❧ ✦ ☙

Irina and Felix's relationship with Bébé was often difficult. They had proved bad parents, unconcerned with the day-to-day doings of their daughter who, like many upper-class children, was shuffled between nannies, tutors and governesses. Severe financial difficulties and frequent changes of residence had added to the problems. Between 1919 and 1924 they hardly saw her at all. She adored her father but the relationship with her mother was more distant.

She had a habit of asking awkward questions. 'Where are the spoons we always use?' Bébé enquired one day. She was told off for asking. The spoons had been pawned.[13]

When it became difficult to educate Bébé at home with a governess she was enrolled in the nearby Cours Dupanloup. This Second Empire building had been owned by Felix's great-grandmother the Countess of Chauveau, then by Irina's uncle Grand Duke Paul until 1912. After the revolution his widow Princess Paley sold the property and it became a girls' school. The Youssoupovs' rue Gutenberg home was one of the outbuildings of the estate.

It became customary for Bébé to go on holiday with Prince Ilarion and Princess Lydia (Dilka) Vassiltchikov and their family. Felix told Dilka, 'You know how to bring up children, and we don't. Take her along!'[14] Bébé went with them to Brittany several times. In 1924 an excursion led them to the Chateau de Kériolet, where a Winterhalter portrait bore a striking resemblance to Bébé. Princess Vassiltchikov then discovered that the chateau had belonged to the Countess of Chauveau, who in 1891 gave it to the town with certain conditions while retaining the right to live there.

On her return to Paris the princess immediately told Felix.

✩

On 21 March 1925 Felix sailed to America on the *Mauritania* with George de Maziroff to fight the Widener case.

It began in the New York Supreme Court in April. Felix's counsel Clarence J. Shearn asked for an interpreter for his client but this was opposed by Widener's Chief Counsel Nathan I. Miller, who insisted that 'he speaks English as well as any of us. I'm told he was educated at Oxford.' As Felix recounted how he smuggled the Rembrandts out of Russia it became apparent that this was not so. Mingling a 'Mayfair clip' with 'the soft sibilancies of the Asiatic', Felix grew almost incoherent as he became more excited.[15]

Questioned by Shearn, Felix insisted that the paintings had been pawned to Widener. They had already been pawned for six months in London for £32,000. He had asked the late Senator William Andrews Clark for £275,000 (just over £11 million today) for *both* pictures but Clark refused, even when the price was reduced by £50,000. At that time Widener offered to lend him £100,000 while he negotiated with an Egyptian millionaire of whom he asked £125,000.

As things became heated the lawyers disposed with courtesies. One of Widener's lawyers said of Felix, 'Any man who paints his face and blackens his eyes is a joke.' Shearn accused Miller of 'framing his questions in such an involved English that the prince would be trapped into misleading answers'.[16]

Calouste Gulbenkian's statement was read, in which he admitted opening a credit line of $520,000 (around £6.5 million today) for Felix so that he could redeem the paintings. Felix said 'that he considered Gulbenkian's offer the fiscal equivalent of a new regime in Russia', feeling that Widener, 'in his insistence on a return of the Romanovs, was being technical'.[17]

After intensive cross-examination Felix commented that 'for the first time in my life, a man has dared to raise a question regarding my veracity'.[18]

Duveen 'testified that he had once offered the prince $550,000 [£150,000 then] for the two Rembrandts and that the prince had wanted a million [dollars]'.[19]

Character witnesses for Felix included Sidney Reilly, the 'Ace of Spies', who took the stand in his capacity as an art dealer. 'Art dealer' is certainly a misnomer; he was more of a con artist and had spent a lot of time in New York since 1923. Much of Reilly's testimony was concerned with the identification of letters, cablegrams and deals which the prince had made with Widener. Reilly said 'that he had enquiries for them prior to the Russian revolution, and that Sir George Donaldson had offered £150,000'.[20] Like other SIS agents, Reilly owed a lot to Felix for his continued silence about British involvement in Rasputin's death.

George de Maziroff insisted that the arrangement with Widener was a mortgage, not a sale. He further testified that the agreement provided for a loan of £100,000 at 8 per cent interest, with the stipulation that Prince Youssoupov had the right to redeem the pictures within two years.

Cross-examined by Miller, de Maziroff maintained that he received a cablegram advising him that the prince's offer had been accepted and instructing him to call on Widener's London agent Sully for the money. The prince then began making plans to dispose of the money, 'which he thought he was getting as a loan'. When the second contract came from Widener he was forced to sign it because he needed the funds. Miller asked whether the letter had not been received first, implying that Felix knew what he was doing when he accepted the terms. De Maziroff refused to be shaken. He also denied that Felix wanted the paintings back so that he could sell them for a larger profit.

As valuable works of art and jewels dominated the proceedings, de Maziroff mentioned various gems which he carried round in his pockets to prevent the prince from pawning them to support the Russian émigré colony in London.[21]

With his lawyers' assurances that the court was bound to find in his favour, Felix returned to Paris. Widener then turned up and asked to settle the case amicably. Felix refused to see him.

The verdict came through in September. Felix had lost. Joseph Widener kept the paintings, which he eventually donated to the National Gallery of Art at Washington. The Youssoupovs called them 'the stolen paintings'.[22]

Worse was to come.

☙ ✸ ❧

The Soviet government had already found Felix's hiding places in the Moika Palace. After it was nationalised in February 1919 an inventory was taken and a search began for hidden artworks and jewellery. Probably with the help of threatened staff, they rapidly found the false ceiling and removed the priceless paintings. By the following month over a hundred huge boxes of treasure had been found.[23] Over the next five years they discovered four more secret rooms, one containing more than 400 pieces of jewellery. In 1925 Sir Martin Conway described a large mirror in one of the ballrooms. 'It clearly hides a cupboard within which a quantity of valuables were hidden,' he wrote, 'but they did not escape discovery and confiscation.'[24]

The Youssoupovs' old valet disclosed the location of the last room on his deathbed. It was a fireproof strongroom concealed behind a folding panel in one of the library bookcases, where Felix had concealed Sèvres dinner services, miniatures, bronzes and jewellery. More jewellery was found in the safe located next to Prince Youssoupov's office and in the basement. A room in the cellar was connected to the billiard room by a secret stairway and a trapdoor. Another secret store concealed even more emeralds, diamonds, rubies and pearls. Many people believe there are still two undiscovered rooms in the Moika Palace.[25]

Then on 17 September 1925 the newspaper *La Liberté* reported that during restoration work in the Youssoupovs' Moscow house hidden treasures had been discovered. The Soviets had searched there for years, even torturing and killing

Gregory Boujinsky for heroically refusing to divulge the location. Then the son of one of the masons who devised the hiding place told the authorities that there used to be a cloakroom under the main staircase. It was now hidden behind a false wall which he had helped his father to build.[26] When the wall was torn down it revealed seven leather trunks containing '255 diamond brooches, 13 tiaras, 42 bracelets and 462 pounds of assorted *objets d'art*, including trinkets by Fabergé and gold dinnerware'.[27] Among the items were the Sunburst tiara, the Cartier rock crystal tiara which Irina wore for her wedding, the Lovers' Knot diamond tiara with pearl drops, an emerald and diamond stomacher, two large Fabergé swans and many unique diamond necklaces. The total value of the booty was put at 50 million roubles. Newspapers worldwide published the photograph of the hoard spread out on a table.

La Liberté reported that cunningly hidden steel doors concealed a gallery leading to two underground vaults. 'In the first cellar were piled up paintings by masters, antique furniture and a collection of porcelain of unique beauty. The second cellar concealed … all the jewels of the Youssoupoffs [sic], collections of snuffboxes, old coins, watches … and a profusion of *objets d'art*.' According to the Soviet commissioners, 'two hundred and ten kilograms of gold objects, 21,441 grammes of jewellery [and], a group of silver weighing one thousand pounds alone were collected. There were twenty-five necklaces of sixty-three large emeralds each, eighty-seven diamonds of marvellous water, two hundred and fifty-five platinum brooches, thirteen ruby diadems, etc.'[28] *The Geelong Advertiser* called it 'a discovery rivalling the magnificence of the Arabian Nights…'[29]

The Soviets extracted the larger stones to sell. The result was the depression of the European jewellery market even further.

This discovery removed any hope that the Youssoupovs could one day return to Russia and retrieve their valuables, which had effectively been stolen.

☙ ✶ ❧

One day Felix suggested to Irina that they take the car and go on a trip. They ended up in Marseilles, where a boat was leaving for Calvi in Corsica.

Exposed to gales from the Mediterranean, Calvi was a remote location seldom visited by tourists. The old town is surrounded by a massive wall dating from the Middle Ages and dominated by the imposing Citadel. It had been ruled by the Genoese at one point and the old houses were huddled together on steep slopes reached by uneven steps. Some of these houses, which had been the homes of Genoese merchants and officials, still maintained their former grandeur.

Irina and Felix were immediately charmed by the place and the friendliness of the people. One of the pink-walled houses inside the Citadel was for sale and on 20 December 1926 they bought it from Achille Giuliardi for 15,000 francs.[30] The two-story Maison Giuliardi had a garage, a granary dwelling and other adjoining dependencies. There was no electricity, no water and no bathroom but, as Irina said, they could bathe in the sea.

Until 1928 when she left for America, one of their regular guests was Grand Duchess Marie Pavlovna. Taking the steamer from Nice she endured a long, dusty drive in an old car but the view of Calvi in the morning light was 'worth it'. Marie felt the discomfort as soon as she arrived, describing Maison Giuliardi as 'a ridiculous half-tumbledown building', almost a shack, yet they managed to enjoy themselves swimming and boating.[31]

The Youssoupovs also bought or leased other properties. On 23 January 1928 Felix paid 15,000 francs for the first and third floors of another house in the Citadel, which he sold on 22 September for the same price to Count Foulques de Balliardei de Lareinty Tholozan and his wife, Zizi.[32]

Count Foulques had turned up at rue Gutenberg in 1927, introducing himself as one of Felix's cousins. It turned out that Zizi, the former Zenaide Pavlovna Demidov, had a tenuous family relationship with Felix through the Soumarokoff-Elstons.[33] Tall, good looking and sporty, Foulques had been an officer in the French Air Force. In 1925 the Lareintys moved into the Chateau du Lac at Sigean in the south of France, which became a meeting place for Russian aristocrats. One of their most famous guests was Felix. He and Foulques struck up a deep friendship and sometimes went on holiday together, although their political views were miles apart and they had heated discussions.[34]

On 12 April 1928 the Youssoupovs bought from Marc Antoine Giudicelli a garden place called Donateo near Calvi and the first floor of a house in the garden for 20,000 francs,[35] then engaged Restitude Orsini as housekeeper. When Mme Orsini heard about their financial difficulties she travelled to Paris to give the Youssoupovs her savings.

There was also a lease for the rental of a farm named Donateo and Cordella Soprana 'located on the territory of Calvi' and its cultivation rights in Calvi dated 1928.[36] Their only regret was that the farm had no flowers in its gardens. The following year when they returned, flowers had been planted by the local people.

 C3 ✱ 80

In the mid-1920s Felix was approached by Hélène Izvolsky, daughter of the tsar's ambassador to France, who wanted to write a book about Rasputin and the fall of the Romanovs. 'He talked for several hours about the assassination,' she recalled, 'and seemed quite pleased to reminisce, going over all the horrifying details.'[37] With Purishkevich's supposed diary already published, Felix now saw no reason why he should not write his own book.

Only Dmitri and Lazovert were still alive. Purishkevich had died from typhus in 1920. Sukhotin, after escaping from Bolshevik imprisonment, married as his second wife Sofia Tolstoy, granddaughter of the famous writer, but in 1921 he suffered a stroke and she divorced him. Sofia's aunt Alexandra Tolstoy wrote to Felix for help and he invited Sergei to Paris where he died in 1926, leaving no memoirs.[38]

With no apparent obstacles in his way, Felix began work on his own book about Rasputin's murder. He asked Alexandra Lebedinsky, Princess Kropotkine, to translate it into English but after some time she returned the manuscript claiming she was unable to do the work. She then tried to publish extracts, so Felix applied for an injunction to prevent her. Princess Kropotkine had recently published an article called 'Unpublished Letters of Rasputin's Murderer, by Princess X' largely based on the memoirs, which had never been authorised. The case in the High Court of Justice was stood over for a week in order for the defendant to respond. Then on 16 February *The Times* reported that 'the plaintiff had discontinued his action'.[39] Why Felix dropped the case was not stated.

Oswald Rayner then stepped into the breach. Although Rayner's name appears as translator in the English edition, it does not appear in the American publication.[40] Rayner also approached the publisher Jonathan Cape with a proposal for the book and some people believe he actually wrote it.

Rasputin, His Malign Influence and His Assassination appeared in 1927 and stirred up strong emotions among the émigrés. Although some supported him, there were also anonymous letters full of insults and threats, especially from the far-right. The book was described in some quarters as a scandal and Felix was accused of insulting the memory of the imperial family, especially the empress whose portrayal was unflattering. Many believed he was wrong to use Rasputin's brutal murder for monetary advantage, while others blamed him for 'contributing directly to the collapse of the Russian monarchy and thus to their present woeful condition'.[41]

Grand Duchess Olga Alexandrovna was sickened. 'He believes himself to be a hero and he wants to show himself to the world in this way. Now he wants to "whitewash" but if you knew the real details, they're disgusting,' she told her former tutor.[42]

Grand Duke Dmitri again accused Felix of breaking their oath of silence. 'Not a single person, including members of my own family, has heard from me about the events of that terrible night,' he told a Russian paper published in Paris. Felix hadn't seen him for six years. When Dmitri married American heiress Audrey Emery in November 1926 neither Felix nor Irina was among the guests.[43] The rift was permanent.

The negative reactions came as a great surprise to Felix and Irina, who had supported her husband. Even worse, Maria Rasputin lodged a formal complaint against Felix and Dmitri for 'vilest calumnies', saying her father had been deliberately lured to the Moika Palace with the aim of murdering him. She sought substantial damages.

❧ ✴ ☙

Felix now turned his attention to the Chateau de Kériolet.

On her death in 1893 the Countess de Chauveau left it to the *département* of Finistère. Clauses in her will stipulated that various lands must be conserved intact, the furniture must remain in the chateau and the trees in the park must remain standing. If these conditions were not complied with the property would revert to the countess's heirs. These, of course, were her granddaughter Princess Zenaide and Felix.

Zenaide had examined the question after Princess Vassiltchikov's visit to the property, but her lawyer Maître Imbert said it was too late. The chateau was now a museum and the *département* had the right of prescription through long-term use and enjoyment, which annulled those rights of the natural heirs.

In 1926 Felix inspected the chateau, which had been reconstructed for the countess at enormous cost in the rather heavy Gothic Revival style. Felix and his secretary Katalay were shown around by an old attendant who had worked for the countess. Felix was the first member of the family he had seen since her death. Little of the original interior remained except some old panelling and magnificent tapestries. The furniture had been sold and Felix hoped this would give him a loophole to reclaim the property.

Meanwhile, Irina and Bébé were in England. Since April 1925 Grand Duchess Xenia had been living in Frogmore Cottage, a grace-and-favour residence in Windsor Home Park granted to her by George V. The move was intended to be temporary. Living with her were Andrei, Elsa and their children Xenia, Michael and Andrew, plus the Elsa's other children Betty and Sandrick Friderici.[44] The overcrowded cottage was open house for Xenia's large family and their friends. Irina and her brothers played tennis (sometimes in pyjamas) and golf even on Sundays and rode on bicycles around the mausoleum of Queen Victoria's mother the Duchess of Kent. Nearby was a small river where they bathed. The king had ordered that 'no restrictions' were to be placed on the grand duchess and her guests; they could go where they liked and do what they wanted. Most of the expenses were charged to the Privy Purse.[45]

CR ✱ ꙮ

Between 1927 and 1929 Felix repeatedly mortgaged the Youssoupov jewels. Jacques Cartier, Pierre's younger brother who ran the London branch, often complained that he went to Paris to visit the Youssoupovs only to find that Felix was away and Irina was 'at a friend's house – says she's sick'.[46]

Felix and Irina approached Jacques with a collection of pearl earrings and necklaces, including the famous La Pelegrina pearl. In 1927 Cartier worked jointly with Thomas M. Sutton Ltd of London, a 'dealer in precious stones' according to the company's notepaper but actually a high-class pawnbroker, to advance £37,807 (around £1.5 million today) for the pearls.[47] The Polar Star diamond, once owned by Joseph Bonaparte and bought by Princess Tatiana Youssoupov, was among the jewels lodged with Cartier and pledged to Sutton in 1924.[48]

While in London one morning Felix passed the kennel where he had bought his now deceased bulldog Punch. Popping in to see the owner, he saw a bulldog exactly resembling his former pet. Unfortunately, the price was too high. Dejected, he went to meet King Manoel for lunch. The king asked why he was so disconsolate and Felix told him. The following day Felix received a cheque from Manoel for the exact amount required. Delirious with excitement, he threw a raincoat over his pyjamas and hurried to the kennel. He called the dog Punch in memory of his predecessor.

Although Felix loved dogs, Irina preferred cats.

Around this time a campaign of defamation began against Felix.

Towards the end of 1927 a relative of Irina claimed to have been warned by the Minister of the Interior that Felix would shortly be named in connection with a scandal concerning forged Hungarian banknotes. She told Felix to leave the country immediately, to avoid further scandal. Irina was immediately suspicious but, given the woman's sincerity, Felix felt obliged to comply.

He placed their affairs in the hands of his business manager Yakovlev and left for Spain armed with visas for himself and his valet. Suddenly he received desperate letters from Irina begging him to return. Yakovlev was constantly demanding that she sign authorisations and give him authority to sell their remaining jewels. Felix warned her not to listen to others and not to sign anything. He had received no reply from Yakovlev but had been told that Irfé was on the verge of bankruptcy. There was also a scandal brewing at the Monolix porcelain factory, whose deliberate sale of defective porcelain to a famous French establishment had caused outrage in the newspapers.

When Felix tried to return home he had to leave his luggage behind and be smuggled across the border because of an alleged problem with his passport. In Paris a thin, nervous Irina met him at the Gare du Nord accompanied by Prince Michael Gorchakov. They told him that Yakovlev had fled and Irina's relative had gone to America. Enquiries through friends at the Ministry of Interior confirmed that Felix's name had never been mentioned in connection with the Hungarian scandal.

Then in January 1928 the Russian newspaper *Dni* (Days), printed in Paris and owned by Alexander Kerensky, published allegations that Felix had been expelled from France after involvement in a financial and sexual scandal, having 'seduced the underage son of a French politician'. The father had allegedly caught his son and Felix *in flagrante delicto*, whereupon he beat both of them. The paper reported that the politician was reluctant to attract publicity by taking the matter to court, so Felix offered him hush money. The following day *Dni* alleged that Felix had fled to Switzerland after paying a large amount of money to keep the story quiet and that Irfé's employees were out of work because the business had closed in mysterious circumstances.[49] These stories resulted in the banks refusing Felix all credit.

The allegations were then published by newspapers abroad. Felix hired the renowned lawyer Maître de Moro-Giafferi to issue a denial in the Paris newspapers and sue for libel. He asked for damages of half a million francs, stating that this was the latest in 'an unremitting campaign of rumour and slander' which had been going on for the past eight years. He won the case but the judge ordered only a symbolic fine of one franc.[50]

Several London newspapers reported that Felix had been expelled from France and was going to Belgium, 'where he has business interests'. The story was published as far afield as Australia.[51] In London Felix engaged Mr Norman Birkett KC and sued the proprietors of *The Sunday Express*, *The Daily News* and *News of the World* for libel. The case came to the High Court of Justice in May 1928, where the King's Bench Division upheld Felix's claim. The defendants profusely apologised, giving the unlikely excuse that they had been misled by 'a confusion of names'. They indemnified his costs and paid damages, which Felix gave to Russian charities in France.[52]

'Poor Irina, who loves him very much, suffers from all these disgusting stories,' Grand Duchess Olga wrote, 'but he himself is delighted to be the one everyone is talking about right now, he loves popularity in all aspects, so since this story everyone in Paris has rushed to see their store Irfé...'[53]

At the insistence of Maître Moro-Giafferi, Felix sent a letter of protest to the Minister of the Interior – but the French government was not interested.

Who was responsible for all these stories, and why, is unknown.

ᦞ✷ᦟ

With Yakovlev's disappearance the couple's business affairs were entrusted to Arcadi Polounine. Despite his own parlous finances Felix continued to help the émigrés. He gave his cousin Zenaide an allowance of 5,000 francs a month and his mother helped several exiled families pay their rent.

With the date of the payment to redeem their pawned jewellery shortly falling due, the Youssoupovs were again saved by Mrs Vanderbilt. She wrote Felix a cheque to cover the losses on Irfé, whose apparent success had been affected by the defamation stories. However, they were still in serious financial trouble.

Mrs Whobee then suggested a way out. Although she could be an absolute tyrant, when the mood took her she was excessively generous. Once she sent Irina a bouquet of roses attached to a diamond brooch. She already owned an apartment and a country house. Now she suggested buying Irina and Felix's house and letting them live in the pavilion above the theatre.

The idea of having Mrs Whobee on their doorstep did not really appeal but Irina and Felix could see no alternative.

The offer was accepted.

13

Anastasia

'These false pretenders ought to be gathered up and sent to live together
in a house somewhere.'

Felix to Grand Duke Andrei[1]

In the mid-1920s rumours circulated among the émigré community that one of
the tsar's daughters had escaped from Ekaterinburg. The resulting investigations
divided Irina's family.

On 17 February 1920 an unidentified young woman was pulled from Berlin's
Landwehr Canal after attempting suicide. It was believed she was Russian but
she refused to answer questions or speak the language. Her body bore marks of
violence. 'Miss Unknown' was sent to an asylum, where in 1921 she told a nurse
that she was Grand Duchess Anastasia.

A recently discharged patient then claimed she recognised Tatiana among the
inmates. Baroness Sophie Buxhoeveden, who had been with the imperial family
in Tobolsk, visited and pronounced her too short for Tatiana, but the girl told
one of the émigrés that she was Anastasia.

For the next three years she was shuttled between the émigrés and various
hospitals, thin, anaemic and tubercular. Although she knew many intimate
details of court life the Romanovs greeted news of a survivor with great
scepticism. The enquiry conducted by Nicholas Sokolov had established that all
the tsar's family were dead.

Against the wishes of the dowager empress (who believed the family were in
hiding), Olga Alexandrovna visited her 'just to clear up the case once and for
all'.[2] Afterwards she wrote: 'It is a story so tangled that I cannot say exactly, but
I see no resemblance and could not get any word from her mouth to make me
believe that this may be her.'[3]

By the spring of 1927 the claimant, now calling herself Mme Tchaikovsky,
was staying with Romanov descendant Duke George of Leuchtenberg at Castle
Seeon in Bavaria. Locals said that Grand Duchess Xenia and Princess Irina
would visit. Instead, Felix arrived.

He went first to Berlin to see Harriet von Rathlef and Professor
Serge Rudnev, two of Mme Tchaikovsky's most ardent supporters, before

accompanying Rudnev to Seeon. Felix had not known Anastasia well. His meetings with the tsar's youngest daughter had been limited to a few occasions in the Crimea, his wedding and one or two of Olga Alexandrovna's gatherings.

Recounting the events to Pierre Gilliard, the imperial children's tutor, Felix said that according to Rudnev, her reaction to news of his arrival was excitement. "'Felix! Felix! What a joy to see him again! I will get dressed and come down immediately. Is Irina with him?" This joy at seeing me again seemed exaggerated,' Felix told him.[4] In fact Mme Tchaikovsky had been horrified and, remembering his role in Rasputin's murder, only agreed to meet him in the garden on condition she was not alone. Their conversation was 'banal and short'. Felix spoke to her in Russian. She answered in German, a language which he said the tsar's daughters did not know well. Questions in French or English, in which the grand duchesses were fluent, elicited no response. He told her about Irfé and asked if she would like some new dresses. After about thirty minutes he left.[5]

The woman later claimed that she had fled screaming as Felix tried to kill her, a statement that like other claims she made (including a meeting with Hitler) can be dismissed as pure fantasy.

'Nervous, hysterical, vulgar and common' was Felix's verdict. Like many others, he believed she was really the Polish-born Franziska Schanzkowska.[6]

'From the first impression, which was disastrous, I realized that I was dealing with a *comedienne* [actress] playing her role very badly,' he told Gilliard. 'Nothing in her was reminiscent, even from afar, of any of the young grand duchesses, neither her features, nor her appearance, nor her bearing. She was so far from that natural simplicity which is the gift of those to whom she belongs from birth and by atavism. So characteristic a trait in the family of our emperors.'[7]

Writing to Xenia's cousin Grand Duke Andrei Vladimirovich, Felix went further, calling her 'an adventuress, a sick hysteric and a frightful play actress ... If you had seen her, I am convinced that you would recoil in horror at the thought that this frightful creature could be a daughter of our tsar...'[8]

Gleb Botkin, son of the tsar's doctor who had been murdered with the family, met the young woman at Seeon and was convinced that she *was* Anastasia. Botkin said that as soon as Felix heard he had recognised the woman he 'hurried by aeroplane from Paris [to New York] to see me, and tried to induce me to ... go over to the camp of ... Grand Duchess Xenia. When he saw that his efforts were in vain, he invited me to an informal little party in his room promising me some very good wine.' Botkin declined, 'recalling Felix's playful habits with his guests' wine'.[9] In fact the meetings took place in Berlin and Felix's first aeroplane journey was not until 1934.

Felix was said to have written an introductory letter to the empress's sister Victoria, now Marchioness of Milford Haven, and asked Botkin to take it to London with his (Botkin's) documentary evidence in favour of the claimant. Although Botkin believed in her, Felix wrote to Victoria, 'I cannot understand how anyone can make such a mistake, since she is very common and has absolutely nothing to remind one of the grand duchess ... I feel such a situation should not be allowed to continue, and that something should be done about it.'[10]

These were the first salvos in a long war.

‍‍‍‍ **⊂ℜ✳℥⊃**

Irina's father was still determined on a divorce. 'He begs to be given back his freedom and threatens to obtain it through his own actions just as before,' Xenia told Irina in March 1928.[11]

Irina and Felix spent Easter at Roquebrune. Sandro, who was nearby at Carnolès, wanted a heart-to-heart talk with his daughter and asked her to come over.

In the spring Irina went to Copenhagen to see her grandmother. While she was away Felix went down with food poisoning. Count Foulques and Countess Zizi invited him to convalesce at the Chateau du Lac. He took with him Hélène Trofimoff and his valet Pedan, but was soon called away to meet a banker in Vienna who seemed willing to advance a large sum of money to support his businesses. After discussions, a contract was prepared for signature the following day, when Felix would receive the money. Overnight the banker called off the deal, having heard rumours about Felix which aroused his mistrust.

The following year an extraordinary story was published in the *Kingston Gleaner* in Jamaica, which appears to refer to events in 1928. Under the heading 'Poison Plot to Avenge Rasputin', the article printed a report from Paris dated 28 April which claimed that Felix and some of his friends had been poisoned. 'The Countess de Lareinty ... her husband, and a number of friends staying at the Countess de Lareinty's chateau near Sigean ... have been on various occasions seized with a mysterious illness...' The doctor diagnosed poisoning by belladonna.

The countess told police that when her husband and Felix were in Marseilles the prince suffered the same symptoms. Felix made light of the suggestion. 'Nevertheless,' the newspaper continued, 'the countess persists in her theory that the motive for the supposed poison plot is to revenge Rasputin's tragic death in 1916, and that she and her husband are among the intended victims because they are friends of Prince Youssoupoff [*sic*].'

A member of the count's household was arrested and declared he was under the domination of a man who made him swear to poison Foulques and Felix. 'He added that the man had given him poison, and had promised him 400 [francs] if he would put it into the count's coffee ... The prisoner has since retracted this statement and refuses to say any more. The police are meanwhile continuing their investigations.'[12]

Paris-Soir reported that a temporary employee had poisoned Felix at the instigation of Ilya Pedan, who had promised the man 50,000 francs. Yet, the paper asked, why would Count Foulques be poisoned if this was a revenge attack for Rasputin's murder? Moreover, the count's father stated that he always refused to receive Felix at the Chateau du Lac.

One of Felix's students from the Russian School in Paris told a reporter: 'The prince himself suffered the beginnings of poisoning ... last November, shortly after the lawsuit brought against him by the heirs of the monk

Rasputin, and some of our friends concluded that it was a criminal attempt ... Prince Youssoupov himself took care to deny this legend, and we heard him affirm to us, on various occasions, that he had only had a rather serious malaise after having eaten mussels, some of which no doubt were not of the first freshness.'[13]

Irina, questioned in Paris, corroborated this and said that until the return of the prince and his valet it would be impossible to add anything specific.[14]

This is just one of the curious stories that always seemed to follow Felix around.

෬ ✸ ෨

In May 1928 Felix picked up Tao Kerefoff and Hélène Trofimoff and arranged to meet Irina in Calvi. In Marseilles he bought some cheap furniture from an antique dealer, hired a guitarist and a pan-flute player whom he heard in the Old Port and put the whole lot into his car. In Nice they met up with Foulques and Zizi, and Michael and Nona Kalachnikoff and headed to Corsica.

In Calvi, Felix hired an open lorry to ferry his friends around. The sedate town had never seen anything like it, especially in the evenings when Felix's musicians played outside the cafés and the men danced with the fishermen on the quayside.

By the time Irina arrived in early June many of Felix's guests had left. A few days later Princess Zenaide telegraphed that Felix senior, who had recovered from a stroke in 1924, was failing fast. Felix left for Rome where he found his father in a serious condition.

Zenaide said that in the event of his death she wanted to rent a small apartment so that she could remain in Rome. Felix immediately saw a trap. He told Irina that if she received a telegram saying that Felix senior had died, she was *not* to come to Rome or they would not be able to return to Corsica. Potential problems with his mother may not have been Felix's only fear. It is possible that Irina still knew nothing about Zina Gregoriev. His wife's presence would be a complication he did not need.

By 9 June Felix's father was out of danger. Then two days later he died after another stroke.

A coded telegram informed Zina Gregoriev, who lived nearby, of his death. Felix now had to ensure that his mother and Zina did not meet during the funeral in the Cimitero acattolico, the Protestant cemetery in Rome.

Felix had given his father an undertaking that he would look after the needs of Zina and her children Tatiana and Olivier. For about two years Zina received transfers of money from Felix junior. Then the payments stopped. As his resources dried up Felix gradually forgot about his commitment.

Before leaving Rome, Felix visited Grand Duchess George. He was annoyed to hear that her daughters had recognised the false Anastasia, calling them both mad, acting as if under hypnosis.

෬ ✸ ෨

Felix was recalled to Paris by the ongoing lawsuit brought by Maria Rasputin (now Maria Soloviev). She was claiming 25 million francs in damages (some £12 million today) for the murder of her father in a premeditated plot.[15]

Felix again hired Maître de Moro-Giafferi and issued a statement. 'I admit I killed Rasputin,' he said. 'But it was a purely political act, motivated by the conscientious conviction that I was fulfilling my duty to my country, my sovereign and to the allied nations.' He added that he had possessed information, which was corroborated, that Rasputin 'had become the evil genius of Russia, an enemy of the imperial family and a tool in the hands of Germany'. Since then, he continued, 'everything I have learned has only strengthened my opinion'.[16]

'No one should have told the story,' Dmitri retorted. 'Even if it had good results those who accomplished it should have regarded it as a duty to keep the story of the drama a secret. Prince Yusupov [*sic*] was wrong in writing a book...'[17]

Irina was incandescent at Dmitri's comments but in the end it did not matter. The court decreed they had no jurisdiction over something which occurred in imperial Russia and refused to hear the case.

ରେ ✳ ଛେ

Felix joined Irina in Calvi. Ilya Pedan had been dismissed as steward and in his place came Gregory Stolaroff (Grisha), a young Russian from the Ukraine. When he heard of the couple's financial difficulties Grisha refused to accept any payment. In 1935 he married Denise Labanère, a girl from the Basque country, who came to work for them as a cook. Grisha and Denise became almost part of the family.

Felix returned to Rome where he found his mother in a bad state, her health worsened by defamatory accounts about him in the newspapers. Felix convinced her to come and live with them in Paris.

Irina was at Frogmore Cottage. When she returned to Paris her mother came with her. Then in September an anxious letter arrived from Denmark. The eighty-year-old dowager empress's health was deteriorating and Olga Alexandrovna asked them to come immediately. They set out at once for Hvidøre.

The dowager empress was delighted to see them and got out of bed. But by the following month her strength was failing and there was little anyone could do. Irina joined Felix in Calvi while Xenia remained at her mother's side. The empress slipped into a coma and died on 13 October without regaining consciousness.

This was a bitter blow to Irina, who had idolised her grandmother. She and Felix immediately made arrangements to travel to Denmark for the funeral but here they came up against a snag. Her mother's cousin King Christian X, who was married to Irina's cousin Alexandrine, refused to grant an entry permit to Felix because he had been involved in the murder of Rasputin. Irrespective of Felix's stated patriotic motives, the king did not wish to shake hands with a murderer. However, at the last moment he relented and allowed Felix to attend the funeral. The king's diary makes no mention of whether he shook his hand.[18]

The funeral on 19 October was attended by the largest gathering of Romanovs since the revolution.

It was the end of an era.

ᘓ ✱ ᘔ

Irina remained in Denmark while Felix visited the Berlin branch of Irfé. Here he received a shock.

The Soviet government was organising a sale of works of art at Galerie Lemké and among the items in the catalogue were several from the Youssoupovs' palaces. Felix alerted his mother. 'We must be very vigilant and attentive to the identification of objects belonging to us,' she commented, 'because otherwise our protests and our steps will not be taken seriously. What I am sure about and can perfectly certify on are the following items...,' and she attached a list.[19]

Felix hired Maître Vangemann to forbid the sale of their stolen property. The objects were then confiscated by the police, as under German law they would have to be returned to their rightful owners. The Soviet government argued that the items had been confiscated under a law of 19 November 1922. They won the case. It was yet another blow for the Youssoupovs.

Another problem was the sale of Empress Marie's jewels, which had been taken to Buckingham Palace. Hennells of Bond Street were asked to sell them discreetly but the market was flooded with Russian artefacts. Felix approached Cartier about one of the jewels, which the jeweller said could be sold 'at great profit' because it had belonged to Empress Marie. Irina told her father but, reporting this conversation to Xenia, Sandro could see only greed on the part of Felix and Cartier.[20]

ᘓ ✱ ᘔ

The gathering in Copenhagen for the dowager empress's funeral provided an opportunity for members of the family to issue a statement about the so-called Anastasia.

Based on the testimonies of the 'numerous witnesses' who had visited the young woman, it said that 'we declare our firm conviction that the woman named Mrs Tchaikovsky, who is now in the United States ... is not the Grand Duchess Anastasia Nicolaievna. The declaration was approved by Her Majesty the Empress Marie Feodorovna.' The signatories were Xenia and Olga; Marie and Dmitri; Sandro, Irina and all her brothers; and Empress Alexandra's brother Grand Duke Ernest Ludwig of Hesse and sisters Victoria Milford Haven and Princess Irene of Prussia.[21] Irina's cousins Princess Xenia Georgievna and Grand Duke Andrei Vladimirovich, who supported the woman, were not consulted.

The response was an ill-advised letter to Xenia from Gleb Botkin, accusing her of a 'conspiracy to defraud your own niece' and trying to gain possession of the tsar's fortune 'by fraudulent methods'.[22]

There were rumours that the tsar had a vast amount of money in a London bank but in fact there was only a small sum in Berlin. The tenth anniversary of Ekaterinburg had just passed and the imperial family could officially be declared dead. Part of Felix's motive for trying to discredit the young woman was alleged to be 'his interest in seeing that there were no challenges to Xenia as executrix of [tsar] Nicholas's estate or to her claims to any funds which might later be discovered'.[23]

Sandro accused Botkin of 'trying to claim money in England that was rightly his wife's'. Gleb was grateful to Sandro for admitting that there was 'money at stake'.[24]

By February 1929 Sandro was on a lecture tour of America. He told Irina that he knew nothing about the so-called Anastasia 'but Botkin can invent a story, it does not matter'.[25]

CR ✶ ஐ

The 1929 New York stock market crash engulfed the money Felix had invested there. With the main house in Paris sold to Mrs Whobee and all their lodgers gone, the theatre pavilion would be their new home. Princess Zenaide was also without money, so a room in the pavilion was arranged for her.

By the summer Irina was in Menthon-St. Bernard on Lac d'Annecy where she had a surprise. 'Completely unexpectedly I found myself in Olga Tchirikov's house, the most wonderful ancient house with twisted stone stairs,' she told her mother.[26] Olga Tchirikov had rented the house for the summer. Irina stayed there for about a month and they explored the area in a friend's car. 'We saw old churches, climbed down into the caves of hermits, or simply gazed at the incredible loveliness of the world,' Olga wrote rapturously.[27]

Irina and Felix were reunited in Corsica but Calvi had been invaded by tourists. The house in the Citadel soon became too small to accommodate their friends, and the bar and restaurant opened by Tao Kerefoff was noisy in the evenings. Felix and Irina moved out to the farm at Donateo.

They were recalled to Paris by news of Princess Zenaide's imminent arrival. She was accompanied by a nurse, her old maid Pélagie (who changed her name to the more elegant Pauline) and her Pomeranian dog. The pavilion met with her approval but she had not been prepared for the smallness of her room. A shed nearby had to be rented for her countless crates, trunks and suitcases.

Irina now had to accustom herself to having her mother-in-law nearby. Zenaide got on well with Mrs Whobee and her eccentric niece Valerie, who dressed as a man and smoked a pipe. Mrs Whobee told Valerie to choose some dresses from Irfé. It made little difference.

From America, Sandro sent news of Irina's brothers. Rostislav married Princess Alexandra Galitzine in Chicago in 1928. Vassili, who had also gone to America, was thinking of settling there. Sandro was especially proud of Dmitri, who was doing well.

CR ✶ ஐ

On 26 January 1930 the Russian émigrés were shaken by the kidnapping on a Paris street of the White General Alexander Kutepov. Soviet agents lured him into a car and he was never seen again. The émigrés began to panic. Paris was a known hotbed of anti-communism and Kutepov had frequented Irina and Felix's restaurant La Maisonette.

There is little doubt that the exiled Romanovs were under constant surveillance by the OGPU, who reported their daily activities to Moscow. Irina and Felix must have been very worried indeed. *Le Petit Gironde* reported that the British police had taken special security measures around Frogmore Cottage, where several suspect strangers had been seen.[28]

Then Felix became embroiled in another lawsuit. On 7 August an article appeared under his name in *The Detective*, attributing to Empress Alexandra political steps which were harmful to Russia and her allies. The article had neither been written, signed or inspired by Felix. He immediately wrote a letter of protest. The editor did not print it so he began legal action. After two summonses by the bailiff Felix's letter was published. The newspaper apologised for its late publication, stating that the article was obtained from *Opera-Mundi-Press* who guaranteed its authenticity. They, in turn, put responsibility onto the *Neues Wiener Tageblatt* in Vienna. Finally, a letter from the guilty Austrian journalist absolved Felix but this did not stop him being violently condemned by the monarchist journal *The Double-headed Eagle*. He won the resulting lawsuit for defamation.

ର ✳ ଛ

On 29 January 1931 the world was shocked to hear of Anna Pavlova's death. Felix, who had visited her frequently at Ivy House, felt her loss keenly, later claiming that 'the only women he ever loved were his wife and Pavlova'.[29]

The depression following the stock market crash was having its effect. Irina and Felix continued to help the émigrés but the money procured by Arcadi Polounine was running out and the situation became worse every day. Irfé's wealthy American clients disappeared and the Youssoupovs' remaining jewels were in the hands of moneylenders. The banks refused credit and they were forced to send Andrew Bull to ask Irfé's clients to pay on delivery, a situation unheard of in couture houses. So when the American tenants of the Villa Tatiana on Lac Leman made an offer to buy it Princess Zenaide accepted, although it was heavily mortgaged.

Catherine the Great's pearl necklace had been pawned and the time to redeem it was fast approaching. Felix waited all morning for Polounine to arrive with the money and was finally forced to pledge his car to redeem the necklace. Unable to cope with the couple's tangled finances amid worsening illness, Arcadi Polounine resigned.

Finally, they were forced to close all the Irfé shops. Felix had tried to save the business by merging it with Yteb but Slavic style was out of fashion, Russian émigrés were not as popular in France and both failing couture houses went bankrupt. The restaurants were sold and the Youssoupovs even lost the furniture and pictures taken from Boulogne to furnish La Maisonette.

Then Mrs Whobee gave them eight days to leave the pavilion. When Felix said they were moving to England she claimed a misunderstanding, saying she needed to put a bedroom and bathroom on the ground floor for them. They could move to a hotel while the work was done.

Irina spent part of the summer at Frogmore, where she heard about Vassili's wedding. Vassili had worked as a cabin boy and a shipyard worker before becoming a New York stockbroker. On 31 July 1931 he married the Hollywood film actress Princess Natalia Galitzine, a distant cousin of Rostislav's wife. Unable to afford a taxi, Natalia went to church in a delivery vehicle with a bathrobe covering the dirty seat. Vassili finally settled in California, making wine and running a chicken farm, which he said he enjoyed most.

Irina returned to Paris in time for thirty-year-old Dmitri's wedding to eighteen-year-old Countess Marina (Myra) Golenitschev-Koutouzov. They had become reacquainted that summer while Dmitri was managing the Chanel shop in Biarritz for which Myra was modelling. The wedding reception was held in the Youssoupovs' pavilion and the newlyweds settled in Paris. Afterwards Irina and Bébé returned to Frogmore while the building works began.

Felix continued the perfume business for a while. 'When I knew him in the 1930s he did not look quite the same,' Guy Burgess recalled. 'He was making scent, before he made £20,000 out of libel actions against Hollywood for its film of the assassination of which he gave me his account.'[30] How Felix met Burgess, an undergraduate and later one of the famous Cambridge spies, is an intriguing question, although they likely had some homosexual friends in common.

જ✷ஐ

Their financial situation was now dire, with Irina frequently wondering whether she had anything they could pawn. Into the breach stepped Sir Paul Dukes, the former SIS agent and member of the Bolshevik Liquidation Club.

Dukes had been sent to Russia after the Bolshevik revolution with a King's Messenger passport, ostensibly to see what relief Britain could bring but really to report back. On his return to London he was invited to join the Secret Intelligence Service. One of his missions had been to help liberate some of the art treasures confiscated by the Bolsheviks. His meeting with Felix, said to be by chance, was surely not coincidental. Was Felix hoping to free some of the Youssoupovs' paintings? Did John Scale (now retired) recommend Dukes to Felix knowing how much the SIS owed for his silence?[31]

On 12 June 1932, Felix wrote to his lawyer Sergei Korganoff: 'I ask you to officially consider Sir Paul Dukes as my business manager having all power in the sale of my precious jewels.'[32] Dukes was chairman of British Continental Press in London, so he travelled between London and Paris as scheme after scheme for raising funds or selling jewels failed. As well as transactions for the jewels, Dukes's diaries also chart the deteriorating relationship between Felix and his mother.

Things did not start well. In mid-July Dukes lamented that some diamond earrings and pendants had been taken to Switzerland, causing him to miss an opportunity to sell them. The earrings, turned down by the Maharani of Baroda as 'of inferior quality', were finally sold to a French lady.[33] Meanwhile, Mrs Whobee was threatening to evict Felix, who Prince Michael Gorchakov called 'amoral'.[34]

The jewels were taken to Geneva, where they hoped to sell them to Haile Selassie, the Emperor of Ethiopia. By the end of July all the proposals had fallen through and Princess Zenaide accused Felix of 'drunkenness and riotous living'.[35] Irina urged Felix to keep the seriousness of the situation from her.

To keep Mrs Whobee happy, Felix moved to the Hotel Vouillement without telling his mother. As more sale propositions failed he remained there hiding from his mother *and* Mrs Whobee. Then suddenly Mrs Whobee invited him to stay with her in the country for the weekend. Things seemed to be better but she again threatened eviction and Felix remained in the hotel.[36]

News then arrived of some prospective Egyptian clients. Another lady was interested but said the prices were high. During a meeting with Dukes she discovered the recent history of the jewels and offered a much lower price. The deal failed. 'Felix in despair. Mother furious,' Dukes recorded.[37]

The situation worsened. Felix remained at Hotel Vouillement while Zenaide thought he was with Mrs Whobee, a fiction Dukes maintained when he had lunch with the princess on 13 August.

Sandro had returned to Europe the previous autumn and published *Once a Grand Duke*. Shortly afterwards he fell seriously ill with a lung malady.

There was a real intimacy between Sandro and his only daughter. Worried about her father's condition, Irina joined him at the Tchirikovs' home, the Villa St Thérèse at Carnolés. Olga Tchirikov nursed Sandro devotedly and there was still a fondness between them. 'For months he lay there suffering,' she wrote. 'He wanted his bed moved so that he could look out of the window to the hills...'[38]

Then the Anastasia affair surfaced again.

ᴄꙗ ✱ ᴇᴏ

On 4 September 1932 the *News of the World* published an article under the heading 'Imposter Unmasked! "Princess" Confesses She Is a Fraud!' It claimed that Anastasia (now calling herself Anna Anderson) had confessed she was a Romanian actress who had been hypnotised into playing the part of the grand duchess by a former imperial manservant. The story was printed all over Europe. The *News of the World*, faced with legal action, discovered that the Paris lawyer acting for the Romanovs had given the information to the newspaper's Paris correspondent. This put the spotlight firmly on Xenia's cousin Grand Duke Cyril Vladimirovich.

He suggested to Felix that she might be persuaded to renounce her claim 'in return for a substantial settlement and a periodic allowance'. At a meeting with lawyers in Berlin in May 1933 Anna Anderson turned down the offer, stating that if she had a horsewhip she would happily use it on Cyril.[39]

The mystery is why Cyril wrote to Felix about this. Felix and Irina did not support Cyril's proclamation as emperor, although they *were* hostile to the woman's claim. If Cyril was hoping that Felix could put up the money for the settlement and provide the allowance, he was disappointed.

ᴄꙗ ✱ ᴇᴏ

Felix's relationship with his mother had deteriorated further. 'Youssoupovs worse than ever,' Paul Dukes recorded on 19 September. Zenaide had her trunks packed and was threatening to leave. She was in such a mood that Felix rarely visited and when she spoke to him it was only to say something rude or offensive. He was 'terrified of [his] mother', Dukes noted, 'and only wishes to see her in my company for protection'.[40]

On 20 September Felix received a letter stating that the 26th was the absolute final day for a particular payment. After desperate efforts to raise the funds failed, according to Dukes, Felix decided to pass 'his nephew Marcel' off as a rich Argentinian jeweller who was willing to advance the money on 1 October, adding to this a post-dated cheque for 13,000 francs. As a last resort Dukes agreed. They set off but then a worried Dukes pursued them in a taxi to stop the cheque.[41]

Felix decided it was impossible to live in the pavilion with Mrs Whobee on one side and his mother on the other. He remained in the hotel.

Arriving at the pavilion one day Felix found the bailiffs already there. The prince dealt with the situation in his own inimitable style, insisting they do things the Russian way. He put some gypsy music on the gramophone and poured the vodka. After a few drinks the bailiffs were performing Russian dances and left without seizing anything. They paid several more visits but none ever resulted in more than an inventory of the furniture.

Princess Zenaide was now 'violently opposed' to Felix's way of life. She threatened to move to Vouillement if he failed to find the money to pay another debt. Although Felix was 'deeply offended', the threat made an impression and three unsuccessful days of trying to raise funds followed.[42]

Irina was also having a bad time in Menton. Despite borrowing from her father, she had not been able to pay the Tchirikovs for a week and, as their financial position was similar to her own, felt this was unfair.

Felix's latest money-making venture was to become a 'sort of high-class tout, entertaining customers' at the Russian tea room of Princess Eristova. Felix then persuaded the princess to advance 15,000 francs on some pawn tickets for his jewels, with Dukes standing the other 3,000. Dukes obtained more money from other friends but kept it secret from Felix, 'who would certainly have wanted to keep part of [the] 15,000 for himself'.[43]

By November Felix had been at the Hotel Vouillement for four months without paying his bill, even though it was owned by relatives of some friends. The money lent by Dukes was eventually refunded by Princess Zenaide.[44]

Finally, a pair of large earrings and a five-row necklace were sold. 'Policy of desperation,' Dukes recorded. But when he expressed sadness at seeing the necklace go, Felix replied: 'I'm not – I'm damn glad.' He was sick of the whole business and had a huge row with his mother.[45]

As the saga of trying to sell more jewellery continued into 1933, the association with Dukes did not last. He walked out, allegedly after a few 'thoughtless words' from Princess Zenaide.[46]

Sergei Korganoff then took over the Youssoupovs' tangled affairs. He and his wife only had modest means but Korganoff did not hesitate to mortgage his property, while his wife did the same with her jewellery. Between 1932 and 1939 there are many references to receiving jewels on deposit, selling jewels to Korganoff, or pledging them to pawnbrokers.

ɔ✱ɕ

Grand Duchess Xenia arrived at Villa St Thérèse to find that Sandro's state of mind was terrible. The doctors told Irina to try to keep him interested in things around him but it proved impossible.

On 25 February 1933 Irina kept her father company while her mother was guest of honour at an evening function. At 3 a.m. on 26 February he suddenly complained of terrible pains. Irina summoned the doctor and sent for her mother but Xenia arrived too late. Sandro died at 3.45 a.m. The death certificate does not show the cause of death but it was undoubtedly cancer.

Irina was devastated. She immediately telegraphed Felix, who left for Carnolès with Andrei, Feodor and Dmitri.

Despite his last wishes, Sandro was given a religious funeral at the small Orthodox church nearby. On 1 March he was buried with military honours in the cemetery at Roquebrune-Cap-Martin in the presence of Xenia, Felix and Irina, four of Irina's brothers (Rostislav sent a telegram), King Christian X and Queen Alexandrine of Denmark, the Tchirikovs and the major-domo Karabassov.

○ ✦ ○

With the building work finished, Felix moved back into the pavilion but his mother refused to speak to him for two days. She did not understand why he had left her alone there, although she had a nurse, two maids and a cook.

Irina refused to return until she had reimbursed the Tchirikovs. She was still in Carnolès in June. With Sandro's affairs in considerable disarray Xenia was unable to help. 'If I had the money I would give it to you to pay your debts and the ticket,' she told Irina.[47] Felix was living in a continuous nightmare, still awaiting the arrival of the moneylender.

Irina returned to Paris in October. Princess Zenaide now needed constant care from two nurses. Irina and Felix therefore moved to a small flat at 19 rue de la Tourelle where they remained until the eve of the war. Bébé was a boarder at '*l'ecole de jeunes filles de la princesse Mestchersky*', a finishing school at Auteuil.

It is apparent that the Youssoupovs had brought out of Russia more than just a handful of jewels but Irina and Felix had now sold most of their treasures. These included a Buddha carved out of a ruby said to have been looted from the summer palace of the emperor of China near Peking, a statue of Jupiter ascribed to Cellini and the Blue Venus carved from a sapphire and mounted on a ruby base, but they were unable to settle their bills. Generous as always, Felix once gave the money set aside for this purpose to a needy refugee who knocked on the door.

A list of 'Bills to be Paid' dated 19 December 1932 lists forty-six items totalling 178,158.38 francs, including expenses for the properties at Calvi and tax payments for Irfé perfumes, as well as more mundane things like the butcher, the baker, the dentist and the garage.[48]

Felix went to Calvi, stayed at the Citadel and visited the farm. He would have to think about selling. A document notes 'the purchase contract for a dwelling house in the citadel in Calvi signed in 1932'[49] but this property was not sold at that time. The following year there was a lease on 'Donateo et Cordella Soprana situated in the territory of Calvi' which mentions a 'kitchen garden there belonging to the property given in renting to Prince Youssoupov...'[50]

In Paris the bailiffs were still a constant presence. Felix telegraphed to an unnamed recipient in London: 'I have received a share. I will bring you Thursday the rest received beginning of November.'[51]

Then just when it seemed that things had reached their lowest ebb help came from a most unlikely source.

Irina and Felix were saved by Rasputin.

14

Youssoupov *versus* MGM

'It is extraordinary to consider that this libel case was won by an admitted murderer who objected to the portrayal of the murder.'[1]

Around Christmas 1932 the Metro-Goldwyn-Mayer film *Rasputin and the Empress* opened at the Astor Theatre in New York. Purporting to tell the story of the murder of Rasputin, it was produced by Irving Thalberg and starred three huge Hollywood stars: Ethel, John and Lionel Barrymore.

Mercedes de Acosta was originally going to write the film's scenario. Some years earlier she had met Felix in Paris and heard the story of Rasputin's murder. Learning that Thalberg insisted on a scene in which Rasputin tries to seduce Irina, Mercedes asked Felix whether he 'objected to the inclusion of the use of any of the comments made to her several years earlier and more specifically, if he objected to the inclusion of the seduction scene'. Felix replied that she could write whatever she wanted about him and Rasputin but under no circumstances could Irina feature. He threatened to sue if Irina even appeared in the film.[2] When Mercedes informed Thalberg, he summarily fired her.

The film went ahead. In a key scene Rasputin (Lionel Barrymore) hypnotised and then violated the tsar's beautiful niece Natasha (Diana Wynyard), whose fiancé Prince Paul Chegodieff (John Barrymore) murdered Rasputin in his cellar in revenge. Ethel Barrymore was cast as Empress Alexandra. On set she was so autocratic that the crew called her 'the Empress of all the Rushes'.[3]

Although the picture bore little resemblance to the facts, a dramatic preface was shown on screen at the beginning. It said: 'This concerns the destruction of an empire, brought about by the mad ambition of one man. A few of the characters are still alive. The rest met death by violence.'

Critics gave the film a mixed reception but the *New York Times* reviewer remarked on 'the fight between Prince Chegodieff, as Prince Youssoupov is known here, and the Mad Monk'. The inference was clear. He believed that the character of Chegodieff was the real-life Prince Youssoupov – and everyone knew that Felix was married to the tsar's niece Princess Irina.

The events depicted in the film were relayed to Irina and Felix and when it was released in Paris they went to see it.

After all other attorneys had refused to take the case they were introduced to the New York lawyers Neufeld & Schlechter. They wrote to MGM on behalf of Felix, asserting libel because 'the incidents surrounding the historic drama and the manner and method of the killing of Rasputin were neither fair nor true'.[4] On 19 January 1933 MGM rejected the complaint.

In March Neufeld & Schlecter wrote on Irina's behalf, affirming that Princess Natasha was 'a thinly disguised impersonation' of their client and 'the whole world is appraised of the alleged desecration' of Princess Irina. They demanded that MGM withdraw the film immediately, issue an apology worldwide and recompense Irina for the incalculable damage to her reputation.[5]

It was also disrespectful to her family's memory. Two of Irina's maternal uncles, three paternal uncles, five cousins and several other relatives had been murdered by the Bolsheviks only fifteen years earlier. Many others had barely escaped with their lives. Irina was left deeply traumatised.

This was not the first time the Rasputin murder had been filmed. Having already turned down Hollywood's proposal to play himself in a silent feature, in 1932 Felix objected to the depiction of himself in the Alfred Trotz film *Rasputin*, in which the central character was played by Conrad Veidt. Felix's lawyer began negotiations but the prince reputedly later broke off discussions. The *Berliner Nachtausgabe* reported that Felix had asked that 'his person should be deleted from the Rasputin film at present being shown in Berlin, on the grounds that the representation does not correspond with the facts, and that, in any case, he objects to his name and person being used in a partly inaccurate rendering of history'. *The Times* reported on 29 February that the prince's solicitor said that he would not take legal action provided they pay him an indemnity of £2,500.

It was impossible to take Felix out of the film, which had already been released, and the case was dropped. In November it was shown in London with English subtitles.[6]

Thalberg's film, now retitled *Rasputin the Mad Monk*, opened in London in 1933. It was expected to be profitable, as England accounted for half of MGM's foreign revenue.[7] MGM refused to consider the Youssoupovs' claims and the American lawyers dropped out of the picture.

In the summer of 1933, Irina was in the south of France after her father's death. Olga Tchirikov had just completed her memoirs with the help of the ghostwriter Frank Scully, who was staying in the area. One of Scully's visitors was the American lawyer Fanny Holtzmann. Olga sent an urgent message to Scully asking Fanny to contact the Tchirikovs. They then put Fanny in touch with Irina.

Brooklyn-born Fanny Holtzmann was a diminutive brunette of about thirty with a very acute mind. She was a specialist in film and copyright law, with clients including Noel Coward and Fred Astaire. Irina told Fanny that, according to friends, the character of Natasha was clearly recognisable as herself. She had never met Rasputin and expressed outrage at the film's content and the defamation of her character. She was leaving details of the compensation to Felix, as in a press interview John Barrymore 'had imprudently announced that his portrayal was indeed that of Prince Felix Youssoupov'.[8]

Fanny met him at the Ritz in Paris. Over lunch (paid for by Fanny) Felix 'ate like a prince' and they discussed the matter in her broken French and his faulty

English.[9] He then suggested that Fanny meet his mother-in-law, whose English was excellent. At Frogmore Cottage Grand Duchess Xenia explained everything.

After trying to persuade MGM to settle out of court, Fanny and Felix attended a private screening at the MGM executive theatre in London.

Felix was convinced that the characters of Prince Paul and Princess Natasha were himself and Irina. Fanny was not so certain but she saw a possible cause for action in the dramatic preface, which contradicted MGM's claim that the story was fictional. Also, the only *principal* characters still alive were Irina and Felix. 'Furthermore, the sexual episodes in the picture were hardly ambiguous; if "Natasha" was indeed a thinly disguised Irina, then Irina had grounds for libel.'[10]

The film was still showing in London, so Fanny convinced Irina and Felix that they could take action in England. Meanwhile, legal papers were filed in New York seeking an injunction against any further public showing of the film.

The matter was complicated by the fact that Irina was a close relative of King George V. Having heard the story from Xenia and knowing Felix's reputation, the king decided it was imperative to avoid being involved in any possible scandal involving relatives of the British crown. He consulted the Lord Chamberlain, Lord Cromer, who referred Fanny to Sir Reginald Poole at Lewis & Lewis, King George's personal solicitors.

Poole, having seen the film, said that there was no case to answer in England, as 'the prospects wouldn't justify the risk of public scandal'. Perhaps Fanny might be more successful in America.[11]

Fanny made several more attempts to settle out of court but MGM refused to consider even a minimal settlement, maintaining that Princess Natasha was fictional and they were covered by clearances. To obtain damages Irina would have to go to court. Fanny decided to bring the case in London where she felt royalty would be treated more sympathetically.

As an American, Fanny could not conduct the case herself so she approached Sir Patrick Hastings KC, a distinguished barrister with 'charm, nerve and imagination' but whose fees were high. Jowitt charged MGM £2,625 (around £200,000 today) for his brief alone and Hastings' fee was believed to be higher.[12]

Hastings agreed that there was no case Felix could bring, as the circumstances surrounding Rasputin's murder in the film were so different to the account in his book, but he agreed that Irina had grounds to sue for libel. As solicitor, Fanny instructed Harold Brooks, a partner in the firm of J. D. Langton & Passmore. Henry St John Field, Irina's junior counsel, submitted the necessary documents to begin legal action.

In the meantime, MGM's English subsidiary began eliminating references or inferences in the film that might imply that Princess Natasha had been seduced by Rasputin. By doing so, they 'removed elements of the plot that made several subsequent scenes awkward and lacking in meaning'.[13]

Fanny now needed background material so Irina, Feodor and Dmitri took her on a round of visits to the Russian émigrés in Paris. Meanwhile, many Russians received a letter from Metro-Goldwyn-Mayer, who were obviously canvassing opinions.

The Youssoupovs now had to think about how to fund the case and they were obviously broke. Felix suggested Irina could apply to the League for the Defence of Women's Rights. Instead, Irina wrote to her cousin Lady Zia

Wernher. Born Countess Anastasia de Torby, she was a daughter of Grand Duke Michael Michaelovich (Miche-Miche), whom Felix had visited while he was at Oxford. In 1917 she married the extremely wealthy Sir Harold Wernher, 3rd Baronet, whose family had made their fortune through South African diamonds. Lady Zia and her husband 'turned down the suggestion' of helping Irina fund her lawsuit. Sir Harold was allegedly 'touchy when Zia received begging letters from impoverished Russian relatives'.[14]

Nevertheless, Irina was determined to go ahead. 'I have had enough of being silent,' she told Prince Lieven in March 1934. 'I had to sue. I don't want to suffer any more if my personality or even a semblance of me is dragged around the world. I was in London for a hearing at the end of October. I am going back for the same reason. It's boring, a lawsuit, but I prefer to go through this effort to try to end it all. I have hired a lawyer to handle the case. It's complicated with cinema. I have to sign a bunch of papers. I had to protest in several countries, in Italy in particular.'

Irina received Prince Lieven in 'a small mansion at Boulogne ... The dining room, half lit by the reddish light of a chandelier, is separated by a bay from the small living room ... The walls are covered with photos, the furniture of all styles clutters the two rooms in a semblance of disorder.'[15] Irina and Felix did not want the world to know how impoverished they really were.

ॐ ✱ ॐ

The first salvo came from MGM, who demanded security against costs. On 5 February 1934 it was reported that an order had been made by the Appeal Court that Princess Irina pay '£1,000 security for all costs from the issue of the writ up to and including the trial'. It is believed that this payment came 'discreetly from Buckingham Palace, which also paid for the initial costs of retaining the British counsel'. Felix said that Nikita introduced him to Baron d'Erlanger, who either gave or lent him the money.[16] However, a suspicion remains that Irina came to an arrangement whereby Fanny advanced the costs 'in return for a share of the proceeds of the judgement or any compromised settlements'. For her own fees Fanny was relying on 'follow-up judgements against the movie company in other parts of the world', where she was Irina and Felix's sole representative.[17]

Irina had to be in London fifteen days before the hearing, so after a brief stay at Frogmore she moved to the Ritz Hotel. On 24 February *The Times* reported Felix's arrival from Paris. To reach London in time and despite suffering from vertigo, Felix took his first ever aeroplane journey accompanied by Andrew Bull. It did nothing to dissuade him that he preferred trains and boats.

The action was for damages for libel alleged to have been contained in the film. Irina claimed that the picture depicted her as Princess Natasha, who 'had been seduced by and was the mistress of Rasputin'.[18]

The question was, how would the shy Irina fare under cross-examination in the witness box?

ॐ ✱ ॐ

The King's Bench Division was packed to overflowing as the first case alleging libel in a talking picture began on Tuesday, 27 February 1934. It was presided over by eighty-three-year-old Mr Justice Avory with a special jury of nine men and three women, comprising persons 'of the rank of esquire or higher degree, or merchants or bankers'. It was felt that people of a higher social standing would be more likely to understand the case.[19] Irina and Felix sat on the solicitors' bench. Nearby were the representatives of Metro-Goldwyn-Mayer, including their counsel Sir William Jowitt KC.

Sir Patrick Hastings KC opened the proceedings by giving a brief history of the events in imperial Russia and outlining the law of libel. The jury then adjourned to view the film. When the hearing resumed after lunch Sir Patrick called Irina to the witness stand. *The Times* described her as 'handsome' and 'hollow-eyed'. Having established that she was the late tsar's only niece and that she had never met Rasputin, Hastings asked, 'Who was the person who was popularly supposed to have been the cause of Rasputin's death?'

'It was my husband,' Irina replied.

'Who do you think is represented by Princess Natasha?'

'I think that it is myself.'

'Does Prince Chegodieff represent anyone to you in real life?'

'I think that he represents my husband.'

'Did any prince other than your husband own a palace called the Moika Palace?'

'No.'

Irina 'said that the film left no doubt in her mind regarding what was supposed to happen between Rasputin and Princess Natasha. There was still a good deal of mystery, she had found, among people with regard to what happened about that period of Russian history in which Rasputin died.'[20]

Hastings kept his examination to the minimum in order not to confuse the jury but there was a lot of discussion about who the characters in the film might represent and how many of them had met their death by violence.

Then it was the turn of Sir William Jowitt to conduct the cross-examination.

'Do you think that anybody who knew the real circumstances could suppose for one moment that you were portrayed by Natasha?'

'Yes. They might.'[21]

There were questions about the Youssoupov family, who Irina agreed were known to dislike Rasputin, and about Felix. In an attempt to prove that Prince Chegodieff was far more like Grand Duke Dmitri, Jowitt asked the princess if it would be fair to describe her husband as 'frail and effeminate'.

'He does not appear that way to me,' she replied, as the courtroom broke into laughter.[22]

Irina denied that she was bringing the libel suit to obtain money, revealing that 'she was bringing actions in Austria, Germany, France, Italy and the United States'.[23]

❦ ✶ ❦

The following day long queues waited outside the court hoping to be admitted to the public gallery. In the corridor outside Court No. 7 scuffles broke out among those eager to sit in the back of the court itself.

The cross-examination resumed. Irina agreed that when the film was shown in London nobody wrote to her about it. 'She understood that certain scenes had been cut out of the film, but the harm had been done.'

Sir William Jowitt continued: 'Have you also threatened proceedings against some 288 picture houses up and down the country?'

'Yes.'

'If it is a matter of money I can well understand it, but if your object is to remove a slur on your name the present proceedings would remove it?'

'Yes.'

'Then what is the object of your taking proceedings against more than 200 picture houses?'

'I want to stop the film.'

Jowitt suggested that Felix failed to kill Rasputin with the first shot, and that Purishkevich fired four shots, two of which hit him, as he was trying to escape.

'If he was dead before he was pushed into the ice, it was Purishkevich who finally killed him,' Irina replied.[24]

At this point Hastings objected. The testimony was hearsay and technically inadmissible.

After several hours Irina's ordeal ended and she left the witness box with relief.

Next was Eugene Sabline, a former diplomat who knew the imperial family well. He had no doubt that Prince Chegodieff was Felix and that Princess Natasha was Irina. Jowitt's cross-questioning failed to break him.

Then came the eagerly awaited Felix, whose command of English, despite his years at Oxford, was in no way comparable to his wife's. Wearing conventional English morning clothes, he first of all gave his now familiar account of Rasputin's killing, with one important difference. This time he swore on oath that he battered Rasputin with Maklakov's club while he was still alive. This was important as, in the film, Prince Chegodieff battered a still living Rasputin with a poker. By establishing that Felix had done the same, he was more closely identifying himself with Chegodieff and thus helping Irina's case.[25]

Felix testified that Rasputin was working to promote the interests of Germany and had planned to arrange the tsar's abdication so that the empress could act as regent for Tsarevich Alexei. Felix was convinced that Rasputin had to be killed 'for the good of Russia' and agreed that he was acting 'in the service of his country'.[26]

Hasting's questioning lasted little more than ten minutes.

In contrast, Jowitt's three-hour cross-examination was 'detailed, and … tedious' and, because of the language difficulty, Hastings interjected that they might have to call in an interpreter.[27]

As people still fought to get into the courtroom Felix sat with his head bowed throughout. 'No such detailed description of a murder has ever been given from a witness box,' wrote the *Daily Express*. As Jowitt went through Felix's book meticulously, gaining no more than assent from him, Mr Justice Avory intervened.

At one point Felix became so exasperated that he exclaimed, 'I am no professional murderer, even if I did kill Rasputin!'[28]

Felix agreed that the character of Natasha 'was to a certain extent a composite picture' of Anna Vyrubova and Munya Golovina, although it was true other royal princesses, whose names had been noted, were still alive. 'I suggest that no reasonable person, with any knowledge of the facts, could possibly think that the Natasha of the film was your wife?' Jowitt continued.

'I got just the opposite impression,' Felix replied.[29]

Jowitt was growing more and more angry with Fanny Holtzmann, concluding *she* had decided the Youssoupovs should bring the case to add to her own reputation. When Jowitt put it to Felix that Fanny Holtzmann had been exploiting his wife, the question was lost. Felix had no idea what he meant by exploitation.

Felix later told *The Daily Express* that the cross-examination was 'a great trial' and that, although the British justice system was the fairest in the world, it was 'torture' to relive the killing of Rasputin before a courtroom of non-Russians, many of whom attended out of mere curiosity.

More witnesses were called by the prosecution, including Sir John Hanbury-Williams (head of the British Military Mission in 1914), Admiral Sir Aubrey Smith (a naval attaché in St Petersburg) and several people who said they were interested in Russian history. All testified that they believed Prince Paul Chegodieff to be Felix and Princess Natasha to be Irina.

Next was Prince Nikita, who had difficulty in making his way into the crowded courtroom. His contribution was exceedingly brief and largely irrelevant. He took Princess Natasha to be Irina.

Sir William Jowitt then opened the defence before the hearing was adjourned.

ೞ ✦ ഔ

On the fourth day public interest increased, aided no doubt by headlines in the *Daily Express* such as 'Prince Gives Terrible Details of Rasputin's Murder' and 'Princess Says: "I Did Not Want Money!"'

Jowitt's first witness was Colonel Cudbert Thornhill, who had been in charge of the British Intelligence Mission in Petrograd, then worked at the British embassy. He had met the imperial family and in his opinion Prince Paul and Princess Natasha were entirely fictional.

Cross-examined by Hastings, Thornhill said that he went to see the film with Captain and Mrs Knowling (the former Meriel Buchanan, daughter of the British ambassador). Thornhill had no idea whether Mrs Knowling had been trying to help MGM, or whether she had taken many others to see the film. He admitted she had told him about the characters beforehand but said he would see the film before forming an opinion.

Then came George Tchapline, whose father had been the Russian postmaster general. He had never met Prince Felix and originally thought Prince Chegodieff was a fictional character based on Grand Duke Michael but later decided that he was completely fictional. He formed the same opinion about Princess Natasha.[30]

Commander Oliver Locker-Lampson MP had seen active service in Russia but only knew Prince and Princess Youssoupov by sight. He had seen the film with an open mind at a private showing and thought that if Chegodieff represented anybody it was Dmitri and that Natasha was Anna Vyrubova.

Under cross-examination, Locker-Lampson claimed that he had been invited by Purishkevich to murder Rasputin. He added that one of the reasons he did not think Natasha represented Princess Youssoupov was that the actress who played Natasha did not look like the princess. Hastings pointed out that the producers 'would have chosen an actress for her beauty or other reasons...'[31]

Mrs Meriel Knowling thought 'the character of Prince Chegodieff had a certain resemblance to Prince Youssoupoff [*sic*], but it might also be the Grand Duke Dmitri, and she thought it was a combination of the two. Natasha she regarded as a purely fictional character.' She could never have connected the character with Princess Youssoupov, for whom she had the greatest admiration. 'I know she could never be connected with Rasputin or do anything at all which would connect her with scandal of any sort.'[32]

Cross-examined by Hastings, Mrs Knowling denied asking people to give evidence on behalf of the defendants, saying she had only done some historical research for them.

The last witness was Mr Henry Wright from the solicitors Wright & Webb. He was chairman of MGM's English company and was instructing the defence. He maintained that 'the defendant company was closely associated with the American company which produced the film. After he heard from Princess Youssoupov's solicitors, certain cuts were made in the film to do everything possible to satisfy her.'[33]

Under cross-examination, Wright did not think it important that it should be demonstrated that the film's producers never intended to portray Prince and Princess Youssoupov. Nor had he brought anyone from America who could throw any light on the question of whether they deliberately intended to portray the Youssoupovs. He agreed that when the film was produced, some newspapers had already made the connection between Prince Chegodieff and Prince Youssoupov but they did not make any cuts or put anything in to say that the prince was not portrayed. He added that there was no witness present who could say whether during production of the film the American press had said that Prince Youssoupov was being cartooned and he had not asked the American company any questions about their intentions in this matter.

Although Mercedes de Acosta was back on the MGM payroll, 'she was not about to risk her job and career again for the Youssoupovs' and neither Thalberg nor Louis B. Mayer (co-founder of MGM) could have put forward a credible defence.[34]

With the defence concluded, the case was adjourned until Monday and it was arranged for the jury to view the film again.

ℂ✱ℬ

Monday morning brought even more crowds to the High Court to hear the final speeches and the judge's summing-up. Lady Diana Cooper, who had attended every day, was present as Irina sat between Felix and Harold Brooks 'pale, drawn and nervously toying with her lace handkerchief'.[35]

After counsel's speeches, Mr Justice Avory 'said that there was nothing in the case to which the established principles applicable to other libel actions could not be applied. The only question for the jury was whether the evidence had satisfied them that the film character of Natasha would be reasonably understood to represent Princess Youssoupov by persons who knew her ... If the film were a libel, it was a gross, insulting, and injurious libel, and it was difficult to estimate the consequences of a libel published in a film which had been exhibited not only in Great Britain but also in foreign countries.'[36]

The jury filed out. None of the spectators left the packed courtroom, afraid that they would not be readmitted. Irina sat 'white-faced, with clenched fists, staring hard at the floor'.[37]

The court was crowded to suffocation point when, after two hours' deliberation, the nine men and three women filed back in. They found for the princess, awarding damages of £25,000 plus costs – about £1.9 million today. The stunned silence was broken by a high-pitched voice at the back of the courtroom saying, 'Oh-o-o, what a lot of money.'[38]

Mr Justice Avory gave judgement for that amount. 'The defendants gave an undertaking not further to show the film as it was complained of in this action,' reported the *Portsmouth Evening News* on 5 March. '£25,000 Damages for Libelled Niece of Czar,' screamed the *Daily Mail's* headline on the same day. 'Reputation Injured in film *Rasputin, the Mad Monk*.'

The judge assigned costs (estimated at over £20,000) to MGM and ruled that £5,000 should be paid to the princess immediately, 'with the remainder payable after any appeals had been ruled upon'. He also granted an injunction against any further showing of the film in Great Britain and ordered that the sum of £1,000 paid by the princess as security for costs 'should be handed out to her solicitors on her behalf'.[39]

The court's decision stated: 'It is difficult to imagine a worse libel upon a woman than to say she has been seduced by a villain such as Rasputin.'[40]

Felix and Irina had to literally fight their way out of the court, where they were met by another crowd of people. They and their solicitor sought refuge in a consultation room where Irina sat talking to Russian friends, laughing and joking until the crowd cleared. 'Irina's pale cheeks were flushed with her triumph,' reported the *Sheffield Independent*. 'As she drank tea and smoked cigarette after cigarette in her long amber holder, she talked of the fairness of British justice, of the ordeal of the witness box, of offers of film contracts, and of her plans for the future.'

'I have had a great reception in this country. I have had the fairest trial of my case that I could ever expect,' Irina said. 'I am completely satisfied with the verdict.' She confirmed her immediate plans were to stay with her mother at Frogmore, adding that 'during the trial I was very worried at times and I did not have any thrills in the witness box'.[41]

The New York Times published another admission by the princess: 'I knew of the plan to kill Rasputin and of the part my husband was to take some time before the appointed day, and I did not see him for a fortnight after the deed had been accomplished.'[42] (This was not quite true. They were reunited about ten days after the murder.)

She and Felix then left quietly by a side corridor and drove to the offices of Langton & Passmore, from where Irina telephoned the good news to her mother.

૦૩ ✸ ૬૦

The Youssoupovs held a celebration party at Frascati's in Oxford Street, one of London's most prestigious restaurants. Among the guests were Nikita and Marie, Count Vladimir and Countess Merika Kleinmichel (a daughter of Countess Natalia von Carlow who had worked with them at Belgrave Square), Merika's brother-in-law Prince Vladimir Galitzine and Mr and Mrs Harold Brooks.[43]

On 10 March Irina and Felix returned triumphantly to Paris. In New York, Grand Duke Dmitri refused to give an interview about the case.

That was not the end of the affair. On 14 March it was reported that MGM had been granted a stay of execution by the Court of Appeal in respect of the damages to be paid. 'Conditions made by the Judge required that the £25,000 should be paid into Court, and £5,000 of that sum is to be paid to the princess forthwith.'[44] This meant the court would hold £20,000 of the damages.

CR ✶ ℰ

In Paris Irina and Felix found themselves besieged by creditors who were convinced that they now possessed millions. This of course was not true, as they had to await the result of the appeal.

Finally managing to escape, they spent part of the summer in the barge owned by Mrs Whobee's niece Valerie, moored at the Pont de Neuilly on the Seine, away from the hustle and bustle of the city.

They were still broke. Thomas M. Sutton Limited had agreed in May to 'wait settlement of the charges due' of £1,100 and £2,000. In July they agreed to 'hold the goods mentioned on contracts 8626 [a pair of pearl earrings at £1,100] and 9176 [goods unknown] for £2,000 until 31st day of August 1934'.[45]

Later that year Felix authorised Korganoff to release the earrings from Suttons but the items on contract 9176 remained with them for the time being.

On 9 July Irina received a telegram from Harold Brooks. 'Appeal Wednesday very urgent you come at once...'[46]

Irina stayed with the Kleinmichels at what the *Lincolnshire Echo* described as their 'pretentious villa' in Golders Green. Count Kleinmichel, who was in the banking sector, was a friend of Grand Duchess Xenia with whom Irina often stayed when visiting London.

The hearing at the Court of Appeal came before Lords Justices Scrutton, Greer and Slesser on 12 July and lasted for several days. Both Irina and Felix were in court, following the opening statements with keen interest from the solicitors' table. MGM appealed on the grounds that 'there was no defamation, that Mr Justice Avory misdirected the jury, and that the damages were excessive'. It was stated that the sum awarded would bring in an income of £750 a year (about £57,000 today) if invested in government securities.[47]

After several days' deliberation Lord Justice Scrutton gave judgement that there was no reason to interfere with the original verdict and, to Irina's relief, the appeal was dismissed. MGM were ordered to pay the costs, plus an additional £5,000 to the princess. 'You have had a second try and been beaten – is that clear?' he said, giving them three months to pay.[48]

MGM made noises about taking the case to the House of Lords but this never happened.

CR ✶ ℰ

MGM and its exhibitors were now wide open for further damages, as proceedings were to be initiated in America (where the repercussions were enormous), Germany, Austria, Italy and France. 'In every theatre that showed the film, if the projectionist had run it four times a day that meant four separate libels each bearing an established price tag of $125,000' (almost £2 million today). If the Youssoupovs sued everywhere, the cost would be astronomical. 'Overseas showings in the British Empire alone would be enough to put the parent company ... out of business.'[49]

On 10 August it was announced in Britain and America that litigation had ended. The following day it was reported 'that in lieu of further damages to the princess, the American company [MGM] has paid her £150,000 [over £11 million today] and that on her part the princess has ended all further action against that company in any part of the world'. That sum was later said to be 'very wide of the mark', the payment said to be 'only a fraction of this amount'.[50]

This was confirmed by Count Kleinmichel, who was interviewed in his 'picturesque dressing gown' by reporters on his doorstep and 'who thought that perhaps the sum quoted referred to U.S. dollars'. He added: 'Princess Youssoupov is on the whole looking very well. She has recovered excellently from the great strain which the trial undoubtedly imposed upon her and a rest now in the country will do her good. She is very glad it is all over.'[51]

However, before Irina had her rest there was a victory party at the Kinnerton Studios apartment at Hyde Park. Mingling with the Youssoupovs were Violet, Duchess of Rutland (mother of Lady Diana Cooper) and other aristocrats, as well as Hollywood stars including Gertrude Lawrence and Douglas Fairbanks junior.

Felix continued to be a regular guest at Fanny's parties, charming everyone with his stories of treasure stashed away in Russian palaces. At one party given by the Youssoupovs, Fanny introduced Irina to Prince Frederick (Fritz) of Prussia, grandson of the kaiser. According to the United Press, it was the first time since the 1914–18 war that a Romanov and a Hohenzollern had met.

❧ ✹ ☙

The exact sum paid to Irina by MGM was never disclosed, but it was said to be the biggest libel judgement in England since 1684.

According to Sir David Napley, 'MGM's books recorded that of $185,000 ... $125,000 [about £2 million today] went to the princess ... and $60,000 [£919,128] went to Fanny Holtzmann'. Another source stated that $750,000 (£12 million) was paid by MGM to Irina, with Fanny Holtzmann's share 'being correspondingly increased'. A further sum, estimated to be around $380,000 (just over £6 million today) was absorbed by MGM in costs. Fanny Holtzmann later said that the settlement was 'for a lot more' than MGM would admit.[52]

In March 1993 two authors asked for access to the MGM Studio archives to verify the figures quoted in the lawsuit. They were informed that the archives are 'permanently closed to researchers'. However, another author postulated that 'the company could have paid more than the books officially specified out of an unaudited contingency fund of around $1,000,000 that is regularly noted on its annual report'.[53] The *New York Times* stated that 'similar suits were filed in other countries, and the film company eventually settled them all for $750,000', plus the $125,000 awarded to Irina in England.[54]

Pressed to comment on the settlement, Fanny quoted a sum of $250,000 (about £4 million today) plus costs but declined to say how much the costs were. Told later that a Russian émigré had estimated a total figure of $900,000 (just over £14 million today), she remarked that 'he seems to know what he is talking about'.[55] In fact some of the jury held out for a higher settlement figure but changed their mind when they learned that lawsuits were pending in other countries.[56]

Irina told the press that she was putting the money in trust for Bébé and her future children, 'so that she and they shall never know the poverty I have endured'.[57]

Later that day she left for a fortnight's rest with her mother at Frogmore before they went to Calvi with Feodor.

୯ ✱ ୨

The case made legal history and still appears in textbooks today. As Sir David Napley pointed out, the judgement 'established that it was defamatory to assert of a woman that she had been raped'. In the narrower public morals of the 1930s, 'to have been raped was regarded as being only a rung or two above being born illegitimate'. The woman concerned was ruined for life. No mother would have wanted her son to marry someone who had been raped.[58]

Secondly, Sir David said, 'no film maker ever again took the risk of saying that some of the characters were still alive'. Since the Youssoupov case of 1934 every film, where appropriate, publishes a disclaimer on the screen to the effect that any similarity between the characters and living people is purely coincidental and not intended.[59]

Whatever the sums involved, the settlement from MGM saved Felix and Irina's finances in the short term. Although Felix wanted to invest the money, the princess carried out her wish to put part of it in trust, the deed of which provided 'for the transfer of ownership in the event of death of one of the two spouses, their daughter Princess Irina Youssoupov [Bébé] being appointed heiress and all liberty being left to her on the disposition of the capital from which she will inherit'. The trustees were Nikita, Count Vladimir Kleinmichel and Mr J. Passmore of Langton & Passmore.[60]

A further amount was used to pay Felix's debts, which were now serious. Typical of the letters Felix was receiving is one dated 2 November from Paul Piazza, a lawyer in Paris. 'I have received a note from Monsieur Selle [a former Paris notary] telling me to insist on you for the settlement of his interest since 16 July last, that is to say 1,000 francs. I beg you to do your best to pay at least a small deposit. I would be sorry if M. Selle had your property [in Corsica] sold by the court.'[61]

Something had to be done quickly.

On 5 December 1934 Irina asked Harold Brooks 'to account for any moneys due to me after the sum of £25,000 has been paid to the Settlement Trustee, to Maître Fabiani, as I wish him to have such moneys towards the payment of my husband's debts'. She understood that the final settlement figure should be available in January.[62]

Count Kleinmichel has asked me to write to you to inform you that there is a sum ... which could be paid to me and my co-trustees, shortly,' Brooks wrote to Maître Fabiani. 'From this sum there would be available about

5,000 dollars [about £80,000 today] for Prince Youssoupov and if you want to ask him his instructions so that I can send you this sum, I will be very happy to do so.

Moreover, there might be a little surplus available later for Princess Youssoupov, which she would like to transfer to her husband. All I can say is that there is this possibility and if there is a payment, it will be done by yourself. I will obtain permission from Princess Youssoupov to make this payment if the opportunity arises.[63]

On 8 January Irina asked Harold Brooks to transfer to Korganoff, 'for the payment of my husband's debts', any money remaining after the £25,000 had been paid. 'Should the sum remaining after payment to the Settlement Trustees be over £1,500 ... kindly send said sum of £1,500 to Mr S. Korganoff, and for the balance remaining after this ... please send it to Maître Fabiani, to whom special instructions are given on this subject...' She hoped for quick confirmation of this to enable Korganoff 'to come most rapidly to an agreement with my husband's creditors'.[64]

Irina finally agreed to pay £20,000 (just over £1.5 million today) to her trustees but in the end only £16,449 13s 2d was paid, with the princess pledging to pay the remaining £3,539 11s 10d as soon as the pearl La Pelegrina, was sold. This would bring the amount up to £20,000.[65] Putting the money in trust to limit Felix's access was a wise move and there are later references to him waiting for Irina to sign papers so that he could get money.

There was also a clause which stated that the trust was obliged, 'in case of emergency', to advance them £2,000 without any security.[66]

This would prove very useful in future.

15

Tangled Finances and Pawned Jewels

'Without money I cannot appear anywhere…'
Felix Youssoupov[1]

It has always been assumed that the Youssoupovs' finances were secure after Irina's successful court case against Metro-Goldwyn-Mayer. This was far from the truth.

With most of the money in trust, Felix's debts remained unpaid and the matter was pressing. On 11 January 1935 Sergei Korganoff sent an urgent telegram to London: 'Take all steps to have Brooks send the requested confirmation as soon as possible. Absolutely indispensable.'[2]

'Brooks absent. Receive letter next week. Our case commences Tuesday,'[3] Felix replied.

When Brooks contacted Irina he had 'not had the opportunity of settling the matter with my co-trustees, but I am considering the matter and will let you hear from me further in the near future'.[4]

A few days later Brooks told Korganoff that Maître J. de Morinni, the Paris representative of Langton & Passmore, 'has been instructed to … offer £1,500 in settlement of *all* Prince Youssoupov's outstanding debts. This is a final offer and if it is not accepted immediately, it will be withdrawn and nothing further can be done in the matter.'[5]

രെ ✶ ഌ

At the suggestion of the Russian-born Mrs Lythgaw Smith, the Youssoupovs opened a London cosmetic and perfume salon to sell Irfé fragrances. An announcement in *The Times* informed society that 'the Premises at 46, Dover Street for their IRFÉ Perfumes from Paris are now open'. There was a scent for blondes and another for brunettes, with prices ranging from £5 to £16 a bottle.[6] The *Dundee Courier* added, 'One of the perfumes available at this salon has so far been exclusive to the Princess [Irina].'

The Dover Street shop was decorated in Directoire style. Irina and Felix lived in one of the rooms, which was fitted out like a tent. Felix felt this would contribute to the success of the shop but at first it was unsuccessful. Felix 'had no idea how to manage money and it just went through his fingers'.[7]

He had been unable to sell the other jewellery deposited with Boucheron in London. He had received offers of 500,000 francs but Boucheron wanted nearly a million francs. Suttons had agreed to wait for the repayments and interest due under contract 9176 and Felix was still hoping for a successful sale. On 14 May he sent Korganoff a cheque for 20,000 francs but it was possibly as late as 1936 before he was able to repay the remainder of the amount owed plus interest.[8]

In May 1935 the Exhibition of Russian Art was held in Belgrave Square in aid of the old organisation of the Russian Red Cross Society. Among the items on show were Princess Zenaide's jewels. 'Here people are already talking about it in all the newspapers,' Felix told Korganoff. 'Such an opportunity only happens once in life...'[9]

Felix was asked to lend the pearl La Pelegrina, which according to Youssoupov family legend had belonged to Cleopatra. In 1579 it was acquired by Philip II of Spain before passing into the hands of Louis XIV in 1706. It remained part of the French crown jewels until their theft in 1792. It then appeared in Moscow and in 1826 was bought by Felix's grandmother Princess Tatiana Youssoupov.

The Youssoupovs were lucky to have it. Princess Zenaide had taken out some loans from a Paris pawnbroker who took La Pelegrina as security. In 1935 the pawnbroker demanded reimbursement, threatening to sell the pearl. To avoid this, Irina's trust reimbursed Zenaide's creditors almost £2,040, taking the pearl as security. Felix's creditors then blocked this pledge and placed a restraint on the pearl with Boucheron in Paris. The trust then advanced a further £1,500 to pay *them* off. These two advances carried interest of 6 per cent. With the pearl now safely back in their possession, Felix and Irina took it to London.

La Pelegrina was the cause of a lively discussion between Felix and the 2nd Duke of Abercorn who owned a pearl called La *Peregrina* which had belonged to the Habsburgs. Felix had called *his* pearl La Peregrina but according to Hans Nadelhoffer the Youssoupovs' pearl was La *Pelegrina*.[10]

To avoid further financial problems, Princess Zenaide sold La Pelegrina to Irina's trust in December 1935. This transfer of ownership was realized only *vis-à-vis* third parties, the trust considering itself a creditor. Somehow, ownership of the pearl remained with Princess Zenaide.[11]

os ✶ so

When Irina and Felix returned to Paris, Bébé announced that she wanted to marry Count Nikolai Cheremetev, whom she is said to have met when he was briefly working as a taxi driver in Paris.

Nikolai was the son of Count Dmitri Cheremetev (a childhood playmate of Grand Duchess Xenia) and Countess Irina Vorontzov-Dashkov, daughter of the former Minister of the Imperial Court. By the 1930s the Cheremetevs were well established in Rome. Nikolai already had connections with Bébé's family. His sister Prascovia married Prince Roman, son of Grand Duke Peter and Grand Duchess Militza. His cousin Marie Vorontzov-Dashkov was the wife of Nikita.

Felix thought Nikolai was more in love with Bébé than she was with him but he seemed pleased. The only cloud on the horizon was his health. Nikolai had tuberculosis, so the Youssoupovs withheld formal consent until he was cured. He went to Lausanne for treatment but Irina and Felix refused to allow Bébé to join him until they received more reassuring news.

There were other family problems. Feodor's marriage to Irene Paley had disintegrated. On 7 May 1934 she gave birth to a daughter, also called Irene, who was given the surname Romanoff because Feodor was still her husband, but some say he was not the father.

Ten years earlier Princess Irene and her widowed mother Princess Olga Paley had leased a house and opened a school for young Russian girls. When the building became too small, in 1928 Count Hubert de Monbrison offered his chateau at Quincy to the school. After her mother's death in 1929 Irene and Hubert began an affair. Feodor had taken all this passively. According to his son Michael, Feodor was raised in luxury in the Crimea and remained an adolescent who never had a job in his life. His taste for alcohol caused the failure of the marriage.[12]

In the wake of these problems Irina, Felix and several friends spent the rest of the summer at Choisy near Compiègne with Mrs Whobee, who had rented a villa for them near to her own. She then decided to build a house for Irina and Felix next to her villa and asked her architect to draw up the plans.

CR ✦ ဢ

Monetary troubles continued to pursue the Youssoupovs. On 14 August Felix sent Korganoff 25,000 francs and asked for a statement of his assets and a note of what remained at the pawnbrokers. Later that month he sent Korganoff an urgent telegram from Brussels: 'Money tomorrow Bank of Brussels your name.'[13]

That autumn Irina and Felix toured Cornwall with Andrei. In the village of Paul near Penzance they stopped for lunch at the King's Arms and decided to stay the night. Mrs White, the licensee, obviously knew who Irina and Felix were from the newspaper coverage of the libel case. She told a local paper that they made several long-distance telephone calls to London and Paris, and also to Frogmore Cottage. To do this they had to telephone Windsor Castle direct and be put through from there. 'I had the pleasure of doing this for them one night,' she told a reporter proudly.[14]

From Cornwall Felix wrote to Korganoff asking how the money from his last payment had been distributed. He had met an American interested in helping with his business. 'Even a little money could help us,' Felix continued.[15]

Then the bailiffs reared their heads again.

In December 1935 Felix received a demand for payment of 7,500 francs for rent due on 1 October 1934, the date of expiry of the lease he had signed on the property in Calvi in 1928. Failure to comply immediately would mean 'the seizure of all furniture and movable objects and after the thirty-day period expires by the actual seizure of his premises'.[16]

There was also trouble with Maison Guiliardi, owned by Felix, and Maison Guibega, owned by Tao Kerefoff, who had opened Chez Tao, Corsica's first nightclub, in the cellar. In February 1936 the lawyer Paul Piazza informed Felix that Maître Selle 'no longer wanted to wait for the repayment of his loan as well as the interest due for two years. I managed after many explanations to make him agree to wait until the end of March, but he told me there would be no more respite afterwards, "I will sell the property in Calvi". I wanted to inform you about it so that this time you can arrange how you can finally get rid of this nightmare in the course of the next month.' A scribbled note on the letter indicates that the amount owing was 3,000 francs.[17]

Felix promised to pay by 1 March 1937.

The affair dragged on.

ભ ✶ ૭

In January 1936 King George V died. Irina attended his funeral in St George's Chapel, Windsor, with her mother, Andrei, Feodor and Nikita.

His death had a direct impact on Irina's mother. Xenia had been King George's favourite cousin but his son Edward VIII had no such family feeling. He informed Xenia that he wanted to keep Frogmore as a private sanctuary for the family and offered her Wilderness House at Hampton Court Palace. There was no choice.

That summer consequently saw the last reunion of all Irina's family at Frogmore Cottage. Despite her mother's sadness at leaving Frogmore, Irina was delighted to see all her brothers together again. Feodor was present without Irene. They divorced in July that year and she told him not to visit their house in Neuilly or see Michael.[18]

Felix was waiting to receive money from the sale of one of his mother's necklaces. In the meantime, he needed Vladimir Kleinmichel to advance £15 for a few days and pay for the car, which otherwise would be taken away.

Princess Zenaide was refusing to eat or get out of bed. The doctors could do nothing and Felix returned to rue Gutenberg to stay with her. Things came to a head one evening when he refused to go to dinner with Mrs Whobee, saying he had to remain with his mother. Some years earlier Mrs Whobee said she wanted to leave Bébé one of her Paris houses. Now she was so angry that she cut Bébé out of her will and turned Irina and Felix out of the pavilion in rue Gutenberg. She died soon afterwards without seeing them again.

ભ ✶ ૭

'Would you agree to sell pearl at 17,000 pounds sterling, estimate very good price, urgent response,'[19] Boucheron telegraphed from London in October 1936. Irina's trust deposited La Pelegrina with Boucheron in November. They confirmed that it was 'certainly very rare and one could say unique'. They estimated it should fetch several million francs.[20]

The following month King Edward VIII abdicated to marry the 'loathsome' Mrs Simpson, as Xenia called her.[21] He was succeeded by his brother the Duke of York and his wife, who reigned as King George VI and Queen Elizabeth. Although Irina and her mother knew them well, this did not change the position regarding Frogmore Cottage and in January 1937 Irina returned to help with the move. She was anxious about the amount of time she and Felix spent apart but he seemed reluctant for her to join him.

Felix found the constant search for money exhausting. His mother's nurses proved expensive and he was worried that at any moment they could lose the rue de Tourelle apartment. Their lease ended on 8 April but he managed to arrange a six-month extension.

Irina was worried about the illegal sale of La Pelegrina to the trust. She would be in trouble if it was discovered, as she had signed the letter. She dreamed of living at Choisy with Felix and Mickey the dog but this was now in doubt.

☙ ★ ❧

From 1937 to 1967 Sergei Korganoff acted as the Youssoupovs' lawyer and trusted businessman, handling all their finances.

In January 1937 Irina told him that Felix's debt of £1,000 would be paid as soon as the sale of La Pelegrina was concluded. The following month she sent a similar letter to a Mr G. Kammerer regarding Felix's debt of £500.[22]

Felix then told Korganoff that the pearl ('belonging to my wife Princess Irina of Russia') was currently deposited for sale at Boucheron, authorising him to sell it for $100,000 (£1.5 million today). Korganoff would receive 10 per cent commission.[23]

At this point a note arrived from Paul Piazza reminding Felix of his promise to pay Monsieur Selle by 1 March.[24] The deadline came and went with no sign of the money. Piazza wrote again. Selle had telephoned, saying 'that this time he was going to act energetically and that he was going to sell the properties in Calvi'. Piazza was sorry to have to tell Felix this but, he added, 'now I have lost all authority towards Monsieur Selle and I deplore the consequences that will follow'.[25] Something had to be done.

At Irina's request, Harold Brooks sent her a copy of the Trust Settlement document.[26]

After a trustees' meeting, Langton & Passmore informed Irina that 'in certain circumstances, we are permitted under the Settlement by a Clause ... to advance you £2,000, and the Trustees will consider this advance if arrangement can be made for a charge to be taken in favour of the Trustees on the present monies you will be advanced on the Pelegrina'.[27] Irina went to London for a meeting.

If Princess Zenaide signed the papers, they could have £2,000 now and would be able to obtain more after the sale of La Pelegrina. Zenaide's lawyer was against her signing, but if she did not do so they would not receive the money.

Zenaide became very ill in the summer and needed more medical care. Prince Gabriel's wife Antonia was president of Sylvabella, a retirement home for Russian émigrés. She suggested an unfurnished apartment at Sèvres. Zenaide was moved there but could not accustom herself to her new home.

In June the trust advanced £2,000 to Princess Zenaide, without interest, but they demanded custody of La Pelegrina as a guarantee. When the pearl was sold this amount would have to be repaid, plus 'costs and expenses incurred regarding the Pelegrina pearl'.[28]

As Irina and Felix stated in an undated memo: 'It follows therefore from this ... that, in advancing us the sum of £5,500, the difference remains to the Trust, namely £3,500.'[29]

☙ ★ ❧

In the middle of all this, Felix received an urgent letter saying that if they did not pay Monsieur Selle 70,000 francs by 15 June they would lose all their property in Corsica. Felix wanted Irina to pay 10,000 francs immediately, so that it would be easier to persuade Selle to wait for the balance. The only reply was a telegram saying Feodor would be arriving. Felix could not believe that the trustees would not send a further £95 to save Irina's property. It was money she had every right to receive.

On 7 July another urgent letter arrived. Monsieur Selle was going to seize the properties, 'which will be put on sale very soon', Piazza informed him. 'I wrote at once to Monsieur Selle ... but if you do not pay at once 20,000 francs, I do not think that he will stop the proceedings.' Piazza insisted Felix must do everything possible to obtain this money. 'You know that the princess has also signed the mortgage. It is absolutely necessary and within 48 hours that you stop the prosecution otherwise all will be sold for nothing in Calvi and you will assist at the consecration of your ruin. Is that what you want?'[30]

In August Piazza told Irina that 'it is necessary that we send to Monsieur Selle a sum of ten thousand francs, otherwise there is nothing more to do. So tell the prince, I beg you, to send me this sum. I will write to Monsieur Selle to make him pause for breath.'[31]

A way out had to be found. In September 1937 Piazza approached Crédit Foncier to see if they would take over the debt from Monsieur Selle, so 'that would make it possible to refund him'. Documents were enclosed for Felix and Irina to sign immediately, 'because a Crédit Foncier inspector leaves for Corsica at the end of the month and the application must be filed before he leaves'. If this scheme proved successful Felix would be completely released from his debt.[32]

It seemed a solution was in sight.

In February 1938 Paul Piazza obtained copies of the purchase acts of Maison Guiliardi and Maison Guibega. 'These acts accompanied by the notary's letter must suffice to the Consortium which must advance you the sums to be refunded to Monsieur Selle. I am still waiting for him to receive the sums paid and the mortgage bond deeds. As soon as I have them, I will send them to you.'[33]

The farm was also sold. On 6 November 1938 a handwritten letter from Mimi, a former employee, congratulated Felix on the sale and said she had been hired by the new owner, Mme de Buisseret, at 400 francs a month. Mimi also enquired what was happening to the house in the upper town (the Citadel). 'I would be happy to help you,' she added.[34]

There must have been a delay, because records in Corsica show the property at Donateo was sold to Michel de Buisseret, a former guest at Maison Giuliardi, on 26 May 1939 for 17,000 francs.[35]

In December 1937 Princess Zenaide authorised Maître de Morinni to sell La Pelegrina, whose 'sale price should not be fixed below 17,000 pounds sterling'.[36] This should be the *minimum* price, she said, as the price in reality is 20,000 pounds sterling. A few weeks later Maître de Morinni deposited a sealed wooden box with Barclays Bank, Paris on behalf of Count Kleinmichel, as representative of Irina's trust.[37] Inside was La Pelegrina.

On 28 April 1938 the bank asked Count Kleinmichel to remove La Pelegrina from their custody before 9 May. He therefore approached Baring Brothers, the trustees of Grand Duchess Xenia. At the end of May La

Pelegrina was transferred to the Westminster Foreign Bank in Paris 'in the name of Baring Brothers, directors of this bank, and with whom our Trust was in business'.[38]

And there it remained.

☙ ✸ ☞

Bébé had developed a difficult attitude but in 1938 they had to consider her marriage. Nikolai Cheremetev was now completely cured and working in an insurance office in Rome, so there was no reason for Felix and Irina to oppose their union. Nikolai told a reporter that his only problem was 'to find a two-room flat' in Rome for them to live in.[39]

Nikolai's aunt was Queen Elena of Italy and his parents lived in Rome, so it made sense to hold the ceremony there. It was arranged for June 1938.

Grand Duchess Xenia arrived a few days before the wedding, certain that it would be impossible to find a better husband for her granddaughter. He was 'honest, exemplary, kind and Russian to his fingertips,' she assured Irina.[40] It seems that Bébé's parents still needed convincing.

The couple married in a civil ceremony on 14 June, followed by a religious ceremony at the tiny Russian Church of St Nicholas in via Palestro at 5 p.m. on 19 June. 'The lavish days of the Russian court will be recalled tomorrow,' gushed United Press International the day before, in expectation.

Well, not quite.

'The little church was improvised out of the ground floor of an ordinary dwelling-house,' wrote the Hobart *Mercury*. 'The small group of guests represented some of the greatest names in Russian imperial history, but there were no gay dresses, no court ceremonial.' The French press made much of the fact that the bridegroom was a descendant of Peter the Great and that Grand Duchess Xenia, sister of the murdered tsar, was present.

Thirty-three-year-old Count Nikolai, wearing a blue serge suit, waited with his parents on the steps for his twenty-three-year-old bride. Bébé, who was described in one newspaper as an unemployed typist, wore a white satin dress 'with a garland of orange blossoms grown in the gardens of the Italian royal household'.[41]

The hour-long service was conducted by the Archimandrite and attended by Grand Duchess Militza (sister of Queen Elena) and her son Prince Roman, Princess Marie of Greece (the former Grand Duchess George, who in 1922 had married Admiral Pericles Ioannides), along with around three hundred members of the exiled Russian nobility. 'The presence of people with names once famous in Russia, and the deep voices of the male choir, brought back memories of the Imperial Russian court,' Reuters reported. White lilies adorned the altar and there was a wreath with the former tsarist colours.[42]

Afterwards, in a borrowed car, the newlyweds left on their honeymoon at 'what used to be a Russian monastery at Bari, on the Adriatic'.[43]

There were two notable absentees. Nowhere in all the accounts in the French press is there mention of Prince and Princess Youssoupov being present.[44]

Felix had consented to the wedding but perhaps he was not satisfied with his daughter's choice after all. Maybe he was afraid that the tuberculosis would return or affect their children, 'and for this reason, or for some other reason, the bride's parents did not come to their daughter's wedding'.[45]

CR ✶ SO

At the dawn of 1939 Irina was at Wilderness House, where her mother and Elsa were both unwell. The nun Mother Martha was nursing them. Anyone who wanted to see the grand duchess now had to get past Mother Martha, who effectively became the 'gate keeper'.[46] Irina's absence meant she and Felix were apart for their silver wedding anniversary on 9/22 February.

Felix had met a very wealthy lady who wanted to acquire a house in Paris. He was looking for a suitable property, hoping to earn some commission. A letter from the Parisian Office of Real Estate and Insurance Operations set out the terms, which 'will be the same for all business that we could present to this customer and that would be agreed by him'.[47]

The deal seems to have fallen through, as at the end of March Felix took out a second mortgage for 25,000 francs on Maison Guiliardi with Monsieur E. Benoiton. He made it a condition that 'on signature of the mortgage, I receive a letter from Mme the Princess Youssoupov with her personal guarantee based on the Trust in London which disposes of her assets'. If the whole sum, plus interest, was not fully repaid, Benoiton would have the right to reclaim the difference from Irina's Trust. The 25,000-franc loan was made up of 13,000 francs for Felix's personal debt, 'and for the 12,000 francs difference, I will sell you for this sum a ring with a brilliant ... valued by us at 12,000 francs and accepted by you for this sum'. Benoiton added, 'It is understood that the amount of the first mortgage will not exceed the sum of fifty-five thousand francs.'[48]

The Youssoupovs were now renting an eighteenth-century country house at 7 rue Victor Hugo in Sarcelles, about 10 miles north of Paris. While they were in the course of moving, Bébé arrived.

Unknown to Irina and Felix, when Bébé left it would be eight long years before they would see their daughter again.

CR ✶ SO

The time at Sarcelles was among the happiest of their long exile. For the first time they were alone. Felix worked in the garden and lived the life of a countryman, working with Grisha and Denise to grow fruit and vegetables for barter. Irina painted icons, sketched and became a non-stop talker, only pausing to chain-smoke. Thinking themselves free from the comings and goings at Boulogne, they revelled in their new life. However, friends soon discovered their address and the Sunday gatherings, complete with lively singing and dancing, resumed.

Irina became an aunt again when Rostislav and Alexandra had a son, also Rostislav, in Chicago in November 1938 and the following June news came from England that Elsa had been pronounced clear of cancer.

Their carefree existence was disturbed by news from the east, where Adolf Hitler's ambitions for the expansion of Germany had become more apparent. Felix and Irina, who had lived through the First World War and the Russian revolution, could only sit, wait and worry.

On Bastille Day 1939 French and English troops marched along the Champs-Élysées in a show of defiance. The following month Hitler and Stalin signed a Nazi–Soviet non-aggression pact. This caused consternation among the White Russian émigrés, many of whom regarded supporting Hitler as a way to end communism in Russia.

MI5's interest in White Russian activities also intensified, as they sought signs of Nazi collaboration. There was also interest from the INO, the Foreign Intelligence Section of the OGPU (later the NKVD, the Soviet secret police in Moscow), headed by Mikhail Trilisser.[49]

Germany invaded Poland on 1 September and general mobilisation was ordered in France. Stations in Paris seethed with soldiers, while civilians rushed to shops and restaurants as the last days of peace ticked away.

On 3 September 1939 Britain and France declared war on Germany.

16

War and Occupation

'Titi and Felix are doing, and living, not badly in Paris.'
Prince Nikita to Grand Duchess Xenia, 1941[1]

When war broke out Irina's family was scattered. Her mother, Feodor, Andrei and Elsa were at Wilderness House. Feodor's ex-wife Irene and their son Michael were in France. Bébé and Nikolai were in Rome where later they were joined by Nikita, Marie and their sons Nikita and Alexander. Rostislav and Vassili were in America, while Dmitri was a lieutenant-commander in the Royal Navy.

Irina and Felix remained in Sarcelles. As it was on the route taken by the French army Felix offered their house as a billet. The available rooms were converted into officers' dormitories and the Youssoupovs spent evenings with them in the kitchen. On the evening before their departure the men brought champagne to drink with their hosts.

Princess Zenaide needed an operation for acute sinusitis, for which Felix had to pay £30. 'In view of all the sums expended by you over all these years.' Count Kleinmichel told Felix, 'I thought that now, when you are in need, someone would arrange for the doctors to do it practically free, considering what your mother and yourself have done for people in the past.'[2]

Felix had no such luck. Their immediate debts were roughly £600,[3] so they thought of taking £2,000 (about £140,000 today) out of Irina's trust. This proved more complex than they anticipated. It would have to go to court.

Harold Brooks died in 1937 and was succeeded as Irina's trustee by Sidney J. Passmore of Langton & Passmore. Count Kleinmichel therefore forwarded their request to him. Passmore replied that Princess Zenaide's illness and the consequent expense 'should be made the chief reason for you wanting some of the money released from the Trust – ordinary debts and the possibility of what might happen in the future, would not ... be valid reasons'. Irina's allowance had been exceeded due to Princess Zenaide's health problems and there were other debts as well. 'The Court will not even consider the matter unless full information is forthcoming as to how the present situation has arisen,' Passmore added ominously. 'As soon as the information comes to hand we will at once submit the proposals to Counsel for his Opinion.'[4]

One of the debts referred to Irina's tax demands for 1933–37. Her appeal was rejected. 'I have the honour to inform you that, ruling on the contentious point of view on the complaint that you have addressed to me,' wrote an official grandly, 'I have by a decision of 10 October 1939 dismissed said complaint.'[5]

Then on 24 November Princess Zenaide died, with Felix holding her hand.[6] It merited only a couple of lines in the French press. She was buried in the Russian cemetery at St Geneviève-des-Bois. Her death aged seventy-eight removed Felix's lifelong supporter and severely complicated matters.

Count Kleinmichel asked them to 'seriously consider' the wisdom of asking for £2,000 from the trust. Princess Zenaide's illness was 'the only motive which might have influenced the courts to a certain extent,' he pointed out. 'Now this reason does not exist. The fact that you might owe some money in respect of the treatment, operation and funeral could only result in the Court permitting a sum to be released for payment of these debts, but of course they would have to be satisfied that the amounts are owing.' The couple would probably only receive a few hundred pounds and would have to pay around £100 to get counsel's opinion.[7]

Irina and Felix also thought Grand Duchess Xenia could live in a house they proposed to rent in the Pyrenees when they obtained the money. 'This will not work at all,' Count Kleinmichel pointed out, 'as you would have to prove that the grand duchess is dependent on you Irina, which is not the case … She has her own Trust which would also have to be disclosed and it would be of no use bringing this excuse.' Last year, he reminded them, they received income of £537 from the trust. The court would 'look at it from an abstract point of view and would say that such an income (about £10 per week) is sufficient to maintain a family.' This year was expected to be better 'owing to the improvement [of investments] in America'. He also warned that with Princess Zenaide's death, the question of La Pelegrina would have to be revealed and would likely cause them 'endless trouble'. He thought their best course of action would be to 'go to the Pyrenees or some other remote spot, take a maid with you and live quietly in an hotel on your £6 per week [about £236 today] for the time being'.[8]

Felix was worried about his mother's debts. The retirement home wanted 20,000 francs and he wanted to repay the friends who had lent them money. His latest idea was to sell the trust to a bank in Paris. Count Kleinmichel was bewildered. 'I simply don't understand what exactly you mean,' he replied. 'According to the laws here [in England] you have no power to dispose of this Trust or even to mortgage the income you get from it; this is a thing which is absolutely contrary to any British laws, whatever they are in France … What sort of Bank would make an offer to you to that effect I cannot even imagine.' He asked for a list of people to whom money was owing so that he could make some suggestions.[9]

As if out of spite, that winter was particularly severe. Sarcelles had no proper heating and Denise and Irina tried to conjure up a decent meal out of practically nothing.

They remained there for Christmas. Friends brought provisions to celebrate the new year, they heard Midnight Mass on the radio and sat silently, thinking of Christmases in Russia. Suddenly the Christmas tree caught fire but they were so lost in thought that it was a while before anyone moved to douse it.

CR ✶ ℘

France settled into the 'phoney war'. As 1940 dawned theatres and restaurants remained open and those who had fled flocked back to Paris. There seemed little cause for alarm.

On 4 January Felix asked Count Kleinmichel to try and obtain funds without going to court. Kleinmichel found a particular point which, if it proved possible, would give them a smaller sum. He also passed on news of Irina's family. 'Elsa is very bad indeed, but this is nothing new. I had a card from Aleka [Rostislav's wife] yesterday with a charming photograph of little Rostislav. She may have sent you one. The Nikitas do not write at all. Well, anyhow, it is hard for them, it was their own choice.'[10] Nikita and Marie were having a difficult time in Rome.

Irina and Felix anxiously awaited news. 'I am still convinced that it would be to your advantage if possible to take less money without going to court hoping to get more,' Kleinmichel told Irina. 'If my plan works I will make you a proposal by which some of your debts could be liquidated soon, if it does not then there is no other way but to go to court, which will take a long time...' He hated the fact that it was Irina's money that was being spent on counsel's opinion and 'it hurts me because all these years I am doing everything I can myself in order to save you expense, but others will not'.[11] He was fighting various regulations. 'You cannot imagine all the difficulties that exist now ... I hope we shall meet one day and perhaps have a good laugh (at the moment it looks more like a good weep).'[12]

Sending Irina 'the usual £6' on 2 February, Count Kleinmichel passed on some worrying news. 'I am sorry to say the grand duchess is not well. I saw her last Sunday and she has her pains again. As usual she looks very weak and vague. She is not as bad as she was last year, but, of course, with her constitution, one gets terribly alarmed whenever she is unwell.'[13]

The following week Count Kleinmichel reported that he should be able to get about £500 without going to court. 'With the sum I mention above and the tax refund you get in the spring I am sure you could manage,' he added. The situation was complicated because a power of attorney had to be prepared for Nikita to sign, 'as without it we would not be able to sell anything'. At the bottom he added reassuringly: 'The grand duchess is looking better.'[14]

To their relief, Irina and Felix learnt that it would be possible to obtain £550.[15] This would mean selling 'one or two small investments but this is much quicker than going to court and waiting indefinitely', according to Kleinmichel, who added: 'I have sent Nikita a Power of Attorney to sign ... I hope he will lose no time, but of course the postal service to Italy is greatly delayed. I have asked him to borrow some money for the Consular fees.' He estimated that after April Irina's monthly remittance could be increased to £8 and 'if you don't contract any new debts, you could live in France on 1400 francs a week. This is for you to decide.' The only other way would be by selling La Pelegrina, paying the trustees the amount borrowed and then 'any amount realised ... over and above the sum of £3,539.11s.10d could go to you'. He suggested that Felix speak to Boucheron 'now that circumstances are altered'.[16]

Going to court would not bring a swift conclusion and they had to decide. 'When I know your decision we shall have to think in what manner the money can be transferred to you – this is by no means simple,' Kleinmichel warned.[17]

Felix and Irina accepted Count Kleinmichel's plan. Irina signed a letter of instructions, the bank applied for the necessary permits and securities were sold.

Kleinmichel still had to find the best way of sending the money, 'which of course you will appreciate is a little complicated during the present emergency'.[18]

At the end of March came more news from Hampton Court. '[I] have seen the grand duchess last Sunday, she says that she is not feeling well and is often giddy,' Count Kleinmichel reported, 'but I must say that she looks better. Elsa – no change, it is impossible to see her [*sic*] for anyone except Andrusha and the children for a short time. It is a nightmare!'[19]

When the money arrived, among the many payments made was £160 to Sergei Korganoff. The balance of the debt amounting to £107 18s 8d was paid in May after the princess's tax affairs were finalised.[20]

∝ ✳ ℘

On 9 April 1940 Hitler invaded Denmark. By the following month Luxemburg, the Netherlands and Belgium had been overrun and in June Norway fell. The Germans rolled towards the English Channel and the British forces were evacuated from Dunkirk.

France was defeated on 10 May and panic seized Paris. As the Germans advanced, four million men, women and children fled south.

In Sarcelles the telephone was cut and the sight of refugees from nearby Luzarches caused alarm. The shops closed and the town emptied. Taking Irina's cat, the Youssoupovs used their remaining petrol to return to Paris and stay with friends. Seeing a friend running a canteen for refugees, they immediately offered to help.

The government left on 8 June and three days later Germany declared Paris an open city. On 10 June, Italy (who had entered the war on the Axis side) declared war on France and Britain. France signed an armistice with Germany on 22 June and with Italy a few days later. As the Wehrmacht took over, the swastika replaced the banned tricolour and Hitler's troops goose-stepped down the Champs-Élysées. France's war was over.

France was divided into the occupied zone and the *zone libre*. General de Gaulle fled to London and began plans for a Free French movement.

In August strict food rationing began. For those without access to the black market the only options were 'hunger and queues'.[21]

Constantin de Grunwald summed up the situation: 'For weeks until the gasoline was exhausted, I saw parading on the road in front of my windows, an interminable cortège: refugee cars fleeing the bombed region of the Loire and Allier; some debris from a large army in retreat; generals surrounded by motorcyclists...'[22]

With no guarantee that they would not be arrested or forcibly repatriated to the Soviet Union, Felix and Irina had real cause to worry. The Germans could also use them for propaganda purposes. Irina's very name would provide a big draw to émigrés and could be used to persuade them to collaborate with the occupying forces. Unwilling to take the risk, Felix and Irina returned to Sarcelles.

∝ ✳ ℘

The occupation brought other problems. Britain's Defence of the Realm Act prohibited money being sent from England to occupied countries. With no means of communication with Irina's brothers in America, the Youssoupovs were unable to obtain funds.

Felix's thoughts returned to the perfume business. On 7 August 1940 he received a letter from Monsieur F. Kataleff concerning the perfume formula that had been created by the Youssoupovs and marketed by the firm of Molinard in Grasse. On 13 November, Molinard outlined their agreement to establish the formula and sell it in the occupied zone through their wholesale company La Spar. The two fragrances would cost 140 and 200 francs respectively and La Spar would pay a royalty of '20% or 30 and 40 francs per bottle sold'.[23]

Meanwhile they were visited by German officers, who respectfully offered Felix food and fuel. He declined their generosity, certain that they would want something in return. He soon discovered the reason for their concern.

La Pelegrina was still in a safe deposit box in the Westminster Foreign Bank. The German *Devisenschutzkommando* (Foreign Exchange Protection Commando), or DSK, demanded to see the contents of *all* safety deposit boxes in the Paris vaults. Everything was then listed and transferred to accounts controlled by the occupying authorities. There was now the distinct possibility that La Pelegrina would be taken by the Germans. Having saved it from the Bolsheviks, Felix had no intention of letting the Nazis confiscate it.

He needed a letter from the trustees to confirm 'that the pearl is my property, that is to say the property of a Russian citizen (since I inherited it from my mother), that it is in the hands of a Trust established for the safeguarding of the capital belonging to the Princess Irina Alexandrovna of Russia, as secured by a loan of 5,500 pounds sterling plus interest. Would you also say that the Trust will not give up the pearl for repayment of the loan during the present war.' He added: 'I hope to be able to sell the pearl and to release it from you, in which case I propose to deposit the total sum in pounds sterling in a foreign bank under the names of the three Trustees. Finally, I need a letter from Baring Brothers instructing the Westminster Bank to give me the pearl against a receipt from the [Westminster] Foreign Bank certifying that the sum in question had been paid to them.' Both letters should be authenticated by the American Consulate in London.[24] America had not yet entered the war.

The bank manager then told Felix that the Germans wanted to see the contents of the box, although they knew very well what it contained. At the bank he was met by two German officers who, when the box was opened, said they would return the pearl if Felix agreed to work as the Germans' society agent. He could live in one of the best houses in Paris, be provided with unlimited money and they could resume their former lifestyle. In return, Felix would entertain guests sent by the Germans, for which he would be provided with the best food and wine.

To his credit Felix refused. He had been living in France for many years, the people had made him and his wife welcome and he would not betray them. The Germans accepted his decision. Outside the bank, one of them congratulated Felix on his courageous stand but La Pelegrina was sequestered for the duration of the war.

Sometimes when they went to lunch with Mrs Whobee's niece Valerie they found Germans there. Several times the Youssoupovs received invitations from the Germans and they were accepted with reservation. They felt it was wise to do so in order to keep the trust of the occupying power. Also, it enabled them to vouch for friends who were threatened with arrest or deportation.

Life at Sarcelles was fine during the summer. They grew vegetables in the garden and were able to survive. In November they returned to Paris, taking a small furnished apartment in rue Agar in the 7th arrondissement. It was one of the few properties with heating, giving them the luxury of a warm bath twice a week. Friends soon took advantage of this in exchange for provisions, which they all shared.

After a few months the Youssoupovs moved on.

ରୟ ★ ℬ

Although communications with England were broken, they could now correspond with Bébé and Nikita. They heard that Grand Duchess Xenia was safe after a bomb landed near Wilderness House on 29 October 1940 but that Elsa lost her long battle with cancer the same day. Xenia moved to Craig Gowan, a house at Balmoral lent to her by King George VI. Only later did Irina and Felix learn that Feodor was in a sanatorium near Aberdeen suffering from tuberculosis. They also learned of the death of their former butler Andrew Bull. Early in 1941 Nikita passed on news of them to Grand Duchess Xenia, assuring his mother that 'Titi and Felix are quite well'.[25]

By February the Youssoupovs were living in an immense empty attic in rue de la Fontaine. Felix's Parisian antiquarian friends deposited their most beautiful furniture there so it would be safe from the Nazi investigations. 'Titi and Felix are alright in Paris,' Prince Nikita assured his mother, also sending her an urgent request for money. Xenia complied and also sent money for Irina. 'She will be so thankful for the sum you give her from G,' Nikita told the grand duchess.[26]

In Paris food prices rose sharply and the black market was in full swing. The Youssoupovs often ate in small restaurants where the menu was sufficient and the price affordable. Old friends invited them to lunch and Felix was sometimes persuaded to play his guitar.

Then on 22 June 1941 Hitler invaded Russia.

ରୟ ★ ℬ

Hitler's launch of Operation Barbarossa divided the émigrés. Some were appalled at the idea of Germans on their native soil, while others saw collaboration with the Nazis as an opportunity to put an end to Stalin's regime. Many joined the Germans as combatants or interpreters. In France stateless Russians could be arrested and repatriated. Irina and Felix tried to keep a low profile.

Felix was asked by an acquaintance to receive Hitler's envoy, who wanted to convey a message regarding the political future of Russia. He agreed to a meeting on neutral ground, where he was told that Hitler intended to free Russia from Bolshevism and restore the monarchy, hinting that Felix would be the best candidate for the restored throne. Felix refused to be drawn, instead offering to provide details of surviving members of the Romanov family living in Paris. He made his excuses and left.

Then on 7 December 1941 the Japanese bombed Pearl Harbour and America entered the war.

ରୟ ★ ℬ

In 1942 the Youssoupovs learned they had become grandparents when on 1 March Bébé gave birth in Rome to a daughter whom she named Xenia (known as Punka). Nikita and the baby's aunt Prascovia (Roman's wife) were the godparents.[27] Irina authorised Bébé to have the money that she was unable to receive from England. 'Bébé and little Xenia need this money,' Nikita told the grand duchess. 'Nikolai's salary not being enough.'[28] They had still not seen a photograph of their granddaughter. 'Unhappily I cannot send any to Mama and Papa,' Bébé lamented.[29]

By November Bébé and her daughter were back in Rome with Nikita's family. 'They came to spend some days with Nikolai, who is going to R[ussia] soon,' Nikita told Grand Duchess Xenia. 'I do envy him, but can't help it as they won't have me.'[30] Nikolai went to Russia in October 1942 as a liaison officer and interpreter.

Bébe had very little news of her parents. 'I only know that they are well,' she told her grandmother, 'and live in the country. Mama draws and Papa I think sells pictures and other things. Anyhow thank God they do not live too badly.' She enclosed some photos of little Punka. When she was born, Bébé said, 'she looked exactly like Mama but now she looks more like Nikolai's family'.[31]

Much of this news filtered through gradually to Felix and Irina, although whether Felix heard that his former friend Grand Duke Dmitri Pavlovich had died on 5 March at a Swiss sanatorium is unknown.

Accounts of Dmitri's death vary.[32] He had been treated for tuberculosis and it is said that he organized a grand, Russian-themed party to celebrate his imminent departure from Schatzalp Sanatorium. The following morning he was found dead in his bathroom. His ex-wife Audrey was notified of his death via telephone by a man who identified himself to her as a German officer. Some family members insist that he succumbed to tuberculosis in the end. 'Most certainly Dmitri Pavlovich died of tuberculosis and any suggestion to the contrary must be ignored,' said Prince Nicholas Romanoff. Others think he was murdered.[33] Whatever the truth, Princess Marina, Duchess of Kent summed it up in a letter to Grand Duchess Xenia: 'What a tragic end.'[34]

◌ ✴ ◌

With La Pelegrina sequestered by the Germans, Felix and Irina tried to get it released.

On 19 March 1942 Edward Peacock, director of Baring Brothers & Co. Ltd, wrote to Westminster Foreign Bank in Paris confirming that La Pelegrina was the 'exclusive property' of Felix and Irina, that it was in safe custody for account of Irina's trustees and that the bank was holding it 'in a fiduciary capacity for the beneficial owners'. Then came the crux of the matter. 'We hereby authorise you to deliver the box said to contain this pearl to Prince Felix Youssoupoff and Princess Irina Youssoupoff [*sic*], whose receipt shall be a full discharge for you. We give these instructions at the request and with the approval of the clients for whose account we hold the box.'[35]

An undated memo was typed, of which Felix retained a copy, giving the history of La Pelegrina, the money lent against it and its transfer to Paris. 'Currently the pearl is in the bank, under sequester by order of the German authorities,' the memo continued. 'We, the owners of this pearl, ask the German authorities to remove the sequestrum to give us the opportunity to take possession of this pearl which currently represents the only asset we have in Paris.' They attached correspondence with the Trust and the affirmations of Maître de Morinni, the Paris representative of Langton & Passmore.[36]

Nothing happened.

☙ ✦ ❧

Irina and Felix decided to leave rue de la Fontaine before the end of their lease. The proprietor asked if they could free the property so that it could be rented again by 1 October if necessary and Felix confirmed that this would be done.[37]

They found an old stable on rue Pierre-Guérin in Auteuil, which had been transformed into a dwelling. The landlady, an old friend, also ceded a group of small adjacent houses to them (some of which no longer exist). The dwelling was surrounded by trees and had a paved courtyard. The place was without any comfort but Felix employed Russian workmen to extend it and make the place habitable. In the meantime, they returned to Sarcelles.

Irina and Felix also had fears for their property in Corsica. In November 1942 Mussolini's Italian fascist troops occupied the island, which came under the control of the German army in response to the Allied invasion of North Africa. There was no longer a 'Free Zone' in France.

In July 1943 Felix had papers drawn up for the sale of Maison Guiliardi for the sum of 300,000 francs. The document, dated by Felix 15 July 1943, does not give the name of the purchaser.[38] A document notes 'the purchase contract for a dwelling house in the citadel in Calvi signed in 1932' and the 'typed promise of sale' for this house in June 1943.[39]

In September Italy surrendered to the Allies and on 13 October declared war on Germany. The Italians in Corsica were joined by German troops, who faced fierce opposition from the Resistance. The island was liberated in October, becoming an Allied air base. The Germans now began to occupy Italy.

Isolated in Sarcelles, Irina and Felix worried that the Russians would arrive in Paris.

The house at rue Pierre-Guérin was still unfinished in December when Felix was diagnosed with trouble in his leg. The surgeon in Paris said he would be immobilised for several months. Luckily Irina proved an excellent nurse. There was no heating in the new house. Smoke from the old stove almost asphyxiated them and the windows had to be left open, day and night. The roof needed repairing and when it rained they slept under an umbrella. If Felix was alone the concierge, Louise, cooked for him and every day the American art expert Rudolph Holzapfel-Ward read to him in English to relieve the boredom.

Food was scarce and the few cars around ran on wood gas. Nevertheless they celebrated Christmas and new year with gaiety.

By March Felix was up and about and the work at rue Pierre-Guérin was almost finished. From the entrance hall, 'decorated with icons, porcelain and prints of Imperial Russia',[40] a door on the left led to an office, a small kitchen and a summer dining room. The winter dining room and living room were on the right. The dining room contained drawings that Felix had done in Calvi and a glass case containing some funny little woollen dolls made by Irina. Felix's drawings of monsters decorated the walls of the living room.

A steep staircase led to the upper floor. Their large sunny bedroom, originally the hayloft, was painted aquamarine. Portraits and engravings lined the walls, including a photograph of Felix in the boyar's costume at the 1912 costume ball. A small shed outside served as a garage. Close by was a narrow house occupied by Grisha and Denise.[41]

Food became harder to obtain, so Grisha and Denise cycled out to Sarcelles with a trailer to bring back provisions from the abandoned vegetable garden. As the situation became desperate, women were accosted in the Paris streets and their furs, jewels, shoes and even clothes seized. People were afraid to open their doors, as false police arrived at apartments and then burgled them. General Rommel and his staff installed themselves opposite the Youssoupovs' home and rue Pierre-Guérin was soon full of German soldiers.

Rome was liberated on 3 June and three days later the Allies landed on the Normandy beaches. The Germans now retreated on both fronts and, harassed by the Resistance, began the arrest and execution of hostages. As the Allied advance continued, the air raid sirens wailed almost continuously. In Paris everyone held their breath. The whole of 24 August was spent waiting for the Allies to arrive.

The following day the German commander surrendered and General de Gaulle, who had won the struggle for leadership of France, made a triumphant entry into Paris, followed three days later by the American army. Although the war in Europe continued, as did strict rationing, Paris was liberated.

On 13 September the new British ambassador Duff Cooper and his wife Lady Diana arrived at the Hotel Berkeley, where Felix soon visited them. It had been requisitioned (while the embassy was refurbished) by their comptroller Freddie Fane, who was none other than Frederick Navarre Fane, Grand Duchess Xenia's former lover. Fane was also secretary of the Travellers' Club,[42] a regular haunt of Felix's, so it is quite possible that Felix ran into him.

Irina's brother Dmitri arrived on a mission for the Admiralty. He had taken part in the evacuation of Dunkirk and accompanied the armament convoys from Britain to Murmansk. He finished the war as military attaché to the Royal Hellenic and Royal Yugoslav navies stationed in British waters. Dmitri told Irina that Andrei had remarried in 1942. His new wife was Nadine McDougall, a member of the wealthy McDougall flour family, whom he had first met before the war. Feodor had suffered a relapse the previous September and was in a sanatorium near Aberdeen. The grand duchess was reasonably well but worried about her large family.

There now seemed no further obstacle to obtaining the release of La Pelegrina from the bank. On 7 September Felix and Irina asked the manager 'to fix the day when we could go to the bank to take back the pearl ... We find it necessary to inform you that our pearl has been in your coffers for too long and that it is high time to put it back in the air as soon as possible.'[43]

The bank replied on 11 September. 'We wish to have the agreement of our General Management for the operation that you envisage and we think to be able to contact him within a few days.'[44] Felix had to wait until the end of 1945 before the pearl was released.

The winter of 1944/45 was another bad one. There were no cars, buses or taxis and the metro stopped running at midnight. Felix and Irina began to socialise at dinners given by Rudolph Holzapfel-Ward, Louise de Vilmorin or

Lady Diana Cooper. Friends opened restaurants in their own homes and when the Youssoupovs missed the last metro Grisha put a board on the trailer and came to meet them with this improvised vehicle.

ca ✱ so

By January 1945 Bébé and two-year-old Punka were at the Hotel Beau-Rivage in Lausanne. They had endured a terrible journey from Italy through bombing and machine gun fire, then spent three weeks in a refugee camp sleeping on the floor without sheets. Bébé spent her days peeling potatoes.

Nikolai suffered an even worse experience. He had worked as a Russian speaker for Italian state radio and was rounded up with Russians who had worked for the wrong side. They were locked into a cattle truck to be taken back to the Soviet Union for almost certain execution. As the unguarded truck rolled on its way through Germany the men prised up the floorboards and, one by one, dropped through onto the tracks and escaped. Nikolai found shelter with a German princely family who had known his parents.

Irina was now able to write to her daughter. 'I got a letter from Mama, that [sic] is well,' Bébé told her grandmother, 'but I wonder why she writes nothing about Papa. I am worried.' Bébé needed money. 'Do you think there is a possibility of getting some money from the Trust?' she continued. 'Shall I write to Mama about it? I do not even know how they are living because Mama did not write anything about it.'[45]

Friends also suffered. Mrs Whobee's niece Valerie, who had entertained the Youssoupovs alongside German officers, later made grave errors and paid with her life. Serge Lifar, Director of the Paris Opéra Ballet, was denounced as a collaborator for continuing to work at the Opéra, though he maintained he had kept it open to stop it being seized by the Germans.

Foulques de Lareinty also paid dearly. In 1930 he had been adopted by Prince Michael Kotchuobey[46] but was then hit badly by the global financial crisis. In 1937 (now a prince) he divorced Zizi and sold his property piece by piece. By 1941 he retained only the two pavilions of the Chateau du Lac. Some Germans lived in the chateau and Foulques reported information gained from them to British Intelligence in Narbonne. Yet if Germany won the war, Foulques hoped to get out of debt by recovering his adopted father's Ukrainian estates, so he joined the Waffen-SS. In 1944 he was arrested, tried by the French Resistance and executed on 6 September as a German sympathiser. Too late, a telegram arrived confirming that he was spying for the British. After his death Felix received a note of farewell, saying, 'In ten minutes I shall be shot.'[47]

ca ✱ so

The war in Europe ended in May 1945. As life returned to normal Irina and Felix leased Villa Lou-Pradot in Biarritz as a holiday home. From the outside it looked like a Swiss chalet but inside they had to clear mountains of corn and rid the place of moths. Irina's nephew Prince Michael Feodorovich recalled buckets placed strategically under holes in the roof. When it was windy Grisha ran around placing other buckets while Felix directed the operation from under a large golf umbrella. 'We were soaked but we laughed!' Michael recalled. He remembered Aunt Titi and Uncle Felix with fondness. Irina, he said, was quiet, but exuded a 'marvellous and subtle perfume'. Felix seemed more of a typical Romanov than Irina's brothers but, above all, he was a true Russian. Irina was devoted to him. In return he was full of attentions to her and in the early days of their exile had refused her nothing, convinced that they would soon be returning to their old life.[48]

In Biarritz using bicycles or walking were the only means of getting around. Although 'the heyday of Biarritz was over',[49] they had lively evenings of charades or *tableaux vivant* with improvised costumes, guitar playing and singing in the basement bar with friends. At the Russian restaurant Chateau Basque, in an atmosphere of Cossack choirs, *zakouski* (*hors d'oeuvres*) and gypsy singers, it was as if old Russia had come back to life.

After spending summer and part of the autumn in Biarritz, they returned to Paris to prepare for their journey to England.

17

The Chateau de Kériolet

'I find this castle very ugly.'

Felix Youssoupov[1]

In April 1946 Irina and Felix arrived at Wilderness House for the first time since 1939. Travelling to England was neither easy nor pleasant. It was only possible to cross the Channel between Dieppe and Newhaven and they were delayed because of numerous complicated formalities.

Grand Duchess Xenia, now in her seventies, had been suffering from a duodenal ulcer and still looked very ill. Feodor was little more than skin and bone, 'eaten up with lung trouble and looks awful', as Queen Mary noted the previous month.[2] Irina and Felix were appalled.

They left England at the beginning of summer, taking Feodor with them in the hope that a better climate would help. The British doctor who accompanied them gave him six months to live. After a medical examination in Paris Feodor was sent to a clinic in Pau where they visited him regularly from Biarritz.

They also received news of Nikita, who was rescued from Berlin by Prince Paul Shouvalov 'because he was in danger of being arrested'.[3] He and Marie were staying with the Duchess of Kent's sister Countess Toerring, trying to obtain British visas. The Red Army was coming dangerously close. Of all Irina's brothers 'Nikita was closest to the Nazis'.[4]

Irina and Felix finally met their granddaughter when Bébé and four-year-old Punka spent the summer at Villa Lou-Pradot. 'I lived with them for two years ... when I was three years old and four years old, here in Paris and in Biarritz,' recalled Xenia Sfiris.[5] Nikolai was a purser for the shipping company founded by Russian émigré Alexander Vlasov.

The ageing process had not been kind to fifty-nine-year-old Felix. He did his best to combat it, spending hours every morning 'applying eye-liner, mascara and rouge to his face and combing his thinning hair into a lattice-work that very nearly covers his scalp'. Noel Coward met him at dinner that summer. Later, 'really quite sweetly', Felix sang and played his guitar. 'I looked at him: a face that must, when young, have been very beautiful but now it is cracking with effort and age. I imagined him luring Rasputin to his door with that guitar and "dem rollin' eyes". It was all a little macabre.'[6] Kenneth Snowman of the jewellers Wartski described him as 'an immaculately tailored wraith'.[7]

In Biarritz Felix met Father Jacques Laval. Born in 1911, he was a priest in Reims before joining the Dominican Order at the Convent of Saint Jacques in Paris. His homosexuality did not preclude his rise in the church and in the early 1950s he was director of the cultural section of Vatican Television. Felix found him interesting and intelligent. A friend of artists and writers, he published several novels under a pseudonym. Their first encounter was brief but they met again in Paris.

Father Laval later said that he had met someone who understood him, the person he had spent his whole life looking for. He wanted to leave the monastery and end his days with Felix. It has been alleged that the prince and the thirty-five-year-old priest became lovers. [8]

ଓ ✦ ଅ

Irina and Felix returned to rue Pierre-Guérin in the autumn with Bébé and Punka. Nikita, Marie and their sons had arrived, Grisha and Denise were in Biarritz, so Felix moved to the Hotel Vouillement, leaving Irina and Bébé to do the cooking.

The war years had been one of the longest continuous periods the Youssoupovs had spent together. When peace came, the separations began again.

In November 1946 Irina, Bébé and Punka left for Villa Lou-Pradot while Felix went travelling with friends. Irina visited Feodor in Pau and drew Christmas cards which she sent to Felix to sell. Feodor was looking better and had gained weight. His ex-wife Irene visited regularly and her sister Natalie sent 25,000 francs after Felix wrote to her for help.

In 1948 Bébé and Nikolai moved to Greece, where the climate was better for his health. Bébé had taken Punka there for a holiday. 'It was a trip we should have done for three months, but we stayed for life,' recalled Xenia Sfiris. 'And so I did not see my grandparents for several years.' The invitation came from the widowed Princess Nicholas of Greece, Felix's old flame Grand Duchess Elena. 'We saw her a lot and we liked her a lot,' Xenia Sfiris continued. 'She loved us and she loved my mother and she was really a great person...' Elena always looked after Felix's family.[9]

ଓ ✦ ଅ

Felix now turned his attention back to the Chateau de Kériolet. Princess Zenaide's lawyer Maître Imbert had died several years earlier and, as he was Jewish, the Nazis had raided his office and burnt his papers. Felix had to travel to Quimper, capital of the Département of Finistère, to find the documents. It seemed that the clauses had been broken, so Felix decided to assert his right to the estate. First he had to commission an expert report.

In May 1949 he received a communication from Maître Queinnec, a solicitor in Quimper: 'I expect to be able to send you very soon if not a complete despatch of the report which is very long, at least the conclusions of this report, and which the expert is sending to the Clerk of the Court...'[10]

Maître Joisson, a Paris lawyer, thought they had a case but, before proceeding, the solicitor required money. 'Send without delay the provision of 8,000 francs requested by Maître Queinnec,' Joisson wrote. 'I look forward to hearing the findings of this report....'[11] Felix received it in July. Although not as favourable as Joisson hoped, in his opinion it allowed them 'to initiate the action against the Département in revocation of the donation' granted on 30 May 1891.[12]

It would be a long-drawn-out process.

CR ✶ ℘

In the spring of 1948 the doctors said Feodor urgently needed an operation to save him. Felix recommended the clinic of Dr Bernou in Châteaubriant. 'It's a very difficult operation, but I will be at his side,' he told Michael.[13] Feodor underwent three operations before he was declared free of danger. By the summer Felix and Princess Irene were paying for him to stay at the Hotel Etchola in Ascain near Biarritz. Irina and Felix came several times and Felix did everything he could to get close to him. It is alleged by one author that Felix was in love with him.[14] Feodor's illness brought Irina closer to her more serious cousin Princess Irene; it was a friendship from which she would benefit later.

After helping Feodor, Felix lost his taste for society and began working for the poor and sick in Paris. Financially there was little he could do but, even though few people knew his identity, he spent hours sitting at hospital bedsides praying and comforting. Many believed he had the power of healing and came to him hoping for miraculous cures. Yet although he set about his faith healing with enthusiasm and believed in the power of prayer, it proved a failure. He was not very skilful.

He often saw Jacques Laval (they were now on first-name terms) and their friendship became stronger, reinforced by their empathy for people in distress. Laval was repeatedly astonished that Felix's life, so full of vicissitudes, had not destroyed him.

Felix became more spiritual and had no doubt that there was an afterlife. He and his brother had promised that the first to die would come back to the other. Shortly before Felix left for Oxford in 1909 he felt an urge to go towards his dead brother's room in the middle of the night. The locked door suddenly opened and Nicholas stood on the threshold, arms outstretched. As Felix moved forward he disappeared. At Oxford he developed an unsettling power of second sight, noticing that certain acquaintances sometimes appeared as through a cloud. These people either died or suffered serious accidents shortly afterwards. To his relief, this ability disappeared as suddenly as it had appeared.

After the war he frequently consulted a Paris clairvoyant. Irina also believed what she said and urged Felix to take her advice. She regularly asked what the clairvoyant had told him and often urged Felix to send her horoscope magazines.

CR ✶ ℘

Felix's latest money-making ideas included a plan to produce home-made cheap port wine and a scheme to sell the chalk soaked out of architectural drawing paper as fine gauze for dressmaking. When these strategies failed, he had no choice but to pledge La Pelegrina.

On 4 May 1945 he had confirmed to Sergei Korganoff that 'our obligation to you is still in force'.[15] In November the pearl was placed in Korganoff's strongbox at Credit Lyonnaise and a new agreement between Felix and his lawyer was signed.

Felix had received two offers, one from a Paris bank and the other from a Swiss bank. By early May 1949 he expected to receive definite propositions but there was no news from Switzerland. Then a lunch appointment with Baron Nicolas de Plantier, an artist and designer from Madrid, produced the names of two other possible buyers. Felix procured a visa from the Swiss consul in case of need. On 8 May the Swiss bank agreed to buy the pearl. The following week Felix and Korganoff took it to Geneva, where Felix's worries were justified. The bank wanted a guarantee from one of the large Paris jewellers. Felix rang Pierre Cartier at his Geneva home but he was staying in the Ritz in Paris. When Felix rang the hotel, he had already left. Jean Dufour in Paris then promised to pay the interest if the deal was without result, provided that the pearl would be kept in a safe place for a year.

Felix returned to Paris on 12 May without any sale, but with Dufour paying the interest at least he could relax.

On 13 May Felix confirmed to Dufour that he had received a loan of 150,000 francs at the rate of 7 per cent per year. 'I promise to reimburse you immediately my fine pearl ... La Pelegrina, is sold ... I have informed my businessman, Monsieur Korganoff ... who is holding this pearl on deposit, to take note of the present pledge, which is formal and irrevocable.'[16] Felix and Korganoff also had a meeting with Pierre Cartier, who had taken over the firm's Paris branch and offered his help.

Then Felix heard that Belgium wanted to offer La Pelegrina as a wedding present to Princess Josephine Charlotte when she married the hereditary Grand Duke Jean of Luxembourg. But the Belgians changed their minds and by November La Pelegrina was still unsold.

In August Felix wrote again to Dufour. This time the loan was 400,000 francs at 7 per cent. This 'could be reimbursed to you, if you desire, in dollars ... at the rate of 900 francs to the dollar and this against the delivery of my two letters (the present one and that of 2 August 1950)'. Reimbursement would be made after the sale of La Pelegrina.[17]

He was also in trouble with the tax authorities. 'Be kind enough to pay to the Tax Collector only a part, because we cannot pay everything,' Felix told Korganoff from Biarritz in June 1949. 'On the 1st of July Dufour must send me 50,000 francs, tell him to deduct from this sum what you have expended for me, plus 500 francs for the identity card.'[18]

This was only one of his worries. Felix then received a letter from Zina Gregoriev-Svetilov. His half-sister Tatiana was about to be married but his half-brother Olivier, whose health was fragile, was unable to work because of illness. Zina was obviously hoping for financial help.

Felix pleaded poverty in order to evade his moral responsibilities. He told Zina that he and Irina only had enough money for food, everything had been sold, their last *objets* had been confiscated during the German occupation and they were living near Biarritz with friends. He wished Tatiana happiness and sent her a small icon. Zina then began selling the jewels given to her by Felix senior in order to support her children. Worse still, she lent Felix junior money which he never repaid. She eventually tore up the IOU.

There was also the perfume business. Molinard were about to launch 'Princess Irina', although 'Brunette' was not yet ready. Felix had another meeting with Molinard, with whom he was planning to launch 'Blonde'. In Paris Felix and Irina would receive 10 per cent of the sales, whereas in London they would only receive 5 per cent. Even this was not plain sailing. Several ladies complained that the perfumes did not smell like Irfé at all.

∽ ✱ ∾

Felix thought Feodor should come and live with them and threatened otherwise to refuse to help him. Feodor did not want to be under their care but they were worried he would start drinking again. Nikita and Marie were leaving for America and Irina had no idea when she would see them or Feodor again. She blamed all their problems on lack of money.

La Pelegrina remained unsold and the battle for the Chateau de Kériolet had hardly commenced. A reporter from the *Evening Standard* described the house at rue Pierre-Guérin as 'chilly and damp with coal economies and dark with self-enforced electricity cuts. The hessian-covered walls display a few yellowing unframed snapshots ... a small tinsel-framed photo of the tsar and tsarina stands in a corner. The furniture is old and nondescript and the mats on the sitting-room floor are threadbare.'

They were trying to sell their house in Corsica. Finally, in 1951 Felix and Irina sold an unspecified property to Hervé Louis Ernest de la Grange for 700,000 francs.[19]

Felix then fell into problems with the National Solidarity Tax. This had been imposed in 1945 to tax the increase in wealth since 1940 of people 'whose wealth had increased to 200,000 francs or whose enrichment exceeded 50,000 francs'. The money raised was used 'to pay the exceptional costs generated by the war'.[20]

Felix explained his position on 7 June. 'As a Russian émigré, I have possessed considerable property in France. For many years, I realized my values, sold my paintings by masters, my jewels and all my other goods including my mansion in Boulogne-sur-Seine ... Most of the money has been spent on charitable works for the benefit of emigrants without money.' He stated that even before 1945 he had not possessed the elements necessary to qualify for the tax.[21]

He was then asked to sign a declaration of inheritance. Once again, he confirmed that, as of June 1945, he did not have 'any of the necessary elements for subscription to the *declaration du Patrimoine*'. Furthermore, he continued, 'as regards the account in question at B.N.C.I. [The National Bank for

Trade and Industry] the largest part of this sum had been collected and was intended for emigrants without resources. If however you judge that this sum is taxable, I beg you not to consider it as a new element, because it is known that I have spent considerable money in France, I never earned neither before the war, neither during the war nor after, any sum whatsoever.' Perhaps the most surprising thing was that Felix stated that 'until 1939, I received from England, from my mother-in-law Grand Duchess Xenia of Russia, some sums [of money]. Recent English laws allow me the hope of touching again the money from England'.[22]

One of the émigrés Felix assisted was Natasha Brasova, widow of Irina's uncle Grand Duke Michael Alexandrovich. Natasha had escaped from Russia and by 1946 was in dire straits, living in a shabby attic box room on Paris's left bank offered rent-free by an elderly émigré. Her granddaughter Pauline sent regular sums and the relatives of Natasha's first husband helped where they could. But the only member of the imperial family who took an interest was Felix. He often brought 'food and cash' to the lady who was, after all, Irina's aunt by marriage.[23]

In November Felix received a demand for 2,446 francs from the tax office in Calvi, covering the period between October 1940 and December 1951. This was 'for construction of a terrace on a parcel of military ground of the citadel of Calvi' and 'for renting a parcel of land to build a cottage'. 'You can pay the total sum of 2,446 francs to my postal account in Ajaccio,' the official added helpfully.[24]

With no end to the monetary problems, they urgently needed a solution.

CR ✱ ℰ

Felix decided to write his memoirs, helped by Irina whose memory was better. By July Irina was complaining that she, her mother and Feodor had worked with his notes all day and had not finished. 'It is not possible to write like you,' she protested, which poses questions as to the eventual authorship of the book.[25] Felix acknowledged that Irina was the better writer. She was gifted and humorous despite her reputation as a quiet woman. She wanted to write her own book, 'What my husband didn't say'. Many years earlier she wrote a spoof account of their life in Calvi which was circulated to friends, and had begun writing *Le Journal de Bull*, a diary as if written by their former butler. Felix thought she would certainly have more success than him.

Felix needed a sensational story to make money. Their annual rent was 3,500 francs, including the legal surcharge. He therefore embellished his earlier book *Rasputin* to heighten the drama. By casting himself as the hero who slayed the devil incarnate, Felix enhanced his notoriety and tried to justify a cold-blooded murder.[26]

Avant l'Exil was published in France in 1952. It did not receive unanimous approval from the Russian community, who believed it was ghost-written. The following year it was published in English under the title of *Lost Splendour*, translated by Anne Green and Nicholas Katkov. With the current money problems, a cheque for £100 sterling for royalties, paid to the Westminster Foreign Bank in Paris by his UK publishers Jonathan Cape in 1953, was very welcome.[27]

Although Felix revelled in the notoriety, when he was approached by Les Films Montmorency, who wanted to interview him for their film *The Intimate Life of Rasputin*, Korganoff declined on Felix's behalf.[28]

All the criticism did not stop Felix from writing a second volume. *En Exil* was published in 1954 but never translated into English.

∝ ✶ ℘

The saga of Le Pelegrina rolled on. In March 1952, Korganoff wrote to the Banque Perrier Lullin in Geneva saying that the jewellers Lombard had a buyer for an historic pearl he was selling. As its value was £20,000 sterling (just over £600,000 today), the owners would like to deposit it in the Banque Lullin. He wondered whether this would be possible.[29]

After contacting Lullin, Jean Lombard wrote to Felix. 'I am delighted at the decision Your Highness has taken to kindly make available to me his marvellous jewel, and I can assure Your Highness that I will do my utmost to reach a satisfactory conclusion.'[30]

The answer from Lullin was obviously no because in May Jean Lombard approached the Director General of the Union of Swiss Banks in Geneva, 'to whom I have requested agreement, for the deposit of the Pelegrina'. Lombard told Korganoff that the Director General had given 'all the guarantees. So please let me know when you arrive, and I reiterate that you will be my guest in Geneva,' he added helpfully.[31]

On 5 February 1953 La Pelegrina was sold to the jeweller Jean Lombard on behalf of an anonymous collector in Europe.[32]

Having disposed of La Pelegrina, Felix resumed the fight for the Chateau de Kériolet.

The extensive report showed that several hundred objects had been sold, fetching around 22,000 francs. The most beautiful Flemish tapestry had been removed and the border of another had been cut off. Trees had been felled in the park and allotment gardens created, then rented out. A hospital was installed in the chateau in 1944 and fairs had been held there.[33] Felix wanted the building returned to him and claimed four million francs for depreciation.

The Département's expert claimed the infringements were only minor and cited the thirty-year prescription on facts prior to 1920 and the period of exemption during the war.[34] On 30 July 1952 a tribunal at Quimper ruled against Felix and ordered him to pay the costs. He decided to go to the Court of Appeal in Rennes.[35]

In May 1954 the Court of Appeal upped sticks and visited the chateau to settle the dispute. 'I feel that I own a property that does not belong to me,' Felix said as he arrived with Irina.[36] Forty witnesses had been called.

Although the *Préfet* of Finistère, Monsieur Laporte, and his predecessors were jointly responsible, their lawyers protested that although Princess Zenaide and Prince Felix had arrived in France in 1920 (which in Zenaide's case was certainly not true) and had known the conditions of the donation, they had made no objection between then and 1940.

Seven or eight grievances were put forward by Felix. The clause regarding the conservation of shade in the park had been violated by cutting down 2,000 chestnut trees (only those diseased or dead, maintained the *Préfet*).

They had installed a sheepfold, sold some of the furniture, substituted an altar in the chapel (the current one was more beautiful, maintained Monsieur Laporte) and removed or mutilated tapestries. The former billiard room was dilapidated and there was a mushroom farm in the basement.[37] And so it went on.

'I live in the Auteuil in a converted stable. I only have three rooms but I find more harmony there than in this mediocre cinema décor,' a reporter quoted Felix saying.[38]

Felix later admitted that they had some bad moments during the trial. One came when the Département disclosed a confidential proposition by which Felix offered to revoke the donation, thus becoming the owner of the chateau, 'provided, of course, that the furniture and works of art remain in his possession'. This caused a disturbance in the court that took some while to calm down.[39]

But finally, after five years of legal wrangling, the court ruled that the conditions *had* been broken. On 13 February 1956, by a judgement of the Court of Appeal, ownership of the Chateau de Kériolet and its estate, worth over half a million pounds, was taken from the Département of Finistère.

∞ ✶ ∞

In the spring of 1954 Irina arrived at Wilderness House to find her mother weak and unwell. The weather was cold and wet, rationing was still in force and there were almost no vegetables. Irina found the situation tiring and Mother Martha's tantrums drove her crazy. Felix understood it was Irina's duty to be with her mother but he still needed to get away with men.

At some point during the 1950s Felix spotted Robert Speller junior, son of the New York publisher, on a beach on the French Riviera. Speller was part of a touring dance group and his lithe figure was obviously attractive to the prince. This resulted in a brief affair, during which Felix told him plenty of stories about the Romanovs. Speller later said that 'the prince was in remarkable shape for a man of his age [his sixties] but that his make-up was apparent'.[40]

Although Irina understood his need she deplored these separations. She addressed her letters to 'dear Monkey', or, when she was cross with him, 'dear Youssoupov'. Occasionally she called him 'little one', ironically the name Rasputin had used for him. She often signed her letters 'your old Irina'.[41]

That year Felix refused an offer to return to Russia. During a meeting with the Soviet ambassador arranged by Serge Lifar, Felix was told that the Soviet government was restoring Arkhangelskoe as a museum. In return for him acting as curator, they could go and live in a flat in one of the wings.

Felix was astonished and intrigued. Arkhangelskoe had always been his favourite home. Irina, however, was having none of it. The Soviets had murdered seventeen members of her family, including the cousins she had grown up with. This left her angry and bitter. She pointed out that the émigrés, many of whom had lost relatives and property, would disown him. The idea never got off the ground.

In November that year sixty-seven-year-old Felix was the victim of a road accident which left him with a head wound. He refused admission to hospital and, after examination by a surgeon, was given a certificate saying that he was forbidden from all work for a period of forty-five days.[42] He was consoled by a new puppy called Mopsy, who joined his dog Gugusse and Irina's cat Minou.

⊱ ✴ ⊰

While living in Paris Irina's brother Dmitri had become a close friend of the Duke and Duchess of Windsor. The duke, as Prince of Wales, had attended parties at Felix's London flat with his brother Bertie, later King George VI.[43] In the mid-1950s, through Dmitri, the Windsors formed part of Irina and Felix's social circle which included J. Paul Getty, Philippe de Rothschild and Sir Oswald and Lady Mosley.

Like Felix, the duke had performed one act for which he would always be remembered. This was his abdication in 1936. Now he and his wife Wallis Simpson, exiled from British society and the royal family, lived in a grace-and-favour house in the Bois de Boulogne. The duke 'hated living in France' said John Julius Norwich. 'His French was execrable, and he makes no attempt to improve it.'[44]

Invitations to the Windsors' mansion allowed Irina and Felix to savour the splendour of former times. They were greeted by liveried footmen and in the hall the duke's Garter banner from St George's Chapel hung proudly over the stairwell. While signing the visitors' book they could not have failed to notice on the table the red despatch box proclaiming 'THE KING' in tooled lettering.

It was with a sense of *déjà vu* that Felix and Irina entered the elegant salon where they were offered chilled champagne, whisky, or a thimbleful of vodka. The furniture was Louis XVI, the silver was old English and the carpet was woven with a design of the Prince of Wales's feathers. Fabergé boxes and jewelled trinkets in ivory, jade or turquoise were dotted around on tables. Wallis rather overdid the splendour. 'There were always too many golden ashtrays.'[45]

The Windsors greeted Irina as 'Your Imperial Highness', which she thought was funny, having once called Felix a snob for addressing a letter to her as H.I.H. Princess Irina Youssoupov. Irina had long given up on titles but she played along, addressing Wallis as 'Your Royal Highness', the title denied to her by George VI.

At precisely 9.15 p.m. the guests headed towards the exotic dining room with its 'blue silk curtains, Chinese panels and coral silk carpet'.[46] They ate the best food served off the finest bone china and prepared by the greatest French chefs. One evening after dinner Felix forgot himself and began clearing the plates ready to wash up. An embarrassed Irina reprimanded him while everyone laughed.

They had many friends in common but the Windsors' dinner parties were 'impossibly tedious', with the duke's conversation mainly devoted to golf and card games.[47] One evening Felix played his guitar and the duchess asked, 'What do you think of me, Felix?' 'I don't think you'd like it if I told you,' he replied. 'But you have no sex, not female or male, but you have a Wallis sex, and without you the duke could not live. You are his oxygen tent.'[48]

It was a strange friendship, especially as the duke was thought to dislike anything smacking of homosexuality, while the fragile Irina seemed to have little in common with the brittle, angular duchess.

According to Cecil Beaton, invitations from the Windsors slowed when Felix became friendly with 'a shabby monk, who was so smelly that it made entertaining Youssoupov impossible'.[49]

It was the closest Felix and Irina came to their old royal life.

18

The Shadow of Rasputin

'I don't want to be remembered for just one thing.'
Felix Youssoupov[1]

On her way to London Irina often called in to Andrei's home Provender, the house near Faversham that Nadine inherited from her mother. To their daughter Princess Olga, Irina was Aunt Titi who amused her by doing funny drawings and caricatures of animals. She was always very elegant, had a wonderful sense of humour, a very deep voice and smelt of Gauloises cigarettes and Chanel No. 5. She wore beautiful pearls and 'was *wonderful* with small children,' Olga recalled.[2]

During one of Irina's visits Andrei and Nadine took her to Torry Hill, nearby home of the Leigh-Pemberton family. There was a small-gauge miniature railway running round the estate with tunnels and a steam engine. They all took a ride but Irina got soot in her eye. 'It was really painful,' her niece recalled, 'and she had to go to the Cottage Hospital to have the soot removed.' Felix was absent from these visits. Andrei 'had never forgiven him for his part in Rasputin's murder' and Olga was never allowed to meet him.[3]

When Irina arrived at Provender in 1956 Bébé was there. Irina and Bébé then spent two days with Rostislav and his third wife Hedwig in London.

On one of her trips to London Irina and Andrei visited Wartski, who in 1945 had re-acquired the Fabergé Coronation Egg of 1897. Irina asked if she could see it. The egg was produced and the 'surprise', the tiny replica of Catherine the Great's gold coronation coach, was taken out and put on the desk. Irina immediately began wheeling it up and down. 'Oh no, no, please don't do that,' one of the assistants begged her anxiously, 'it's *far* too valuable.' 'How *ridiculous*,' she replied. 'I used to play with this in the nursery!'[4]

The Duke of Edinburgh's niece Princess Margarita of Baden occasionally bumped into Irina when she visited Wilderness House. She met Bébé at least once and described Felix as 'unbelievable, out of this world'. He wore make-up, she added incredulously.[5]

Irina also met Prince David Chavchavadze, an officer in the US Army, who visited Grand Duchess Xenia whenever he was in England. His mother Princess

Nina, the daughter of Grand Duke and Duchess George, always said that Irina was her favourite cousin. 'Irina was very shy with me,' Prince David recalled, 'until I took a lorgnette out of my uniform pocket and stared at her through it, thereby looking like my grandmother. Then she smacked me on the shoulder, laughing and calling me *durak* [ass or fool]!'[6]

At Wilderness House stamp collecting was a hobby and a delivery of mail would elicit the question, 'What's the stamp?' Irina frequently asked Felix to buy or send certain stamps. In 1937 she had reminded him to open envelopes with Edward VIII stamps carefully, as they would be scarce.[7]

ଓ ✶ ଶ

Good news travels fast. While the lawsuit against the Département of Finistere was pending appeal Felix heard from his half-sister Tatiana Bonnard. Someone in her family had married in 1953, so Felix sent congratulations and enclosed a small bottle of Irfé perfume. Felix then received another letter from Zina Gregoriev-Svetilov, who had heard of their good fortune. Sergei Korganoff explained that there was third-party opposition from the government to the court's decision and until this was settled the prince was unable to sell Kériolet or any of the lands around it. He also stressed that the amounts quoted in the newspapers were exaggerated and the sum would be considerably diminished once the court costs and inheritance fees were taken into account.[8]

In April 1957 Irina and Felix purchased a house in rue de la Sablonnière in Septeuil, Brittany, although they would not be able to restore it until the business with Kériolet was settled. This was going slowly. By mid-May the lawyer had obtained some money to pay the experts and Felix arranged a meeting. They still had no idea how much money they would receive.

In July the Court of Appeal awarded compensation of twenty-five million francs for the damage done at Kériolet. There was still controversy about the sale of the land at Morau, valued at eighteen million francs, which Felix's great-grandmother had given permission to sell.

Felix began selling Kériolet's contents at auction to pay the lawyers and his creditors. Then he tried to sell the chateau to the Municipal Council of Concarneau but they turned it down. They did accept the gift of the domed well, which was reassembled in the walled town in the government courtyard. The chateau and surrounding lands were finally sold in 1960.[9]

Despite their financial problems the Youssoupovs were never really poor. They may have been strapped for cash but they were always asset rich. The trust fund from the MGM court case, as well as royalties from Felix's books and the sale of the Kériolet estate, gave them a comfortable lifestyle denied to many Russian exiles.

ଓ ✶ ଶ

When she was sixteen Punka returned from Greece to stay with Felix and Irina. 'And that's where I really knew them ... I'll never forget, because it was sensational moments that I spent with these two characters,' she recalled. 'My grandparents never spoke of the past, they only talked about the present and the future, and my parents the same thing. And I think it was a very fair thing, because I learned the story of Russia by growing up and reading books about everything that happened. But we never talked about it in the family ... it certainly hurt, but we never showed it. They were people who had really changed their lives and they turned the page.'[10]

In an interview with Frédéric Mitterrand she said that Felix was charming and extravert, while Irina, like 'almost all the Romanovs' was very calm and shy. And she told the story of how, when the couple received an envelope with their monthly allowance, Felix wanted to be the first man to buy his teenaged granddaughter her first pair of high-heeled shoes. Irina protested that this was all the money they had to live on for the month but Felix insisted. He did not care about spending the money. He bought her the shoes.[11]

While Irina remained quietly at home, almost every night Felix took his granddaughter 'to the Opéra, the theatre, restaurants. When we came back (my grandmother did not go to bed before we got back) she asked us what we did and where we went. I got along very well with my grandfather and I thank the good God that I knew him as well and that he really gave me a lot, many things of his own...'[12]

Through their granddaughter Felix and Irina met seventeen-year-old Victor Contreras, a young art student who had run away from his home in Mexico and was studying in Paris. Punka invited him to Sunday lunch with her grandparents but Victor had no idea who they were. 'I was served like royalty and there was this beautiful old gentleman sitting across from me,' he recalled.[13]

Irina and Felix felt an instant connection with the young man. He was invited to rue Pierre-Guérin and finally they asked him to move in. They treated him like an adopted son and he spent the next five years there, moving out in 1963. They called him their Mexican son, fallen from heaven.

Contreras recalled that security outside consisted of a small sign saying 'Beware of the dogs', although there was now only the pug, Gus. Irina also had the inevitable cat, this time a tailless animal called Muni which she had taken in off the street.

Irina and Felix had accepted their changed circumstances:

'They didn't miss their lives in Russia ... They were realists – they thought that the revolution would fail, but they also thought that they might not get to witness its failure first-hand.' As for the fortune that they were forced to leave behind ... they were never less than philosophical. 'They always used to say, "We were the richest people in the world, but we didn't know who our friends and enemies were. Now, we may not have great riches, but we do have great friends."'[14]

Despite her sixty-three years, the princess had 'an exceptional beauty' with a profile like a cameo. She went out very little, spending her time reading, knitting little woollen dolls, or playing solitaire. She still smoked long Gauloises cigarettes from an amber holder. Contreras remembers her as 'distant, formal and of few words' but with 'beautiful eyes'. Seventy-one-year-old Felix was flamboyant and sociable. Visitors to the house included General de Gaulle, cabaret artist and heroine of the French Resistance Joséphine Baker, Ingrid Bergman, Jean Cocteau and Salvador Dalí.

Sometimes Felix took Contreras on his visits to help the Russian émigrés. '"He was mystical and possessed special powers," insists Contreras, bizarrely echoing one of the main accusations against Rasputin. Special powers or not, the artist admits to having fallen under the prince's spell. "We fell in love," he says. Even though there is plenty of literature about Prince Felix's supposed homosexuality, Contreras says that their relationship was always platonic.'[15]

Another visitor was J. Paul Getty. Felix had known him in the 1920s and took him to Frogmore for dinner. He had visited Russia in 1913 and 1935. 'Had a real Russian dinner with Prince Felix,' Getty's diary recorded. 'He is seventy-three, but doesn't look or act it. He played the balalaika and we sang old Russian songs for hours.' Felix was astounded that his guest knew all the words.[16] He could not understand why Getty, who was certainly not homosexual, was so keen on him and why the parsimonious oil millionaire spent money telephoning him from England. He also sent Felix 'the biggest box of caviar he had ever seen', saying, 'You will never be happy if you go on like this.'[17] Their last meeting was in Paris in 1959.

☘ ✳ ☙

Encouraged by Felix, Feodor's son Michael went into the film business after the war. Whenever he was working at a studio nearby he popped into rue Pierre-Guérin, usually to be greeted by Denise exclaiming, 'Oh, Prince Michael, we were afraid you would not come!' He recalled his uncle Felix sitting in a high-backed armchair, while Aunt Titi was on the couch holding a small deck of cards which had been worn out by interminable games of patience. Everyone gave her 'limitless respect and immense tenderness'.[18]

Michael worked on the Anatole Litvak film *Anastasia*, which in 1956 gained an Oscar for Ingrid Bergman as the heroine.

The Anastasia saga still captured the world.

In January 1958, lawyers met in the High Court of Hamburg where Anna Anderson sued for direct recognition as Grand Duchess Anastasia Nicolaievna. Irina and Felix were appalled. They were 'extremely indignant' about a letter of support for her from Grand Duke Andrei Vladimirovich (who had died in 1956), published in *Le Figaro* some time earlier.[19] Felix made his feelings plain in a postcard to Baron Rausch von Trautenberg, refuting the young woman's claim and calling her 'a half-crazy adventurer in the hands of dishonest or stupid people'.[20]

The following month the Youssoupovs sent an article to *Le Figaro* protesting against the false Anastasia. Pierre Gilliard then suggested it would be a good time for the family to issue another declaration to combat the press campaign in her favour orchestrated by Dr Botkin's daughter Tatiana Melnik. Gillard was adamant that Mme Melnik's efforts must be countermanded. 'If you do not think it is possible to quickly gather the signatures for a new declaration, do you not think it would be a good idea to send to *Le Figaro* the declaration made in 1928 by Grand Duke Alexander Michaelovich...?' Gilliard asked Felix. 'You will recall that it is signed by all the uncles and aunts and first cousins of Anastasia Nicolaievna still living in 1928. But who could take the initiative for such an intervention?'[21]

Felix sent Gilliard a copy of his *Le Figaro* article and on 25 February Gilliard wrote again. 'The silence of the imperial family became oppressive and it is a great happiness that thanks to you it has been broken. The larger public are ignorant of the declaration issued by Grand Duke Alexander. They will now know that for a long time the members of the imperial family were convinced that this is an adventuress. Do you have the memoirs that Mme Melnik published in Russian in Belgrade in 1921? It will be evident from this that Mme Melnik was nowhere near the palace.'[22]

The family was still divided. On 11 March Prince Dmitri wrote to Prince Ludwig of Hesse saying that the irresponsible statement of his cousin Princess Xenia Georgievna should be refuted. 'We know that she left Russia in 1914 aged ten years old,' he told Louis. 'I also know that Nina and Xenia never saw Uncle Nicky's family very often, and when they did see them that was when they were very young.' He enclosed a short, typed statement from Grand Duchess Xenia saying that she was convinced the woman was an imposter and believed in the statements of Felix and others who had met the woman. 'I asked my sister [Irina] and brother-in-law to send their statement from Paris to you,' Dmitri added.[23]

On 7 April *The Times* published a short paragraph under the heading 'No "Princess" file at King Umberto's Home', saying that General Graziani, head of the king of Italy's household, had denied there were any documents relating to Anastasia at the king's residence in Cascais, Portugal. Italian newspapers erroneously claimed that the diplomat Francesco Lecchui had investigated the rival claims some years ago but his report was never published. Xenia called the resurfacing of the Anderson case 'abominable'.[24] Felix then learnt that Nikita had important documents which had been left by Sandro. He asked him to send them to Germany urgently.

In 1959 Judge Heinrich Backen and a rogatory commission travelled abroad to hear witnesses. On 15 July they took a statement from seventy-two-year-old Felix at his Paris home.

After recounting his meeting with the plaintiff at Castle Seeon, Felix repeated his impressions of her which he gave to the family years before. 'Nothing about her reminded me of the youngest daughter of the tsar ... I missed the simplicity in her which is allegedly characteristic of the tsarist family; the language, the posture, the movements and the mannerisms.'

The plaintiff's attorney Dr Kurt Vermehren pointed out that other members of the family had recognised her as Anastasia. 'I believe that those people ... are either idiots, simple-minded or not honourable,' Felix retorted. 'I had the impression that she neither spoke Russian, French or even English since she didn't answer my questions in these languages.' He added that her German seemed poor. 'Due to our close family relationships, I also knew the youngest daughter of the tsar well ... Since I am married to the tsar's niece, I had access to the court of the tsar and also on unofficial occasions. I last saw the youngest daughter of the tsar in 1915.'

Some additional questions, sent via the embassy in Paris, were then put to him regarding his meetings with Gleb Botkin in Berlin. 'I think I remember that I, Professor Rudnev and Gleb Botkin called on Mrs Rathlef-Keilman.' It was Harriet Rathlef-Keilman's conviction about the plaintiff's identity which persuaded Felix to go to Seeon. After his visit he told Botkin that 'the patient in Seeon was not identical with the youngest daughter of the tsar'. At no point did Felix change his mind and decide that he and Botkin 'would agree about the identity'. He had no recollection of writing a letter to Victoria Milford Haven and asking Botkin to take it to London 'and I don't know either, why I should have given him that advice'. Nor did he see Botkin's open letter to Grand Duchess Xenia in 1928.

He declared that the statement Botkin gave on 13 March 1959 in New York, 'was on the whole accurate apart from the threats [to supporters of the plaintiff] which I was being accused of which do not include a single true word'.

Dr Vehmehren then asked whether he had met the Danish Ambassador Herluf Zahle in Berlin. Felix confirmed that he met Zahle before and after his visit to Seeon. 'He thanked me for my visit and stated that he would inform the Danish King', Christian X.

When questioning finished, the statement was approved by Felix.[25]

This was not the end of the affair. In 1961 Felix was contacted by Alexei Milukov, a mysterious Russian émigré who worked for the American military administration in Frankfurt. Milukov, anxious to do a deal with the surviving Romanovs, was under the impression that Felix was either the head or the spokesman of the family.

According to Milukov, Felix now 'promised to recognise Anna [Anderson], providing he could have a share of her money' believed to be in the Bank of England. This angered Gleb Botkin, who pulled no punches in his reply to Milukov. 'Youssoupov is a self-confessed murderer, perjurer and traitor. As everyone knows, he is also a homosexual, a drunkard and a hooligan ... [He] testified under oath that Anastasia is an imposter and that all her supporters are either lunatics or crooks.' His willingness to acknowledge Anderson as the grand duchess in return for money proved he was a scoundrel. Felix, said Botkin, 'knows perfectly well that Anastasia is what she claims to be and his fight against her is a crime more horrible and cruel by far than the murder of Rasputin'.[26]

Judgement was rendered on 15 May 1961. 'The Landgericht-Hambourg dismissed the complaint ... as unsubstantiated' and stated that the counter-charges (based on the finding that the complainant was Franziska Schanzkowska) were inadmissible. 'The court was satisfied that the complainant was not in any case Anastasia, the daughter of Tsar Nicholas II.'[27]

In 1965 Irina's nephew Prince Alexander Nikitich agreed to meet Anna Anderson. Afterwards he said 'he believed she must be the grand duchess, as she so closely resembled his grandmother and his aunt Princess Irina'.[28]

CR ✱ ഇ

By March 1960 Grand Duchess Xenia's health was failing fast. Irina spent her time rushing between Paris and Wilderness House, where she told reporters that a doctor came twice a day and the devoted Mother Martha was assisted by another nurse. On 1 April Xenia suffered a relapse but then there was a slight improvement and bulletins ceased.

Then on 20 April Xenia's condition worsened and her confessor administered the last rites. She died later that day with Irina and Andrei at her bedside.

The coffin was taken to the Church of the Holy Assumption (Russian Orthodox Church in Exile) in Kensington for a memorial service on 26 April, attended by representatives of the queen and other royal families. Irina, heavily veiled and carrying a lighted candle, was accompanied by Andrei and Dmitri with their wives, Andrei's daughter Xenia, Princess Rostislav and Nikita's son Alexander.

The funeral service took place the following day. Afterwards Irina accompanied her mother's body to London Airport (now Heathrow) for the journey to Nice. It was her first flight, recalled Dmitri, and far from being excited, 'she sat away from the window completely oblivious to the flying'.[29]

From Nice they travelled along a narrow, winding corniche road to the cemetery at Roquebrune overlooking the sea. Irina, Andrei and Dmitri were joined by Felix, as on 29 April Xenia was laid to rest alongside her wayward husband Sandro.

Most of Xenia's money went to a trust fund 'from which her children would benefit in equal proportions'. Irina also inherited many of her mother's possessions.[30]

Irina returned sadly to Septeuil. Felix was about to go to Corsica, probably to see Tao, and from there to Spain with some companions. Irina was still unhappy about these long separations.

He occasionally went out in the evenings to bars or fashionable restaurants while Irina stayed at home listening to classical music and reading Russian literature. Even in old age his chauffeur was ordered to keep an eye on him because he liked to pick up attractive young men.

Between 1957 and 1963 Felix and Irina's most frequent journeys were to visit Feodor in Ascain. Irina spent a great part of every year staying at the guesthouse close to her brother.

⊗ ✶ ℬ

In 1961 Irina's nephew Alexander became the first Romanoff to set foot in Soviet Russia.

Xenia and Sandro's palace on the Moika was a sports club. According to the caretaker, much of the interior was destroyed by a Nazi bomb during the Siege of Leningrad and, Alexander said, 'only the main staircase flanked by potted plants had remained intact'. In contrast Alexander found Arkhangelskoe 'well preserved', calling it 'a beautiful house in a beautiful setting' with everything more or less as it was when the Youssoupovs left.[31] This must have pleased Felix enormously.

Felix kept in touch with old friends. Eric Hamilton's son remembered him visiting his father just after the war, travelling on a Green Line bus. Felix's final meeting with John Scale had taken place in 1948. Scale died the following year[32] but Felix remained in touch with Oswald Rayner, sending him a message in his idiosyncratic English on the back of a postcard of the Arc de Triomphe.

My dear W. W.
I hope you will be quite well soon. What sort of operation did you have? Many thanks for your lovely card, it looks like if it was you and I having a little trip in the air. I often think of you, & whatever should happen I shall never forget the good moments we have had together. I completely

changed my life. I am no more interested in political or social life, but only in sick & poor people & this takes all my time. Thank God I have a very good health & plenty of energy. My wife helps me. Next time when I go to England I shall let you know & hope that you will do the same when you come to France.

Ever yours, Felix.[33]

There is one further postcard, sent to Rayner from Septeuil in 1960. 'Many wishes and kisses for Christmas, from Felix.'[34]

Oswald Rayner died on 6 March 1961 at his home in Abingdon. Felix immediately wrote to his widow Margaret (his second wife).

Dear Madame. I have just received your letter giving me the sad news of the death of Oswald. I am all the more distressed as I was joyfully looking forward to seeing him again shortly. My wife and I have you much in our thoughts and with all our hearts wish you the courage to bear your sore trial. May God keep you. Youssoupov.'[35]

Rayner took his secrets to the grave. When he was diagnosed with terminal cancer he 'destroyed everything' to do with Russia, Gordon Rayner said, adding, 'By that I mean burnt!'[36] Both Felix and Rayner claimed to have a ring containing a bullet which shot Rasputin. It is probably no coincidence that he named his son John Felix Hamilton Rayner.

Eric Hamilton died in 1962.

CR ✖ ෨

During the latter years of his life Felix became obsessed about money. American broadcaster James Critchlow recalled seeing him on French television quiz shows trying to win prizes. Noel Coward described Felix in these years. 'During the dinner, whenever Felix smiled or laughed, the heavy make-up which he wore cracked and kept dropping to the table and into the food.'[37]

Cecil Beaton photographed him in 1964. Felix thought the photograph 'is very successful and everybody likes it'. He added he would be pleased to see the rest of the batch and had nothing against the idea of putting one of the photos in a magazine.[38]

The following April, Beaton returned to rue Pierre-Guérin. Felix's condition had deteriorated. He only heard the doorbell at the second ring, his sight was failing, his badly shaved face had 'white whiskers covered with powder' and he no longer wore eye make-up. During their conversation he claimed to have never made a friend in Paris and said that 'people were only interested in money and power'. On his previous visit Beaton noticed a book about Anna Pavlova on his bedroom table. It was still there and, Beaton recorded delightedly, 'luckily the prince asked if I would like to borrow it'. Beaton left with Felix's laughter ringing in his ears after a young Frenchman asked why he was wearing a table napkin in his breast pocket. Felix had been unable to find a handkerchief in the cupboard.[39]

CR ✖ ෨

In 1965 Felix sued the Columbia Broadcasting System in the New York Supreme Court. Again, the subject was the murder of Rasputin.

The Youssoupovs were now far from the glamourous young couple who had won a similar case in London. Felix was a seventy-nine-year-old man with tinted glasses to protect his failing eyesight, 'thin and nearly bald, with a sharply pointed nose, a finely edged chin, skin drawn tightly over his cheekbones and thin hands that looked like porcelain'.[40] Seventy-year-old Irina was grey and bent.

Once more the redoubtable Fanny Holtzmann came to their aid, promising to underwrite the expenses of the trial for half of the proceeds if they won. Felix claimed $1,500 (just over half a million pounds then) under a section of US State Civil Rights Law known as the 'right of privacy'. He complained that a half-hour play about Rasputin's murder, *If I Should Die*, screened on CBS television in 1963, 'utilized his name without his permission for commercial reasons and invaded his privacy in what he called a "sexual" drama'[41] offensive to him and Irina. According to fictional dialogue in the play, Irina was used by Felix as 'seductive bait' to lure Rasputin to the Moika Palace. He had not authorised the use of his name and the script was inaccurate, although CBS claimed it was based on Felix's books. Lawyers for CBS maintained that the killing was part of history, in the public domain and open to interpretation in both literary and dramatic works.

The case began on 16 October and lasted several weeks but American newspaper reporters were more interested in Vietnam than in something that happened almost fifty years ago.

Felix spent five days in the witness box telling his oft-repeated story, although, *The Times* reported, the proceedings were complicated by the prince's 'failing hearing ... and inadequate English'. Many of his more difficult answers had to be translated from French.[42] He admitted bringing Rasputin to the Moika Palace and testified that Purishkevich shot him when he fell down into the snow. His physical and mental frailty soon became apparent and he stumbled over the answers as the questioning continued.

When the lawyer for the defence insisted that 'Rasputin had expected to meet the princess', the statement was 'vehemently' denied.[43] During cross-examination about Irina's role he collapsed into the arms of a court attendant and a doctor was summoned.

Significantly, this time Felix changed his stance, giving his motive for the murder as 'distaste for Rasputin's debaucheries' rather than a patriotic gesture. He claimed that when he pleaded with him to leave Petrograd Rasputin admitted he was a German agent. He claimed to have shot Rasputin once in the heart and once in the liver, but he never said 'precisely how or where the almost indestructible monk [*sic*] died'.[44] Even after all these years, he took Maklakov's advice and concealed the details.

Irina took the stand wearing a plain black dress. In faultless English she denied her name had been used in connection with the invitation to the palace, saying that she was in the Crimea.

Looking at the frail old couple, it was difficult to believe that Irina could have been used as a sexual lure for Rasputin. Yet in refusing to say why Rasputin had come and denying that it was because of Irina, Felix admitted that he had lied about the reason for Rasputin's visit to the Moika Palace.

The defence called as witnesses the scriptwriters, the producer James McGinn and a history professor but it soon became apparent that none of them had realised that Felix was still alive. McGinn, cross-examined by Felix's lawyer, stated that it was an historical event and no permission was necessary providing it was reasonably accurate.[45]

The jury took over three hours to unanimously reject the Youssoupovs' claim. A rather jaundiced view was taken by the New York correspondent of *Izvestia*, the Soviet newspaper, who commented that the Youssoupovs 'are now living off the Rasputin murder'. Yet the case was equally as historic as the 1934 ruling. It opened to television 'those avenues of communication and comment which had been barred to films' by Irina's win in the suit against MGM.[46]

Irina and Felix went quietly back home, where they learnt that on 20 June Punka had married Ilya Sfiris in Athens. The bride and bridegroom spent their honeymoon in Paris, where Felix rented them a room in a nearby hotel. They spent every day together and Felix gave Ilya a sapphire and silver ring with the Youssoupov monogram.

✩

On 28 December 1965 *The Times* announced that early in 1966 the BBC would screen 'a 90-minute documentary about the events leading up to the assassination of Rasputin'. It was written by Kiernan Tunney, who made 'at least eight visits to Paris' to speak to Felix, who had approved the script.[47] *In Search of Rasputin* would deal with Felix's relationship with the peasant, about which Tunney believed Felix had not told the truth. When Tunney questioned Felix, he admitted that Rasputin had intense affection for him. Tunney also believed that Felix had concealed the truth about the murder and the reason for Rasputin's presence in the palace that night.

Suddenly, after eighteen months' work, the project was dropped by the new BBC head of drama who, Tunney said, 'wanted to use only the more sensational aspects of the story and I had been commissioned to do a serious documentary drama'. During long talks with Felix he had found 'much new material ... The reason Rasputin came to the prince's palace ... was not to meet the prince's wife, but because the monk wanted to see the prince.'[48]

Meanwhile, Felix had made a deal with the French company Epinal Studios for Robert Hossein to make a film depicting 'the first authorized version' of Rasputin's death, starring Gert Froebe (famous as Goldfinger) as Rasputin, to mark the fiftieth anniversary of the murder. Felix agreed to appear fleetingly in the opening of the film.

The historical consultant Dmitri Fedotov arranged for Peter Lennon of *The Guardian* to briefly interview Felix, who was now partly paralysed following a stroke. Lennon arrived with Fedotov at rue Pierre-Guérin.

A Swedish secretary led us into the salon and I was presented to the prince: a polished head, refined features, his knees covered by a rug in an armchair, his withered right arm lying across his lap. But his eyes seemed very much alive and intelligent and smiles of amused anticipation shivered continually across his mouth...

The princess made an appearance, walking with the aid of a stick. She is tall, thin, with bobbed white hair, dressed in a cardigan, a plain skirt, and sensible shoes – very much the style of an English lady. She took up a watchful position in a far corner. It was all a very long way from Siberia.

Lennon had been rationed to just a few questions, so as not to tire his host. He asked if it really had been so difficult to kill Rasputin. 'But it is in my book!' Felix replied. 'It is all, all true. Why else should I have written it?'

He asked the second question: 'Would you, if necessary, do it again?' Felix 'stretched forward shakily and for a moment his voice took on a deep baritone note: "Yes!" he shouted. "And how."'

Lennon insisted, 'But you would do it again?' 'Yes, Yes,' was Felix's emphatic reply.

Felix was still grinning when Lennon shook his hand on departure. Fedotov 'clicked his heels and kissed the raised hand of the princess. What must she have thought of my plebeian handshake?' Lennon wondered.[49]

Felix gave another interview to the American journalist E. M. Halliday. Published in *Horizon* in the autumn of 1967, 'Rasputin Reconsidered' challenged Felix's version of events. Halliday did not believe that Rasputin went to the Moika Palace to meet Irina and he disputed Felix's stated motive for killing him.

The interview, Halliday wrote, 'was interesting but unproductive'. He came 'close to admitting that there are indeed aspects of the famous story that are still wrapped in mystery ... "We cannot say why," was the closest he ever came to admitting that he had deliberately lied' about the motive for the murder.[50]

In 1966 the Hammer film *Rasputin the Mad Monk* was released with Christopher Lee in the title role. This was a different film to that featured in the 1930s court case. Hearing that it was being shown in London, Felix asked some friends to see it and report back. He was quite disappointed to learn that there were no grounds on which he could bring a lawsuit.[51]

Felix had apparently met Christopher Lee in London many years earlier. One of Felix's friends was Countess Estelle Carandini, an Italian aristocrat. One evening Estelle hauled her young son Christopher out of bed to meet two Russian aristocrats. 'You probably won't remember what they look like, but one day you will remember that you met them,' she said. The men were Felix and Grand Duke Dmitri.[52]

CR ✱ ℬ

In 1966 the Youssoupovs sold the house at Septeuil and in the following months they made their last public appearances together.

The couple were interviewed by Alain Decoux for *I Killed Rasputin*. Felix, now almost blind, wore dark glasses while Irina seemed almost intimidated by the presence of strangers. When asked why he had finally consented to participate in the film Felix replied that he had agreed to tell the truth because of the false stories circulating. Yet he said nothing new.

Although Irina had remained in the Crimea, she admitted knowing what was about to happen.

Decaux: 'Princess, were you aware of your husband's plans?'
Irina: 'Yes.'
Decaux: 'Did you approve?'
Irina: 'Yes.'[53]

The film was shown at the opening of the 1967 Cannes Film Festival and broadcast the following year. The reviews were critical and the audience was modest. When Tunney heard about this film, he instructed a French lawyer to sue Felix.

It was Rasputin's last stand.

When Irina's nephew Prince Michael Andreievich was asked if Felix ever spoke about Rasputin, his answer was unequivocal: 'My boy, that's all he ever talked about.'[54]

ଓ ✸ ଓ

By September 1967 Felix had been ill and in great pain for some time. He went into a coma and his family gathered at the bedside. On 27 September he suddenly opened his eyes, smiled and died peacefully.

Hundreds of mourners attended his funeral on 30 September. Irina, looking frailer than ever, was accompanied by Bébé, Nikolai and Xenia Sfiris. After a service at the Orthodox Church of Notre-Dame de la Dormition at St Geneviève-des-Bois, Felix was buried alongside his mother. As Father Nicholas Obolensky said prayers over the simple wooden coffin a busload of pupils from the local orphanage arrived to pay their respects. Unknown to Irina, Felix had helped them financially for some considerable time.

When Irina returned to rue Pierre-Guérin, she found a single rose and a letter of condolence from Stanislas Lazovert. Despite living in Paris, the only remaining conspirator in Rasputin's murder did not attend Felix's funeral.[55] Lazovert's was among many letters Irina received expressing condolences, as well as gratitude for the help Felix had extended to various people.

Irina remained in Paris, totally lost without Felix. She had stood by him throughout everything – the murder of Rasputin, the trauma of exile and the constant money problems. Despite frequent separations they had been devoted to one another. Now he was gone.

Speaking of his wife to a magazine interviewer some years earlier, the prince picked up a photograph of her. 'Isn't she beautiful?' he said. 'We live as happily together as we did the first day. This is love, true love – something I've felt for no one but her. When she dies, I will die.'[56]

Irina refused to move to Greece to be near Bébé; she wanted to be close to Felix. On 28 August 1968 she became a great-grandmother when Xenia Sfiris gave birth to a daughter, Tatiana, in Athens.

Irina remained a fragile figure, dressed in undistinguished black garments that betrayed neither age nor price. Her cousin and former sister-in-law Irene Paley stepped into the breach.[57] She invited Irina to stay with her at Balindus, the Biarritz villa Princess Olga Paley had bought in 1923. The women enjoyed each other's company and rarely missed celebrating the Russian Easter with traditional coloured eggs, *kulich*, and *paskha* made in a pyramid-shaped mould by the old Russian nurse.

Feodor was living in Ascain, too ill to work. Irina and Princess Irene helped to pay his medical bills. It was Irene's sister Natalie, living in America, who after the war delivered the penicillin (unavailable in France) which enabled him to survive. He was looked after by a local woman who stayed with him until he died in 1968.[58]

When not in Biarritz, Irina remained at rue Pierre-Guérin with her servant Bernice. She had always loved cats and never failed to feed the strays that came into her yard. One morning in February 1970 their meowing woke her and she went outside in her negligee to feed them. She caught a cold which turned to pneumonia. Her condition worsened and she was bedridden.

Princess Irina died on 26 February at the age of seventy-four.[59]

Just nine days earlier Anna Anderson's appeal to be recognised as Anastasia was rejected by the court. In 1994 DNA testing proved that she was indeed Franziska Schanzkowska.

ೞ ✳ ❧

Irina's funeral took place on 2 March at St Geneviève-des-Bois. She was buried beside Felix. Five days later, Bébé arranged for a Mass to be said in the Russian Church on rue Daru, which was attended by royalty from all over Europe.[60]

Irina is remembered today, if at all, for her once staggering beauty and for the court case against MGM. Felix, however, is remembered for one thing – the murder of the so-called 'Mad Monk'.

After the revolution it was claimed that Rasputin had cursed Felix's family, so that from then onward the only heir would always be a daughter.[61] At the time of writing, no sons have been born in the family since the birth of Felix in 1887.

Felix died as he had lived, in the shadow of Rasputin.

Postscript

Most of the Russian homes Irina and Felix knew are still there.

After the revolution the Moika Palace was nationalised and opened as a museum in August 1925. A guide to the works of art was published, yet it was the notorious basement which drew visitors. The government closed the museum in 1926 and dispersed some of the furniture. At one point the basement room was divided into lavatory cubicles.[1]

The artist Robert Byron visited in 1932. It was then the clubhouse for the Trade Union of Educationists and men were eating soup in the winter garden. A safe had recently been discovered under the floor in Felix senior's rooms. Byron asked about 'the hoard of treasure found in 1925' and 'our guide replied that the whole place was honeycombed with secret passages'. He went down the spiral staircase to the basement but a thaw had set in and it was under 6 inches of water.[2]

By 1937 the palace served 'as a kind of doss-house for engineers visiting Leningrad', with rows of iron beds in the elegant rooms and corridors. The contents had been perquisitioned.[3] After the war it became home to the St Petersburg Cultural Centre for Educational Workers.

During the Second World War a hospital was situated in the palace but in 1941 German bombs damaged some of the rooms, including the theatre.

The palace has now been restored and is one of St Petersburg's most popular attractions, where tourists can admire the splendour of the interiors and see waxworks of the conspirators and their victim in the infamous cellar and study.

Xenia and Sandro's palace at Moika 106 is the Lesgaft National State University of Physical Education, Sport and Health. The interiors have not survived and the former chapel became a gym.[4]

In Moscow, Arkhangelskoe came under state protection in 1919 after the estate manager appealed to Lenin. At the end of the civil war it became a resort for senior communist officials. Two new side blocks were built and Stalin had his own special suite constructed. Later it was used as a sanatorium for officials from the Ministry of Defence. Cambridge spy Guy Burgess was treated there in the spring of 1960. He wrote that the main house was 'a museum full of Hubert Robert's [paintings] but one good Titian, one very good Tintoretto'.[5]

Arkhangelskoe has now been restored and is open to the public. It is said to be haunted. The unfinished mausoleum has been used for exhibitions and concerts but the crypt is empty. The Church of the Archangel Michael also survives. A marble grave once contained Princess Zenaide's son Nicholas and her sister Tatiana with her baby. During the revolution their bodies are believed to have been thrown into the Moscow River.[6]

The Youssoupovs' house in Moscow became the offices of the Academy of Agricultural Sciences. The interior decor has remained in all its oriental splendour, 'although the living quarters have been changed beyond all recognition'.[7] The golden lions on the main staircase still stand proudly[8] but the seven leather trunks of Youssoupov diamonds they once guarded are long gone.

In the Crimea much damage was done during the Nazi occupation between August 1942 and mid-October 1944. When a group of us toured the Crimea in 1999 many of the palaces had never received a visit from foreign tourists before.

Koreiz came under the aegis of the Ministry of Foreign Affairs after the revolution. Estimating their losses in exile, the Youssoupovs estimated that Koreiz alone, with its 22 hectares of land (222,000 square metres), lost them 1.5 million roubles. In February 1945 it was Stalin and Molotov's base during the Yalta Conference at nearby Livadia. Fearful of attack, Stalin used an inconspicuous side entrance and had a bomb shelter specially built. Furniture, china and silverware had to be brought from Moscow hotels for Stalin's grand dinner in the 50-foot-long dining room with its half-moon window and Moorish-style fireplace.[9] Stalin used a large room, partitioned in two so that he could sleep and work there. His desk was still there in 1999.[10] The billiard room was converted into a cinema. In 1945 several foreign ministers' meetings were held at Koreiz. It later became a resort for Levrentii Beria's NKVD staff.[11] In 1999 it was a high-class hotel and by 2010 it was the guesthouse of the President of Ukraine. Most of the interior has been drastically changed.[12]

Part of the Koreiz estate now belongs to the Crimean Nature Reserve. The Eagle's Flight rock and the observation platform remain, although the little teahouse which Felix gave Irina in 1913 was destroyed, possibly during the Second World War.[13]

Ai-Todor became a Soviet spa, with communist blocks covering the vineyards and hills where Irina and her brothers once ran around and played. When their grandson Prince Alexander Nikitich went there it was 'a sanitorium or something', with people walking around in prison-style uniforms. It was so depressing that he did not even get out of the car. In 1999 tourists were not allowed anywhere near the estate.[14]

In 2013 Alexander's cousin Princess Olga Andreievna Romanoff was allowed inside the security fence. The little chapel where her father married Elsa had gone but the gravestones in the floor were still visible among the woodland. Ai-Todor was a rehabilitation home for abused older teenage children. Along the drive were huge silos with windows, crammed with bunkbeds. 'In one quite small area ... was the chalet where Amama and Apapa [Xenia and Sandro] lived, which was beautiful, like a Swiss chalet although slightly larger.' It was also crammed with bunkbeds. 'Then next door was the ancient cookhouse, which still had the frieze of hand painted drawings around the top where the cornice was.'[15]

In November 2015 the Russian government sold Ai-Todor to the politician Oleg Tsarev, who was planning to construct a four-storey building and swimming pool. The land on the lower part of the estate was bought by the billionaire Arkhady Rotenberg.[16]

Kokoz became administrative buildings, a Tartar school and later a club and headquarters for the police. Most of the original furnishings disappeared but anything left was taken to the Khan's Palace at Bakhchisaray. In 1999 it was a children's home, with the dining room divided horizontally and the upper part used as a dormitory. The room's wonderful ceiling remained and the blue-eye motif was still there. Nearby, the Tartar mosque built by the Youssoupovs still stands.[17]

Since 2014 Kokoz has been the Artek International Children's Camp.[18] The village of Kokoz is now called Sokolinoe.

Sosnovaya Roshcha, where Felix and Irina never had chance to live, was demolished in 1970. There is now a large sanatorium near the site of the house.[19]

In Yalta on 11 April 2009 a granite obelisk was erected on the waterfront by the Yalta Friends Club to mark the ninetieth anniversary of the departure of HMS *Marlborough*. Under a double-headed eagle is a metal plaque with the inscription: 'On April 11, 1919 the British Battleship HMS *Marlborough* departed from Yalta, taking into exile the surviving members of the Russian Imperial Family among them the Dowager Empress Marie Feodorovna.' The double-headed eagle on top of the obelisk has now disappeared and has been replaced with a granite cone.

On a rainy day ten years later, a small crowd gathered in Yalta to commemorate the centenary of this historic departure. Speeches were made and, as women sang 'God Save the Tsar', wreaths and roses were tossed into the grey waters of the Black Sea.[20]

More than seventy years after the departure of Irina and Felix, their granddaughter Xenia Sfiris visited the Moika Palace in St Petersburg. In the 1990s she gave a DNA sample to help identify the remains of Nicholas II (her great-great-uncle) and his family found near Ekaterinburg. In 2000, she was granted Russian citizenship by the President of the Russian Federation.

The Youssoupovs had come full circle.

Notes

Introduction

1. Napley, p 121.

1 The Tsar's Niece

1. Mandache, p 186.
2. Alexander, *Once,* p 203.
3. The *Church Times.* 15 July 1895. Ian Shapiro Collection. H.I.H. stands for His/Her Imperial Highness.
4. Kleinpenning, p 202.
5. Kleinpenning, p 204.
6. Kleinpenning, p 205.
7. The Coster sisters were from a large family in Eastbourne, Sussex, where their father William was a carpenter. Jane returned to Eastbourne to care for her widowed mother until her death in 1893, then about eighteen months later she returned to St Petersburg to become nurse to Irina. Frances Coster was nurse to Grand Duchess Olga, remaining with her all through 1896 before returning to the Platouines as housekeeper, a post she held until her retirement in 1912. www.Eliotsofporteliot.com; Welch, *Tea Party,* p 51.
8. Tegulle, In *Royal Russia* No. 13. p 131.
9. *Maria Feodorovna, Empress of Russia* Exhibition catalogue, p 174.
10. Van der Kiste & Hall, p 47.
11. Kleinpenning, p 24.
12. Obolensky, p 79.
13. Alexander, *Once,* p 133; His wine list itemised six red and seventy-eight white vintages. Wine list courtesy of Prince Michael Romanoff.
14. Bing, p 146.
15. Maylunas & Mironenko, p 245.
16. GARF 643-1-49. Irina to Olga Alexandrovna, 20 Oct. 1904. Trans. by George Hawkins.

17. Hawkins. Irina to Marie, 21 May 1905.
18. GARF 611-1-87. Irina to Olga Nicolaievna, 21 May 1905. Trans. by George Hawkins.
19. *London Daily News*, 6 April 1907.
20. Maria Pavlovna to Prince William of Sweden, 22 Aug 1907. In *How Lovely it is to be a Bride*.
21. Hawkins. Tatiana to the dowager empress, 13 Aug. 1909.
22. Hawkins. Olga to Petrov, 24 Sept. 1909.
23. Hawkins. Irina to Olga Nicolaievna, 26 March 1909.
24. GARF 651-1-75 Irina to Tatiana, Biarritz, 26 March 1909. Trans by George Hawkins.
25. GARF 651-1-75 undated. Irina to Tatiana. Trans. George Hawkins.
26. Hawkins. Irina to Tatiana, 3 Feb. 1910.
27. Hawkins. Olga Nicolaievna to Xenia, 30 March 1910.
28. Hawkins. Irina to Tatiana, 30 March 1910
29. Hawkins. Irina to Olga Nicolaievna, undated.
30. Hawkins. Olga Alexandrovna to Tatiana. 8 July 1910.
31. GARF 651-1-79. Olga Alexandrovna to Tatiana, 23 Aug. 1910. Trans.by George Hawkins.
32. Hawkins. Olga Alexandrovna to Tatiana, 23 Sept. 1910.
33. Kamarovskaia, p 177.
34. 'Letters of Marie Alexandrovna to Missy.' Talk given by John Wimbles at the Royalty Digest Conference, Ticehurst, April 2004.
35. Hawkins. Olga Nicolaievna to the dowager empress, 18 July 1911.
36. Hawkins. Olga Alexandrovna to Tatiana, 27 Nov. 1911.
37. Some sources erroneously say that Olga wore pink, but her diary makes it clear that she wore a long white dress for the first time. See Olga's diary entry in Rappaport, *Four Sisters*, p 158.
38. Hawkins. Olga Alexandrovna to Tatiana, 27 Nov. 1911.
39. Kamarovskaia, p 175.
40. Fane was born in Pau, France in 1871. His family were descended on the wrong side of the blanket from the 8th Earl of Westmoreland. He attended the Beacon Preparatory School in Sevenoaks before entering the army, serving with the Queen's Own (Royal West Kent Regiment) until resigning his commission in 1893. In 1896 in New York he married Scharlie Thorne and later served in one of the Volunteer Battalions in the Boer War. Kamarovskaia calls him an officer in the Indian army and a relative of Warburton. Ancestry.co.uk; *The London Gazette; The New York Times*.
41. Various editions of the *Gazette de Biarritz;* Information from Courtney West; Maylunas & Mironenko, p 313.
42. The picture is in The Ricketts Collection at the National Media Museum, Bradford; *Le Figaro*, 2 Dec. 1910.
43. In 1896 Mary married Barclay Harding Warburton I, one-time owner of the Philadelphia Evening Telegraph, by whom she had two sons and a daughter, Minnie, who was a year younger than Irina. The Ellis Island records show that Mrs Warburton returned to New York from Europe in 1911.
44. Kamarovskaia, pp 126/7.
45. Kamarovskaia, p 127.

2 The Richest Man in Russia

1. Ferrand, *Youssoupovs*, p 3; *The Yusupov Palace. Museum Guide*, p 21; Radzinsky, *Rasputin*, p 106.
2. In June 1718 Tsarevich Alexei was found dead in his cell in the SS Peter & Paul Fortress, probably as a result of torture. According to the Russian Nobility Association of New York, Princess Zenaide's father may have been the Don Juan of St Petersburg Prince Anatole Ivanovich Bariatinsky. Princess Zenaide always maintained that the two families shared the same lineage and that Anatole's descendant Prince Alexei Scherbatov, who lived near them in Rome in the 1920s, was Felix's cousin once removed. See Moe, *Prelude*, p 246, note 48.
3. Ferrand, *Youssoupovs*, pp 3 & 207.
4. 27 June 1888. www.Kulturologia.ru
5. Information from Elizaveta Krasnykh.
6. Xenia Sfiris interview with Anna von Lowzow, 2009.
7. *The Yusupov Palace. Museum Guide*, pp 5, 20 & 37.
8. Haskin. 'Seneca, D. H. Lawrence and the Yusupovs.' In *Atlantis*, Vol. 4, No. 2. p 5.
9. Haskin. 'Seneca, D. H. Lawrence and the Yusupovs.' In *Atlantis*, Vol. 4, No. 2. p 7.
10. *The Yusupov Palace. Museum Guide*, p 37.
11. Eric Hamilton's diary. 3 Sept 1910. University College Archives, 25/MS/1.
12. Information from Elizaveta Krasnykh.
13. Eric Hamilton's diary. 15 Sept. 1910. University College Archives, 25/MS/1.
14. Haskin. 'His Brother's Keeper.' In *Atlantis*, Vol 2, No 3, p 10.
15. Obolensky, p 68.
16. Haskin, 'His Brother's Keeper', Part 2. In *Atlantis*, Vol 2, No. 4, p 15.
17. Moe, *Prelude*, p 227.
18. 31 August 1908. Courtesy of Dr William Lee.
19. There is another man who comes up in connection with Felix's efforts to learn English. Frank Walter Cooke (born 31 Dec. 1865) applied for a passport in 1888 and came to St Petersburg to teach English. In 1902 he married Edith Wilton (sister of the Times correspondent Robert Wilton) and in 1909 they and their daughters moved to Moscow. Frank and Edith then gave English lessons. Among Frank's pupils were Felix and, later, Grand Duke Dmitri Pavlovich. Details are sketchy but it is interesting that Cooke's younger daughter was given the middle name of Zenaide, while his son (born in 1909) was called Dmitri. Pitcher, pp 135/6; Horsbrugh-Porter, pp 39/46; ancestry.co.uk.

3 The Dreaming Spires of Oxford

1. Nicholson, 'The Assassin in the Computing Room.' In *The Martlet*, Spring 2017.
2. Clarke, *Saving*, p 30.
3. *The Times*, 5 October 1967.

4. University College Archives Admissions Register, p 184B.
5. University College Archives. UC: BU3/F3/88. Six guineas is six pounds and six shillings (£6.30 today).
6. *New York Times*. 'Prince Youssoupoff Defended in Rasputin Case.' 17 Jan. 1917.
7. In 1940 the current incumbent crawled 'flat on his stomach into a remote inaccessible corner at the back of the cupboard' and found 'a large stone pot with metal clasps labelled "Finest Astrakhan Caviar"'. There is, unfortunately, no proof that it was left by Felix but the students like to believe that it was. Until recently the Club was a computer room for the students. Nicholson, 'Assassin' and personal visit with Dr Michael Nicholson, 2019.
8. Nicholson, 'Assassin'.
9. *New York Times*, 17 Jan. 1917.
10. University College Archives; Nicholson, 'Assassin'.
11. Yudin, 'Knyaz Feliks Yusupov v Oksforde (1909-1912).'
12. Nicholson, 'Assassin.'
13. *New York Times,* 14 Jan. 1917.
14. Yudin, 'Knyaz Feliks Yusupov v Oksforde (1909-1912).'
15. Van der Kiste & Hall, p 198.
16. Timetable in Krasnykh p 178; details from U.C. Archives and conversation with Dr Michael Nicholson, 2019. There were very few actual professors during Felix's time at Oxford.
17. *New York Times*, 14 Jan. 1917.
18. Haskin, Gretchen. 'Seneca, D. H. Lawrence and the Yusupovs.' In *Atlantis Magazine*, Volume 4, No. 2, p 11.
19. Information from Martin Ellfolk, Arkivsamlingarna, Åbo Akademis bibliotek; Cook. *Rasputin,* pp 76/7.
20. Hamilton memoir, U.C. Archives. 25/MS/2 (1956)
21. Hamilton memoir, U.C. Archives. 25/MS/2 (1956)
22. It was linked to the story of a beautiful Polish girl held prisoner in the khan's harem. Marie Potocki became Khan Qirim Giray's favourite, with her own luxurious apartments and a private catholic chapel. When she was stabbed to death by jealous rivals the grief-stricken khan had a marble fountain constructed, from which two oval spouts gushed a steady stream of water representing his tears.
23. Hamilton diary, Sept. 1910. U.C. Archives. 25/MS/1.
24. Haskin. 'Seneca, D. H. Lawrence and the Yusupovs.' Atlantis Vol. 4, No. 2, p 11.
25. Hamilton memoir, U.C. Archives. 25/MS/2 (1956)
26. It has been said that before her marriage to Prince Nicholas of Greece she ran away with an army officer and had to be brought back from the frontier. Information from Elizaveta Krasnykh. Galina Korneva, an expert on the Vladimir family, doubts this story.
27. Xenia Sfiris interview with Anna von Lowzow, 2009.
28. Hamilton diary, 31 Aug. 1910. U.C. Archives 25/MS/1.
29. Khrustalev, p 31.
30. Information from Dr Michael Nicholson; Hamilton memoir, U.C. Archives. 25/MS/2 (1956)

31. Yudin, 'Knyaz Feliks Yusupov v Oksforde (1909-1912).'; Chris Danziger, 'The Oxford alumnus who helped assassinate Rasputin.' In *Oxford Today* magazine, December 2016.
32. *New York Times,* 17 Jan. 1917. Haskin, 'Seneca, D. H. Lawrence and the Yusupovs.' *Atlantis,* Vol. 4, No. 2 p 10; Yudin, 'Knyaz Feliks Yusupov v Oksforde.' One of his hunting costumes survives in Russia.
33. Sebastian Earl's memories of Felix. UC Archives. Accession No. 1089.
34. Nicholson, 'Assassin.'
35. Dobson, p 30.
36. Information from Elizaveta Krasnykh & Prince Michael Romanoff.
37. Sebastian Earl's memories of Felix. UC Archives. Accession No. 1089.
38. *New York Times,* 14 Jan. 1917
39. Clarke, *Saving,* p 30.
40. 28 February 1911, qtd in Khrustalev, p 42.
41. Cooper, *Darling Monster,* p 405. In 1912 Marjorie married Charles Paget, later 6th Marquess of Anglesey.
42. Victoria to Grand Duchess Eleonore of Hesse. Grand Ducal Family Archives in the Darmstadt State Archives, D24 No. 45/1 8 January 1911.
43. Xenia Sfiris interview with Anna von Lowzow, 2009.
44. Vassiliev, p 268.
45. Yudin, 'Knyaz Feliks Yusupov v Oksforde.'
46. Hamilton diary, 7 Sept. 1910. U.C. Archives 25/MS/1.
47. Sebastian Earl's memories of Felix. UC Archives. Accession No. 1089.
48. Yudin, 'Knyaz Feliks Yusupov v Oksforde.'
49. Yudin, as above; C. S. Lewis Diary, 9 Feb. 1927, (Geoffrey Bless, 1966); Nicholson, 'Assassin.'
50. Sebastian Earl's memories of Felix. UC Archives. Accession No. 1089.
51. University College Archives. UC:BU9/C1/1. This is the only letter they have in Felix's own hand.

4 Irina and Felix

1. Erté, p 56.
2. *Iz semeynoy perepiski Yusupovykh,* p 125.
3. Xenia Sfiris interview with Anna von Lowzow, 2009.
4. *The Aberdeen Journal,* 14 September 1911.
5. *Iz semeynoy perepiski Yusupovykh,* p 128.
6. *The Dundee Evening Telegraph,* 31 Jan. 1912 [NS] & others.
7. Dept of Written Sources, State Historical Museum, Moscow. GIM OPI. Fund 411. Op. 1. D. 39. L. 1–2 vol. 14, qtd in Khrustalev, p 47.
8. *The Daily Mirror,* 10 Nov. 1916.
9. Krasnykh, p 285.
10. Kamarovskaia, p 214.
11. Hawkins. Olga Alexandrovna to Tatiana. 5 July OS 1912.
12. Hawkins. Tatiana to the dowager empress, 13 Aug. OS 1912.
13. Letters of Marie Alexandrovna to Missy.' Talk given by John Wimbles at the Royalty Digest Conference, Ticehurst, April 2004.

14. Van der Kiste & Hall, p 73; Accounts of the Xenia Association. Copy in author's possession.
15. Kamarovskaia, p 207.
16. Hawkins. Tatiana to Xenia. 18 Nov. 1912 & Xenia to Tatiana. Copenhagen. 22 Nov. 1912.
17. Hawkins. Olga Alexandrovna to Tatiana. 12 April 1912.
18. Hawkins. Olga Alexandrovna to Tatiana. 23 Aug. 1910.
19. Azar, *Diary of Olga Romanov,* pp 91/92.
20. Kamarovskaia, p 194.
21. Romanoff, Prince Roman, p 321.
22. Kamarovskaia, p 207.
23. Diary. 11 April 1913. Maylunus & Mironenko, p 376.
24. Xenia Sfiris interview with Anna von Lowzow, 2009.
25. Information from Elizaveta Krasnykh.
26. 'Letters of Marie Alexandrovna to Missy.' Talk given by John Wimbles at the Royalty Digest Conference, Ticehurst, April 2004.
27. Xenia Sfiris interview with Anna von Lowzow, 2009.
28. Information from Dr William Lee & letters in Krasnykh.
29. Quoted in Khrustalev, p 52.
30. Maylunus & Mironenko, p 378.
31. GARF 642-1-1676. To the dowager empress, 3 June 1913. Translated by George Hawkins.
32. Krasnykh, p 299.
33. Radzinsky, *Rasputin,* p 196.
34. Haskin, 'Seneca, D. H. Lawrence and the Yusupovs.' Atlantis Vol. 4, no 2, p 13.
35. Krasnykh, p 303.
36. Haskin, 'Seneca, D. H. Lawrence and the Yusupovs.' Atlantis Vol. 4, no 2, pp 13/14.
37. Information from Elizaveta Krasnykh.
38. *Ruslands Skatte,* p 168.
39. Khrustalev, p 55.
40. Khrustalev, p 55.
41. See Youssoupov, *Lost Splendour,* p 160.
42. Haskin. 'Seneca, D. H. Lawrence and the Yusupovs.' Atlantis Vol. 4, no 2, p 15.
43. Dept of Written Sources, State Historical Museum, Moscow. GIM OPI. F. 411. Op. 1. D. 84. L. 104-105. Qtd in Khrustalev, p 58.
44. Olivier Coutau-Begarie auction catalogue, Dec. 2015, p 67.
45. Dept of Written Sources, State Historical Museum, Moscow. GIM OPI. Fund 411. Op. 1. D. 84. L. 102-103. Qtd in Khrustalev, p 54.
46. GARF 642-1-1676. Irina to the dowager empress, 21 July/3 Aug. 1913. Trans. by George Hawkins.
47. Maylunas & Mironenko, p 381.
48. Maylunas & Mironenko, p 383.
49. Maylunas & Mironenko, p 384.
50. Radzinsky, *Rasputin,* p 196.
51. GARF 642-1-1676. Irina to the dowager empress, 11 Nov. 1913. Trans. by George Hawkins.

52. Haskin. 'Seneca, D. H. Lawrence and the Yusupovs.' Atlantis Vol. 4, no 2, p 14.
53. Krasnykh, p 330.
54. Ian Shapiro collection. Olga Alexandrovna to Princess Marie Louise of Baden. No date.
55. *The Aberdeen Journal*, 5 Jan. NS 1914.
56. Radzinsky, *Rasputin*, p 209.
57. *Russlands Skatt*, p 311.
58. Kleinpenning, p 318.
59. Betteley & Schimmelpennick van der Oye, p 94.
60. Stolitsa i usad'ba No. 5, 1914, p 9; Ferrand, *Youssoupovs*, pp 246/57.
61. Nadelhoffer, pp 71/2; Cartier Brickell, p 86. Stolitsa i usad'ba, No. 5, 1914, p 9, listed an emerald and diamond brooch given by Grand Duchess Olga Alexandrovna. From Queen Alexandra, a miniature portrait of herself. Her daughter Princess Victoria sent a bracelet. Grand Duke Nicholas Michaelovich gave a diamond pendant with a pink pearl, and his brother George a diamond bow brooch. Grand Duchesses Olga and Tatiana presented a diamond ring. There was a lily of the valley diamond and pearl brooch from Grand Duchess Ella. A list of Irina's wedding jewellery is given in Tillander-Godenheilm, pp 214/215. See also Ferrand, *Youssoupovs*, pp 246/257, & Nadelhoffer. Sources disagree on descriptions of the items.
62. '...almost nothing of Marie Antoinette's wardrobe escaped the onslaught [of the French revolution] intact.' See Weaver, p 7; Xenia's diary entry is in Maylunas & Mironenko, p 39.
63. Van der Kiste & Hall, p 83; Softky, 'Growing up Royal...'
64. Maylunas & Mironenko, p 391.
65. M. Buchanan, *Victorian Gallery*, p 185.
66. M. Buchanan, *Victorian Gallery*, p 184.
67. A poem dedicated to the couple is preserved in the Youssoupov archives.

5 Early Married Life

1. GARF 642-1-1676. Irina to the dowager empress, 11/24 Feb. 1914. Trans. by George Hawkins.
2. Tatiana to Xenia. 29 April OS 1914. Hawkins.
3. Tatiana to Xenia. 8 July OS 1914. Hawkins.
4. The Duchess of Saxe-Coburg to Crown Princess Marie of Romania, 12 July 1914. Horwood. 'Half a Century of Royal Letters'. *Royalty Digest Quarterly*, 2016.
5. Anon. *Russian Court Memoirs*, p 146.
6. Udaltsov, p 63.
7. Alexander, *Once*, p 228.
8. Anon. *Russian Court Memoirs*, p 55. In 1925 the Bolsheviks found a secret door in the bedroom leading to a room where a coffin contained a man's skeleton. Gossips said it was a young anarchist who had been the lover of Felix's great-grandmother the Countess of Chauveau. In her youth she had an affair with a young revolutionary who was later imprisoned in the Sveaborg Fortress in Finland. She helped him escape and then hid

him in the Liteinaia house until his death. Ferrand, *Youssoupovs*, p 148; Youssoupov, *Lost Splendour*, p 32.

9. Xenia Sfiris interview with Anna von Lowzow, 2009.
10. Byron, pp 84/88; King, *Rasputin*, p 148.
11. Tatiana to Xenia, 3 Sept. 1914. Hawkins.
12. Xenia to Tatiana, 5 Sept. 1914. Hawkins.
13. Napley, p 108; Anon, *Russian Court Memoirs*, p 56.
14. *Edinburgh Evening News*, 6 Jan. NS 1915.
15. GARF 642-1-1676. 25 Dec. 1914. Trans. by George Hawkins.
16. Bokhanov, *Romanovs*, p 240; Azar, *Diary of Olga Romanov*, p 23.
17. *Ruslands Skatte*, p 315.
18. Fuhrmann. *Wartime*, p 98; Azar & Nicholson, *Tatiana Romanov*, p 105.
19. Baschkiroff, p 15; Maylunas & Mironenko, p 422.
20. Fuhrmann, *Wartime*, p 121.
21. The appointment replaced the post of Special Military Governor and gave Felix senior an inflated idea of his own importance, believing he was equivalent to a viceroy.
22. Hamilton diary, 7 Sept. 1910. U.C. Archives 25/MS/1.
23. Hall, *Little Mother*, p 265. *Poslednie Novosti*, July 1933; Radzinsky, *Rasputin*, p 339.
24. Quoted in Nelipa, p 88.
25. Hamilton memoir, U.C. Archives. 25/MS/2 (1956)
26. Haskin. 'Seneca, D. H. Lawrence and the Yusupovs.' *Atlantis*. Vol 4 No. 2, p 14.
27. When our group visited Koreiz in 1999 we were told that Ai-Petri was still considered the private property of Princess Zenaide.
28. Baschkiroff, p 18; Khrustalev, p 80.
29. Dokumenty po Istorii Kryma Vtoraya Polovina xix – Nachala xx Veka v Yusupovskom Fonde v Rossiyskom Gosudarstvennom Arkhive Drevnikh Aktov.
30. Tatiana to Olga Alexandrovna, 17 November 1915. Hawkins.
31. GARF 642-1-1676. To the dowager empress, 6 April 1916. Trans.by George Hawkins.
32. Krasnykh, p 354.
33. Xenia to Olga Nicolaievna, 24 May 1916. Hawkins.
34. Tatiana to Xenia. 10 June 1916. Hawkins.
35. GARF 642-1-1676. To the dowager empress, 8 July 1916. Trans. by George Hawkins.
36. GARF 642-1-1676. To the dowager empress, 8 July 1916. Trans. by George Hawkins.
37. Olga Alexandrovna to Xenia, 3 & 4 Oct. 1916. Copy in author's possession.
38. Zillah was a daughter of William Henton, an engineer, and his wife Sarah Devereux. The family moved to Leicester and then Nottingham and by the age of thirty-two Zillah was working as a domestic nurse in Yorkshire with the family of the Rev. G. T. Whitehead. www.Ancestry.co.uk; 'Zillah Henton' by Ian Stevenson. *The Huddersfield & District FHS Journal*, April 2017.
39. 12 Aug. 1916. Fuhrmann, *Wartime*, p 557.
40. See Coutau-Begarie auction Catalogue, 4 November 2016, p 101 & p 110.

41. See Coutau-Begarie auction catalogue, 4 Nov. 2016, pp 101 & 110.
42. Hall. *Little Mother,* p 267.
43. 14 Aug. 1916. Fuhrmann, *Wartime*, p 560.
44. Xenia to Tatiana. 10 Sept. 1916. Hawkins.
45. Tatiana to Xenia. 15 Sept. 1916. Hawkins.
46. Pitcher, p 135.
47. D. Smith, p 190.
48. Moe, *Prelude,* p 495.
49. Vulliamy, p 105. Undated from Petrograd; Moe, *Prelude,* p 495.

6 Rasputin

1. In a somewhat spooky twist Bobby Farrell, the lead singer of Boney M, died in St Petersburg on 30 December 2010 – by the Western calendar the ninety-fourth anniversary of Rasputin's death in 1916.
2. Hamilton memoir, U.C. Archives. 25/MS/2 (1956)
3. Qtd. in D. Smith, p 450.
4. Qtd. in Radzinsky, *Rasputin,* p 400.
5. See Youssoupov, *Rasputin,* p 59; D. Smith, p 450.
6. *The Times,* 30 Sept. 1967.
7. Vulliamy, p 105.
8. Vulliamy, p 108.
9. Vulliamy, p 109.
10. Salisbury, p 289.
11. Nelipa, pp 102/4; Moe, *Prelude,* p 496.
12. Sukhotin, who was the same age as Felix, was raised by his step-mother Countess Tatiana Tolstoy, daughter of the writer, and studied at the University of Lausanne. Galina von Meck called him a 'distant relation' with whom she used to dance as a child. von Meck, p 183.
13. Others have claimed it was to cure Felix of his homosexual tendencies. See Cook, *Rasputin,* p 40.
14. Youssoupov, *Lost Splendour,* pp 218/9 & 227/8.
15. Langer, 'Fighting the Future'; Salisbury, p 290.
16. Vulliamy, p 111.
17. Naryshkin-Kurakin, p 215; Marie, *Education,* p 280.
18. *Reka vremen 2,* p 149, qtd. in D. Smith p 573.
19. Vulliamy, pp 115/6.
20. *Reka vremen 2,* p 149, qtd. in D. Smith p 576.
21. 31 December NS 1916. FO371/2994 (705).
22. There is no surviving evidence that Rasputin was under 24-hour surveillance at the time, although Douglas Smith says he had Okhrana bodyguards to keep him out of harm's way. See Cullen p 120, D. Smith p 424. There were Okhrana surveillance diaries covering the period January 1915 to February 1916. Nelipa, p 49.
23. Vulliamy, p 113.
24. Qtd. in Radzinsky, *Rasputin,* p 444/45.
25. Radzinsky, *Rasputin,* p 447.
26. Vulliamy, p 110.

27. Quoted in Radzinsky, *Rasputin,* p 447.
28. Vulliamy, p 115. Olga Vassiliev claimed to have met Irina at the Ekaterinsky Institute in their youth. However, Irina was never a pupil at the Institute, although along with other members of the imperial family she received students of the Institute at Gatchina. Information from Valentina Nabok, The Youssoupov Palace.
29. Nelipa, p 105.
30. Dobson, p 13; Nelipa, p 122. Maklakov testified to Nicholas Sokolov in Paris in 1920. Sokolov, the former Court Investigator into the deaths of the imperial family, had expanded his investigation to include the circumstances leading up to their deaths, one of which was the murder of Rasputin. This was a purely personal project, cut short by his death in 1924. His dossier, which fell into the hands of the Russians in 1945, remained hidden in a Soviet Archive until 1991. See Nelipa, p 101.
31. See Youssoupov, *Rasputin,* p 142.
32. Beloborodov, Diary. In Russkaya mysl, Paris, No. 941. 21 August 1956.
33. Youssoupov, *Lost Splendour,* p 233.
34. *The Times.* 30 September 1967.
35. Cook, *Rasputin,* p 168.
36. *The New York Times,* 23 Sept. 1918.
37. Cullen, p 76.
38. Ruud & Stepanov, p 311; Tomaselli, 'Britain Helped Rasputin's Killers.'
39. Since 1916 part of the Moika Palace was occupied by the Special Department for the Care and Pension Provision of Soldiers and their Families. See Nabok, 'Khudozhestvennaya kollektsiya knyazey Yusupovykh v dvadtsatom veke'. The old Moika 92 building has now been replaced by a four-storey apartment building set further back. See Moe, *Prelude,* p 542, note 151.
40. Konshine & King, 'The 1916-17 Diaries of Grand Duke Andrei Vladimirovich.' *Atlantis,* Vol. 5, no. 1, p 38.
41. Konshine & King, 'The 1916-17 Diaries of Grand Duke Andrei Vladimirovich.' *Atlantis,* Vol. 5, no. 1, p 38.
42. TNA FO371/2991 (705) 31 Dec. NS 1916 & (FO 371/2994 (1187). 1 Jan. 1917.
43. The entire letter is in Moe, *Prelude,* pp 556/7.
44. Vera Karalli, a ballerina with the Bolshoi Ballet, was born on 27 July 1889 in Moscow and made films from 1914 (in Russia) until 1921. She died on 16 November 1972 in Baden, having left no memoirs and never having given an interview. Information from Dr William Lee; Moe, *Prelude,* p 540.
45. See Cook, *Rasputin,* pp 53/4.
46. Paleologue, Vol 3, p 142.
47. Shishkin, Chapter 26. Citing Archive of GTsTM. A. A. Bakhrushina. F. 563. D. 186-314808/9. L. 6 & L. 8.
48. Nelipa pp 294 & 409; www.forum.alexanderpalace.org 'Rasputin's Murder.' Richard Cullen's post of 2 Jan. 2006.
49. www.forum.alexanderpalace.org. 'Rasputin Killed by British Agent.' Cullen's post of 5 Oct. 2004.
50. In *Nicholas & Alexandra* Exhibition Catalogue, p 328.
51. Stopford, pp 87 & 83.

52. See Cullen, pp 210/211.
53. Hall. *Little Mother*, p 274.
54. Aldrich & Cormac, pp 169/70.
55. Aldrich & Cormac pp 170 & 172.
56. *The Times*, 1 December 1921. 'Assassins of Rasputin – Rasputin's Fate.'
57. Cook, *Rasputin*, p 80 and Andrew Cook's interview with Gordon Rayner, Oswald's nephew, on 13 March 2004. I am grateful to Andrew Cook for making this interview available to me. I have used the more familiar term MI6, although at the time it was MI1c.
58. Collection Donner, Uno and Olly, 35. Vån.II2: L:1. Åbo Akademi University Library, Finland. For some unexplained reason Rayner addressed his letters to Anna Sinebrychoff to 'Dear Granny' and signed himself 'yours affectionately, Billy'. Finland was at this time part of the Russian empire so this may have been done to avoid curious eyes, looking as if he was a grandson writing to his grandmother. His work for the SIS may have necessitated this deception.
59. Cullen, pp 16/17; Cook, *Rasputin*, pp 79/80; M. Smith, p 196; Aldrich & Cormac p 169.
60. Email from Dr David Lockwood, 2 Oct. 2020; Jeffery, p 9; Aldrich & Cormac, p 157.
61. Cook, *Rasputin*, p 82.
62. Preston Manor Archives.

7 Cover-up

1. Youssoupov, *Rasputin*, p 149.
2. Courtesy of the Youssoupov Palace.
3. Collection Donner, Uno and Olly, 35. Vån.II2: L:1. Åbo Akademi University Library, Finland. 16 May 1916.
4. Collection Donner, Uno and Olly, 35. Vån.II2: L:1. Åbo Akademi University Library, Finland. To Anna Sinebrychoff, 14 & 29 May 1916.
5. Milton, pp 12 & 15; Hoare, p 108.
6. Milton, p 13 & 114; Jeffery, p 103.
7. M. Smith, *Six*, p 197.
8. Scale papers. Qtd in M. Smith, p 199/200.
9. Andrew Cook interview with Muriel Harding-Newman, 28 May 2003. I am grateful to Andrew Cook for making this interview available to me.
10. Andrew Cook interview with Muriel Harding-Newman, 28 May 2003.
11. Email from Andrew Cook 16.11.2020; M. Smith, *Six*, p 187.
12. www.forum.alexanderpalace.org 'Rasputin's murder'. Post by Phil Tomaselli, 18 Jan. 2006.
13. Cullen, p 193; Cook *Rasputin*, p 155.
14. Lockhart, pp 119/20.
15. Gosudrstvennyi istoricheskii muzei, otdel pis'mennykh isochnikov 411.66. 24-24ob. Courtesy of Douglas Smith.
16. See Cook, *Rasputin*, p 156.
17. 15 Oct. 1916. Preston Manor archives; Collection Donner, Uno and Olly, 35. Vån.II2: L:1. Åbo Akademi University Library, Finland. 16 October 1916.

18. 29 Nov. 1916. Preston Manor Archives; Oxfordshire History Centre. P23/1/C/3/3.
19. Cook. *Rasputin,* pp 216 & 156.
20. RGADA. Fond 95. Op. 1.D. 63. List 51. Quoted in Shishkin, *Poslednyaya tayna Rasputina.* Chapter 19.
21. 14 Dec. 1916. Oxfordshire History Centre. P23/1/C/3/4.
22. Email from Dr David Lockwood, 27 July 2018. According to Gordon Rayner, his father had a book about Rasputin on his bookshelf and 'when Uncle Oswald came to visit he always removed it' so not to 'enrage uncle Oswald.' Andrew Cook interview with Gordon Rayner, 13 March 2004. I am grateful to Andrew Cook for making this interview available to me.
23. Cook, *Rasputin,* p 230.
24. Cook, *Rasputin,* p 220; www.ancestry.co.uk
25. John Penycate, Letter in *Oxford Today,* 8 April 2017; Moss. 'Who Was Rasputin?'
26. Cullen, p 108.
27. Nelipa, p 108; Dorrill, p 611.
28. 14 Feb. 1917. Preston Manor archives.
29. 14 Feb. 1917. Preston Manor archives.
30. Email from Dr David Lockwood, 15 Oct. 2020; Collection Donner, Uno and Olly, 35. Vån.II2: L:1. Åbo Akademi University Library, Finland. 13 June 1916.
31. 2 Oct. 1919. Preston Manor Archives.
32. D. Smith, pp 631/2 & 610.
33. Milton, p 24.
34. D. Smith, p 632.
35. Nicholas Michaelovich to Frederic Masson, 7 Feb. OS 1917. Courtesy of Dr William Lee.
36. Private information; Email from Dr William Lee.
37. www.forum.alexanderpalace.org Rasputin Murdered by British Agent. Post by Phil Tomaselli, 4 Oct. 2004.
38. Buchanan, Vol II, pp 36/37.
39. Hoare, pp 67/68 & 137/8.
40. Hoare, p 156; Cook, *Rasputin,* p 74.
41. See Cook, p 275 note 21.
42. TNA FO371/2994 (1187) 19 Dec 1916/1 Jan. 1917.
43. www.forum.alexanderpalace.org British Foreign Office Files and Rasputin, post by Phil Tomaselli, 9 Jan. 2006.
44. Norwich, p 45.
45. Tomaselli, 'Britain Helped Rasputin's Killer.'
46. M. Smith, p 205.
47. See letter of 25 Dec. 1916 from Misha Soumarokoff-Elston to Felix in Ganina, *Arkhiv Feliksa i Iriny Yusupovykh.*
48. Private information.
49. Xenia Sfiris interview with Anna von Lowzow, 2009.
50. Nelipa p 257 & 211.
51. D. Smith, p 600.
52. Youssoupov, *Lost Splendour,* p 239.
53. Yusupov. *Konets Rasputina,* p.114.

54. Yusupov. *Konets Rasputina*, p.114.
55. Qtd. in Radzinsky, *Rasputin,* p 460.
56. Yusupov. *Konets Rasputina*, pp 115/6.
57. Russkiy Istoricheskiy Muzey. No. 85. Qtd. in Krasnykh p 441.
58. Harmer, pp 59 & 177.
59. Hasken, 'Seneca. D. H. Lawrence and the Yusupovs.' *Atlantis*, Vol 4, No. 2, p 17.
60. Konshine & King. 'The 1916-17 Diaries of Grand Duke Andrei Vladimirovich.' In *Atlantis,* Vol 5, No. 1, p 38.
61. Stopford, pp 77/8.
62. Warwick, p 286.
63. Extract from a decipher of a telegram from Sir George Buchanan, Petrograd, 14 January NS 1917.
    www.forum.alexanderpalace.org British Foreign Office Files and Rasputin, post by Phil Tomaselli, 3 March 2006.
64. Nelipa, p 100; Khrustalev, p 93; Cockfield, p 179. Her brother Dmitri, who spent the night of the murder at Koreiz, said she received a telegram at 4.00am on 17 December saying, 'It's all over' Obituary of Prince Dmitri. *Daily Telegraph*, July 1980. Welch, *Russian Court*, p 114.
65. Cockfield, p 178.
66. Vulliamy, p 116.
67. Vulliamy, p 116.
68. Nelipa p 274, citing the police protocols copied and published in French in 1930. The original autopsy report disappeared from an archive in Leningrad some years ago. According to Douglas Smith, p 609, the copy of Kosorotov's report published by Alain Roullier is fraudulent. Cook and Cullen both cite this version as authoritative. (Smith, p 777). Smith says the only reliable sources are the interview Kosorotov gave to Russian Liberty in 1917, and Sereda's account of an interview with Kosorotov which was given to Grand Duke Andrei. (Smith, p 610). The British Intelligence Service received a copy of the autopsy report. See Nelipa, p 13/14.
69. Vulliamy, p 117.
70. Marie, *Education,* p 265.
71. Marie, *Education,* p 266.
72. Alexander, *Once,* p 277.
73. Welch, *Russian Court,* p 114.
74. Konshine & King, 'The 1916-17 Diaries of Grand Duke Andrei Vladimirovich.' *Atlantis,* Vol 5, No. 1, p 40.
75. Anon. *Fall,* p 269.
76. Grand Duke Dmitri's Diary, 24 Dec. 1917. Trans. by Dr William Lee.
77. Stopford, p 93.
78. Konshine & King, 'The 1916-17 Diaries of Grand Duke Andrei Vladimirovich.' *Atlantis,* Vol 5, No. 1, pp 43/44.
79. Quoted in D. Smith, p 615.
80. Olga Alexandrovna to Xenia. 26 Dec. 1916. Copy in author's possession.
81. Belyakova, 'Letters from Grand Duke Alexander...' *Royalty Digest* No. 161, p 137. 29 Dec. 1916.
82. Courtesy of Huw Owen-Jones.

8 Rakitnoie and Revolution

1. Coutau-Begarie auction catalogue, 4 Nov. 2016, p 5
2. Maylunus & Mironenko, p 524.
3. Hawkins. Xenia to Grand Duchess Tatiana. 9 Jan. 1917.
4. D. Smith p 623, citing GARF, 102.00191.6g.246.37a3,6,12,16-17.
5. Information from Martin Elifolk, Abo University Library.
6. 30 Jan/12 Feb 1917. Courtesy of the Youssoupov Palace.
7. D. Smith, p 660.
8. *переписка членов императорского дома 1894-1918*, p 183.
9. Cook, p 217/8 quoting the original in GARF.
10. Maylunus & Mironenko, p 534
11. Maylunus & Mironenko, p 530.
12. D. Smith, p 623.
13. Van der Kiste & Hall, p 101.
14. Translated and quoted in Nelipa, p 363.
15. *Istoricheskii Vestnik*, April 1917. Translated and quoted in Nelipa, p 363.
16. de Robien, pp 31/32.
17. Stopford, p 141.
18. Nabok. 'Khudozhestvennaya kollektsiya knyazey Yusupovykh v dvadtsatom veke.'
19. Hall, King, Wilson & Woolmans, pp 528/9.
20. Collection Donner, Uno and Olly, 35. Vån.II2: L:1. Åbo Akademi University Library, Finland. To Anna Sinebrychoff, 6 April 1917.
21. *Novoye Vremya* No. 14726, p 164. April 1917. Translated & quoted in Nelipa, p 365.
22. Vulliamy, pp 127/8 & 129/30.
23. Clarke, *Saving*, p 80. Stopford saved many of Grand Duchess Vladimir's jewels from her Petrograd palace.
24. Norwich, p 62; Payn and Morley, p 656; de Robien, p 29.
25. Dorr, pp 104/5.
26. *The Times,* 30 Sept. 1967.
27. Blunt, p 108.
28. King, *Rasputin,* p 203, qtg figures provided by the Moika Palace, 19 May 1992.
29. Xenia to Grand Duchess Tatiana. 6 July 1917. Hawkins. See also 18 Sept. 1917 & 11 Nov. 1917.
30. Stopford, pp 189/90.
31. Ulstrup, p 96.
32. Van der Kiste & Hall, p 118.

9 Last Days in Paradise

1. 20 March OS 1917. Preston Manor Archives.
2. Collection Donner, Uno and Olly, 35. Vån.II2: L:1. Åbo Akademi University Library, Finland. 30 Oct. 1917.

3. Since 1916, part of the palace had been occupied by 'The Special Department for the Care and Pension Provision for Soldiers and their Families.' Other organisations occupied outbuildings. In 1917 the garden pavilion was rented to a hairdresser. The German Revolutionary Workers and Peasants' Committee moved into the Moika Palace in 1918. Nabok, 'Khudozhestvennaya kollektsiya knyazey Yusupovykh v dvadtsatom veke.'

4. Krasnykh, p 495.

5. Ulstrup, p 128.

6. Langer p 50; Grand Duke Dmitri's diary. 15 Nov. 1917. Translated by Dr William Lee.

7. He was tried in December 1917 for plotting to overthrow the Bolsheviks and restore the monarchy and released under an amnesty for political prisoners on 1 May 1918. See Langer, p 51. He died of typhus in 1920.

8. Azar. *Tatiana Romanov*, p 220. 26 Feb. 1918. This seems to be the only time the tsar's daughters mentioned Felix by name after the murder of Rasputin.

9. 6 Nov.1917. Courtesy of the Youssoupov Palace.

10. Collection Donner, Uno and Olly, 35. Vån.II2: L:1. Åbo Akademi University Library, Finland. To Anna Sinebrychoff, 13 Dec. 1916. Rayner and Scale later served together in Stockholm, recruiting agents to report on Bolshevik policy and intentions. Cook, p 225. Rayner and Alley later worked together at British American Tobacco.

11. Collection Donner, Uno and Olly, 35. Vån.II2: L:1. Åbo Akademi University Library, Finland. To Uno & Olly Donner, 18 Nov. 1917.

12. Author's notes from Xenia's diary, 31 Dec. 1917.

13. Udaltsov, p 111.

14. The *Yorkshire Post*. 18 January 1930; Welch, *Russian Court*, p 160.

15. Olga Nicolaievna to Xenia, 1/14 April 1918. Hawkins.

16. The bust was made and exhibited in an exhibition called 'Art and the Crimea' organised by the art critic Sergei Makovksy in Yalta in 1918, along with the marble busts of Irina and Felix. See Vertepova, 'Bust of the Commissioner for the Empress's Order.' www.oldyalta.ru

17. Romanoff, Prince Roman, p 490.

18. von Meck, p 179.

19. Many sources incorrectly state that the wedding took place in May 1918, possibly to cover up the scandal of a pregnant bride. The dowager empress's diary of 12/25 Nov. 1918 makes it plain that 'Andrusha's wedding is this evening' in the little church at Ai Todor. Ulstrup, p 267; Prince Roman, p 491, gives the incorrect date.

20. Vertepova 'Bust of the Commissioner for the Empress's Order.' www. oldyalta.ru The fate of the bust is unknown but the one of Felix is in the collection of the Alupka Palace Museum.

21. Olivier Coutau-Begarie auction catalogue Dec. 2015, p 53.

22. Krasnykh, p 525.

23. National Archives of Malta. Pridham, p 161, gives Thespé, Topin and Latt. Maids: Jovravloff and Lata. He doesn't make it clear whether this was for Felix senior or junior.

24. Olivier Coutau-Begarie auction catalogue 4 Nov. 2015, p 101 gives the date as 25 March OS 1918, but 1919 makes more sense.

25. Krasnykh, p 534.
26. Welch, *Russian Court*, p 43.
27. Cook, *Rasputin*, pp 225 & 274; Collection Donner, Uno and Olly, 35. Vån. II2: L:1. Åbo Akademi University Library, Finland. To Anna Sinebrychoff, 7 April 1919. Rayner arrived in Vladivostok on 28 January 1919 and the last letter from there is dated late July. Information from Martin Ellfolk, Åbo Akademi University Library. He arrived in San Francisco from Vladivostok on 8 January 1920.
28. Romanoff, Prince Roman, p 502.
29. Pridham, p 67.
30. Romanoff, Prince Roman, p 503.
31. Van der Kiste & Hall, p 147.
32. Youssoupov, *Lost Splendour*, p 279.

10 A Nomadic Existence

1. Felix to Mrs Ethel Earl, from Biarritz, around Aug. 1919. Courtesy of Mrs Cordelia Uys.
2. Van der Kiste & Hall, p148.
3. Prince Dmitri's unpublished memoirs, qtd. in Welch, *Russian Court*, p 51.
4. Ulstrup, p 350.
5. National Archives of Malta. This differs from the list given in Pridham.
6. D. Smith, *Former*, p 205.
7. Skipwith, p 55.
8. Skipwith, p 55.
9. Ingham, p 60.
10. King, *Rasputin*, pp 102 & 213; Van der Kiste & Hall, p 153.
11. Lieven, pp 51 & 133.
12. Xenia Sfiris interview with Anna von Lowzow, 2009. There is another version. When they tried to escape from Paris Marie Antoinette's diamonds were in a casket which was entrusted to the queen's hairdresser Léonard, who travelled separately and was supposed to deliver it in person. He unwisely gave the casket to a soldier, who the next day was found 'murdered and empty handed.' Weber, pp 230/1. Some of the queen's jewels eventually reached Austria and were given to her daughter Madame Royale. 'L'affaire des bracelets de Marie-Antoinette.' Vincent Meylan. *Point de Vue* No. 3813, p 47.
13. Grand Duchess George to Xenia. 24 Feb/9 March 1919. Copy in author's possession.
14. Grand Duke Dmitri's diary, 19 June 1919. Trans. by Dr William Lee.
15. Xenia Sfiris interview with Anna von Lowzow, 2009.
16. Felix to Mrs Ethel Earl, from Biarritz, around Aug. 1919. Courtesy of Mrs Cordelia Uys.
17. Grand Duke Dmitri's diary, 5/18 June 1919. Trans. by Dr William Lee.
18. Grand Duke Dmitri's diary, 23 June 1919. Trans. by Dr William Lee.
19. Grand Duke Dmitri's diary, 24 June 1919. Trans. by Dr William Lee.
20. Clarke, *Saving*, pp 115/6.

21. Olga Alexandrovna to Xenia,13/26 May 1919. Copy in author's possession.
22. Dobson, pp 121/2.
23. Marie, *Exile,* p 104.
24. Dmitri Obolensky, p 162.
25. Qtd. in Zinovieff, *Red Princess,* p 100.
26. Serge Obolensky, p 231.
27. Serge Obolensky, pp 203 & 89/90.
28. Marie, *Exile,* pp 105 & 120
29. Norwich, pp 108 & 121.
30. Grand Duke Dmitri's diary. 16 Dec. NS. 1919. Trans. by Dr William Lee.
31. Conversation with Dr Idris Trayler & Dr Ronald C. Moe, 2006; email from Andrew Cook. 16.11.2020.
32. The visitors' book shows a visit on 20 February. *The visitors' book of princes F.F. and I.A. Yusupov. London-Paris. June 1919 – June 1945.* www. nashaepoha.ru
33. Statement qtd. in Dobson, p 125.
34. Marie, *Exile,* p 103.
35. Felix to Dmitri. 26 Feb. NS. 1920 Trans. by Dr William Lee.
36. Dmitri to Felix. 17 Feb OS. 1920. Trans. by Dr William Lee.
37. *The Times,* 25 June 1920.
38. Grand Duke Dmitri's diary, 17 April/4 May 1920.

11 Bohemian Rhapsody

1. Marie, *Exile,* p 20.
2. TNA FO 371/4026. Sir Arthur Davidson to the Under-Secretary of State, 13 Aug. 1919.
3. Norwich, p 148.
4 Sebastian Earl's memories of Felix. UC Archives. Accession No. 1089.
5. Behrman, 'The Days of Duveen.'; *En Exil* p 38, says Felix wanted £200,000. Widener said this was too high and offered £120,000.
6. Coutau-Begarie auction catalogue, 11 Dec. 2015, p 53. Irina was godmother to the couple's son Sandrik, born on Lemnos in 1920. Sandro was his godfather. Her second child, also Olga, was born in Menton in February 1922.
7. Vassiliev, p 271; Metternich, p 56.
8. Metternich, p 56.
9. Metternich, p 56.
10. Erté, p 271.
11. Marie, *Exile,* pp 271/2.
12. Jeffery, p 18; Shirokorad, p 60.
13. 'Summary of the Foreign Department of the Cheka on the Russian intelligence organizations in Berlin, their activities and agents', 21 January 1922. In *Russian Military Emigration of the 30s and 40s. Documents & Materials,* Book 2, p 482. http://militera.lib.ru/docs; Botkin, pp 295/6.
14. Marie, *Exile,* p 270.

15. Welch, *Russian Court*, pp 218/9. The prince's mistress Zina had arrived in Constantinople with her children under false papers which stated she was the wife of Felix senior's secretary Svetiloff. Finding it impossible to abandon that name, she and her family moved to Via Umbria in Rome, not far from where the Youssoupovs were living. The prince took an active part in his children's life and education, a fact attested by the photographs he gave them and the numerous love letters he wrote to Zina, meanwhile giving his mistress instructions about where to go to avoid bumping into his wife. See Olivier Coutau-Begarie auction catalogue 14 Nov. 2007, pp 16/17.
16. Van der Kiste & Hall, pp 167/8.
17. Van der Kiste & Hall, p 162.
18. Van der Kiste & Hall, p 168.
19. Xenia Sfiris interview with Anna von Lowzow, 2009.
20. Alexandra was the daughter of Henry Coombs, a British businessman who was working in Russia before the First World War. Gwendoline Digby had come to Rome with Madame Wolkoff's family in 1919 and then been employed by the Youssoupovs.
21. The *Bluefield Daily Telegraph*. 14 Dec. 1923; The *Dundee Courier*. 14 Dec. 1923.
22. Shoumatoff, pp 181/82.
23. Cartier Brissov, pp 260/1; Nadelhoffer, p 286.
24. Nadelhoffer, p 124.
25. Mrs Peter Gerry of Washington was reported to have purchased the forty-two black pearls in 1924, said to be the most perfectly matched pearl necklace in the world. There is no record of who purchased Marie Antoinette's earrings but they were later acquired by Marjorie Merryweather Post, who bequeathed them to the Smithsonian Institute.
26. *Excelsior*, Paris, 21 Jan. 1925.

12 The House of Irfé & Other Ventures

1. For several years Kitmir, the firm of Dmitri's sister Marie, did exclusive embroidery for Chanel using patterns based on folk designs. Legend says that Dmitri was behind the iconic design of the bottle for Chanel No. 5 perfume, which was based on the Russian army hip flask. Personal visit to Chanel, Paris, 2006.
2. Qtd in Vassiliev, p 272.
3. Vassiliev, p 188.
4. Menegaldo, p137.
5. de la Haye, p 100; Ekaterina Guseva, *Russian Emigrants in France. (1900-1950)*, qtd in Menegaldo, p 138.
6. Vasiliev, p 272.
7. Dunne. *Vanity Fair*, 1987; Vassiliev, p 282.
8. de la Haye, p 100.
9. Irishkokov, Protsai, & Shelayev, p 327.
10. Qtd. in Vassiliev, p 280.
11. Vassiliev, p 277.

12. Skipwith, p 88/89; Zinovieff, *Red Princess*, p 158.
13. Metternich, p 57.
14. Metternich, p 57.
15. *New York Evening Post,* 14 April 1925.
16. Behrman, 'The Days of Duveen'; *New York Evening Post.* 14 & 15 April 1925.
17. Behrman, 'The Days of Duveen.'
18. *New York Daily News,* 22 April 1925.
19. Behrman, 'the Days of Duveen'; *New York Times,* 22 April 1925.
20. Email from Andrew Cook. 16.11.2020; *The New York Daily News,* 22 April 1925; *New York Times,* 22 April 1925.
21. *New York Times,* 25 April 1925; *Beckley Post Herald.* 21 April 1925.
22. *The Times*, 16 Sept. 1925; Dobson, p 142.
23. Nabok, 'Khudozhestvennaya kollektsiya knyazey Yusupovykh v dvadtsatom veke.'; *Krasnaya Gazeta*, 7 March 1919.
24. Conway, p 139/40. In one of Prince Felix senior's private rooms a safe was discovered under the floor in 1932. Cross, p 254.
25. Email from Valentina Nabok, 2021; Clarke, *Romanoff Gold* p 230; Moe, 'Notes from Old Russia', p 9.
26. *La Liberté,* 17 Sept. 1925.
27. Nadelhoffer, pp 286 & 319.
28. *La Liberté.* 25 Sept. 1925.
29. *The Geelong Advertiser,* 15 Sep. 1925.
30. Parcels C132 & C 133. *Registres de la conservation des hypothèques. Archives de la collectivité de Corse.*
31. Marie, *Exile*, p 273.
32. *Registres de la conservation des hypothèques. Archives de la collectivité de Corse.*
33. https://kotchoubey.com
34. *Sigean. Le Sombre Destinee du Chateau du Lac* by Jean-Pierre Géa Torres. Editions Géa 2016; https://sites.google.com/site/sigeanchateaulareinty/home/le-chateau-du-lac-des-origines-jusqu-au-xviiieme-siecle/sigean-le-chateau-du-lac-du-xixeme-au-xxeme-siecle. Jean-Pierre Géa, 2013.
35. *Registres de la conservation des hypothèques. Archives de la collectivité de Corse.*
36. Geoff Teeter Collection.1 October 1928.
37. Qtd. in King, *Rasputin*, p 230.
38. Moe, *Prelude,* pp 650 & 682. Lazovert was denied permission to enter Canada to visit relatives on his way to Siberia, where he had volunteered to accompany the allied intervention. By 1918 he was in New York. He returned to south Russia, gave up his medical career and became part of the circle surrounding Queen Marie of Romania. He then became a broker in the oil business.
39. *The Times.* 22, 27 & 29 Jan, and 16 Feb. 1927.
40. Moe, *Prelude,* p 533.
41. Moe, *Prelude,* p 664.
42. Olga Alexandrovna to Ferdinand Thormeyer. Hall. 'A Loyal and Affectionate Friend.'
43. Welch, *Rasputin*, p 189; *Gazette de Biarritz,* 22 Nov. 1926.

44. Information from Stephen Patterson, Royal Collection Trust, Oct 2019; Andrei moved in when he was declared bankrupt after the failure of his Regent's Park Country Club. See Hall, 'Courting Disaster.'
45. Information from Stephen Patterson, Royal Collection Trust. Oct. 2019.
46. Cartier Brickell, p 298.
47. Nadelhoffer p 124; Cartier Brickell, p 573 note. The pearl market had collapsed and it was 1934 before Cartier bought the pearls. Cartier Brickell, p 333.
48. It was redeemed by Cartier in 1928, set into a necklace and sold for £48,000 to the Dutch oil magnate Henri Deterding for his Russian-born wife Lydia, although he bought the diamond without the necklace. Cartier Brickell, pp 296/7 & 322; Nadelhoffer, p 319. It was sold to a Mumbai collector in 1980 and has not been seen since. Cartier Brickell p 574, note.
49. Dobson, pp 147/8.
50. D. Smith, p 675.
51. *The Herald*, Melbourne; *The Western Australian*, Perth; *The Telegraph*, Brisbane, 17 Jan. 1928.
52. The *Yorkshire Post*, 9 May 1928; Dobson, pp 147/8.
53. Olga Alexandrovna to Ferdinand Thormeyer. Hall, 'A Loyal and Affectionate Friend.'

13 Anastasia

1. Welch, *Fantasy*, p 141.
2. Vorres, p 174.
3. Olga to Ferdinand Thormeyer. Hall, 'A Loyal and Affectionate Friend.'
4. Kurth, p 186.
5. Youssoupov, *En Exil*, p 115.
6. Kurth p 186.
7. Felix to Pierre Gilliard. Rome. 10 Dec. 1928. Ian Shapiro collection.
8. Felix to Grand Duke Andrei. Qtd. in Kurth, p 186.
9. Botkin, p 295.
10. Anon. *I Anastasia*, pp 227/8.
11. Xenia to Irina. Olivier Coutau-Begarie auction catalogue Dec. 2015, p 60.
12. *Kingston Gleaner*, Jamaica, 31 May 1929.
13. *Paris-Soir*. 29 & 30 April 1929.
14. *La Tribune de l'Aube: journal républicain independent,* 28 April 1929; *La Revue Hebdomadaire,* 28 April 1929.
15. *New York Times*, 15 June 1928; Moe p 630 says $800,000.
16. *New York Times*, 22 June 1928.
17. *New York Times*, 17 June 1928.
18. Jespersen, pp 345/6. For the dowager empress's death and funeral see Hall, *Little Mother of Russia*, pp 349/52.
19. Olivier Coutau-Begarie auction catalogue Feb. 2007, p 45.
20. Van der Kiste & Hall, p 187.

21. Ian Shapiro collection.
22. Van der Kiste & Hall, pp 183/4.
23. Letter from Ronald C. Moe to the author, 28 October 1994.
24. Welch, *Fantasy*, p 149.
25. Olivier Couteau-Begarie auction catalogue, Dec 2015. p 54.
26. Van der Kiste & Hall, p 192.
27. Tchirikov, pp 253 & 256.
28. Information from Elizaveta Krasnykh; *Le Petit Gironde,* 4 Feb. 1930.
29. Vickers, *Beaton in the Sixties*, p 31.
30. Lownie, p 393, note 26.
31. Cook, *Rasputin,* p 225; Dobson pp 160/62. For Dukes's career see Jeffery, pp 175/8; Milton pp 228/81; and M. Smith *Six pp 239/50.* He was knighted by George V in 1920.
32. Olivier Coutau-Begarie auction catalogue Feb. 2007, p 41.
33. Sir Paul Dukes papers, Box 5, 1932 diary, 14 July, 29 Sept & 1 Oct. Hoover Institution Library & Archives. Dukes's handwritten diary is not easy to read.
34. Sir Paul Dukes papers, Box 5, 1932 diary, 15 & 19 July. Hoover Institution Library & Archive.
35. Sir Paul Dukes papers, Box 5, 1932 diary, 29 July. Hoover Institution Library & Archive.
36. Sir Paul Dukes papers, Box 5, 1932 diary, 30 July, 13 & 23 Aug. Hoover Institution Library & Archive.
37. Sir Paul Dukes papers, Box 5, 1932 diary, 24 Aug. Hoover Institution Library & Archive.
38. Tchirikov, p 266.
39. Kurth, p 277.
40. Sir Paul Dukes papers, Box 5, 1932 diary, 19 Sept. Hoover Institution Library & Archive.
41. Sir Paul Dukes papers, Box 5, 1932 diary, 24 Sept. Hoover Institution Library & Archive. Dukes calls the man Felix's 'nephew Marcel' but it has been impossible to discover whether Felix did have a nephew of this name.
42. Sir Paul Dukes papers, Box 5, 1932 diary, 9, 12 & 17 Oct. Hoover Institution Library & Archive.
43. Sir Paul Dukes papers, Box 5, 1932 diary, 23 Oct. Hoover Institution Library & Archive.
44. Sir Paul Dukes papers, Box 5, 1932 diary, 6 & 14 Nov. Hoover Institution Library & Archive.
45. Sir Paul Dukes papers, Box 5, 1932 diary, 26 & 30 Nov. Hoover Institution Library & Archive.
46. Youssoupov, *En Exil,* p 165. Further diaries are not extant. Dukes helped Madame Nadine Legat with the Legat School of Russian classical ballet whose patron was Grand Duchess Xenia.
47. Olivier Coutau-Begarie auction catalogue Dec. 2015, p 58.
48. Geoff Teeter collection.
49. Olivier Coutau-Begarie auction catalogue Feb. 2007, p. 41.
50. Geoff Teeter Collection. 1933.
51. Geoff Teeter Collection. November 1933.

14 Youssoupov *versus* MGM

1. Unnamed source qtd. in Traylor & Moe, 'Tartars versus Moguls,' p 27.
2. Qtd. In Traylor & Moe, 'Tartars versus Moguls,' p 18.
3. Traylor & Moe, 'Tartars versus Moguls,' p 19. There was even a novel, *Rasputin and the Empress* by Val Lewton, based on the screenplay.
4. Napley, p 66.
5. Napley, p 67.
6. *The Times*, 28 Nov. 1932. Dobson, p 163 says it is possible that Felix received an out of court settlement. Traylor & Moe p 17 gives details of other Rasputin films.
7. Traylor & Moe, 'Tartars versus Moguls,' p 19.
8. Traylor & Moe, 'Tartars versus Moguls,' p 30, note 27.
9. Berkman, p 138.
10. Berkman p 143.
11. Berkman, p 144.
12. Traylor & Moe, p 22 & *The Times*, 6 Feb. 1934.
13. Traylor & Moe, 'Tartars versus Moguls,' pp 21/2.
14. Trevelyan, pp 337/8.
15. *Excelsior,* Paris, 6 March 1934.
16. *Sutherland Daily Echo*, 5 Feb. 1934; King, *Rasputin,* p 246; Youssoupov, *En Exil,* p 177.
17. Napley, p 202; Berkman, p 151.
18. *The Times,* 28 Feb. 1934.
19. Napley, p 195.
20. Report in *The Times,* 28 Feb. 1934
21. *The Times,* 28 Feb. 1934.
22. Traylor & Moe, 'Tartars versus Moguls,' p 23.
23. *Aberdeen Journal*, 28 Feb. 1934.
24. *The Times*, 1 March 1934.
25. In *Rasputin,* Felix says he battered Rasputin after he was already dead. In *Lost Splendour* he grabs hold of the club but fails to use it. See Youssoupov, *Rasputin, p* 180 & *Lost Splendour,* p 230.
26. Traylor & Moe, 'Tartars versus Moguls,' p 24.
27. Napley, p 129.
28. *Daily Express,* 2 March 1934; *Chicago Tribune.* 2 March 1934.
29. *The Times,* 2 March 1934.
30. *The Times,* 3 March 1934.
31. Napley, pp 166/7.
32. *The Times,* 3 March 1934; Napley, pp 170/1.
33. *The Times,* 3 March 1934.
34. Traylor & Moe, 'Tartars versus Moguls,' p 25.
35. Napley, p 181.
36. Report in *The Times,* 6 March 1934.
37. Napley, p 195.
38. The *Daily Mail,* 5 March 1934.
39. The *Sheffield Independent,* 6 March 1934.
40. The *New York Times* obituary of Prince Felix Youssoupov, 28 Sept. 1967.
41. The *Western Daily Press,* 6 March 1934.

42. The *New York Times*, 5 March 1934.
43. *The Sphere*, 10 March 1934 & information from Katya Galitzine.
44. *Taunton Courier and Western Advertiser*. 14 March 1934.
45. Thomas M. Sutton, 17 May & 23 July 1934. Geoff Teeter collection.
46. Telegram 9 July 1934. Geoff Teeter collection.
47. *Gloucestershire Echo*, 17 July 1934; *Nottingham Evening Post,* 12 July 1934.
48. King, *Rasputin*, p 255; Berkman, p 159.
49. Berkman, p 159.
50. *Lincolnshire Echo*, 11 Aug. 1934.
51. *Lincolnshire Echo*, 11 Aug. 1934.
52. All quotations from Napley, p 202.
53. Traylor & Moe, 'Tartars versus Moguls, p 31; Crowther, p 229.
54. The *New York Times* obituary of Prince Felix Youssoupov 28 Sept. 1967 & 11 Aug. 1934.
55. Berkman, p 161.
56. Traylor & Moe, 'Tartars versus Moguls, p 28; *New York Times,* 11 Aug. 1934.
57. Napley, p 197.
58. Napley, p 200.
59. Napley, p 203.
60. Document dated 8 Jan. 1941. Geoff Teeter collection.
61. Paul Piazza to Felix, 2 Nov. 1934. Geoff Teeter Collection.
62. Irina to Brooks. 5 Dec. 1934. Geoff Teeter collection.
63. Harold Brooks to Maître Fabiani, 22 Nov. 1934. Geoff Teeter collection.
64. Irina to Brooks. 8 Jan. 1935. Geoff Teeter collection.
65. Kleinmichel to Irina 9 Feb. 1940. Geoff Teeter collection.
66. Undated memo from Irina and Felix re La Pelegrina. Geoff Teeter collection.

15 Tangled Finances and Pawned Jewels

1. Olivier Couteau-Begarie catalogue Feb. 2007, p 41.
2. Korganoff to Brooks for Prince Youssoupov. Geoff Teeter collection.
3. Felix to Korganoff. 12 Jan 1935. Geoff Teeter collection.
4. Brooks to Irina. 23 Jan. 1935. Geoff Teeter collection.
5. Brooks to Korganoff, 27 Feb. 1935. Geoff Teeter collection.
6. *The Times,* 21 Feb. 1935; *The Mail*, Adelaide. 23 March 1935.
7. E. Zinovieff, p 156.
8. See Olivier Couteau-Begarie catalogue Feb. 2007, p 42.
9. Olivier Couteau-Begarie catalogue Feb. 2007, p 41.
10. Dobson p 173; Ferrand, *Youssoupovs,* p 119; Youssoupov, *En Exil,* pp 186/7. James Hamilton, 2nd Duke of Abercorn, was a great-grandfather of Diana, Princess of Wales. For the sake of clarity, Felix's pearl will be called La Pelegrina in this book.
11. Document of 8 Jan. 1941 and annexes. Geoff Teeter collection.
12. Toscano, p 46.
13. Felix to Korganoff, 20 Aug. 1935. Geoff Teeter collection.

14. *The Cornishman*, 19 Sept. 1935.
15. Olivier Coutau-Begarie auction catalogue, Feb. 2007, p 42.
16. Command for all Purposes, 16 December 1935. Geoff Teeter collection.
17. Paul Piazza to Felix, 6 Feb. 1936. Geoff Teeter collection.
18. Feodor left the marital home in 1937 (Toscano, p 43) and went to America, where it was proposed that he became a test driver for an automobile company. Unlike his brothers, he was unable to adapt to the American way of life. He soon realised that he was being used and that his automobile demonstrations on second-rate circuits served only the public relations of a band of unscrupulous men. He returned to his mother in England. Mitterand, *Exil*, pp 239/40.
19. Telegram to Youssoupov, 20 rue Nungessercolli Paris, 28 Oct. 1936. Geoff Teeter collection.
20. Boucheron to Felix, 21 Nov. 1936. Geoff Teeter collection.
21. Xenia to Irina. Olivier Coutau-Begarie auction catalogue Dec. 2015, p 58.
22. Irina to Korganoff, 8 Jan 1937 & unsigned and undated draft, Windsor, Feb. 1937. Geoff Teeter Collection.
23. Felix to Korganoff, 18 Feb. 1937. Geoff Teeter collection.
24. Piazza to Felix, 27 Feb. 1937. Geoff Teeter collection.
25. Piazza to Felix,15 March 1937. Geoff Teeter collection.
26. Brooks to Irina, 10 May 1937. Geoff Teeter collection.
27. Langton & Passmore to Irina, 8 May 1937. Geoff Teeter collection.
28. Count Kleinmichel to Irina, 9 Feb. 1940. Geoff Teeter collection.
29. Geoff Teeter collection.
30. Piazza to Felix, 7 July 1937. Geoff Teeter collection.
31. Piazza to Irina, 7 September 1937. Geoff Teeter collection.
32. Piazza to Felix, 15 Sept. 1937. Geoff Teeter collection.
33. Paul Piazza to Felix, 1 Feb. 1938. Geoff Teeter collection.
34. Letter from Mimi to Felix, 6 Nov. 1938. Geoff Teeter collection. Handwritten and not easy to read. Michel de Buisseret does not appear to have been married at this time.
35. *Registres de la conservation des hypothèques. Archives de la collectivité de Corse.*
36. Authorisation from Princess Zenaide, 5 Dec. 1937. Geoff Teeter collection.
37. Receipt from Barclays Bank, & undated memorandum by Felix and Irina regarding La Pelegrina written during the 1940s. Geoff Teeter collection.
38. Letter from Count Kleinmichel to Felix, 28 April 1938; Receipt from Westminster Foreign Bank, 30 May 1938; Undated memorandum by Felix and Irina written during the 1940s. Geoff Teeter collection.
39. *The World's News*. Sydney. 13 Aug. 1938.
40. Olivier Couteau-Begarie auction catalogue Dec. 2015, p 61.
41. *The Mercury,* Hobart. 6 Aug. 1938.
42. Associated Press report in the *Chicago Tribune; The Western Morning News and Daily Gazette*, 20 June 1938; *Le Matin*, 20 June 1938.
43. *The Mercury*. Hobart. 6 Aug. 1938.
44. *Paris-soir, Le Matin & L'Intransegeant*, 17-20 June 1938.
45. Krasnykh, p 625.
46. Van der Kiste & Hall, pp 210 & 233.

47. *Office Parisien d'Operations Immobilieres et d'Assurances* to Felix. 7 March 1939. Geoff Teeter collection.
48. Benoiton to Felix, 28 March 1939. Geoff Teeter collection.
49. Information from Andrew Cook, 21.4.2006.

16 War and Occupation

1. Prince Nikita to Grand Duchess Xenia, 9/22 May 1941. Copy in author's possession.
2. Count Kleinmichel to Felix. Undated, but appears to be 1939. Geoff Teeter collection.
3. Count Kleinmichel to Irina, 9 Feb. 1940. Geoff Teeter collection.
4. Passmore to Count Kleinmichel, 23 Nov. 1939. Geoff Teeter collection.
5. *Le directeur des Contributions directes* to Irina, 19 Oct. 1939. Geoff Teeter collection.
6. Youssoupov, *En Exil,* p 198.
7. Count Kleinmichel to Irina & Felix. 5 Dec. 1939. Geoff Teeter collection.
8. Count Kleinmichel to Felix & Irina, 5 Dec. 1939. Geoff Teeter collection.
9. Count Kleinmichel to Irina and Felix, 19 Dec. 1939. Geoff Teeter collection.
10. Count Kleinmichel to Irina, 16 Jan. 1940 & 9 Feb. 1940. Geoff Teeter collection.
11. Count Kleinmichel to Irina, 23 Jan. 1940. Geoff Teeter collection.
12. Count Kleinmichel to Irina, 26 Jan. 1940. Geoff Teeter collection.
13. Count Kleinmichel to Irina, 2 Feb. 1940. Geoff Teeter collection.
14. Count Kleinmichel to Irina, 8 Feb. 1940. Geoff Teeter collection.
15. Telegram from Count Kleinmichel, 12 Feb. 1940. Geoff Teeter collection.
16. Count Kleinmichel to Irina, 9 Feb. 1940. Geoff Teeter collection.
17. Count Kleinmichel to Irina, 13 Feb. 1940. Geoff Teeter collection.
18. Count Kleinmichel's office to Irina, 1 & 8 March 1940. Geoff Teeter collection.
19. Count Kleinmichel to Irina, 27 March 1940. Geoff Teeter collection.
20. Count Kleinmichel to Korganoff, 10 April & 15 May 1940. Geoff Teeter collection.
21. Sebba, p 62.
22. Constantin de Grunwald to Grand Duchess Marie Pavlovna, 20 December 1940. Courtesy of Jacques Ferrand.
23. Olivier Coutau-Begarie auction catalogue, 14 Feb. 2007, p 39.
24. Undated letter handwritten by Felix to unnamed 'Messieurs.' Geoff Teeter collection.
25. Nikita to Xenia, 13 Jan NS 1941. Copy in author's possession.
26. Nikita to Xenia, 14 March 1941 & 9/22 May 1941. Copies in author's possession.
27. Nikita to Xenia, 22 May 1942. Copy in author's possession.
28. Bébé to Xenia, Dec. 1942; and Nikita to Xenia. attached to letter of 22 May 1942. Copies in author's possession.
29. Bébé to Xenia, Dec. 1942. Castello di Corbara, Orvieto. Copy in author's possession.

30. Nikita to Xenia, Nov. 1942. Copy in author's possession.
31. Bébé to Xenia. Lausanne, Jan. 1945 postmark. Copy in author's possession.
32. Accounts of Grand Duke Dmitri's death from Prince Michael Romanoff, Prince Nicholas Romanoff, Jacques Ferrand & Dr William Lee, the authority on Dmitri.
33. Email from Prince Nicholas Romanoff, 29 Sept. 2005 and information from Dr William Lee.
34. Princess Marina to Xenia, 4 April 1942. Copy in author's possession.
35. Sir Edward Peacock to Westminster Foreign Bank, 19 March 1942. Geoff Teeter collection.
36. Undated memo from Felix and Irina. Geoff Teeter collection.
37. M. Romanet to Felix. 2 Aug. 1943; & Felix to M. Romanet, 10 Aug. 1943 Geoff Teeter Collection.
38. Promise of Sale; and declaration by Felix dated 15 July 1943 giving the sale price. Geoff Teeter collection.
39. Olivier Coutau-Begarie auction catalogue Feb. 2007, p 41.
40. King, *Rasputin*, p 263.
41. Ferrand, *Youssoupovs*, pp 298/9. Part of the building later collapsed during construction work nearby and the house was altered. The site of the former garage became a kitchen.
42. Fane had been Comptroller of Duff and Diana Cooper's household in Algiers from January 1944 until the end of August 1944. He died on 6 February 1945 after a fall. Information from Blandine Turbellier, *Secrétariat des Membres*, The Travellers' Club, Paris.
43. Felix and Irina to Westminster Foreign Bank Paris, 7 Sept. 1944. Geoff Teeter collection.
44. Westminster Foreign Bank to Felix, 11 Sept. 1944. Geoff Teeter collection.
45. Bébé to Xenia, postmarked January 1945. Copy in author's possession; Van der Kiste & Hall, p 221.
46. He was the second husband of Foulques's mother-in-law, née Olga Cheremetev.
47. https://kotchoubey.com; Youssoupov, *En Exil*, p 138.
48. Toscano, p 103.
49. de La Cerda, p 144; Ferrand, *Youssoupovs*, p 1.

17 The Chateau de Kériolet

1. Unattributed newspaper report dated 25 May 1954. Geoff Teeter collection.
2. Van der Kiste & Hall, p 224.
3. Information from Prince Michael Romanoff; Van der Kiste & Hall, p 222.
4. Van der Kiste & Hall, p 222.
5. Xenia Sfiris interview with Anna von Lowzow, 2009.
6. Craig Brown, p 135; Payn & Morley, p 61.
7. Snowman, p 128.
8. See letter of 1 Dec. 1949 in Olivier Coutau-Begarie auction catalogue Dec. 2015 pp 66/67. The catalogue says the letter is from Irina, but this makes no sense at all. Lariviere, p 474, alleges they were lovers.
9. Xenia Sfiris interview with Anna von Lowzow, 2009. Information from Elizaveta Krasnykh.

10. Maître Queinnec to Maître Roger Joisson, 21 May 1949, forwarded to Felix. Geoff Teeter collection.
11. Maître Joisson to Felix, 25 May 1949. Geoff Teeter collection.
12. Maître Joisson to Felix, 7 July 1949. Geoff Teeter collection.
13. Toscano, p 103.
14. Lariviere, p 474.
15. Irina and Felix to Korganoff, 4 May 1945. Geoff Teeter collection.
16. Felix to Dufour, 13 May 1949. Geoff Teeter collection.
17. Felix to Dufour, 2 & 3 August 1950. Geoff Teeter collection.
18. Felix to Korganoff, 24 June 1949. Geoff Teeter collection.
19. *Registres de la conservation des hypothèques. Archives de la collectivité de Corse.* 19 June 1951.
20. Inventaire d'archives: Impôt de solidarité nationale (1484 W). https://francearchives.fr
21. Felix to *Impôt de solidarité nationale,* 7 June 1951. Geoff Teeter collection.
22. Felix to Monsieur A Vors, *Inspecteur de l'enregistrement,* 28 June 1951. Geoff Teeter collection.
23. Crawford, pp 394/5; Pauline Gray p 145; King, *Rasputin,* p 269.
24. *Direction Generale des Impôts, Bureau de Calvi* to Felix, 30 November 1951. Geoff Teeter collection.
25. Olivier Coutau-Begarie auction catalogue Dec. 2015, p 68.
26. Douglas Smith pp 592/3 discusses this point.
27. Felix to *l'Inspecteur des Contributions Directes,* Paris, March 1953; Payment advice dated 18 May 1953. Geoff Teeter collection.
28. Monsieur Saurel to Felix, 17 March 1953; & Korganoff to Saurel, 21 March 1953. Geoff Teeter collection.
29. Korganoff to Lullin, 27 March 1952. Geoff Teeter collection.
30. Lombard to Felix, 31 March 1952. Geoff Teeter collection.
31. Lombard to Korganoff, 27 May 1952. Geoff Teeter collection.
32. Memo from Felix, 5 February 1953. Geoff Teeter collection.
33. Undaed handwritten assessment of Kériolet. Geoff Teeter collection.
34. 'Therefore, a person who, without having any title deed, has occupied for a period of thirty years a real estate or land, knowing that he did not own it, may, at the end of this period, become the owner through usucapion [the acquisition of a title or right to property by uninterrupted and undisputed possession for a prescribed term] and to the detriment of the legitimate owner of the property.'
35. Unattributed newspaper cutting of 24 May 1954. Geoff Teeter collection.
36. *France-Soir,* 26 May 1954; Unattributed newspaper cutting dated 24 May 1954. Geoff Teeter collection.
37. Unattributed newspaper reports dated 24 & 25 May 1954. Geoff Teeter collection.
38. Unattributed newspaper report dated 25 May 1954. Geoff Teeter collection.
39. Unattributed newspaper report dated 25 May 1954. Geoff Teeter collection.
40. Information from Griff Henninger, who heard the story from Speller.
41. Information from Valentina Nabok, The Youssoupov Palace.
42. Certificate from *Hôpital Boucicaut,* Paris, 8 November 1954. Geoff Teeter collection.

43. After his divorce in 1947 Dmitri returned to London. He rekindled his friendship with Sheila Chisholm, whom he had met at Felix's parties in the 1920s. They married quietly in October 1954.
44. Pasternak, p 257.
45. Pasternak, p 255.
46. Menkes, p 27.
47. Pasternak, p 244.
48. Vickers, *Beaton in the Sixties,* p 31.
49. Vickers, *Beaton in the Sixties,* p 30.

18 The Shadow of Rasputin

1. Dorr, pp 104/5.
2. Princess Olga Romanoff, p 34; Montefiore, p 550 footnote.
3. Princess Olga Romanoff, p 49.
4. Princess Olga Romanoff, p 145.
5. Telephone conversation with Princess Margarita, 3 June 2001; Van der Kiste & Hall, pp 226/7.
6. Letter from Prince David Chavchavadze, 14 May 2001; information from Dr William Lee.
7. Conversation with Prince Alexander Romanoff.
8. See Coutau-Begarie auction catalogue 4 Nov. 2016, p 110.
9. Ferrand, *Youssoupovs,* p 39. Of the 43 hectares recovered by Felix only 2.5 hectares remain today. By an administrative error, one of the seven old posterns which were part of the crenelated walls was forgotten when Felix sold the property. It was still owned by the family in 1991.
10. Xenia Sfiris interview with Anna von Lowzow, 2009.
11. Frederic Mitterand, *Mémoires d'exil,* documentary. CasaDei Productions, 1999.
12. Xenia Sfiris interview with Anna von Lowzow, 2009.
13. The *Moscow Times,* 25 May 2007.
14. 'From Mexico with Love', Adam Thomson, The *Financial Times.* 26 May 2011.
15. 'From Mexico with Love', Adam Thomson, The *Financial Times.* 26 May 2011.
16. Getty, p 69.
17. Vickers, *Beaton in the Sixties,* p 31.
18. Ferrand, *Noblesse Russe,* p 345; Toscano, pp 102/3.
19. Draft telegram from Felix to Pierre Gilliard dated 7 April, no year. Ian Shapiro collection.
20. 2 February 1956. www.Hermitagefineart.com
21. Pierre Gilliard to Felix, 18 Feb. 1958. Ian Shapiro Collection.
22. Gilliard to Felix, 25 Feb. 1958. Ian Shapiro collection.
23. Van der Kiste & Hall, p 232, quoting. Prince Dmitri to Prince Ludwig of Hesse. Hessisches Staatsarchiv Darmstadt, 11 March 1958.
24. Coutau-Begarie auction catalogue Dec. 2015, p 59.
25. Grand Ducal Family Archives in the Hessisches Staatsarchiv Darmstadt. D 26 No. 97/1.

26. Welch, *Fantasy*, p 240/41; Lovell, pp 252/3 quoting Botkin's unpublished letter to Milukov.
27. Ian Shapiro collection.
28. King &Wilson, *Resurrection*, p 241.
29. Welch, *Russian Court,* pp 216/7. Details of Xenia's death and funeral are in Van der Kiste & Hall, pp 238/9.
30. Will & codicil. Van der Kiste & Hall, p 239.
31. Prince Alexander Romanoff, 'A Romanoff in Soviet Russia. *Sunday Telegraph,* 27 Aug. 1961 & 'Moscow Paradox,' *Sunday Telegraph,* 1961.
32. www.ancestry.co.uk; Cook, p 269 note 6.
33. Oxfordshire History Centre. P23/1/C/9. 30 Jan. 1959.
34. Oxfordshire History Centre. P23/1/C/10. Postmark appears to be 23.12.1960.
35. Quoted in Moe, *Prelude,* p 164.
36. Andrew Cook interview with Gordon Rayner, 13 March 2004. Rayner's first wife was Tatiana Glubokovskaya Marek. They married in Moscow on 30 January 1923 and divorced in London on 12 August 1940. Andrew Cook interview with Alexis Caroline Rayner, 26 September 2004. I am grateful to Andrew Cook for making these available to me.
37. Crichlow, James. *Radio Hole in the Head/Radio Liberty.* (Washington DC. American University Press, 1995), p 130; Quoted in Welch, *Russian Court,* p 216.
38. https://archiveshub.jisc.ac.uk/data/gb275-beaton/beaton/a/a1/597. 22 Feb. 1964. Papers of Sir Cecil Beaton. St John's College Library Special Collections, University of Cambridge. GB 275 BEATON/A/A1/597.
39. Vickers, *Beaton in the Sixties*, p 31.
40. *New York Times* obituary, 28 Sept. 1967.
41. *New York Times* obituary, 28 Sept. 1967.
42. *The Times,* 9 Nov. 1965.
43. *San Francisco Chronicle,* 9 Nov. 1965.
44. *New York Times,* 2 Oct. 1965. 'Rasputin's Killer Tells His Story'.
45. *New York Times* obituary, 28 Sept. 1967.
46. Dobson, p 192
47. *The Times,* 8 Dec. 1966.
48. *The Times,* 8 Dec. 1966.
49. *The Guardian,* 29 Dec. 1966.
50. *Horizon* autumn 1967. Vol IX no. 4.
51. Private information.
52. 'Horrors that Haunted Dracula' by Guy Walters. *Daily Mail,* 12 June 2015. In 1930 Estelle married as her second husband Harcourt Rose, uncle of Ian Fleming.
53. The interview is available on YouTube.
54. *The Times* obituary of Prince Michael Andreievich, 11 October 2008.
55. Moe, *Prelude,* pp 650/51. At one point Lazovert returned from holiday to find that a restaurant called 'Rasputin' had opened opposite his apartment. Welch, *Rasputin,* p187. He died in 1976 and was buried in the Pere-Lachaise Cemetery, Division 93.
56. The *New York Times,* 12 March 1970.

57. Princess Irene set up home with Count Hubert de Monbrison after her divorce from Feodor. They used his chateau at Quincy-sous-Senart to house refugee girls from the Russian and Spanish civil wars, as well as forty German Jewish refugee children who arrived in July 1939. The chateau became a Jewish children's home until it was requisitioned by the Germans in September 1940. Irene married Count Hubert in Biarritz in 1950 but they later separated.
58. Mitterand, *Exil*, pp 249 & 241.
59. Krasnykh p 659, using information from Prince Michael Romanoff. Mitterand, *Exil* p 259 has a slightly different version.
60. *Guide des Russes en France*, pp 302 & 293. Plot No. 391, section N3 holds Princess Zenaide, Irina and Felix, & Countess Irina and Count Nikolai Cheremetev. Felix senior remains in the Protestant Cemetery in Rome; *L'Intransigeant*, 7 March 1970.
61. Private information.

Postscript

1. Nabok, Khudozhestvennaya kollektsiya knyazey Yusupovykh v dvadtsatom veke; King, *Rasputin*, p.280.
2. Byron, pp 84/88 gives full details of his visit.
3. Una Pope-Hennessy, p 214.
4. Van der Kiste & Hall, p 240.
5. Moe. 'Notes from Old Russia'; Lownie, p 311.
6. Information from Elizaveta Krasnykh.
7. Moe, 'Notes from Old Russia.'
8. Personal visit 2001.
9. D. Preston, pp 103/4, 184 & 252.
10. Personal visit to Koreiz, 1999.
11. D. Preston, pp 102/5, 200 & 246.
12. Personal visit 1999; Moe, p 202
13. Information from Tatyana Bukharina.
14. Conversation with Prince Alexander Romanoff; personal visit to the Crimea, 1999.
15. Princess Olga Romanoff, pp 140/41.
16. Hall, King, Wilson & Woolmans, p 655; information from Tatyana Bukharina.
17. Personal visit 1999; Hall, King, Wilson & Woolmans, p 348.
18. Information from Tatyana Bukharina.
19. Information from Tatyana Bukharina.
20. Information from Tatyana Bukharina.

Bibliography

Aldrich, Richard J. & Cormac, Rory. *The Secret Royals*. (Atlantic Books, 2021)

Alexander, Grand Duke. *Once a Grand Duke*. (Cassell, 1932.)

Alexander, Grand Duke. *Always a Grand Duke*. (Cassell, 1933.)

Anon. *I Anastasia*. (Michael Joseph, 1958)

Anon. *Russian Court Memoirs 1914-1916*. (Cambridge: Ian Faulkner, 1992)

Anon. *The Fall of Romanoffs*. (Cambridge: Ian Faulkner, 1992.)

Anon. *The Russian Diary of an Englishman*. (New York: McBride & Co, 1919)

Azar, Helen (ed.). *The Diary of Olga Romanov*. (USA: Westholme, 2015)

Azar, Helen (ed.). *The Journal of a Russian Grand Duchess*. (CreateSpace, 2015.)

Azar, Helen (trans.) & Nicholson, Nicholas (annotator). *Michael Romanov. Diaries and Letters 1916-1918*. (Washington: Academica Press, 2020)

Azar, Helen (trans.) & Nicholson, Nicholas (annotator). *Tatiana Romanov. Daughter of the Last Tsar. Diaries and Letters 1913-1918*. (Pennsylvania: Westholme Press, 2016)

Baschkiroff, Zenaide. *The Sickle and the Harvest*. (Neville Spearman, 1960)

Belyakova, Zoia. *The Romanovs. The Way it Was*. (St Petersburg: Ego Publishers, 2000)

Berkman, Edward O. *The Lady and the Law*. (USA: Little, Brown. 1976)

Betteley, Marie, & Schimmelpennick van der Oye, David. *Beyond Fabergé*. (Pennsylvania: Schiffer Publishing, 2020)

Bing, Edward J. (ed.). *The Letters of Tsar Nicholas and Empress Marie*. (Ivor Nicholson and Watson, 1937)

Blunt, Wilfred. *Lady Muriel*. (Methuen, 1962)

Bohhanov, Alexander & others. *The Romanovs. Love, Power & Tragedy*. (Leppi Publications, 1993)

Boland, Terry (with contributions by Arturo Beéche). *Death of a Romanov Prince*. (California: Eurohistory.com, 2018)

Botkin, Gleb. *The Real Romanovs*. (Putnam, 1932)

Boulay, Cyrille. *Les France des Romanov*. (France: Editions Perrin, 2010)

Brown, Craig. *Hello Goodbye Hello. A Circle of 101 Remarkable Meetings*. (Simon & Schuster, 2011)

Buchanan, Meriel. *Victorian Gallery.* (Cassell, 1956)

Byron, Robert. *First Russia, Then Tibet.* (Macmillan, 1933)

Cartier Brickell, Francesca. *The Cartiers. The Untold Story of the Family Behind the Jewellery Empire.* (N.Y: Ballantine Books, 2019)

Cerda, Alexandre de la. *La Tournée des Grand-Ducs.* (Biarritz: Editions Atlantica, 1999)

Clarke, William. *Hidden Treasures of the Romanovs. Saving the Royal Jewels.* (Edinburgh: National Museums of Scotland, 2009)

Clarke, William. *The Lost Fortune of the Tsars.* (Weidenfeld & Nicolson, 1994)

Charles-Roux, Edmonde. *Chanel.* (Johnathan Cape, 1976)

Cockfield, Jamie. *White Crow.* (Connecticut: Praeger, 2002)

Conway, Sir Martin. *Art Treasures in Soviet Russia.* (Edward Arnold, 1925)

Cook, Andrew. *The Murder of the Romanovs.* (Stroud: Amberley Publishing, 2011)

Cook, Andrew. *To Kill Rasputin.* (Stroud: Tempus Publishing, 2005)

Cooper, Lady Diana, *Darling Monster.* (Chatto & Windus, 2013)

Crawford, Rosemary & Donald. *Michael & Natasha.* (Weidenfeld & Nicolson, 1997)

Cross, Anthony. *St Petersburg and the British.* (Frances Lincoln Ltd, 2008)

Crowther, Bosley. *The Lion's Share. The Story of an Entertainment Empire.* (N.Y: E P Dutton & Co. 1957)

Cullen, Richard. *Rasputin. The Role of the British Secret Service in his Torture and Murder.* (Dialogue, 2010)

de Jonge, Alex. *The Life and Times of Grigorii Rasputin.* (William Collins, 1982)

de la Haye, Amy; Taylor, Lou; & Thompson, Eleanor. *A Family of Fashion. The Messels: Six Generations of Dress.* (Philip Wilson Publishers, 2006)

de Robien, Louis. *The Diary of a Diplomat in Russia. 1917-1918.* (Michael Joseph, 1969)

de Stoeckl, Agnes. *Not All Vanity.* (John Murray, 1950)

Dobson, Christopher. *Prince Felix Yusupov.* (Harrap, 1989)

Dorr, Rheta Childe. *Inside the Russian Revolution.* (New York: Macmillan, 1917)

Dorrill, Stephen. *MI6. Fifty Years of Special Operations.* (Fourth Estate, 2000)

Engberg, Magnus. *Maria. Sverige ryska prinsessa.* (Sweden: Magnas Engberg Kulturproduktion och Ala Tryck, 2018)

Erté. *Erté: Things I Remember.* (Quadrangle, 1975)

Ferrand, Jacques. *Le Grand-Duc Paul Alexandrovich de Russie.* (Paris: 1993)

Ferrand, Jacques. *Les Familles Comtales de l'Ancien Empire de Russie,* (Paris: 1997)

Ferrand, Jacques. *Les Princes Youssoupoff & les Comtes Soumarokoff-Elston.* (Paris: 1991)

Ferrand, Jacques. *Noblesse Russe: Portraits d'Exil.* (Paris: 2001)

Fomenko, Boris. *The Knight of the Tennis Racket.* (Moscow, 2004) In Russian.

Fuhrmann, Joseph T. (ed.). *The Complete Wartime Correspondence of Tsar Nicholas II and Empress Alexandra.* (Connecticut: Greenwood Press, 1999).

Fuhrmann, Joseph T. *Rasputin. The Untold Story.* (New Jersey: John Wiley, 2012)

Gabriel Constantinovich, Grand Duke. *Memories in the Marble Palace.* (Canada: Gilbert's Books, 2009)

Ganina, Natalia Alexandrovna. *Arkhiv Feliksa i Iriny Yusupovykh* (Moscow: Muzey Nashey Epokhi, 2018)

Getty, J Paul. *As I See It.* (Los Angeles: J. Paul Getty Museum, 2003)

Gray, Pauline. *The Grand Duke's Woman.* (Macdonald & Jane's, 1976)

Hall, Coryne *Little Mother of Russia. A Biography of the Empress Marie Feodorovna, 1847-1928.* (Shepheard-Walwyn, 1999)

Hall, Coryne. *To Free the Romanovs. Royal Kinship & Betrayal in Europe, 1917-1919.* (Stroud: Amberley Publishing, 2018)

Hall, Coryne & Driver, Senta. *Hvidøre. A Royal Retreat.* (Sweden: Rosvall Royal Books, 2012)

Hall, Coryne; King, Greg; Wilson, Penny; & Woolmans, Sue. *Imperial Crimea. Estates, Enchantment and the Last of the Romanovs.* (CreateSpace Independent Publishing, 2017)

Harmer, Michael. *The Forgotten Hospital.* (Chichester: Springwood Books, 1982)

Hawkins, George (ed.). *Correspondence of the Russian Grand Duchesses. Letters of the Daughters of the Last Tsar.* (Printed by Amazon, 2020)

Heyden, Marina. *Les Rubis Portent Malheur.* (Monte Carlo: Editions Regain, 1967)

Hoare, Samuel. *The Fourth Seal.* (Heinemann, 1930)

Horne, Charles F. (ed.). *Source Records of the Great War* (Vol. V, National Alumni, 1923)

'How Lovely it is to be a Bride'. Letters of Grand Duchess Marie Pavlovna to Prince William of Sweden (Insel Mainau: Privately printed.)

Ingham, Robert. *What Happened to the Empress.* (Malta: Privately printed, 1949)

Irishkokov, Mikhail; Protsai, Liudmila & Shelayev, Yuri. *Sunset of the Romanov Dynasty.* (Moscow: Terra Publishing Centre, 1992).

Iz semeynoy perepiski Yusupovykh. (Moscow: N.B. Strizhevoy. Reka vremen, 1995).

Jensen, Bent. *Zarmoder blandt Zarmordere.* (Copenhagen: Gyldendal, 1997)

Jensen, Mette; Jørgensen, Caspar Andreas; Jørgensen, Christoffer; & Lunding, Gitte. *I Dagmars Skygge.* (Denmark: Culturcentret Assistens Copenhagen 2011)

Jespersen, Knud J.V. *Rytterkongen.* (Denmark: Gyldendal, 2007)

Kamarovskaia, Ekaterina Leonidovna. *Vospominaniia.* (Zakharov, Moscow, 2003)

Khrustalev, Vladimir. *Feliks Yusupov i ubiystvo Rasputina.* (Ebook 2014)

King, Greg. *The Murder of Rasputin.* (Century, 1996)

King, Greg & Wilson, Penny. *The Resurrection of the Romanovs.* (John Wiley, 2011)

Kleinpenning, Petra H. (ed.). *The Correspondence of the Empress Alexandra of Russia with Ernst Ludwig and Eleonore, Grand Duke and Duchess of Hesse, 1878-1916.* (Norderstedt, Germany: Books on Demand, 2011).

Krasnykh, Elizaveta. *Knyaz Feliks Yusupov. Za vse blagodayu.* (Moscow: Indrik, 2003)

Kudrina, Julia. *Imperatritsa Mariya Fedorovna. Dnevniki, pis'ma, vospominaniya.* (Moscow: Olma Press, 2001)

Kurth, Peter. *Anastasia. The Life of Anna Anderson.* (Jonathan Cape, 1983)

Lariviere, Michel. *Dictionnaire historique des homosexualles célèbres* (France: Groupe CB, 2017)

Lieven, Dominic. *The Aristocracy in Europe 1815-1914.* (MacMillan, 1992)

Lockhart, Robert Bruce. *British Agent.* (Putnam's, 1933)

Lovell, James Blair. *Anastasia, The Lost Princess.* (Robson Books, 1991)

Lownie, Andrew. *Stalin's Englishman.* (Hodder & Stoughton, 2015)

Mandache, Diana (ed.). *Dearest Missy.* (Sweden: Rosvall Royal Books, 2011)

Maria Feodorovna, Empress of Russia. (Exhibition catalogue. The Royal Silver Room, Copenhagen, 1997)

Mansvelt, Jean-Marc; Bern, Stéphane; & Vauchadez, Christophe. *Chaument in Majesty. Jewels of Sovereigns since 1780.* (Paris: Flammarion, 2019)

Marie, Grand Duchess of Russia. *Education of a Princess.* (New York: The Viking Press, 1931)

Marie, Grand Duchess of Russia. *A Princess in Exile.* (N.Y: Viking, 1932]

Maylunas, Andrei & Mironenko, Sergei. *A Lifelong Passion.* (Weidenfeld & Nicolson, 1996)

Menegaldo, Helene. *Les Russes à Paris 1919-1939.* (Paris: Editions Autremont, 1998)

Menkes, Suzy. *The Windsor Style.* (Grafton Books, 1987)

Metternich, Tatiana. *Full Circle in a Changing World.* (Elliot & Thompson, 2004)

Miles, Jonathan. *St Petersburg. Three Centuries of Murderous Desire.* (Windmill Books, 2017)

Milton, Giles. *Russian Roulette.* (Sceptre, 2013)

Mitterand, Frédéric. *Mémoires d'exil.* (Paris: Editions Robert Laffont, 1999)

Montefiore, Simon Sebag. *The Romanovs.* (Weidenfeld & Nicolson 2016)

Morel, Thierry & Renne, Elizaveta. *The Splendour of St Petersburg.* (N.Y: Rizzoli Electa, 2019)

Munn, Geoffrey. *Tiaras. A History of Splendour.* (Antique Collectors' Club, 2001)

Nadelhoffer, Hans. *Cartier, Jeweller Extraordinary.* (Thames & Hudson, 1984)

Naplcy, Sir David. *Rasputin in Hollywood.* (Weidenfeld & Nicolson, 1989)

Naryshkin-Kurakin, Elizabeth. *Under Three Tsars.* (New York: E. P. Dutton, 1931)

Neerbek, Hans. *Søstrenes Slot.* (Copenhagen: Hernovs Forlag, 1990)

Nelipa, Margarita. *Killing Rasputin. The Murder that Ended the Russian Empire.* (Colorado: Wildblue Press, 2017)

Nicholas and Alexandra. The Last Imperial Family of Tsarist Russia. Exhibition catalogue. (Booth-Clibborn Editions, 1998)

Nicolson, Juliet. *The Perfect Summer.* (John Murray, 2006)

Norwich, John Julian. *The Duff Cooper Diaries.* (Weidenfeld & Nicolson, 2005)

Obolensky, Dmitri. *Bread of Exile.* (Harvill Press, 1999)

Obolensky, Serge. *One Man in His Time.* (Hutchinson, 1960)

Paleologue, Maurice. *An Ambassador's Memoirs.* 3 volumes. (Hutchinson, 1925)

Paley, Princess. *Memories of Russia, 1916-1919.* (Reprinted by Royalty Digest, Ticehurst, 1996)

Pasternak, Anna. *The Real Wallis Simpson.* (New York: Atria Books, 2019)

Payn, Graham and Morley, Sheridan. *The Noel Coward Diaries.* (Weidenfeld & Nicolson, 1982)

perepiska chlenov imperatorskogo doma 1894-1918. (Russia: no date)

Perry, John Curtis, & Pleshakov, Constantine. *The Flight of the Romanovs.* (New York: Basic Books, 1999)

Pitcher, Harvey. *When Miss Emmy Was in Russia.* [John Murray, 1977]

Pope-Hennessy, Una. *Leningrad. The Closed and Forbidden City.* (Hutchinson, 1938)

Ponfilly, Raymond de. *Guide des Russes en France.* (Editions Horay, 1990)

Preston, Diana. *Eight Days at Yalta.* (Picador, 2019)

Pridham, Vice-Admiral Sir Francis. *Close of a Dynasty.* (Allan Wingate, 1956)

Purishkevich, Vladimir. *The Murder of Rasputin.* (Ann Arbor: Ardis, 1985)

Radzinsky, Edvard. *Rasputin. The Last Word.* (Weidenfeld & Nicholson, 2000)

Rappaport, Helen. *Caught in the Revolution.* (Hutchinson, 2016)

Rappaport, Helen. *Four Sisters.* (Macmillan, 2014)

Robinson, Paul. *Grand Duke Nikolai Nikolaevich.* (Illinois. Norther Illinoie University Press, 2014)

Rogers, Peter. *Mr Stewart and the Romanovs.* (Pocklington: The Stewart Museum, 2014 & revised edition 2015)

Romanoff, Prince Roman. *Det var et rigt hus, et lykkeligt hus.* (Denmark: Gyldendal, 1991)

Romanoff, Princess Olga, with Coryne Hall. *Princess Olga. A Wild and Barefoot Romanov.* (Shepheard-Walwyn, 2017).

Ruud, Charles A. & Stepanov, Sergei. *Fontanka 16. The Tsar's Secret Police.* (Stroud: Sutton Publishing, 1999)

Ruslands Skatte – Kejserlige Gave. (Exhibition catalogue. The Royal Silver Room, Copenhagen, 2002)

Saenz, Jorge F. *A Poet Among the Romanovs.* (California: Eurohistory.com, 2004)

Salisbury, Harrison E. *Black Night, White Snow.* (N.Y: Da Capo paperback, 1977)

Sebba, Anne. *Les Parisiennes.* (Orion, 2016)

Schneer, Jonathan. *The Lockhart Plot.* (Oxford University Press, 2020)

Shishkin, Oleg. *Poslednyaya tayna Rasputina.* (Russia: AST Publishing, 2019)

Shoumatoff, Alex. *Russian Blood.* (Vintage Books, 1990)

Skipwith, Sofka. *Sofka. The Autobiography of a Princess.* (Rupert Hart-Davies, 1968)

Smith, Douglas. *Former People.* (Macmillan, 2012)

Smith, Douglas. *Rasputin.* (Macmillan 2016)

Smith, Michael. *Six. A History of Britain's Secret Intelligence Service.* Part 1. (Dialogue, 2010)

Snowman, A. Kenneth. *Carl Fabergé. Goldsmith to the Imperial Court of Russia.* (New York: Greenwich House. 1983)

Stopford – see Anon. *The Russian Diary of an Englishman.*

Tchirikov, Olga. *Sandrik. Child of Russia.* (N.Y: Dodd, Mead & Co., 1934)

The Yusupov Palace. Museum Guide. (St Petersburg, 2005)

Tillander-Godenhielm, Ulla. *Jewels from Imperial St Petersburg.* (St Petersburg: Likki Rossi, 2012)

Toscano, Anna. *Michel Romanoff de Russie. Un destin français.* (Paris: Harmattan, 2015)

Trevelyan, Raleigh. *Grand Dukes and Diamonds.* (Secker & Warburg, 1991)

Udaltsov, M. *Belikaya Knignya Olga Aleksandrovna Romanova-Kulikovskaya.* (Moscow: Forum, 2011)

Ulstrup, Preben (ed.). *Kejserinde Dagmars fangenskab på Krim.* (Denmark: Gyldendal, 2005)

Van der Kiste, John & Hall, Coryne. *Once a Grand Duchess. Xenia, Sister of Nicholas II.* (Stroud: Sutton Publishing, 2002)

Vassiliev, Alexandre. *Beauty in Exile.* (N.Y: Harry N. Abrams, 2000)

Vaughan, Hal. *Sleeping With the Enemy.* (Chatto & Windus, 2011)

Vickers, Hugo (ed.). *Beaton in the Sixties.* (Weidenfeld & Nicolson, 2003)

Vickers, Hugo. *Cecil Beaton. The Authorised Biography.* (Weidenfeld & Nicolson, 2002)

von Meck, Galina. *As I Remember Them.* (Dobson Books, 1973)

Vorres, Ian. *The Last Grand Duchess.* (Hutchinson, 1964)

Vulliamy, C. E. (ed.). *From the Red Archives.* (Bles, 1929)

Wainwright, Robert. *Sheila. The Australian Ingenue Who Bewitched British Society.* (Allen & Unwin, 2014)

Warwick, Christopher. *Ella. Princess, Saint and Martyr.* (Chichester: John Wiley, 2006)

Weber, Caroline. *Queen of Fashion. What Marie Antoinette Wore to the Revolution.* (N.Y: Henry Holt & Co., 2006)

Welch, Frances. *A Romanov Fantasy. Life at the Court of Anna Anderson.* (Short Books, 2007)

Welch, Frances. *Imperial Tea Party.* (Short Books, 2018)

Welch, Frances. *Rasputin.* (Short Books, 2014)

Welch, Frances. *The Russian Court at Sea.* (Short Books, 2011).

Youssoupov, Prince Felix. *Lost Splendour.* (Jonathan Cape, 1953)

Youssoupov, Prince Felix. *En Exile.* (Paris: Plon, 1954).

Youssoupov, Prince Felix. *Rasputin. His Malignant Influence and his Assassination.* (Jonathan Cape, 1927)

Yusupov. *Konets Rasputina.* (Russia: Otechestvo, 1990)

Zeepvat, Charlotte. *From Cradle to Crown.* (Stroud: Sutton Publishing, 2006)

Zinovieff, Elizabeth. *A Princess Remembers.* (Y.N. Galitzine & J. Ferrand, 1997)

Zinovieff, Sofka. *Red Princess.* (Granta Books, 2007)

Articles

Behrman, S. N. 'The Days of Duveen'. In *The New Yorker*, 22 September 1951.

Belyakova, Zoia. 'Letters from Grand Duke Alexander Mikhailovich to Grand Duchess Xenia, 1916-1917.' In *Royalty Digest,* No. 161.

Bennett, Vanora. 'A Label to Die For,' In 'You' Magazine. *The Mail on Sunday.* 16 June 2013.

Danziger, Chris. 'Rasputin Dispute: Did Oxford Aluminus Really Kill Him?' In *Oxford Today* magazine, April 2017.

Danziger, Chris. 'The Oxford Alumnus Who Helped Assassinate Rasputin.' In *Oxford Today* magazine, December 2016.

Dunne, Dominick. 'The Rockefeller and the Ballet Boys.' *Vanity Fair,* February 1987.

Hall, Coryne. 'A Loyal and Affectionate Friend – Ferdinand Thormeyer and the Family of Alexander III.' In *Royal Russia,* No. 8. Summer 2015.

Hall, Coryne. 'Courting Disaster – The Russian Prince and the Regent's Park Country Club.' In *Royalty Digest Quarterly.* Vol. 4, 2016.

Hall, Coryne. 'Pistols at Dawn. The Curse of the Youssoupovs.' In *Royalty Digest Quarterly.* Vol 2, 2006

Hamilton, Eric. Extract from memoir. 'Oxford and a Glimpse of Russia.' University College Archives, 25/MS/2 (1956)

Hamilton, Eric. Diary. 'Felix and I.' University College Archives, 25/MS/1. (1910)

Haskin, Gretchen. 'His Brother's Keeper.' In *Atlantis Magazine,* Volume 2, Nos 3 & 4.

Haskin, Gretchen. 'Seneca, D. H. Lawrence and the Yusupovs.' In *Atlantis Magazine,* Volume 4, No. 2.

Horbury, David (ed). 'Half a Century of Royal Letters', collected by John Wimbles from the Romanian National Archives and other sources. In *Royalty Digest Quarterly,* 2016.

Konshine, Larissa (trans) & King, Greg (annotator). 'The 1916-17 Diaries of Grand Duke Andrei Vladimirovich' In *Atlantis Magazine,* Vol 5, No. 1.

Langer, Jack. 'Fighting the Future: The Doomed Anti-Revolutionary Crusade of Vladimir Purishkevich,' In *Revolutionary Russia,* Vol. 19. No. 1. June 2006.

Moe, Dr Ronald C. 'Notes from Old Russia. Rediscovering the Yusupov Family Legacy.' (Washington: privately printed, 1992)

Moss, Vladimir. 'Who Was Rasputin?' 2018. www.academia/edu/

Nabok, Valentina. Khudozhestvennaya kollektsiya knyazey Yusupovykh v dvadtsatom veke (Transcript kindly provided by the author.)

Naryshkina-Bulatsel, Irina. 'The American Sculptor Gleb Deruzhinsky.' In *Our Heritage,* No 74, 2005.

Nicholson, Dr Michael. 'The Assassin in the Computing Room.' In *The Martlet,* Spring 2017.

Penycate, John. 'Rasputin Disputed'. In *Oxford Today,* Trinity term, 2017.

Romanoff, Alexander. 'A Romanoff in Soviet Russia.' *Sunday Telegraph,* 27 August 1961.

Romanoff, Alexander. 'Moscow Paradox of Old and New.' *Sunday Telegraph* 1961. Date unknown.

Signorelli, Olga. 'La famiglia Jussupov,' in *La Strenna dei romanisti* 1977.

Softky, Marion. 'Growing up Royal in Imperial Russia.' *The Imperial Russian Journal,* Vol. 2 no. 3.

Tegulle, Marie. 'The Romanovs in the Caucasus.' In *Royal Russia No. 13,* 2018.

Thomson, Adam. 'From Mexico, with Love: Russian Art and Rasputin.' In *The Financial Times,* 24 May 2011.

Tomaselli, Phil. 'Britain Helped Rasputin's Killer.' In *BBC History Magazine,* April 2003.

Traylor, Dr Idris Jnr & Moe, Ronald C. 'Tartars versus Moguls,' in *Atlantis* Vol. 2 No. 1.
Walters, Guy. 'Horrors that Haunted Dracula'. *Daily Mail,* 12 June 2015.

Archives & Collections

Åbo Akademi University Library, Manuscript Collections. Finland
GARF (The State Archives of the Russian Federation)
Geoff Teeter Collection
Ian Shapiro Collection
Oxford History Centre
Preston Manor Archives, Brighton
Hoover Institution Library & Archives, California
The Grand Ducal Family Archives in the Darmstadt State Archives
The National Archives, Kew (formerly the Public Record Office)
The National Archives of Malta
University College Archives, Oxford

Internet

T. Lapteeva. 'Dokumenty Po Istorii Kryma Vtoraya Polovina Xix – Nachala Xx Veka V Yusupovskom Fonde V Rossiyskom Gosudarstvennom Arkhive Drevnikh Aktov.' www.cyberleninka.ru
Shirokorad, Alexander. 'Sud'ba Dinastii' www.litmir.me
Vertepova, Larisa. 'Bust of the Commissioner for the Empress's Order.' www.oldyalta.ru
Yudin, Evgeny Evgenievich. 'Knyaz Feliks Yusupov v Oksforde (1909-1912).' In fuidamental'naya nauka vuzam, 1. 2010 pp 257/263. www.cyberleninka.ru
Yudin, Evgeny Evgenievich. 'Rossiyskaya Modernizatsiya i Aristokratiya: Sostoyaniye semi Yusupovykh v Nachale XX.' www.cyberleninka.ru
www.Eliotsofporteliot.com
The Alexander Palace Discussion Forum. www.forum.alexanderpalace.org
www.firstworldwar.com
https://kotchoubey.com

Newspapers & Journals

Atlantis. In the Courts of Memory.
Poslednie Novosti
The Times
Romanov News
Royal Russia
Royalty Digest
Royalty Digest Quarterly
Sovereign
The European Royal History Journal

Index

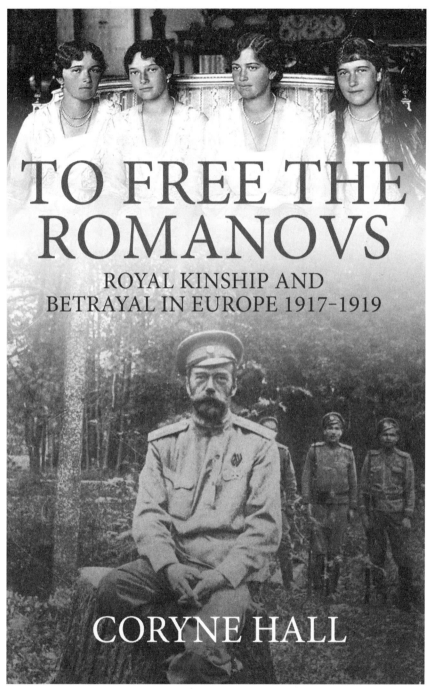

TO FREE THE ROMANOVS

ROYAL KINSHIP AND
BETRAYAL IN EUROPE 1917–1919

CORYNE HALL

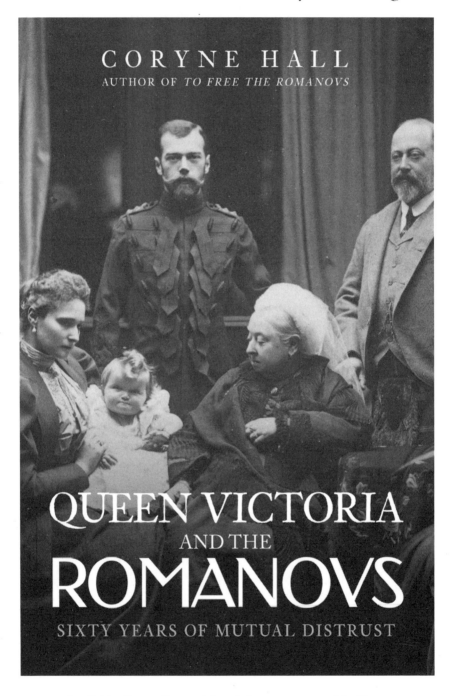